29.95

CD-ROM TECHNOLOGY

CD-ROM TECHNOLOGY

A Manual for Librarians and Educators

by CATHERINE MAMBRETTI, PH. D.

McFarland & Company, Inc., Publishers
Jefferson, North Carolina, and London

British Library Cataloguing-in-Publication data are available

Library of Congress Cataloguing-in-Publication Data

Mambretti, Catherine, 1950–
    CD-ROM technology : a manual for librarians and educators
/ by Catherine Mambretti.
        p.   cm.
    Includes bibliographical references and index.
    ISBN 0-7864-0501-5 (sewn softcover : 50# alkaline paper) ∞
    1. School libraries—United States.   2. Libraries—United
States—Special collections—CD-ROMs.   3. Computer-
assisted instruction—United States.   4. CD-ROMs—United
States.   I. Title.
Z675.S3M238   1998
025'.00285—dc21
                                          98-10321
                                            CIP

Manufactured in the United States of America

McFarland & Company, Inc., Publishers
  Box 611, Jefferson, North Carolina 28640

In memory of E. Bob Cole

Table of Contents

Introduction   1

Part One: Administrator's Guide   7

1   Designing CD-ROM Systems for Libraries and Schools   9
    Overview of Issues and the Planning Process   9
    Avoiding Obsolescence and Planning for the Future   11
    Public Access Issues and Policies   13
    Networking CD-ROMs in Libraries and Schools   17
    Integrating CD-ROM and the Internet   23
    Public CD-ROM Workstation Design   24
    Advanced Uses of CD-ROM: Special Collections, Archiving,
        and Local Databases   29
    Financial Planning   30
    Chapter Summary   32

2   The CD-ROM Title Evaluation Process   34
    Introduction to CD-ROM Title Selection   34
    CD-ROM Title Evaluation Criteria   35
    How to Evaluate Reference Titles   41
    How to Evaluate Educational Titles   50
    Sources of Reviews, Previews, and Demos   52
    Distributors and Other CD-ROM Sources   55
    Chapter Summary   56

**3   Selecting the Right CD-ROM Titles for a Library
    or School**   58
    Introduction to Compatibility and Licensing Issues   58
    Understanding "Compatibility"   58
    Interpreting CD-ROM Title "Requirements"   67
    Obtaining and Maintaining Serialized CD-ROM Titles,
        Updates, and Supporting Software   68
    CD-ROM Copyright and Licensing Issues   70
    Chapter Summary   75

Part Two: Practitioner's Guide   77

4   Supervising the CD-ROM Title Installation Process   79

Introduction to the Installation Process   79
Understanding CD-ROM Device Drivers   81
Other Preparations for Installation   86
Basic Steps in an Installation   87
Typical Installation-Program Warning Messages   88
Chapter Summary   90

5   CD-ROM Workstation Maintenance and Upgrades   91

Supervising Workstation Maintenance and Enhancements   91
Basic Maintenance Requirements and Techniques   91
CD-ROM Title Maintenance   97
Enhancing CD-ROM Workstations   98
Preparing Printed Support Materials for CD-ROM
    Workstation Users   105
Chapter Summary   108

**6   Troubleshooting a Library or School's CD-ROM
    Workstation**   109

Essential Preventatives and Basic Solutions to CD-ROM Title
    Problems   109
CD-ROM Problem-Analysis Techniques   109
Understanding Error Messages   112
Problem Analysis   115
Sources of Assistance Beyond This Book   118
Chapter Summary   124

Part Three: Technical Guide   125

7   Preparing to Install CD-ROM Titles   127

7.1   The Key to Successful Title Installation   127
7.2   How to Download Software for a CD-ROM
      Workstation   127
7.3   Determining a Workstation's Capabilities   134
7.4   CD-ROM Drive Specifications   141
7.5   Device Drivers   150
7.6   Chapter Summary   157

8   Installing CD-ROM Titles   158

8.1   Introduction to Advanced Title Installation
      Techniques   158

8.2   Installation of DOS Titles   158
8.3   Installation of Windows 3.X Titles   171
8.4   Installation of Windows 9X Titles   183
8.5   Installation of Macintosh Titles   192
8.6   Chapter Summary   198

9   How to Solve Many Common DOS Problems   199
9.1   Introduction to This Chapter   199
9.2   Improving DOS Performance   200
9.3   DOS Troubleshooting   201
9.4   The Most Common DOS Problems   207
9.5   Chapter Summary   215

10 How to Solve Many Common Windows 3.X Problems   216
10.1 Introduction to This Chapter   216
10.2 Improving Windows 3.X Performance   217
10.3 Windows 3.X Troubleshooting   218
10.4 The Most Common Windows 3.X Problems   224
10.5 Chapter Summary   235

11 How to Solve Many Common Windows 9X Problems   236
11.1 Introduction to This Chapter   236
11.2 Improving Windows 9X Performance   237
11.3 Windows 9X Troubleshooting   238
11.4 The Most Common Windows 9X Problems   243
11.5 Chapter Summary   248

12 How to Solve Many Common Macintosh Problems   249
12.1 Introduction to This Chapter   249
12.2 Improving Macintosh Performance   250
12.3 Macintosh Troubleshooting   252
12.4 The Most Common Macintosh Problems   254
12.5 Chapter Summary   261

Appendices
A: Optical Disc and Related Technologies for
       Libraries and Schools   263
B: Glossary   269
C: Directory of Resources   280
D: Recommended Reading   285

Index   289

Introduction

A GUIDE FOR LIBRARY AND SCHOOL SYSTEM ADMINISTRATORS, LIBRARIANS, AND TEACHERS

The purpose of *CD-ROM Technology* is to provide a single source of information to help library and school administrators and practitioners manage CD-ROM and related technologies. This book is a manual with step-by-step methods and processes to guide administrators of library and school systems, directors, parent associations, librarians, teachers and other educators. Beginning with the decision-making process, *CD-ROM Technology* attempts to clarify and simplify the enhancement of institutional knowledge resources through the use of CD-ROMs.

In particular, this book is designed for librarians and educators who do not have the luxury of a large technical support organization or a large system-wide mechanism for managing CD-ROM technology. If you have to "do-it-yourself," this book can serve as your primary guide to establishing and maintaining CD-ROM resources. In addition, libraries and schools with upgraded, older-model CD-ROM workstations will find the information in this book to be essential.

It is recommended that you read Part One, Administrator's Guide, as an introduction to the issues involved in CD-ROM technology before you acquire CD-ROM titles or CD-ROM workstations. Then, as you proceed to design and establish your CD-ROM resources, refer to Part One for guidelines and practical advice.

Read Part Two, Practitioner's Guide, to create strategies for managing CD-ROM workstations and CD-ROM disc collections. Part Two explains procedures that are needed to install, maintain, and troubleshoot CD-ROM titles.

It is recommended that you familiarize yourself with Part Three, Technical Guide, so that you will know what help is available in this book for managing your CD-ROM resources after you have acquired them. Keep this book close at hand for resolving problems and answering questions as they arise. Where specific answers are not supplied, refer to the appendices for further help with CD-ROM technology.

The appendices, such as "Appendix D: Recommended Reading," are designed to help you identify sources of advanced or specialized information.

"Appendix B: Glossary" defines terms used in this book and is also intended to support your further readings, especially in information technology periodicals, which tend to rely heavily on jargon and acronyms. "Appendix A: Optical Disc and Related Technologies for Libraries and Schools" is an overview of Kodak Photo CD, IVI, DVD, CD-R, and CD-WR, optical disc technologies similar to CD-ROM, but less-widely used than CD-ROM. "Appendix C: Directory of Resources" lists addresses, phone numbers, and e-mail addresses for CD-ROM title producers, CD-ROM title distributors, CD-ROM hardware manufacturers, periodicals, and organizations that may be of use to you.

THE STATUS OF CD-ROM TECHNOLOGY

The first commercial CD-ROM was produced in 1985, The Library Corporation's *BiblioFile*. Since then the optical disc technology on which it relied has advanced dramatically. Thousands of CD-ROM titles have been issued, and new technologies have emerged.

CD-ROM technology has achieved a high degree of stability and standardization in the intervening years. The fundamentals of CD-ROM technology will no longer *change* as much as they will *improve*. The problem of rapid obsolescence of CD-ROM platforms (that is, the "player" devices, such as CD-ROM drives installed in computers) is probably behind us. For the foreseeable future, upgrades to CD-ROM workstations, such as adding DVD capabilities, should only be required in order to enjoy additional performance benefits—a matter of choice for each library and school.

This means that libraries and schools can now confidently acquire CD-ROM technology. With adequate planning, a CD-ROM workstation can have a useful life of many years. *CD-ROM Technology* is intended to assist you in designing a long-lasting, durable, and valuable knowledge resource.

THE ROLE OF CD-ROM IN LIBRARIES AND SCHOOLS

CD-ROM as a medium for storing and retrieving information has several qualities, which taken together are unique. CD-ROM not only stores vast amounts of data, it stores several forms of data simultaneously, and it allows its users to access specific items quickly in personalized combinations. This makes CD-ROM an especially powerful tool for librarians and educators.

A single CD-ROM disc stores about 650 megabytes of data, the equivalent of over 200,000 printed pages (depending upon the way in which the information is stored). CD-ROM, however, is not limited to text. It stores photographic-quality images, motion video, and high-fidelity audio. Users can search through all of this information in seconds and retrieve data cross-referenced specifically to meet their needs.

Given these characteristics, CD-ROM has a place in every library and classroom, supporting and enhancing books and other media. Like any medium requiring a player mechanism (audiotape, videotape, and all digital media), CD-ROM is unlikely ever to be as inexpensive or easy to use as printed material. It will, however, be highly cost-effective and eventually a lot easier to use than it often is now. This book is intended to help librarians and teachers over the remaining barriers to effective CD-ROM use.

CD-ROM technology also has a role as an archival medium (to some degree at this time, but certainly to a greater degree in the future). Document imaging systems can be used to reproduce perishable, transitory materials, and the resulting images can be stored with near permanence on CD-ROM discs. Local records and databases can also be transferred to CD-ROMs very inexpensively. It is even possible (if not yet entirely practical) for individuals to create their own CD-ROMs, using special "write-able" CD-ROM discs and drives on a personal computer workstation.

The role of CD-ROM technology in libraries and schools is expanding to include more and more sophisticated applications: storage, reference, and multimedia. At the same time, it is becoming more feasible to use CD-ROM for these applications. *CD-ROM Technology*, it is hoped, will guide library and school systems in making informed choices about how best to use CD-ROM technology.

New technologies continue to be developed, which will have a significant impact on libraries and schools. The Internet and DVD are only two of these. Rather than replacing CD-ROM, these technologies represent the continuing diversification of media available for presenting information. DVD is primarily for high-quality motion video and audio information: the cost of developing DVD titles is currently quite high, so it is unlikely that it will replace CD-ROM any time soon.

As the Internet becomes an important resource and tool in both libraries and schools, CD-ROM can also be used to enhance the "online experience." The introduction of the Internet into libraries and schools doesn't make CD-ROM technology redundant or obsolete. The two are not mutually exclusive resources. Each has its place in providing information.

CD-ROM and the Internet differ in several ways. Most importantly, they provide access to different sorts of information and tools. The Internet is a medium for personal communication, while CD-ROM is a medium for publication. The Internet is a medium for traffic, the "Information Superhighway," over which products can be purchased and software can be distributed to individuals. The Internet is a medium for e-mail, for newsgroups, for automated mailing lists, for electronic publication of periodicals, for entertainment, and many other purposes. CD-ROM is a format for the presentation of information, education, training, and interactive applications. You might liken these differences to the differences between books and periodicals: one is highly authoritative and designed for permanence, while the other is ephemeral and designed for currency. CD-ROMs, in this way, are more like books; they've been carefully and expensively produced and, therefore, are intended to have a long shelf life. Information posted on Web pages on the Internet, however, may lack any authority and is often intended to be disposable.

Currently, CD-ROMs are sometimes easier to access than the Internet, as well. Access to an item of data on a CD-ROM disc can be faster than over the Internet. There are fewer barriers between a CD-ROM user and specific information than between an Internet user and the same information. Eventually, accessibility for both technologies will be comparable, but in the meantime, as a practical matter, CD-ROM is often faster.

CD-ROM Technology provides suggestions and guidelines for integrating Internet workstations and CD-ROM workstations.

Owing to advances in technology, libraries and schools have a steadily increasing range of options for the presentation of information and education. Along with each new option comes the need to make informed decisions and the need to be able to cope with special complexities. Nationwide initiatives to bring technology into libraries and classrooms, such as Schools 2000 and Libraries 2000, will put the Internet and multimedia (especially CD-ROMs) in the hands of educators and learners, librarians and researchers. *CD-ROM Technology* is designed to make one of these options, CD-ROM, less challenging for librarians and educators and more beneficial to knowledge seekers.

AUDIENCE

CD-ROM Technology is written specifically with the nontechnical librarian and educator in mind. Part One is appropriate for all information- and learning-resource professionals. Part Two is appropriate for nontechnical professionals with day-to-day responsibilities in the area of learning technologies; this may include school media specialists as well as librarians and educators who have only a single CD-ROM workstation to supervise. Part Three is technical, but it is written with nontechnical professionals in mind. With the assistance of one of the computer manuals listed in "Appendix D: Recommended Reading," a previously untrained individual should be able to perform all of the important maintenance and troubleshooting tasks required for a CD-ROM workstation. In addition, Part Three may serve as a guide to technical support staff within a library or school system who are responsible for maintaining a wide range of types of workstations and for supporting older-model computers for which documentation is now difficult to find.

A NOTE ABOUT TERMINOLOGY

Computer jargon is rapidly becoming part of our language. While *CD-ROM Technology* is written as much as possible in standard English, this book does rely heavily on computer jargon. Technical terms are defined in the text when they first occur and also in "Appendix B: Glossary."

Throughout this book reference is made to "CD-ROM title" and "CD-ROM title producer." These terms mean, respectively, the CD-ROM discs containing intellectual properties and the publishers of those discs. For example, Microsoft developed, publishes, and markets the *Encarta* encyclopedia: Microsoft is the CD-ROM title producer of the CD-ROM title, *Encarta*.

In addition, rather than use the term "computer" or "computer system," this book refers throughout to "CD-ROM workstation," "workstation," or "system." These terms are essentially synonymous. Occasionally, depending upon context, "CD-ROM workstation" or "workstation" refer not only to the computer equipment but also to the furniture in which it is housed. For example, when discussing appropriate locations, the term workstation is used to mean both the computer and the furniture. When the software, such as the operating system, running on the workstation is being discussed, the term "system" is often used.

Operating systems covered include DOS, Windows, and the Macintosh. Windows 3.0 and 3.1 are collectively referred to as Windows 3.X. Windows 95 and its successors are referred to as Windows 9X. The Macintosh operating system is referred to as the Mac OS or System 6, System 7, or System 8, as appropriate.

Finally, the operating systems discussed in detail in Part Three each have their own vocabularies. In most cases, operating-system-specific terms are highlighted in bold and spelled and punctuated exactly as they might appear on a computer screen. Most of these terms are not included in "Appendix B: Glossary." Instead, you are directed to the software vendor's user manuals for more information. In addition, discussions of the DOS operating system include numerous examples of commands and statements: these are printed in a typeface that simulates their appearance on a DOS computer screen. When following these examples, always include spaces and punctuation marks exactly as shown in the text.

Part One
ADMINISTRATOR'S GUIDE

Part One addresses issues important to the design and implementation of CD-ROM technology in libraries and schools. It is intended for nontechnical readers who are interested in establishing a valuable resource for learners based either upon existing computers and workstations or upon new multimedia workstations. Chapter 1, "Designing CD-ROM Systems," provides a blueprint for selecting computer equipment and workstation furniture, for modifying facilities to accommodate CD-ROM workstations, for deciding between stand-alone workstations and networked workstations, and for financial planning. Chapter 2, "The CD-ROM Title Evaluation Process," provides guidelines for acquiring CD-ROM titles to add to a library or school's collection, but without specific title reviews, which are readily available elsewhere. And Chapter 3, "Selecting the Right CD-ROM Titles," focuses on two critical issues in addition to title quality: technical compatibility of titles and workstations and licensing and use legalities.

If you are an administrator or involved in a decision-making committee, Part One may provide all the information you need to accomplish your goals. If you are a librarian or educator who will implement the plans of administrators, read Parts One and Two.

1. Designing CD-ROM Systems for Libraries and Schools

OVERVIEW OF ISSUES AND THE PLANNING PROCESS

The successful implementation of CD-ROM technology in a library or school system depends upon the thoroughness of the planning process. This chapter presents a methodology for both large and small institutions, which is based upon well-established principles of planning for organizational information and multimedia systems in corporations, large public libraries, and institutions of higher education.

Introducing any new technology into a public information and education environment is a highly complex project, which must be carefully managed. CD-ROM is doubly complex because it is a technology that brings with it both the complexities of a computer presentation platform and the complexities of intellectual content. Having established a high-quality computer system on which to run CD-ROM titles, the librarian and educator must also manage a growing library of titles, each with the same benefits and drawbacks of a book or periodical, as well as unique technical requirements of its own. Successful planning and implementation is possible, though, and the rewards of the effort can be manifold.

Many readers may be involved in the planning process not for a system of libraries or schools, but rather for a single institution in which only one or two CD-ROM workstations are under consideration. The planning process for a single, small institution is the same as that for a system of institutions or an institution with multiple locations or one with several CD-ROM workstations. Only the implementation of the plan is different—it can be simpler.

The most successful planning and implementation projects within library and school systems have been those modeled upon large-scale computer-technology acquisition processes. The temptation to treat the CD-ROM technology acquisition process as something less complex is great. Often, the CD-ROM industry promotes CD-ROM as being similar to other media and tends to overestimate its ease-of-use, thus leading to unrealistic expectations about the technology. Unfortunately, CD-ROM technology is complicated. No

9

single, existing turnkey package of hardware and software can meet every library's or school's needs with equal ease. Only a careful planning process, which takes into account the true nature of the technology, can produce a successful result. This means that the planning process must follow information systems methodologies, such as those presented here.

In general, the process of planning for CD-ROM technologies must include the following phases. The first phase is *needs assessment*. The CD-ROM system must be designed to meet specific current and future library patron and learner needs. The goals of the system must be established, and the number of potential users must be estimated. Decisions must be made about the integration of CD-ROM-based resources into the traditional system of printed materials and other media; CD-ROM may replace some resources, while it may supplement or duplicate others.

In addition, the place of CD-ROM technology in the total computer system must be determined. CD-ROM can be implemented on free-standing workstations, as part of a single-location local area network ("LAN"), as part of a multiple-location wide area network ("WAN") or "intranet," or in connection with the Internet. The CD-ROM system should also be designed to allow for future changes and enhancements; the hardware should be designed as an "open system" which can be adapted to changing needs.

The second phase of the planning process is *design* of the physical systems and support systems (personnel, procedures, and so forth). A design document should be written that contains a list of the program goals, a general description of the physical systems needed, and a description of how these systems will be maintained and supported for the next several years.

The next phase of the planning process is *specification*. Two parallel processes should be inaugurated during this phase: planning for the CD-ROM hardware and planning for the CD-ROM title collection. A detailed set of requirements and specifications must be developed for both the CD-ROM equipment and the CD-ROM titles that will be acquired. When planning the hardware system, not only the computer, but also the type of monitor, printer, input devices, CD-ROM drive, the operating system, and security software must be taken into consideration and specified. A CD-ROM title specifications document should also list the requirements of the presentation platform (the CD-ROM workstation) and licensing requirements.

Based on the design document, *budgets* and *schedules* must be developed. Project staff must be assigned and their roles and responsibilities determined. Ongoing maintenance and support needs must be projected, and budgets and staff for them must be determined.

A search must be conducted for sources of equipment and titles. The system design must be reevaluated in light of the results of this search. There may be conflicts between the CD-ROM titles that are available and the plans for the equipment, for example.

A *pilot program* should be undertaken. One or two sample CD-ROM titles and a limited number of workstations should be set up and tested. Among the aspects of the plan that must be tested are acquisition processes, installation of titles, running of titles, use of titles by patrons or students, technical support, and security.

Eventually, the plan must be "worked": a project manager must ensure that the implementation of the CD-ROM system is conducted according to the plan and schedule.

A *maintenance and support plan* must be developed prior to the implementation of the system. A plan must be in place to handle problems that may occur at every step in the process from purchasing and acquisition to de-installation and archiving of outdated CD-ROM title discs. Technical support must be available and easily accessible, whether that support is provided by hardware and CD-ROM title vendors or by in-house staff. Procedures must be in place for problem-resolution. Thorough technical documentation of the process, as well as user guides, must be supplied.

The *implementation* phase includes physical setup of the equipment and workstations, installation of the CD-ROM titles and related software, preparation of documentation and other printed support materials, and their distribution. Often this phase must be conducted when the location is not in use, such as in off-hours or during school vacation periods.

A final *testing* phase should be included in the plan. After the pilot test and after the full system is implemented, a test period must be allowed during which users expect to encounter some additional problems. Additional technical support must be available during this period.

This chapter presents information critical to each of these phases. Refer to Appendix C for sources of assistance with each of these phases.

AVOIDING OBSOLESCENCE AND PLANNING FOR THE FUTURE

While CD-ROM and other optical disc technologies have become relatively stable, change is inevitable in all computer technology. New types of optical disc standards may evolve; the recent development of DVD (Digital Video Disc) is one example. Manufacturers will continue to enhance the performance and speed of CD-ROM drives. Operating systems and software will become more powerful and sophisticated, leading to increasingly sophisticated CD-ROM titles, which in turn will require increasingly powerful and sophisticated computer equipment.

Fortunately, the computer industry, and especially the CD-ROM industry, has learned that so-called "backward-compatible" (in time) and "downward-compatible" (in power) products are essential to their market. This means that most advances in the technology will not make existing equipment, software, and CD-ROM title collections obsolete. It won't be necessary to upgrade or replace most CD-ROM systems when advances take place. Most DVD drives, for example, will be designed to "play" CD-ROM titles as well as DVD titles, so you won't need to replace your title collection when you add a DVD drive to your system. CD-ROM titles will continue to be produced, so your CD-ROM drives will be useful for many years to come, not only with your existing collection of titles, but also with new titles.

Nonetheless, if you have the luxury of designing a CD-ROM system completely from scratch, you should take into consideration the fact that the technology will continue to evolve, and you will probably want to be able to take advantage of these advancements. This means two things. First, a well-maintained CD-ROM system and title collection can have an extremely long useful life; it need not be discarded before the equipment fails beyond repair or before the discs are physically damaged. Second, a computer system with hardware and software modules that can be exchanged or upgraded can accommodate several generations of optical disc technology; new types of drives can be added, for example.

An easily upgraded CD-ROM system, which will accommodate future technologies, can be designed for both stand-alone computer workstations and networked workstations. A stand-alone system should be selected which allows the addition of new components, preferably simply by plugging them into empty slots and bays in the computer. Several such slots or bays should be provided in order to accommodate more than one new component. Old equipment and drives should be able to remain in place after new components are added. Even the most critical components of the computer, such as its ROM chips, should be easily replaceable or upgradable.

Networked systems are inherently modular. The CD-ROM server is separate from the network server and the networked ("client") workstations. The network server can be upgraded without making the other computers obsolete. The client workstations can be less-powerful, less-expensive computers that can be easily removed from or added to the network. The CD-ROM server can be replaced without making the client workstations obsolete. The client workstations, however, should be as easily upgraded as stand-alone workstations should be, in order to accommodate increasingly high-resolution monitors and disk drive speeds, for example.

Not only can you assume that computer and CD-ROM technology will continue to advance, you can also assume that frequency of use of the technology will increase. Library patrons and students will demand greater access to workstations with an ever-wider range of titles available to them and increasingly sophisticated title content. CD-ROM users will begin to depend on digital information rather than printed information for many research needs. They will expect a wider range of means of access to the titles (such as via modem from their home computers as well as in the library or school), and they will expect a wider range of output options (such as color laser printers). A well-designed CD-ROM system should anticipate increased use of workstations, by ever more-knowledgeable users, with increasingly sophisticated requirements.

Systems must be designed to withstand heavy use and even abuse. Systems should also provide a wide range of "ports," network adapters, and connectors so that new input and output devices can be added.

PUBLIC ACCESS ISSUES AND POLICIES

A primary objective of the design of any CD-ROM system is accessibility. This issue poses a conflict: individual library patrons and students must have access to workstations, but workstations must be secure. The issue isn't unlike the problems involved in providing a secure library of books, magazines, or videotapes, except that CD-ROM resources involve not only the physical medium itself (the disc) but also a player device (the workstation). Both security and access to discs are fairly easy to provide. Security and access to workstations may be more difficult to design.

Few institutions today give users direct access to CD-ROM title discs: titles are rarely available to be checked out for home use, for example. Discs are rarely ever directly manipulated by users. In most cases, CD-ROM titles are permanently installed in the system (either in locked, secure CD-ROM drives, towers, and jukeboxes, or at a central CD-ROM server secured away from the public). Most users are also restricted to accessing the titles from a workstation only by selecting the title from a menu of options. In classrooms, the teacher often selects the title from a menu, or may be the only person with any type of access to the disc. Sometimes CD-ROM title programs are "broadcast" from a central server into classrooms at prearranged times, thus preventing direct access to the disc.

The choice of a means of access to CD-ROM titles must be made very early in the design phase, following a careful needs assessment. More than one means of access may be needed. For example, a library might have a stand-alone workstation dedicated to a single multi-disc CD-ROM title, and a number of networked CD-ROM workstations providing access to a menu of several popular reference titles.

Among the considerations for determining access to CD-ROM titles are:
- What are the licensing options available for a specific CD-ROM title you need? Is a network version available? Is the license for single copies so expensive that it prohibits purchasing more than one copy or a multi-site license?
- Are the titles you need designed for use over a network? How well does

a given CD-ROM title perform on a network? Is it virtually unusable when more than one workstation attempts to access it over a network?

• How many users at how many different locations will need access to the same title? Does demand for the title justify a possibly more expensive network license?

• Will the CD-ROM titles be constantly in demand or only in spurts or seasonally? Can titles be scheduled for use at one location at a time?

• Are alternative media available for a given title's content? For example, is a printed version or a videotape version also available to users who may be precluded from accessing the CD-ROM title?

• Will titles be used for long periods of time in one session or will users need rapid, occasional use of the title?

Access methods must be designed based on specific user needs: the types of titles to be included in the system, the nature of the user group that will need access to the title, and the frequency of use. Security must be designed based upon considerations such as budget, physical location, technical support, and licensing considerations.

The physical location of the CD-ROM workstation in the institution will determine much of its security needs. If the workstation is placed in a highly visible, accessible location, vandalism is less likely because staff can supervise its use. Computer equipment can be "hardened" to withstand considerable abuse, but at a cost. For example, a CD-ROM workstation could be designed to resemble a bank card automatic teller machine ("ATM"), with a touch screen and all equipment secured inside metal casings. If keyboard access is required, hardened keyboards are available, including ones that withstand the conditions of desert warfare. These measures, however, can be quite costly.

Less costly hardened systems can be designed which allow users to access a standard computer keyboard and mouse (which of course are easily damaged by moisture and dirt, but which are also easily replaced), while the computer system unit and the monitor are secured inside a cabinet and behind a glass window.

In a classroom or other setting where a teacher, librarian, or administrator may need frequent access to the CD-ROM drives, the other disk drives, or even other software running on the computer, the CD-ROM drive, and computer switches (such as the power switch) can be kept under lock and key.

PLANNING FOR SECURITY OF CD-ROM RESOURCES

Several types of security must be considered: security of the hardware and discs from physical damage, security from theft, security from corruption of the software by computer viruses and misuse, confidentiality of some information, limitation of access to authorized users, protection against copyright violations, and protection against licensing violations.

Each of these requires different safeguards, as discussed below.

Physical Security

CD-ROM title discs can be protected from physical damage and theft by securing them out of the reach of all users. Discs should be permanently installed inside secure drives, such as jukeboxes or towers. No one, not even the network administrator, should remove discs from the drives. Individual CD-ROM drives installed in stand-alone workstations should be physically locked, or the system unit or CD-ROM drive case should be locked inside a cabinet that cannot be opened by users of the workstation. Archived title discs should be stored in an area accessible only to authorized personnel. CD-ROM title discs should never be circulated to the public.

CD-ROM workstations should be located in an area where staff can observe the manner in which the workstation is being used. Portable workstations, such as ones on wheeled carts for use in classrooms or other public presentations, should be kept under lock and key until being released to an authorized individual; the public should not be allowed to move a workstation—not only can such equipment be vandalized when moved to a secluded location but the motion itself can loosen internal computer connections and damage equipment.

CD-ROM workstations should be "hardened." Inexpensive, soft, plastic coverings are available to protect keyboards from dust, oil from fingers, and spills of liquids. Desks and cabinets are available to secure the monitor and system unit inside glass doors to prevent users from touching them. All cables and connections and all power switches should be locked out of the reach of users.

Software Security

Every CD-ROM workstation includes many software programs, each of which has to be installed and configured for proper performance. Users must be prevented from making any changes to the software on the workstation. In addition, the software must be protected from computer viruses. Data stored on the system must be protected from unauthorized access and unwanted changes.

The key to safeguarding software and data is preventing access to the operating system on the workstation. Users should access CD-ROM titles from a menu or shell program that restricts the use of the workstation only to CD-ROM titles. Password-protection software can also provide several levels of access to software on a workstation. For example, a system administrator can be given a password that permits access to all of the software and operating system, while users have passwords that permit access only to specific CD-ROM titles.

Computer viruses can only be introduced to a workstation through a network connection or from a diskette inserted in the diskette drive of the workstation. If the workstation doesn't have a network connection (including a modem connection) and if the diskette drive is locked, no unauthorized data or programs can be introduced to the workstation, and no viruses can corrupt the system. If not, then the workstation must include virus detection software.

Copyright and license violations can only be prevented by establishing policies and ensuring that all users are familiar with the policies. If copyright is a significant concern, then the CD-ROM workstation should not have access to a printer so that users cannot print material from CD-ROM titles (and, in any case, users should not have access to a diskette drive for copying purposes). Most CD-ROM title licenses clearly state who may have access to the title: to prevent license violations, do not install a restricted title on a workstation with network access.

LOCAL VERSUS REMOTE ACCESS FOR USERS OF THE SYSTEM

The CD-ROM system design must specify whether remote access will be available. Remote access is access via modem and phone line from the home or locations other than the library or school system. In some instances it may be desirable to allow authorized individuals to dial in from remote locations via modem to access a networked CD-ROM server. In other cases, the option of adding remote access in the future should be considered and anticipated.

Many CD-ROM title licenses specifically prohibit public, unlimited access to the title via remote dial-up. For example, it would generally be a violation both of copyrights and the license of an encyclopedia CD-ROM title to open up access to the public via modem.

Some public-domain databases on CD-ROM, however, may be legally provided to the public via modem. In addition, if your institution is a public library that may in the future archive local records onto CD-ROM or CD-R discs for your community, you may wish to design your CD-ROM system so that remote access to a networked CD-ROM server is possible in the future.

INTERLIBRARY LOAN, RESERVE, AND OTHER SYSTEMS

If access to some CD-ROM resources is limited for any reason, you may also need to plan for a means of scheduling access by special request. A reserve system might be required for CD-ROM titles; such a system can probably be accommodated by existing reserve systems for books and videotapes so long as the reserve system includes the ability to reserve time at a specific CD-ROM workstation.

Interlibrary loan of CD-ROM titles is a rare option at the time of this writing. First, CD-ROM titles are unlikely to be allowed to circulate among individual users, but rather are limited to access in the library or classroom. As the size of CD-ROM collections increases, it may be economically necessary for library and school systems to devise a means of circulating discs among individual institutions. If so, recognize that all circulating titles would have to be installed on and de-installed from workstations at each location. At this time, however, the cost of most CD-ROM titles is low and multiple copies can be purchased at lower cost than would be required to establish and manage such a circulation system. Individual title licenses may prohibit public circulation as well. Networked systems provide a better means of multi-location access to CD-ROM titles than physical circulation of discs does.

A potential problem on networked systems, though, is that the number of titles available on the network server at any given time is limited to the number of CD-ROM drives or the number of discs that the network jukebox accommodates. For example, a network may only be able to allow access to a dozen titles at the same time. As a result, a schedule may have to be developed for availability of titles, as an institution's collection grows. Or, a procedure might be designed to allow access to a permanent list of titles from the CD-ROM server, while individual workstations on the network also have their own local CD-ROM drives installed for a variable list of titles. Teachers in a classroom or lab could then choose titles from the central server or could insert special titles into their local CD-ROM drives as needed.

NETWORKING CD-ROMs
IN LIBRARIES AND SCHOOLS

This section provides a high-level overview of CD-ROM networking, including basic concepts, planning issues, and budgetary issues for both local area networks ("LANs") and (in the following section) the Internet.

ESTIMATING THE NUMBER OF SIMULTANEOUS USERS

Determining whether or not to network CD-ROMs involves several types of considerations, for example, number of simultaneous users and the need for remote access. In order to determine whether a network system is needed or whether multiple copies of a title should be purchased instead, it's necessary to be able to estimate the number of users who will simultaneously desire access to a given title. Information about use can be obtained by noting the number of people simultaneously accessing a similar reference book, from library transaction records, and so on. Schools may also need to consider the setting in which students and teachers will use a given title: if in a computer lab where students must access the title individually (as opposed to a classroom setting where teachers present or control the computer and CD-ROM disc), then clearly the number of users will be greater. In all cases the number of simultaneous users will be physically limited to the number of CD-ROM or networked workstations.

You will also need this information when deciding on the type of license to purchase for any given CD-ROM title. There's no need to purchase a site license, network license, or multi-user license if the title is going to be installed on a single, stand-alone workstation.

Networks are also useful as a means of isolating the CD-ROM discs and drives from users in public places. As mentioned above, one of the best means of securing CD-ROM titles away from the public in a library or school is to provide access to discs over a network. Even in a small library, a CD-ROM network can be designed in which one or two workstations in the reading rooms are only able to access CD-ROM titles over the network, and discs are controlled by librarians in a remote location, such as behind the circulation desk or in an administrative office.

MULTIPLE LOCATIONS, MULTIPLE DISCS, AND MULTIPLE USERS—DEFINING THE PROBLEM

CD-ROM is a medium for both multimedia and large databases. As a consequence, the computer platform on which CD-ROM titles run must be designed to accommodate the demands of multimedia (images, animation, video, and audio) and provide access to vast amounts of data, including multimedia databases. The computer platform must have the capacity to process and display high-resolution, full-screen video, to process and play many audio file formats, and to access and process data rapidly.

For the purpose of this discussion, a database is a structured collection of data: for example, a CD-ROM encyclopedia is a type of a multimedia database in which data is organized and stored in video files, audio files, text files, and other file formats. In a library or a classroom individual users of the CD-ROM may search the database for information stored either in several locations on a single CD-ROM disc or on several discs. For example, more than one disc of a multi-disc encyclopedia title is likely to contain related information. Several users may simultaneously seek information on the same topic, requiring access simultaneously by several users of a single disc or of several discs simultaneously.

Whether the need is for a single user to access more than one disc at a time or for several users to access one disc simultaneously, the result is that a single CD-ROM drive dedicated to a single-user workstation is inadequate. In either case, the CD-ROM system must be designed so that more than one disc is accessible and more than one workstation at a time can access each CD-ROM disc.

Not all libraries or schools will be faced with this issue, though. Solutions, such as the following, may be adequate for a small library or school:

- Acquire only single-disc titles
- Install multiple CD-ROM drives in each workstation
- Provide enough stand-alone CD-ROM workstations for each CD-ROM title for the user population
- Schedule access to CD-ROM titles to avoid conflicts

During the needs assessment phase of your CD-ROM implementation project, you should determine whether the CD-ROM titles you plan to acquire include multi-disc titles and how likely it is that more than one user at a time will desire access to a single title. CD-ROM companies are producing a growing number of multi-disc titles. In the future higher-capacity discs (such as DVD) will enable title producers to place larger databases on single discs (although, inevitably, this will lead to multi-disc DVD titles, as well). The number of users desiring simultaneous access to information, though, is likely to increase exponentially. In addition, libraries and schools are being encouraged to establish LANs as they become connected to the Internet, and the presence of a LAN in a library or school will facilitate the adoption of networked CD-ROMs.

TECHNOLOGY OPTIONS

Solutions to the multi-disc, multi-user problem form a matrix. On one axis of the matrix are multiple CD-ROM drives versus disc changers, and on the other axis of the matrix is the stand-alone workstation versus the networked workstation. Each cell in the matrix represents a viable alternative, and all of these alternatives may coexist happily within an institution. Your library or school may have a stand-alone workstation dedicated to a multi-disc title using several internally installed CD-ROM drives. You may also have a CD-ROM network providing simultaneous access to a popular, single-disc title and a collection of over 100 other titles. Some technology options have been available for several years and may already be in place, while you may also wish to consider some of the newer options. All of these can coexist, given careful planning and good technical support.

The simplest and oldest option is multiple CD-ROM drives dedicated to a single workstation. All operating systems for PCs since DOS 4.0 and for the Mac since System 6 accommodate multiple CD-ROM drives. DOS and Windows PCs can theoretically accommodate twenty-six drives (one for each letter of the alphabet); excluding diskette drives (A and B) and a hard drive (C), all remaining drives may be CD-ROM drives. The Mac operating system accommodates a SCSI chain of up to seven CD-ROM drives.

As a practical matter, more than four CD-ROM drives would be difficult to accommodate inside a single system unit, and a long chain of external

SCSI drives is considered to be unwieldy. Therefore, older multi-disc options included disc changers, stackers, and jukeboxes. These worked something like old-fashioned record-changers and music jukeboxes: Several discs are held in reserve and swapped in and out of the drive on request. This option allows a single user to access a large collection of discs, but access is relatively slow, and only one disc at a time can be accessed. Disc changers and stackers tend to hold about a dozen discs, while jukeboxes hold many dozens.

Many jukeboxes are still in use and available. An appropriate use for a CD-ROM jukebox would be to provide access to a large collection of single-disc CD-ROM titles that may have been acquired over several years and which are infrequently used. Many educational freeware and shareware CD-ROM titles fall into this category. Archived telephone directory CD-ROM titles might also fall into this category.

A more-recent technology option is the CD-ROM drive tower. A tower looks like a number of disc drives in a single case, typically a dozen. While the tower may be attached to a single, stand-alone workstation, it is intended for use on a network. The tower's case usually has a locking door or locks on each disc-drive drawer to prevent unauthorized access to discs and to prevent a disc from being removed from the system while it is in use. Often the tower consists of a stack of bays into which drives can be installed and removed, allowing for easy upgrades to the drives.

A CD-ROM network requires more than simply a tower: it must include several other hardware and software components. A network consists of one or more "servers," one or more "client" workstations, and the wiring or cabling that connects the servers and clients. There are several options for accomplishing this—several types of networks. Networks may be one of several widely used commercial systems such as those offered by Microsoft and Novell, or closed, proprietary systems designed specifically for libraries.

If your library already has a LAN, it may be one of several types, not all of which will easily accommodate a new CD-ROM server. For example, a proprietary card-catalog system (consisting of both network hardware and software, including a card-catalog interface system for patrons) probably isn't able to accommodate additional functions, such as CD-ROM access for patrons, as well. As another example, older Macintosh networks are of the type called "peer-to-peer" and based on the AppleTalk protocol (a technology standard). Peer-to-peer networks involve no central servers; each workstation is independent and equal but may share and transfer files and share peripherals, such as a printer. A Macintosh AppleTalk network will allow users to access a CD-ROM drive that is physically attached to any Macintosh in the network, but access is restricted to one user at a time and is consequently rather slow. An AppleTalk network would not accommodate a CD-ROM tower and CD-ROM server.

Older PC networks may be based on one of several protocols and use a network operating system, such as Banyan Vines or Novell (as do newer networks). The earliest such networks are configured around a file server, which allows users with networked workstations to share and transfer files and share peripherals. Each workstation on the network, though, has its own application programs, including CD-ROM titles, installed on its hard drive. A CD-ROM network can be designed so that the file server has a tower or a number of CD-ROM drives installed, so you could add several CD-ROM drives to an older network based on a file server architecture.

Networks can be structured to allow for many types of servers—not just file servers but also application servers and CD-ROM servers. In such networks the workstations access applications, such as word-processors and spreadsheets, stored on the application server, as well as access and store documents and other files on the file server. A central server may combine these functions.

A separate CD-ROM server can also be added to many types of networks, with the sole purpose of providing access to CD-ROM discs in a tower. The CD-ROM server provides enhanced performance through specialized software, so that access to discs by several users is faster than in other types of systems.

A CD-ROM network usually is made up of a number of different hardware and software components. An older Macintosh network based on AppleTalk requires only a small connector and ordinary phone cabling to connect several Macs. The operating system running on each Mac workstation handles the network traffic. More complex, sophisticated networks require a good deal more. Each workstation must have a network adapter card installed and cabling to connect to the central server. A separate computer must act as the server, with the appropriate network adapters installed in it and a network operating system to manage the system. The CD-ROM tower (or jukebox) can be attached directly to the central server; or a separate CD-ROM server (to which the tower is attached) can be attached to the central server. The CD-ROM server need not be a separate computer, but is often simply a compact box with only the necessary hardware and software for managing CD-ROMs.

Network performance is another critical consideration when dealing with multimedia CD-ROMs. Many CD-ROMs provide multimedia materials, which require high-performance networks. In part this means fast networks. Before implementing multimedia CD-ROMs on an existing network, it is important to understand how this will affect the network as a whole, not only for the CD-ROM users, but also for other applications running on the network.

This is a greatly simplified description of CD-ROM network options. It is provided only to give you an understanding of the components of such a system so that you can include all necessary items in your budget and select a system that fits in with the architecture of your library's or school's existing systems.

CD-ROM network components are becoming increasingly easy to install and use. Nonetheless, since every network is unique, made up of unique components in a unique environment, networks are technically complex and not easy to support. In almost every case you should consider having a designated network administrator available if you plan to implement most types of CD-ROM networks. Networking expertise can be acquired from external consultants and system-wide technical staff, not just as in-house staff (which may not be necessary and may often be impractical). This individual can help you select the best hardware and software for the network, install the network, and maintain it. Only the simplest types of networks (such as AppleTalk networks and other peer-to-peer networks at a single location) can be managed by untrained or nontechnical staff.

WHEN TO CHOOSE A NETWORK SOLUTION

CD-ROM networks are probably inevitable for most libraries and schools. Multi-location library and school systems which can afford a technical support staff can readily benefit from the CD-ROM network technologies now available. Costs are relatively low for the equipment, and CD-ROM title licenses provide many cost-effective network options. As more and more libraries and schools connect to the Internet, it will make economic sense to include a CD-ROM tower and server in the system.

Smaller libraries and schools and those without a technical staff may find that stand-alone CD-ROM workstations with multiple CD-ROM drives are actually more cost-effective and considerably easier to manage. Most newer-model multimedia computers include at least one internal CD-ROM drive, and adding other drives can cost less than $200 per drive (about the cost of a four-color art-print book, for example). Keep in mind that the cost of workstations and titles continues to fall, while the cost of personnel continues to rise, and personnel time can be a significant part of the cost of any network.

SUMMARY OF NETWORKING

This section has not attempted to be a discussion of network technology, nor has it attempted to survey network protocols, topologies, or operating systems. Instead, this section described for the nontechnical reader the general types of equipment options available for single users accessing multi-disc titles and multiple users accessing a single disc. These options include multiple CD-ROM drives installed in a stand-alone workstation, multiple CD-ROM drives accessible from several workstations over a simple network, disc changers (such as stackers and jukeboxes), and CD-ROM network servers plus a CD-ROM tower.

INTEGRATING *CD-ROM* AND THE INTERNET

CD-ROM is only one of many technologies that may be included in a library's or school's information systems. For some purposes, CD-ROM can be treated as an independent source of information and education; for example, a single, stand-alone CD-ROM workstation might be dedicated to an encyclopedia. For other purposes, CD-ROM may be integrated into a network that provides access to several types of databases at several locations. In many instances, budget constraints may dictate that computers in a library or school be used for several purposes; a stand-alone CD-ROM workstation dedicated to a single information resource may be a luxury that can't be afforded.

Several benefits result from designing workstations to include both CD-ROM access and Internet access. Such workstations allow users to take advantage of educational and information resources that have both a CD-ROM and an Internet component. Most CD-ROM encyclopedia titles, for example, also have an Internet component. Users can access a World Wide Web site from within the CD-ROM encyclopedia's environment to obtain updated information, new information, online chat conferences with experts, and message bulletin boards.

Users also will find it easier to learn to use a single, integrated CD-ROM/Internet workstation rather than two different workstations. For example, a user must learn to print from each workstation: network printers may be accessed differently from printers dedicated to a single workstation. Learning to print information obtained from a CD-ROM and from a Web page is easier if both are available at the same workstation.

The Internet is also the best source of technical support for CD-ROM workstations, operating systems, and CD-ROM titles. Individuals responsible for maintaining a CD-ROM workstation can benefit from being able to access Internet technical resources directly from the CD-ROM workstation.

There are, however, a few drawbacks to integrating CD-ROM and Internet technology within the same workstation. Security is more difficult to establish and maintain on an Internet-connected workstation than on a stand-alone workstation. An Internet connection allows access to the workstation from outside the library or school, potentially compromising any confidential information that may be stored on the workstation and also increasing the risk of computer viruses. Some CD-ROM title licenses may prohibit public access or access by more than one workstation. The operating system and other software on a dual-purpose workstation are more complex than a single-purpose workstation's, making maintenance of the system more difficult. And, finally, the greater the number of resources available from a single workstation, the greater the demand for access to the workstation. Wear-and-tear on dual-purpose workstations will be greater than on single-purpose workstations, and users will experience more scheduling conflicts.

If you plan to provide both CD-ROM and Internet access from a single workstation, you will need the following special hardware and software. The workstation will require an interface card for network access, either an Ethernet card for access to a LAN that is, in turn, connected to the Internet via a router and dedicated line; or an adapter for direct access to the Internet via the router; or a modem (either internal or external). The workstation must either be connected by cable to the LAN or the Internet or by phone line. Each workstation will need Internet-access software, such as a browser, an e-mail program, a news reader program, an FTP program, a Telnet program (some programs integrate these into a single package), and a filter program to prevent access to objectionable materials.

If access is provided via the phone lines, the workstation must also have a dialer program and separate phone lines for this purpose. Keep in mind that each use of a modem is a phone call. Only one call is possible per line simultaneously. If the library or school is directly connected to the Internet, then the cost of access is essentially the fees for the dedicated line, usually obtained from a telephone company or regional network company. If the connection is through phone lines, costs include the charges for each phone call, as well as service fees to an Internet service provider ("ISP") or online service such as America Online.

In either case, budgets must also include the cost of individual workstation hardware and software. Of course, if the CD-ROM workstation is already part of a LAN, no additional equipment is required for the workstation. In such a case, the additional equipment is required for the CD-ROM server system. If the library or school is also part of a WAN, such as a regional library network, Internet access may be available through the WAN. In such a case, even the CD-ROM server may not need additional hardware, but the connection may be made through software changes only. In all cases, however, the individual workstations must have the Internet software applications listed above.

PUBLIC CD-ROM WORKSTATION DESIGN

Having considered the number and type of CD-ROM drives to be included in your institution's workstations, and whether to include network connections, you now have a general idea of the basic hardware necessary for the workstation. CD-ROM workstations are essentially personal computers configured for use by more than one person. This places special burdens on both the hardware and software. This section discusses these additional workstation design considerations.

SELECTING THE OPERATING SYSTEM FOR A LIBRARY OR SCHOOL

After assessing needs such as the number of drives and network requirements, the next decision is which operating environment is most appropriate for your school's or library's needs. Current needs may be modest, but you may have plans for future local area networking or the Internet. The operating system chosen should be easily upgraded to future networking environments. A sophisticated system could be based on UNIX or LINUX, but in most cases this means that the system will require a significant amount of technical support. A more practical approach would be to choose between the Intel/Windows environment ("WinTel") and the Macintosh environment. The only critical issue is the ease with which the chosen operating system can be adapted to the addition of a LAN or Internet connectivity. Be sure to explore this issue with any vendor from whom you plan to purchase new systems.

In reality, your library or school probably already has either PCs or Macintoshes, and you will base future systems on existing systems. Both environments can be successfully incorporated into a CD-ROM technology plan.

PUBLIC LOCATIONS

Each workstation must be located in an open, but traffic-free, area. The workstations must be visible at all times to supervising staff in order to prevent misuse and abuse of the equipment. As tempting as it may be to provide enclosed cubicles for CD-ROM workstations (for example, to prevent multimedia sounds from disturbing others in the library or classroom), secluded CD-ROM workstations tend to be damaged more frequently than do public ones. To eliminate disturbing sounds, provide headphones attached to the computer's sound card and keep users from manipulating the volume controls by securing them in locked cabinets. Simply turning off sound isn't a good idea: many video segments in multimedia titles rely heavily on the accompanying audio.

The workstations must not be placed in high-traffic areas, such as near doorways or in aisles. Traffic near a workstation will distract workstation users and can jostle users. There must be adequate space around a workstation for one or more chairs to be positioned comfortably in front of the screen. If groups are expected to be gathered around a workstation, adequate floor space must be provided.

ENVIRONMENTAL CONTROLS

Workstations must be kept in an area with a stable temperature, away from doors opening to the outdoors, out of breezes, and away from all humidity and moisture. For example, no workstation should be in close proximity to a water fountain or coffee urn. Since the workstation must have a good power supply and possibly connections to a network, it must be located next to a wall, unless floor outlets are available: never allow cables and cords to be taped across a floor or carpet, even when rubber insulation covers them; this is acceptable only as a temporary solution to cabling needs.

Heat is an enemy to all electronic equipment. Even computer components with built-in fans can quickly overheat in an overheated room. Keep in mind that, if an environment is uncomfortably hot for you, it is undoubtedly much hotter inside the computer equipment. Elements can easily fuse, melt, and short-circuit. Keep the workstation cool—no more than 80 degrees Fahrenheit, in most cases.

Moisture is also an enemy of computer equipment. In a cool or moderate-temperature room with high humidity, the heat generated turning on a computer and its components is likely to cause condensation inside the equipment. This condensation can cause the equipment to malfunction, sometimes temporarily, sometimes permanently. Never position a workstation near a vent, fan, or air-conditioning unit.

A particularly dry environment allows static electricity to build up on shoes, clothing, skin, and inside electrical equipment. Provide an antistatic mat or other antistatic devices for each workstation and chair. Static electrical charges can short-circuit the system and damage computer chips.

The electrical lines into every building are fairly volatile. The amount of amperage transmitted through the wires fluctuates. A power surge can short-circuit equipment and destroy it. Lightning striking in the vicinity is a common source of damage to computers. If the power slackens and browns out or completely blacks out, not only can data be lost if a workstation is in use, but the sudden and improper shutdown of the computer can damage components. Some CD-ROM drives may respond poorly to having the power shut off while a disc is in the drive, for example. You may have difficulty removing the disc or may damage the drive while attempting to do so, even after power is restored.

Provide a surge-protecting power strip for all workstations. Instruct staff to shut off the equipment during thunderstorms and when the lights fade or brighten. Attach all equipment to a backup power supply that gives you at least several seconds to shut down the system properly in the event of complete power failure. External power supplies also help to filter the power reaching a workstation.

Dust and smoke in the air can do damage to computer equipment. Besides maintaining as clean an atmosphere as possible, require periodic dusting and vacuuming around the computer with a small computer-sized vacuum cleaner (a large vacuum cleaner's motor can generate a magnetic field that can damage the data stored on disks of all kinds except CD-ROM discs, of course).

ERGONOMICS OF CD-ROM
WORKSTATION DESIGN FOR THE PUBLIC

For workstations intended to be used by one person at a time, the ergonomic considerations are similar to those for any personal computer. For workstations intended for group presentations, the considerations are very different.

Workstations for Individuals or Groups

A public CD-ROM workstation can be designed for use by one person at a time (either as a stand-alone computer or a networked computer) or by a group of people, such as in a classroom or laboratory setting. When intended for use by only one person at a time, the workstation must be hardened against heavy usage and careless abuse. When intended for a group, the workstation must also be designed with additional equipment or nonstandard components, such as a large monitor or projection unit.

Single-User Workstations

Individual CD-ROM workstations should be designed to reduce back strain, reduce wrist strain, reduce eye strain, and reduce exposure to magnetic fields from the monitor. To reduce back strain, provide a chair that can be easily adjusted by the user to a comfortable height and position. Since most public CD-ROM workstations are intended for use only for short periods, such as a quick search of a database, most users won't experience back strain. Wrist strain is a common problem, though, that can cause pain almost instantly. To reduce this problem, the desk should have an easily adjustable shelf for the keyboard and mouse; the mouse should have a long cord that can be repositioned on either side (to accommodate the ten-percent left-handed population); and a wrist support or rest should be supplied.

To reduce eye strain, never locate a workstation directly under ceiling lights that can cause glare; make sure the monitor is a high-resolution monitor with a rapid "refresh" rate (that is, the speed with which the screen is repainted or refreshed); and consider placing an antiglare screen over the monitor's screen.

To prevent exposure of users to strong magnetic fields, configure the workstation with a low-magnetic emission monitor. Shield the back of the monitor from the public, since most magnetic waves are emitted from the rear rather than front of the monitor.

Workstations for Group Presentations

Workstations intended for group presentations should also include either an extra-large monitor or a projection device for screen images. Stereo speakers should be detachable and moveable so that they can be spread out and allow the whole group to hear the presentation. Input devices should be available for interacting with the software from a distance—for example, an infrared, cordless mouse can be used by a teacher conducting a class from the rear of a group of students gathered in front of the workstation. A wheeled cart with electric sockets should be provided to allow for repositioning the workstation. The monitor should be positioned at shoulder-height.

Access to CD-ROM Workstations for the Disabled

Computer technology is particularly powerful for addressing the special needs of the physically disabled. Unfortunately, most technology is designed for the use of one person, making it difficult to accommodate the needs of the disabled public. At minimum, workstations should be designed to allow wheelchair access—wide spaces should be available under the workstation's desk; the chair should be easily pushed aside by wheelchair users.

A wide range of input devices are available for the disabled. If your library or school has a large population that requires assistance with input, you can obtain joysticks and straws to replace mouse and keyboard. Braille keyboards are widely available. Voice input is also possible, although be aware that most voice-activated software is designed for use by a single individual who "trains" the software to recognize his or her voice.

Several special output options are also available. Both the Windows and Macintosh operating systems provide large-type fonts for text displays. Digitized voice software can read text from the screen. Headphones and amplifiers can provide assistance for the hearing-impaired.

All of these options impact the individual CD-ROM workstations, not the CD-ROM server or network systems. So, for example, a few specially equipped workstations can be provided within a network of more-standard CD-ROM workstations.

PLANNING FOR MAINTENANCE, UPGRADES, AND REPAIRS OF LIBRARY AND SCHOOL CD-ROM WORKSTATIONS

As mentioned above, workstations can and should be designed with future modifications in mind. Components should be modular so that they can be replaced if they become outdated or damaged. Computer cases and cabinets housing the system should provide easy access to interior components.

Expect to replace some components of a system frequently, including the mouse, keyboard, hard drive, headphones, and power supply. These are heavily used on every system and tend to wear out, but are also relatively inexpensive.

Establish a regular maintenance schedule for all hardware and software. Clean dust off monitor screens (it is attracted by the magnetic field). Vacuum keyboards and disk drive doors. Use diskette and CD-ROM drive head cleaning kits regularly. Clean the mouse ball weekly, if not daily, and make sure the surface on which the mouse ball rolls is kept clean.

Run hard drive de-fragmentation programs on a regular schedule. Verify that the surface of the hard drive isn't deteriorating (software utility programs can check this for you).

Regularly back up the hard drive onto diskette or tape. Be sure to include a heavy-duty backup system as part of the CD-ROM system's budget: Zip™ drives and tape backup systems are good choices. Store some backups off site so that data can be recovered in the event of disasters, such as fire and flooding where the workstations are located.

Network servers must be backed up even more often than stand-alone workstations. Provide redundancy in the network wherever possible: this includes backup or alternative server systems, power supplies (both external and internal), and off-site storage.

ADVANCED USES OF CD-ROM: SPECIAL COLLECTIONS, ARCHIVING, AND LOCAL DATABASES

Public libraries often (less often schools and school libraries) house local-interest special collections and databases, such as historical archives of city directories, local historical memorabilia, and local newspaper and newsletter archives. Imaging and optical disc technologies (including CD-ROM, CD-R, CD-WR, and DVD-R) are highly suitable for these archives and databases. In addition, the technology required to digitize and create optical discs is becoming increasingly inexpensive and accessible. In planning your CD-ROM system, you may wish to consider including facilities to create your own CD-ROM titles, DVD titles, or other types of discs.

Some disc formats are extremely easy to produce, even in the home, let alone in a professional library or school setting. For example, Kodak Photo CD can be created with a standard 35-mm camera and film, simply by sending the undeveloped film to a Kodak Photo CD processing facility.

More technical skill and specialized equipment is needed to produce a CD-ROM disc, but the cost is not prohibitive, and the technology is fairly easy to use. Your plans for CD-ROM technology could, for example, include at least one workstation equipped with a CD-R drive and software. You could purchase a high-quality scanner (prices tend to be below $1000 for a good scanner) with which to digitize documents; then, to archive the digital files, use the CD-R system to write or save the files to a special type of CD-ROM disc (available for a few dollars apiece).

Alternatively, service bureaus located throughout the United States can take a set of diskettes containing digital archives and transfer them to CD-ROM for you, usually at a cost of a few dollars to a few hundred dollars per disc (depending upon the number of discs ordered).

FINANCIAL PLANNING

Financial planning for CD-ROM technology must include not only the cost of initial acquisition of the technology, but also the cost of maintenance and upgrades. As with any technology resources, costs must include personnel costs, not just hardware and software costs.

COSTS OF EQUIPMENT, TITLE DISCS, AND PERSONNEL

A good CD-ROM financial plan should include the following categories: workstations, title licenses, supplies, installation and setup costs, maintenance and repair, and administration. Depending upon your library's or school's financial reporting requirements, these costs will be classified as capital or expense and will be allocated to the period in which the cost is incurred or at the time of the expense. Planning should cover at least a three year period, but it should be recognized that the actual useful life of any given item is probably one year, depending upon the amount of use the system will receive. The CD-ROM system should be viewed as a permanent resource that will undergo continuous change.

Workstation Costs

If a CD-ROM workstation is purchased new solely for the presentation of CD-ROM titles, you can expect its cost to fall within the high end of the range of prices for any multimedia computer on the market. The workstation should include the highest-resolution monitor available, the largest hard drive, the most memory, and the fastest, most powerful processor, in order to avoid rapid obsolescence and allow it to run CD-ROM titles that are not only on the market today but for several years to come.

If the CD-ROM workstation is being configured from existing computers, the budget should allow for upgrades to the graphics adapter and monitor, hard drive, memory, and (if possible) processor, as well as the addition of the CD-ROM drive or drives or adapter card for a CD-ROM network. Networked workstations require a network card (usually an Ethernet adapter card) and network cabling.

The costs of the workstation will also include the desk and cabinet in which it is secured, the operating system software, and other programs to be installed on it. Such software may include a menu or shell system, a virus detection utility, other utilities to aid in the installation and deinstallation of CD-ROM titles.

Each workstation should be provided with a surge protector, line filter, and backup power supply.

License Costs

The cost of CD-ROM title licenses may actually be the least of any of the costs for which you must plan. Most CD-ROM titles cost under $100. Standard reference titles and network or multi-user licenses are more costly. On a per-user basis, however, they may be highly cost-effective. Budgeting for titles should be done on a per-workstation basis. Many title licenses also cover a limited number of updates and editions or versions. Some licenses may charge an extra fee for technical support, an option which should be purchased when it is available. User manuals and documentation may sometimes be purchased separately, and for networked CD-ROM titles separate user guides may be desirable for each workstation on the network.

Supplies Costs

Supplies for each workstation include diskettes, disk-drive cleaning kits, keyboard and mouse cleaning kits, antistatic sprays and mats, printer ink and paper, and cables and power cords (which break easily). Some equipment, which has to be replaced frequently may also be treated as supplies—including the mouse and hard drive. Depending on your style of financial reporting, software may be considered to be a supply rather than part of the equipment cost.

Installation and Setup Costs

All modifications to existing spaces must be included in the initial installation budget. Wiring for electricity and cabling for networks or phone lines for modems should be included in the installation plan. Staff salaries for the installation or purchase of outside services must also be included.

A training budget should also be included. Training must include not only the use of the workstation or network but also the software and CD-ROM titles to be run on the workstation.

Installation of individual titles should be included in the administrative costs, discussed below.

Maintenance and Repair Costs

Maintenance of the workstation consists of hardware care and software maintenance. Consequently, maintenance involves staff time, supplies, replacement parts and equipment, and warranties of equipment. A budget should be provided for repair of all equipment that includes moving parts since these tend to wear out or break more often than other parts of computer systems. Typical repair items include power switches, keyboards, shorts in circuitry and cabling. The most practical approach is to contract for the costs of parts and labor with an on-site repair service.

Weekly or monthly maintenance procedures should take place regularly and be part of a staff member's responsibilities. The budget should consist of a percentage of salary.

Administrative Costs

Administrative costs consist mainly of the cost of staff to install titles, supervise use of the workstation and collections, maintain and troubleshoot the software, and assist users. Budgets could include full-time equivalent staff dedicated to the technology or a percentage of existing staff salaries.

THE HIDDEN COSTS OF USED AND DONATED EQUIPMENT

It's quite common for libraries and schools to receive donations of computer equipment. Keep in mind that these donations bring with them unexpected costs as well as much-welcome benefits. Used equipment can be more difficult to upgrade and maintain than new equipment. Unplanned additions to a computer system may distract from previously established goals.

Even the gift of CD-ROM titles can result in problems and disruptions to plans. A library of CD-ROM titles must be selected for compatibility with existing equipment or with planned systems. Donated titles may require new equipment in order to be used effectively.

OTHER BUDGETARY ISSUES

A planned CD-ROM system may include phases for the addition of workstations or even a network of CD-ROMs or eventual access to the Internet. If care isn't taken to design stand-alone CD-ROM workstations that are capable of being upgraded and incorporated into more advanced systems, workstations can quickly become obsolete too early.

CHAPTER SUMMARY

This chapter covers a wide range of CD-ROM technology planning issues. A series of phases is suggested for the implementation of CD-ROM technology into a library or school system. The design of workstations and networks is discussed. Specialized equipment for the disabled and advanced optical disc technologies are surveyed. Security of hardware and software is discussed. Placement of workstations is discussed. And, finally, financial plans and budget items are covered.

2. The CD-ROM Title Evaluation Process

INTRODUCTION TO CD-ROM TITLE SELECTION

Before purchasing CD-ROM titles for your patrons and students, you must first determine the specific types of workstations on which those titles will be "played," where the workstations will be located, and who will want to access the titles for what purposes. This information is discussed in detail in Chapter 1. Only after determining the who, what, where, how, and why are you fully prepared to select CD-ROM titles that meet these requirements and that will also run properly on your workstations.

The necessity of selecting appropriate CD-ROM titles can't be over-stressed. No CD-ROM title is suitable for every possible institution, computer system, or public use. Some titles are designed for a single user at a time, while others accommodate multiple, simultaneous users. Some titles run only on one type of computer operating system, while other titles are capable of running on several different systems. Every title is unique in some way—these unique characteristics can make a title especially appropriate for one audience and completely inappropriate for another. With CD-ROM titles "one size does not fit all." Selecting the wrong title is the principal source of most of the problems encountered with this technology.

To ensure successful selection of CD-ROM titles for your library's or school's unique needs, follow an orderly title evaluation process, as described in this chapter. The process should include the following steps:

1. Identify the hardware and other physical requirements for all CD-ROM titles. For example, determine whether the titles you need must be compatible with both a Macintosh and a PC operating system.
2. Identify the user needs that must be met by the CD-ROM titles. For example, determine whether an encyclopedia disc will be needed more often by secondary school students or by adult researchers.
3. Determine what choices are currently available for each type of title. For example, find out whether there is more than one encyclopedia available in CD-ROM format.

4. If the CD-ROM title isn't a unique, standard work (a "must-have"), evaluate the quality of competing titles and how well they meet your other needs. This normally involves studying detailed product information, reading reviews, and obtaining demos and previews of the title discs.
5. Having decided which specific titles you wish to purchase, verify that they are technically compatible with your computers (matching the specifications identified in step 1 above). If necessary, determine whether you must purchase more than one version of the title in order to run them on different computer systems or whether a special network version is available. See Chapter 3 for details on how to ensure compatibility of titles with your computer system.
6. Obtain information on sources and the licensing options available for each title. In most cases, CD-ROM titles aren't distributed by the same organizations that sell books, and many CD-ROM titles (like most desktop computer software) are intended for single-users, not public use. Consequently, you may need to make special arrangements in order to purchase certain titles.

Take the time to evaluate the CD-ROM titles you plan to buy. In the long run you will save time: by avoiding installation problems, by preventing the need to return unusable or inappropriate discs, and by choosing titles with "a long shelf life."

This chapter discusses steps 3, 4, and 6 in the selection process described above. (Step 5 is covered in detail in Chapter 3 and Chapter 7, section 7.3.) CD-ROM title evaluation criteria are discussed, along with some industry jargon you may encounter during your research. Then, good sources of reviews and previews are discussed. And, finally, sources for purchasing CD-ROM titles are discussed.

CD-ROM TITLE EVALUATION CRITERIA

How do you judge a CD-ROM title? Are CD-ROM titles evaluated exactly the way you evaluate a book or other information media? The answer is that CD-ROM, while it is essentially nothing more than a storage medium, must be evaluated according to standards that take into account not only the quality of the content of a title but also the fact that CD-ROM is a digital medium and that the amount of data that can be stored on a single CD-ROM disc is significant.

GENERAL CRITERIA

Below, a number of evaluation criteria are discussed. Use these criteria to formulate a list of specific criteria to use in your own CD-ROM title search.

These criteria apply to most CD-ROM genres. Criteria specific to certain categories are covered later in this chapter.

Reputation of the Title Producers

Just as the reputation of a publisher may indicate the quality of a book, the reputation of a CD-ROM producer may also be an indication of the quality or characteristics of a CD-ROM title. Most producers specialize in certain types of titles. They have a track record of user acceptance and customer support, or lack thereof. Use your own experiences with a producer's CD-ROM titles, just as you would use your experience with a well-established book publisher.

Of course, you can't rely entirely upon the reputation of the CD-ROM producer when selecting discs. Your needs may not match those of most of the producer's customers. Different titles within a producer's catalog may vary in quality.

These differences in the quality of titles are often between those titles actually designed by a company and those titles that are only marketed and distributed by that company.

You need to be able to judge a specific CD-ROM title based on its own merits, not those of its producer. In part, this means you have to determine if the internal structure of the CD-ROM software has been designed specifically for the medium, and if the overall organization of the information is developed with both the limitations and the potential of CD-ROM in mind. A CD-ROM title must not only have high-quality content, but it must be useful and suitable to its users. General selection criteria include: whether the amount of data on the disc is sufficient (including whether the amount of data justifies the extra complexities of presentation on a CD-ROM disc); whether the type of data on the disc is appropriate to CD-ROM; speed and ease of access to that data; appropriateness of the content for interactivity (defined below); and whether the program code that underlies the title has been thoroughly tested, is error-free, and adequately supported with good documentation or a technical support hotline. Each of these evaluation criteria is discussed below.

Technical Quality

The technical quality of a CD-ROM is very important but very difficult to determine before you buy it. The video and audio production quality can be determined by previewing the disc. The quality of the underlying program code rarely can. You also have no way of knowing whether a title was adequately tested before it was released to the public. Reviewers are unlikely to spend enough time with a title to uncover the hidden bugs and program quirks.

The manual may be difficult to understand or poorly written. The technical support personnel may not be well trained or knowledgeable. Yet, these are important considerations in evaluating a CD-ROM title. When you can obtain information about the quality-assurance procedures used in developing the title, be sure to take this into account. Always examine the manuals supplied with the discs. Be sure a technical support phone number is given to customers.

Amount and Type of Data

CD-ROM is first and foremost a storage medium. A single CD-ROM disc can store a massive amount of information in a very compact form. One disc can hold over 600 megabytes (Mb) of data, which is equivalent to approximately 600 million individual printed characters, or several complete books.

The quality of a CD-ROM title is rarely entirely dependent upon the amount of information it contains (just as the quality of a library isn't entirely dependent on the number of books it houses). A CD-ROM, however, like a library, is especially useful when it collects in a single place a relatively large amount of information.

A CD-ROM title should contain a large amount of high-quality information. Many CD-ROM titles (especially many older titles) are merely massive amounts of printed information "dumped" almost without any changes to a CD-ROM disc. Only in rare instances would such a CD-ROM title, regardless of how much data it contains, be considered a high-quality title.

Conversely, a CD-ROM containing little data would probably not be considered a high-quality title, no matter the quality of the data. A CD-ROM's storage capacity makes it most appropriate for applications that require massive amounts of data. If the content of a CD-ROM title can be stored equally well on a single diskette, then the diskette is preferable to the CD-ROM. Think of it this way: if all the information on a certain topic can be printed in a two-hundred page book, it would be absurd to print it in two volumes with extraordinarily wide margins and lots of blank pages. A CD-ROM disc is the equivalent of many volumes, while a diskette is the equivalent of a single volume.

If the diskette version is identical to the CD-ROM version, then the amount of information is probably inadequate. Even in a compressed format consisting of several diskettes, a diskette version cannot possibly approach 600 megabytes. If the program is compressed in order to be stored on diskettes, it will have to be expanded and installed on a hard drive before it can be used. Not only is that an unnecessary complication for your workstation's system manager, but it indicates that the final product will contain only a few megabytes of information, not 600 Mb.

How do you know if a CD-ROM title under consideration contains sufficient data to make it worthwhile? How do you determine if the content actually requires the massive storage capacity of a CD-ROM? You can't look at a CD-ROM and tell how much data it contains. If it were a book you could clearly see how many pages long it is. If it were a videotape, you could look for some indication of its run-length. Because of the way in which a CD-ROM disc is structured, it's even difficult to examine the amount of data on the disc using a computer.

To further complicate matters, the data on a CD-ROM may be stored in a variety of formats. Some of these formats inherently may require massive storage. For example, audio and video take up a lot more space on most CD-ROMs than do program code or text information. So, the more video on the CD-ROM or the more audio, the less conceptual information it may contain. This means that—for example—an encyclopedia with lots of video and audio may actually contain fewer reference articles than a printed encyclopedia. An instructional disc with numerous animations may actually contain fewer learning activities than one with text-based drill-and-practice. (See Table 2.1 for further information on the storage capacity of a CD-ROM disc.)

Table 2.1 Approximate Capacity of a CD-ROM Disc

Maximum	Data Type
2.4	hours of 8-bit stereo LP album sound
4.8	hours of 4-bit stereo FM radio sound
9.6	hours of 4-bit stereo, speech or AM radio sound
16	CD-I audio tracks (at various lengths, different fidelities)
19.2	hours of mono sound
74	minutes of CD audio
100	Kodak Photo CD images
400	3.5 inch floppy disks' worth of data
150,000	typeset book pages
250,000	typewritten pages
600	Mb of data
600	million typewritten characters

Richness of Content

The issue, then, is whether a CD-ROM disc is as content-rich as possible. Advertising and promotional materials for a CD-ROM title will provide some indication of the amount of content: highly touted features of a title often include the number of minutes or hours of full-motion video and high-fidelity audio, the number of photographic-quality images, and the number of articles or "pages" of text information. Remember that there is a substantial trade-off between audio-video length and overall intellectual content.

Nonetheless, one measure of the quality of a CD-ROM title's content is the "number of hours" of play or "hours" of education or training. The number of hours of learning on a single CD-ROM disc is often assumed to be an indication of quality or of the amount of information on the disc. This may not always be true.

This so-called "hour" is not a precise measurement of the actual amount of time anyone will actually spend using the disc. It is only a very general estimate of how much time a typical member of its intended audience may spend on average using the disc.

The advertised number of hours is also potentially misleading when comparing the depth of content on different discs, especially ones produced by different companies. Each producer bases its estimates on different standards. For instance, one company may conduct a validation study with a user sample in order to document the number of hours. Another company may base the estimate of hours on a multiple of some physical component of the program, such as the number of full-screen images, "interactions," modules, challenges, minutes of video, audio and animations, and so on.

In some cases, a description of the number of hours on a disc can help you compare discs produced by the same company—if you have some experience with that company's other titles. For example, a teacher may have used a certain company's educational titles before (most of which were advertised as four hours of instruction) and found that, on average, it takes students only about two hours to complete all of its activities.

The hours of information or learning advertised for a given CD-ROM title also do not indicate the quality of the information or educational experience. For example, a given five-hour-long CD-ROM may actually cover the same concepts or skills as one advertised as ten hours long. There is no relationship between the time it takes to complete a CD-ROM interactive educational disc and its quality. This is because CD-ROM titles are "interactive." Among other things, this means that the learner completely controls the speed at which he or she moves through the information—users can easily back up, repeat activities, replay video segments, and skip over information.

Any good CD-ROM should be content-rich. Depending on the type of information, this richness may be present in the size of its database (the number of items or records stored, often cited in terms of megabytes), the number of "pages" of text information, the number of articles, the minutes or hours of video and audio, the number of images and animations, and the "hours" of learning.

Degree of Interactivity

Interactivity is any *meaningful* participation by the user in determining the outcome of the program. The best way to understand this concept is by a comparison to most books. A reader does not participate in the outcome of the plot of a novel. A computer program, however, can be designed either to have a number of possible "endings" or theoretically even an infinite number of outcomes, and the user can determine or control the choice of outcome.

Interactivity is one of the most misused words in the CD-ROM industry. Some people seem to think that anything on a CD-ROM is interactive or that anything involving a computer is interactive. As a consequence, when a CD-ROM is described in advertising as "interactive," the term tells you little about the quality. Actually, the degree of interactivity of a title may be its single most important quality.

Interaction, as defined here, is exactly the quality that makes a CD-ROM multimedia title worth having. It is the characteristic that makes a CD-ROM title something more than a costly, high-tech sequence of pages to be turned. Interactivity provides an exciting, involving experience—like an old-fashioned "page-turner" novel, something you just can't put down.

If a book is a "page-turner," that's good: it means the reader feels compelled to turn page after page until he or she reaches the end, without putting the book down. It means the book is fascinating. If a CD-ROM is a "page-turner," that's not good: it means the CD-ROM is boring. The best CD-ROMs are those that provide interactivity and allow their users to explore many different, exciting options.

Convenience and Speed of Access

Given the vast amounts of information stored on a high-quality CD-ROM disc, a related criterion is the speed and ease with which a user can access the data. Don't confuse this with the speed of the CD-ROM drive (which is characterized as "single-speed, double-speed, quad-speed, 6X, 8X," and so on). Delays of several seconds accessing data are usually due to poor title design, not the speed rating of the CD-ROM drive (although there is, admittedly, a noticeable difference in the speed of an old single-speed drive and a newer 8X drive). A good CD-ROM title is designed so that users won't experience long waits between the time information is requested and the time it displays on the computer screen.

A well-designed CD-ROM title has an easy-to-use menuing system or other "user interface," which provides quick access to all portions of the disc. It's generally considered to be poor design if a user must "climb" through many layers of menus before reaching the desired information. A CD-ROM title should provide multiple means of accessing data to accommodate the different preferences of its users: icons for visually oriented users, text searches for experienced users, audio cues, on-screen highlights to direct the user's attention and indicate progress, "bookmarks," and indices.

Useful Life

Useful life isn't how long the disc will last (manufacturers now claim they will last hundreds of years); it's how long you will find it to be useful; how long before it becomes outdated? Some CD-ROM titles are reissued every year, but it may not be necessary to obtain the latest version of every disc. Reference discs tend to become outdated more quickly than educational discs, so librarians may need more frequent updates than educators do.

SUMMARY OF GENERAL CRITERIA

Keep these general criteria in mind when evaluating the quality of a CD-ROM title's design:

- Reputation of the CD-ROM title producer
- Technical quality, including user manuals and telephone support
- Amount of data
- Type and appropriateness of data (video and audio, for example)
- Richness of content
- Degree of interactivity
- Convenience and speed of access to the data
- Useful life of the product

HOW TO EVALUATE REFERENCE TITLES

Perhaps the best application of CD-ROM technology is to present reference material. Reference titles take advantage of all the characteristics of the medium. CD-ROM discs can be less costly to produce than printed, bound books; a single disc can contain as much information as a whole shelf full of books; information searches on CD-ROM are enhanced by powerful software tools; and otherwise dry facts and statistics can be enlivened with multimedia illustrations. Reference CD-ROMs are among the consumer best-sellers, as well as institutional best-sellers. In fact, CD-ROM was first introduced commercially as a medium for standard reference works, such as *BiblioFile, Facts on File,* and *Books in Print.*

This section discusses several important types of reference discs: standard reference works, dictionaries and other literary tools, encyclopedias, financial data discs, phone books and other directories, and several specialized references, such as atlases and genealogy discs.

HOW CD-ROM REFERENCES DIFFER FROM BOOKS

The purchase of CD-ROM reference titles should be based upon the same general criteria as other titles. Of course, you should also be alert to several additional quality criteria.

More than any other type of title, reference titles must either be significantly different from or superior to printed versions, must be used in conjunction with printed versions and the Internet, have a superior interface and search engine. Among the questions you should ask are the following:

- Is the data contained in the CD-ROM title more or less current than the data in the printed or online versions?
- Is the data more or less comprehensive?
- If a CD-ROM reference title includes video clips and audio, but excludes articles or information to make room for them, does that enhance or dilute its value for our library or school?
- How quickly does the information featured in a particular reference work become outdated, requiring new discs and updates?
- Must we buy each new edition as it is issued? At what cost?
- How easy is it to install new editions or updates to currently installed CD-ROM titles?

Such reference titles are often sold in series, rather than as separate editions. Be sure to read Chapters 3 and 5 for detailed information on serial titles, new editions, and updates to CD-ROM title licenses.

CD-ROM REFERENCES VERSUS INTERNET RESOURCES

Both CD-ROM and the Internet are excellent sources of reference material. Many CD-ROMs make use of the Internet, either for enhancements or updates. Some reference materials are available in printed form, CD-ROM, or on the Internet.

Choosing between CD-ROM and Internet Resources

Occasionally intellectual properties may be available both as a CD-ROM title and as an Internet resource. The decision to choose one over the other may be made entirely on objective considerations, such as the relative cost and ease of access to each one by your library or school. In other cases, differences in content, presentation, and quality may be the deciding factors.

At the time of this writing, most multimedia content (especially video and audio) is accessed more easily, quickly, less expensively, and at higher quality from CD-ROM than over the Internet. Information is more easily updated online on the Internet, though, so World Wide Web information may be more current than a CD-ROM title's. There is no conceptual or theoretical difference, however, between the two digital media, and neither one is inherently superior to the other for purposes of libraries or schools.

Internet Updates to CD-ROMs

Many reference titles are updated via new CD-ROM discs while others are updated via the Internet. In rare instances, a title may be updated by means of a diskette.

If updates to a title are available on the Internet, keep in mind a few special considerations: Updates and new editions of CD-ROM discs are generally handled, installed, and maintained just like any other disc. Internet updates can be more complicated. First, each location where the update must be installed needs an Internet connection. If a location has more than one workstation which is not networked, each workstation probably needs an Internet connection; most updates are password-protected or otherwise protected against being copied to a diskette and then "sneaker-net" transferred from one computer to the next. In addition, someone needs to keep track of updates system-wide and to ensure consistent updates so that none of the workstations in the system is "out of sync" with the others.

Consequently, while updates to reference CD-ROMs may appear to be a benefit, some library and school systems may find they unnecessarily complicate things. The method by which new editions and updates are issued must be taken into consideration when evaluating a CD-ROM reference title. See also Chapter 7, section 7.2 for detailed information on how to update CD-ROM titles via the Internet.

SUMMARY OF GENERAL REFERENCE CRITERIA

While each reference title and each category of reference title may have slightly different characteristics and quality criteria, the following criteria should be considered in the evaluation process of most reference discs:

- Is the content of the CD-ROM title disc identical to the printed reference work?
- How are new editions and updates issued and in what format? Are several different types of updates available so that you can choose the best for your circumstances?

STANDARD REFERENCES

Standard reference publishers pioneered the development and commercialization of CD-ROM. The first commercially available CD-ROM title was the Library Corporation's *BiblioFile,* issued in 1985. Other early CD-ROM titles included *Books in Print Plus, Facts on File, World Facts,* and other indexes to periodicals, especially newspapers, such as the *New York Times* and the *Chicago Tribune.* Many large-circulation newspapers are now available on CD-ROM as well as on microfilm. In fact, almost all of the most popular reference works are issued on CD-ROM as well as in book form.

Standard reference work CD-ROMs tend to be designed and produced for institutional, rather than individual, use. Consequently, their licensing options tend to take into account multiple users, multiple sites, and networked access. Often the titles are issued in series or with frequent, regular updates. Because the companies that sell these CD-ROM titles are familiar with you— libraries and educational institutions—you will probably find that the license options for such titles are flexible enough to meet most of your needs.

Such discs are also often designed with "the lowest common denominator system" in mind, so that no library or school will be prevented from acquiring a title because of hardware or software incompatibility. Most commercial CD-ROM titles intended for consumers (for example, games) generally "push the envelope" of computer technology and, therefore, can only be run on a limited number of the most up-to-date computers.

This attentiveness to the broadest possible range of computers means that a CD-ROM reference title is often easy to install and update. Most are text-only and provide a very simple graphics interface for the user.

In most cases, the only decision you will need to make concerning a standard reference work is whether to acquire the printed version or the CD-ROM version—or both. The quality of the reference material is rarely in question, because, by definition, a standard reference is often unique and is therefore almost always indispensable. (Other important reference works, for which there are competing "standards," including dictionaries and encyclopedias, are discussed below.)

Assuming that the information in the CD-ROM version of a standard reference is identical to the printed version of the reference, you need to consider the following issues when choosing between them: (1) total cost, including updates and editions, (2) cost and convenience of archiving older editions, (3) maintenance, (4) ease of access to data for users, and (5) whether the CD-ROM version provides special, worthwhile benefits for users.

Analyzing cost and pricing options for CD-ROM titles is often more difficult than analyzing the price of printed materials. CD-ROM title producers generally follow software pricing models, which are very different from book pricing models. In addition, CD-ROM updates can be issued at much lower cost by producers than can book updates and new editions. In part this is because it isn't necessary for a CD-ROM producer to manufacture a new disc in order to update or revise a product; updates can be accomplished via the Internet or by distributing a diskette. Remember to take into account not only the cost of the license for the initial CD-ROM title but also the cost of updates, new editions, and of adding additional workstations or users to your computer system (such additions may have an impact on your license for the title).

If you routinely archive past issues of a standard reference work because they may be of use for historical researchers or trend analysis, a CD-ROM title may have substantial benefits as compared to printed titles. Not only is less storage space required for a CD-ROM disc archive, but it is much easier for users of digital archives to conduct historical or trend-analysis research than it is for users of printed archives.

As discussed above, often it's more difficult and costly to maintain and support a CD-ROM title than a book. On the other hand, a CD-ROM title disc is also literally more durable than a book or magazine. As a result, replacements may be less frequently required for references acquired on CD-ROM than in printed form.

Ease-of-access for users of the reference work is another important criterion. First, a single CD-ROM workstation can be used by only one person at a time, as with a single book. A networked CD-ROM, however, can be accessed simultaneously by several users. For high-demand reference titles, a networked CD-ROM title may be the best choice.

Simultaneous access by several users may be the most important benefit for CD-ROM reference titles. Other benefits include superior indexing and searching capabilities, the ability to print customized reports of search results, and simultaneous access to archives or multiple volumes of data.

In summary, it may be appropriate to choose a CD-ROM reference title, either in place of, or in conjunction with, a printed reference title, if:

- The cost, including updates and new editions, is comparable to or less than a printed version
- Older editions of the reference are routinely archived rather than discarded
- Replacement copies of the work are frequently needed, either because of extensive use, fragility of the medium, or theft
- The reference is in such great demand that simultaneous users could benefit from a networked CD-ROM
- The size of the database of information contained in the reference is so great that searches would be facilitated by using a CD-ROM
- Users of the reference would benefit from the ability to print customized reports.

DICTIONARIES AND OTHER LITERARY TOOLS

Many reference works for writers, such as dictionaries, books of famous quotations, and abstracts of great literature, are available on CD-ROM. The first and still among the most popular is Microsoft's *Bookshelf,* which is issued annually with a slightly changing list of contents. *Bookshelf* editions generally include the *American Heritage Dictionary, Bartlett's Familiar Quotations,* and *Roget's II: The New Thesaurus,* among others. Some editions include *The Concise Columbia Encyclopedia, College Edition,* which has 15,000 articles, photos, and animations.

Because the information on this kind of CD-ROM is mainly textual data that consumes only a little disc space, when evaluating these reference titles you should expect more than just text and at least the complete printed work to be available on the CD-ROM disc. There's rarely a good reason for including only an extract or summary of the printed work on a CD-ROM title disc. For example, *Monarch Notes,* which summarizes great works of literature, boasts the complete text of every *Monarch Note Study Guide* ever published. This actually makes the *Monarch Note Study Guide* CD-ROM disc an excellent resource and value, but, for the amount of space available on a disc, the disc could probably also include the full text of some of the summarized works. (Of course, the value of these study guides is that they condense and summarize.)

Often, such discs also have room to include the complete editions of more than one reference work, adding to the overall convenience. The complete text of various versions of the Bible or Shakespeare's works, for example, are excellent applications of CD-ROM technology. These discs provide the equivalent of an index and a concordance to the work.

You may need to decide among several such reference works for your library or school. How do you decide which of these titles to provide in CD-ROM form? Should you acquire more than one in each category? How will you make all of these titles equally accessible to your patrons and students? Most such decisions depend on your institution's needs, not the quality of the CD-ROM title. As a result, you must be sure to examine your options according to the general criteria and procedures discussed above.

ENCYCLOPEDIAS

Several comparable, high-quality CD-ROM encyclopedias are available, so, deciding among them can be difficult. Consider the following: cost, comprehensiveness, level of sophistication, use of multimedia, and frequency of updates. Ask: (1) "Is the CD-ROM version as good as the printed version?" and (2) "Which CD-ROM encyclopedia of those available is best for my library or school's needs?"

You will, of course, first choose among CD-ROM encyclopedias based on the same criteria used to choose among printed encyclopedias. Most of the CD-ROM titles available are, in fact, versions of printed encyclopedias. The quality of the information in the articles contained in each is comparable to, if not identical to, the printed versions. These include the *Encyclopedia Britannica, Grolier's, Compton's,* and *Funk and Wagnall's* encyclopedias.

Compton's Interactive Encyclopedia: Compton's Interactive Encyclopedia includes over 37,000 articles (the complete text of the printed edition), about 14 hours of sound, 8,000 photos and illustrations, and 100 video clips. Two versions are available, one an academic version with lesson guides. Both are priced under $70. Compton's includes software to dial in to a bulletin board or over the Internet for additional updates and real-time educational experiences.

Encarta: Microsoft's *Encarta* contains over 26,000 articles, and is based on *Funk and Wagnall's New Encyclopedia.* Its special appeal is its focus on current events and use of multimedia: 100 minutes of video clips and animations, 45 different spoken language clips in 9.5 hours of sound, and 800 maps. If your computer runs Windows 9X, the *Encarta* disc allows you to dial in to the Microsoft Network ("MSN") or the Microsoft World Wide Web site for monthly downloadable updates. *Encarta* is priced under $50.

Britannica CD: Encyclopedia Britannica's CD-ROM version is called *Britannica CD.* It contains the entire 44 million word text (66,000 articles, 32 volumes) and illustrations. The encyclopedia can also be subscribed to via the Internet, where it is called *Britannica Online.*

Grolier Multimedia Encyclopedia: Based on *The Academic American Encyclopedia,* the *Grolier Multimedia Encyclopedia* contains over 33,000 articles, with 8,000 photos and over 600 maps. It is designed to enhance learning by means of an interactive timeline and expert opinions, linked together via hypertext and hypermedia features. Software is included to allow users to dial in to CompuServe for additional, detailed information searches. The price is under $60.

The choice among these and other CD-ROM encyclopedias may be made based on a number of criteria. Keep in mind, however, that you shouldn't necessarily replace a printed encyclopedia with its CD-ROM counterpart, since the two may be very different. A CD-ROM encyclopedia is often an excellent enhancement to a collection of printed encyclopedias, and because of its low cost may also be an excellent way of adding to the number of different encyclopedias in your collection.

BUSINESS REFERENCES

A wide range of business reference works are available in CD-ROM format: investment listings; real estate listings and title and deed information; portfolio management information; retirement planning data; comprehensive information about general business trends and forecasts; and statistics on industry sectors, corporations, securities, funds, annual reports, and financial statements.

With this type of CD-ROM title, as with others, the design of the disc is probably of less significance in your selection process than the fact that the disc provides unique information or an extremely large database, which would be unwieldy in book form.

Like many standard references (discussed above), business references are often serialized and frequently updated. Like most encyclopedias, many business CD-ROMs are updated via the Internet or can be used in conjunction with Internet information services and databases. For example, both *Hoover's* business directories and *Dun & Bradstreet's* corporate financial information are available on CD-ROM and online on the Internet. Many states maintain databases of corporate, tax, and other business information that can be accessed via the World Wide Web or on CD-ROM disc. Some archives or historical data are only available on CD-ROM, not on the Internet.

This kind of information is almost always easier to access, maintain, and archive in digital form (either CD-ROM or online) than in book form.

PHONE BOOKS AND DIRECTORIES

CD-ROM phone books and directories not only take up less shelf space in your library than printed versions but also give library patrons many different ways to "look up" information. The powerful search and retrieval capabilities of CD-ROM software allow a user to look for very precise categories of items or individuals, their phone numbers, and addresses very quickly.

Many patrons of public libraries benefit from using CD-ROM phone books for genealogical and family research, to create mass-mailing lists for small businesses, to locate companies (including CD-ROM companies) for customer support numbers, to find old friends—applications are virtually limitless. Few people would have the patience to comb through the millions of pages of phone books in search of this kind of information. For example, one CD-ROM title, such as *PhoneCD* or *Phone Select,* combines street maps with a phone book, so that you can use a mouse to click on a location to display a pop-up window with the address and phone number of the resident.

When evaluating directory CD-ROMs, consider how current and complete the information is; how often updates are issued; how well the information is organized into local, regional, national, and international numbers; and the search capabilities offered.

GENEALOGY

Family history applications are well suited to CD-ROM. Many county, national, and even worldwide archives of birth certificates, death certificates, and marriage licenses are now stored on CD-ROMs and are available through genealogical societies and government agencies.

Many of these CD-ROM titles are aimed at the individual consumer, however, rather than the institutional market, which may make them inappropriate for use in libraries and schools. For example, *Echo Lake* by Delrina Software, Inc., is a popular CD-ROM title specifically designed for creating a multimedia family album. It helps individuals organize their photos, clippings, or other items that can be scanned into a computer; in addition the program provides professionally designed backgrounds centering on a vacation theme. Unfortunately, the resulting history must be stored on the hard drive of the computer, or on a diskette.

If the disk drives of your library's or school's CD-ROM workstations are inaccessible to its users, as is most often the case, then such a title is impractical for your situation. On the other hand, many CD-ROM discs are databases of Social Security records; military service records; marriage, birth, and burial records for various locales, and so on. Broderbund's *Family Tree*, which is designed to create family genealogical charts also provides a wealth of reference information. City directories, especially historical archives of large cities, are now available on CD-ROM. The chief criteria for deciding to obtain any such CD-ROM title must, of course, be your local requirements.

ATLASES AND MAPS

A good atlas, containing detailed elevation maps, is an invaluable addition to any library. As long as the world's boundaries are constantly changing owing to politics and war, such atlases tend to become rapidly outdated; and replacing the printed editions can be costly. CD-ROMs provide low-cost alternatives to these books, with the added advantage of providing the capability to print customized maps. The search and retrieval functions can also be efficient and especially useful for locating out-of-the-way places.

When considering the purchase of atlases for your library or school, be sure that maps can be printed from the CD-ROM title easily in "gray-scale," if you don't have a color printer. ("Gray-scale" is the term used by computer technologists to describe the use of various shades of gray to depict color changes when color isn't available.)

In addition, users should be able to conduct searches for place names based on the name of a municipality, county, state or province, and nation (even bodies of water and geological landmarks). The search tools should accommodate variations in search requests using the Roman alphabet for non–Romantic languages. Phonetic equivalents should be acceptable. Numerous indices and menus of selections should be provided.

And finally, keep in mind that graphics of all sorts (which includes maps) require fairly powerful computers for display. Both photographic images (for example, from satellites) and bitmap, four-color elevation maps alike require significantly more computer "power" to display on a computer screen than do simple line drawings. Printing high-resolution copies of such maps can require a very high-quality printer as well.

How to Evaluate Educational Titles

In this book, educational CD-ROM titles, which have a specific educational purpose, are distinguished from reference titles, which are general-purpose collections of information. An educational title is one that is designed to achieve specific learning objectives. A reference title is one that is designed around a topic. The organization and design of an educational CD-ROM title is, as a result, very different from a reference title and must be evaluated against a different set of criteria.

Characteristics of Good Teaching and Learning Tools

A high-quality educational CD-ROM title must, of course, possess the general characteristics discussed above. In addition, however, the title must provide a high-quality learning experience. Interactive multimedia on CD-ROM must adhere to the same quality standards as other self-paced, self-instructional materials, such as videotape, audiotape, interactive video disc instruction ("IVI"), programmed instruction, and paper-based tutorials. All CD-ROM educational titles are not equally effective learning tools.

Apply the same criteria to educational CD-ROM titles that you apply to any self-paced learning materials or classroom support materials. Such criteria include the accuracy of the content, how appropriate it is for the learner group, how well the materials serve your curriculum requirements, whether the title is intended for self-study or group participation, to what extent the material can be customized by individual teachers, and how well the learning outcomes can be documented, for example.

In addition to these general criteria of educational quality, interactive media (such as CD-ROM) should also be judged according some further criteria. First, the content should be appropriate for multimedia presentation: it should require audio and video for some purpose other than entertainment, for example, audio for language training. It should also only include multimedia, that is, audio, video, and animations, that relate directly to the learning experience. While a jazzy CD-ROM title with lots of sound and motion may keep your students' attention, it may not necessarily impart information or skills.

The title must be highly interactive: the pacing should be entirely in control of the user (whether the user is a teacher in front of a class or an individual learner). A variety of practice opportunities should be included to accommodate a range of learning styles (aural, visual, and so on). Frequent and specific corrective or reinforcing feedback must be supplied to the learner (not just irritating beeps when errors are made). Alternative paths through the instruction should be provided to accommodate the abilities of different learners.

The category of educational CD-ROM titles also has a bearing on the characteristics to evaluate. The following are some common categories of educational CD-ROM titles: tutorial, drill-and-practice, testing, exploration, or a combination of these. A tutorial style tends to take a disciplined, task-oriented, topic-oriented approach while an exploration is a free-form, unguided approach. Tutorials should have specific learning objectives and provide a means of assessing whether the objectives have been met by participants. An exploratory title should also have a set of possible learning outcomes, but assessment may not necessarily be included. Drill-and-practice and testing titles tend to present a series of practice exercises or problems for solving, either in a fixed sequence or drawn at random automatically from a pool of activities. If drawn from a pool, the size of the pool must be evident and the odds of repeating an activity must be stated.

It isn't uncommon to find several competing CD-ROM titles on any given subject, each taking a different instructional approach. For example, French-language CD-ROM titles are available for almost any age group. One CD-ROM title may take a tutorial, step-by-step approach. Another may take an exploratory, free-form immersion approach. As long as you know which approach is followed in a title, you should be able to find a title for your needs. The primary consideration when evaluating competing titles is whether it follows a methodology consistently and whether the methodology meets your needs.

A general word of caution is in order. It is commonly assumed that young people who have grown up in an age of computers are all inherently computer literate. If not, it is assumed that they can adapt more readily to computers than do adults. As a result, unfair expectations about a student's readiness to use a self-paced CD-ROM tutorial could produce unnecessary frustration. Keep in mind, if a CD-ROM title is difficult to install, runs poorly on your equipment, or is difficult for a student to use because it's poorly designed, no student, no matter how motivated or interested in the computer, can overcome these problems.

With these guidelines in mind, consider a few specifics about two popular types of CD-ROM titles, "edutainment" and tutorials.

EDUTAINMENT

"Edutainment" is a recently coined term to describe game-like, entertaining CD-ROM discs that have an educational purpose. There is no doubt that young people often respond very positively to these discs. Edutainment titles, which are generally available through retail outlets to the consumer, tend to follow the free-form discovery methodology discussed above. Such titles are intended to be used by a single user at a time, usually making them inappropriate for group activities or classroom presentation. They may be useful in computer labs, for at-home enhancement of a curriculum, or possibly even in a study hall.

The actual educational value of these titles is as yet unproved. Claims for their value are largely anecdotal as of this writing.

TUTORIALS

Tutorials are guided-learning tools that feature instruction according to a linear, classroom-style. The best ones are highly interactive and may feature simulations, drill-and-practice, and self-assessment quizzes. Such tutorials are generally designed to support secondary school and college-level learning. The older the learner, the greater the need for reality-based examples and simulations in a learning aid. Consequently, tutorials are best when they feature video and audio, as well as real-life scenarios and practical applications of the knowledge. Tutorial CD-ROM titles can be effective when used for remediation or as preparation for college-entrance or trade-school and licensing exams.

SOURCES OF REVIEWS, PREVIEWS, AND DEMOS

Before acquiring CD-ROM titles for your library or school, as discussed above, you should develop a checklist of characteristics or quality criteria against which to judge the titles under consideration. With that checklist in hand, the next step is to study reviews of titles and to obtain and evaluate previews, demos, and trial samples of the title.

This section provides information on how to locate the latest reviews of CD-ROM titles. If authoritative sources recommend a title under consideration, you should next obtain a copy of the CD-ROM title to install for a trial period on your institution's equipment. A trial of the title allows you to make certain that the title can be easily installed on your system, runs well on your system, and meets your needs in all respects. Such a trial also allows you to evaluate the technical support supplied with the title, including technical documentation, user manuals, and telephone help lines.

Evaluation periods of this type are more likely to be available for top-of-the-line, expensive, or serialized titles than for inexpensive ones. Providing a trial period to customers isn't cost-effective for most CD-ROM title producers. So, don't be dismayed if you are unable to obtain a free trial period, even if you plan to purchase multiple copies or a multisite license. It is, however, a good idea to ask your sales representative for a trial disc if possible. If not, purchasing a single copy of a title disc and installing it for evaluation before committing to a major purchase is well worth the cost.

Most CD-ROM titles, however, provide "demos" or previews. The disadvantage to a demo or preview as compared to a full trial is that it will not provide you with an adequate test of the technical quality of the title, its ease of installation, or its compatibility with your computers and workstations. Just because a demo or preview runs without problems on your workstations doesn't mean the actual product will run as well. Most demos and previews are designed only to supply you with an advance look at the content of the title, and may actually be significantly different technically.

SOURCES OF GOOD REVIEWS

Books, journals, and magazines regularly review new CD-ROM title releases. Several publishers regularly publish books of CD-ROM reviews, including the American Library Association, McFarland & Company, Inc., Meckler Publishing, Learned Information, Inc., and others. Refer to the bibliography in this book for other books of CD-ROM title reviews.

Reviews are also available in digital form, including online services, on the Internet, and on widely available CD-ROMs, some of which are distributed free of charge. Online services, bulletin boards, and Internet newsgroups have archives of reviews going back several years. Popular online services, such as America Online, host educational forums and technology forums where CD-ROM titles are discussed, promoted, and reviewed, not just by industry experts, but also by current users. One benefit of the reviews available in these public forums is that they are usually written by purchasers of the product, not paid reviewers or others who may have a vested interest in promoting a given CD-ROM title. Bulletin boards or message boards, such as Internet newsgroups dedicated to CD-ROM titles, provide you with a running dialog among users of specific titles. They reveal the bugs, difficulties, and helpful tips from people who have successfully used them.

Refer to "Recommended Reading" for listings of magazines, books, newspapers, and online sources of good reviews.

SOURCES OF DEMOS AND PREVIEWS

Having identified a likely CD-ROM title for your collection by reading reviews, the next step should be to examine a preview or demo of the disc. Previews and demos are not necessarily the same thing. Previews are often slide shows of the screens, with a scripted marketing pitch; taken with a grain of salt, previews can help you determine whether the CD-ROM title in question is likely to serve your needs. Demos, on the other hand, are often fully functional extracts from the title, with marketing information added.

Demos and previews are available from several types of sources:
- Magazines that are issued with free CD-ROMs and diskettes included
- Subscription CD-ROM services

- Online services, bulletin boards, and Internet files that you can download
- Cable TV shows with reviews and previews
- In retail stores, running on demonstration computer systems

Granted, many of these sources are consumer-oriented. Their reviews and the titles provided may not be targeted specifically at the library or education markets. On the other hand, some titles are appropriate for both home computer users and public institutions. Don't overlook such popular sources of information in your evaluation process.

Magazines

CD-ROM Today is a widely available magazine of reviews and technical information that includes a free CD-ROM disc containing freeware, shareware, utilities, reviews, previews, and demos. (See "Recommended Reading.") The magazine also provides the means to download specific demos.

Subscription Services

Subscriptions to *CD-ROM Today* are available. You can also subscribe to services that distribute nothing but CD-ROMs with reviews, previews, and demos. *PC Computing on CD-ROM* and *Nautilus* are magazines published on CD-ROM. See "Recommended Reading" for these and other subscription services.

Online Services

Many magazine and journal ads for CD-ROM titles list the producer's World Wide Web page or Internet address and indicate whether a free demo is available for downloading. (See Chapter 7 for more information about downloading CD-ROM-related files from such systems.) In addition, many CD-ROM companies routinely upload their demos and previews to the most popular online services, such as America Online, for subscribers to the service.

Television

Some cable TV stations specializing in computer-related content, run detailed reviews and demos of CD-ROM titles. Public education channels often feature educational technologies and may provide information about good CD-ROM titles. These programs have the advantage of showing an expert using the CD-ROM, from whom you may pick up hints on installing, running, and maintaining the disc. They also feature numerous full-screen shots of the CD-ROM.

Retail Stores

Stores selling computer equipment, software, and CD-ROMs often allow customers to try out popular CD-ROM titles or have previews running continuously. Most such in-store demos are game titles, but encyclopedias are also popular.

If you have obtained a demo or preview of a potentially good title, how do you evaluate it for your patrons or students? You might install the demo on a workstation and solicit opinions. You might ask a committee of evaluators to help you decide whether the title is appropriate. Just be certain before you open the discussion to committee review that you are confident that you can install, run, and support the title if your review committee selects it. Only you—after following the orderly evaluation process described in this chapter—know for sure that the title is the best of its kind, that it meets the needs of your total constituency, and that it is technically good and compatible with your computer equipment.

DISTRIBUTORS AND OTHER CD-ROM SOURCES

Having identified CD-ROM titles appropriate to your library or school, the next step is to identify distributors or resellers. Most CD-ROM titles are marketed primarily to the general consumer through retail and catalog sales, channels through which you may find it difficult to make purchases of multiple copies or to obtain professional discounts. This chapter provides information on how to find distributors of CD-ROM titles for libraries and schools and where educational and institutional discounts may be available for both multiple-license and single-license purchases.

DISTRIBUTORS TO INSTITUTIONS

If the distributors from whom you obtain books, textbooks, and audiovisual materials do not carry CD-ROM titles, look for advertisements and listings in the journals and periodicals listed in "Recommended Reading." The Interactive Multimedia Association and the Software Publishers Association have directories of distributors available (both associations are listed in Appendix C).

ASSOCIATIONS AND FOUNDATIONS

Many professional organizations and charitable foundations promote the use of CD-ROM technology in libraries and schools. Such organizations as the Software Publishers Association and the National Education Association conduct studies on the effectiveness of multimedia in classrooms and in curricula. Discounts to public institutions are sometimes provided through these associations. (See Appendix C for a list.)

In addition, most computer companies (both hardware and software) make significant charitable contributions to institutions in the form of CD-ROM titles and equipment. The Microsoft Foundation was established in 1997 specifically for the purpose of promoting multimedia usage in schools, including both over the Internet and on CD-ROM. The easiest way to obtain information about such charitable organizations is to visit a corporation's World Wide Web site (see Appendix C for a list of URLs). Or, contact the educational sales and marketing division of most corporations for information about possible discounts and other special programs.

UNSOLICITED CONTRIBUTIONS — RISKS AND BENEFITS

Gifts of computer equipment and CD-ROM titles from both charitable organizations and individuals often help to introduce this technology into libraries and schools. Many institutions postpone becoming involved in the technology until a gift makes the effort worthwhile. Furthermore, if the gift is specifically solicited by an institution or if the choice of equipment and CD-ROM titles is left up to the decision-makers in the institution, the potential benefits probably far outweigh the risks associated with involvement in any new technology.

It is the unsolicited gift of computer equipment and CD-ROM titles that may pose some risks. If you have read Chapter 1 you know that the costs of the computer, the CD-ROM drive, and the CD-ROM title discs are insignificant in comparison to the costs of personnel for installing and maintaining them.

In addition, planning is essential to the successful introduction of CD-ROM technology into a library or school. Unsolicited gifts can be difficult to integrate into a plan.

Be sure to keep your long-term goals in mind when accepting gifts of technology. In some cases it may be wise to refuse a gift that falls outside the scope of your plan, or to postpone attempting to incorporate such gifts into your system until your system is prepared to accommodate it.

CHAPTER SUMMARY

This chapter discussed the importance of choosing the best CD-ROM titles for your library or school. The selection process is an important part of the complete project; it should be conducted in an orderly manner; and selection criteria should be established before you begin. The chapter also discussed how to judge the quality of a CD-ROM title, how CD-ROM titles should be evaluated differently from printed material, and specific issues related to reference and educational CD-ROM titles.

Having established the selection criteria, the chapter next discussed ways to evaluate specific CD-ROM titles before you purchase them: reading reviews, obtaining free trial periods in which to use a title, and obtaining demos and previews.

Finally, sources from which to purchase the titles were explored.

3. Selecting the Right CD-ROM Titles for a Library or School

INTRODUCTION TO COMPATIBILITY AND LICENSING ISSUES

Purchasing CD-ROM titles more closely resembles purchasing software than purchasing books. Once your content needs have been assessed, both the technical requirements and license requirements must also be assessed before a CD-ROM title can be safely acquired. This chapter explains what the term "compatibility" means in relation to CD-ROM titles, how to determine the technical requirements for a collection of CD-ROM titles, and how to assess the licensing requirements for a library's or school's CD-ROM system.

It is absolutely essential to acquire CD-ROM titles that are 100% compatible with your computer systems. Even minor deviations from the standards can prevent a title from being successfully installed or run.

UNDERSTANDING "COMPATIBILITY"

A CD-ROM title must be "compatible" with the computer system on which it runs. This means that (1) the workstation must have a CD-ROM drive capable of reading the CD-ROM title disc's physical format, and (2) the computer's operating system software and device-driver software (see "Glossary" and section 7.5) must be capable of running the CD-ROM title.

Most CD-ROM drives are capable of reading a number of different physical disc formats, including what is commonly called simply "CD-ROM," as well as CD-ROM-XA format, Kodak Photo CD format, audio CD format (sometimes called "CD-A" or "CD-DA"), and CD-Plus. Some drives read other optical disc formats in addition to CD-ROM; for example, DVD drives often also read several CD-ROM formats. Unfortunately, the older or less-expensive a drive is, the less likely it is to read a range of formats. Many older CD-ROM drives, for example, read only Macintosh-formatted CD-ROM discs or only PC-formatted CD-ROM discs. Before acquiring a CD-ROM title, you must know exactly which formats the CD-ROM drives on the network and individual workstations are capable of reading.

Even if a drive is capable of reading a given CD-ROM title's physical disc format, the workstation still may not be capable of running the software that comprises the title. Each CD-ROM title's software is unique. Every CD-ROM title has specific minimum requirements for the computer equipment on which it can run. These requirements include the type of video, type of audio, amount of memory, amount of hard drive space, type of input and output devices, and, most importantly, the operating system of the workstation. (For example, System 7 is available for only certain Macintoshes. See Table 3.1.)

The following section discusses each element of the technical requirements for most CD-ROM titles. These elements can be isolated and discussed individually, because most workstations are, in fact, systems made up of many different, distinct elements. Any given workstation may have one or more of these elements in almost any combination. As used in this chapter, the term "computer system" means either a stand-alone CD-ROM workstation or a networked CD-ROM system.

This chapter focuses on PCs (with Intel-type processors and Microsoft operating systems) and Macintoshes, not so-called "high-end" computer workstations such as Sun Microsystems or computers running UNIX. Much of the information in this chapter is supplied for users of older computer systems (including DOS PCs and Macintoshes running the MAC OS systems 6 and 7), but not Apple II computers for which CD-ROM drives are rare, if not nonexistent. Newer computers, including Macintosh Power PCs, tend to be designed for full compatibility with a wide range of CD-ROM multimedia titles and software applications, while these older computers were not.

Even the oldest Macintoshes are compatible with at least some older CD-ROM titles. The Macintosh was designed to excel in the display of graphic information and also had built-in audio capabilities. The oldest PCs have no multimedia capabilities. Determining compatibility of a CD-ROM title with a Macintosh is, therefore, considerably simpler than determining compatibility for a PC.

Starting in 1991, the computer hardware industry labeled its multimedia computer systems with "MPC" labels. MPC stands for "Multimedia Personal Computer": a set of minimum standards developed by hardware and software manufacturers to promote a degree of consistency among computers and software. The MPC standard was enhanced and reissued in 1993 as the MPC 2 standard. Look for CD-ROM titles that are described as MPC or MPC 2 compatible, if your institution's PC or Mac also meets MPC or MPC 2 specifications. A complete list of the standards appears in the "Glossary."

Table 3.1 System 7 Versions/Model Compatibility

N=No
Y=Yes
E=Yes, with Enabler Software

Model	7	Pro	7.1	7.0	Enabler	Version
128k	N	N	N	N	—	
512k	N	N	N	N	—	
512KE	N	N	N	N	—	
XL/Lisa	N	N	N	N	—	
Plus	N	Y	Y	Y	—	
SE	Y	Y	Y	Y	—	
SE/30	Y	Y	Y	Y	—	
Classic	Y	Y	Y	Y	—	
Classic II	Y	Y	Y	N	—	
Color Classic	Y	Y	N	N	401	1.0.5
Portable	Y	Y	Y	Y	—	
II	Y	Y	Y	Y	—	
IIx	Y	Y	Y	Y	—	
IIcx	Y	Y	Y	Y	—	
IIci	Y	Y	Y	Y	—	
IIfx	Y	Y	Y	Y	—	
IIsi	Y	Y	Y	Y	—	
II vi	E	E	N	N	001	1.0.1
II vx	E	E	N	N	001	1.0.1
LC	Y	Y	Y	Y	—	
LC II	Y	Y	Y	Y	—	
LC III	E	E	N	N	003	1.0
LC 475	E	E	N	N	065	1.1
LC 520	E	E	N	N	403	1.01
Quadra 605	E	E	N	N	065	1.1
Quadra 650/610	E	E	N	N	040	1.1
Quadra 660AV	E	E	N	N	088	1.1
Quadra 700	Y	Y	Y	N	—	
Quadra 800	E	E	N	N	040	1.1
Quadra 840AV	E	E	N	N	088	1.1
Quadra 900 series	Y	Y	Y	N	—	
Powerbook 100	Y	Y	Y	N	—	
Powerbook 140	Y	Y	Y	N	—	
Powerbook 145	Y	Y	Y	N	—	
Powerbook 160	E	E	N	N	131	1.0.3
Powerbook 170	Y	Y	Y	N	—	

N=No
Y=Yes
E=Yes, with Enabler Software

Model	7	Pro	7.1	7.0	Enabler	Version
Powerbook 180	E	E	N	N	131	1.0.3
Powerbook Duo	E	E	N	N	Duo	1.0
Powerbook 200 series	E	E	N	N	Duo	1.0

In addition, most recently-manufactured computers, which include the following equipment, are compatible with most CD-ROM titles:

- For PC users—a "386" or faster PC, purchased within the last three or four years, with 4 Mb RAM, DOS 5.0 or later or Windows 3.X or later, a CD-ROM drive, sound card, and a mouse.
- For Mac users—a Mac with 2 Mb RAM, 32-bit color, usually System 7 or later, and a CD-ROM drive

Consider the above computer technical specifications to be a "minimum" for running most CD-ROM titles of interest to libraries and schools. (The most recent game CD-ROMs will require far more computer power than these minimums, but few libraries or schools are likely to acquire such titles.)

If the workstation in question is an older computer (for example, more than three years old), it is highly likely that its technical specifications are no longer available to you: the original purchaser or installer of the equipment may have left your organization, the computer's manuals are lost, or the external labels on the equipment may no longer even be readable. In such cases, there are several ways to determine whether the workstation in question is capable of running a given CD-ROM title, as explained below.

In addition to the technical specifications of the specific computer system on which a given CD-ROM title is to run, the technical requirements of the CD-ROM title must also be taken into consideration. The two sets of specifications must match, that is, be "compatible." Marketing literature for CD-ROM titles and CD-ROM title packaging usually itemizes the title's technical requirements. Study these carefully before acquiring any CD-ROM title.

COMPUTER TYPE

The first consideration when buying a CD-ROM title is the type of computer (specifically, its processor). Some CD-ROMs can only be used on PCs or Macintoshes, but not both. Some CD-ROM titles can be played on both a PC and a Mac, because they include data in both computers' formats and retrieval or player software for both platforms (these are sometimes called "hybrid" discs; see "Glossary" for definitions). Keep in mind that PC and Mac CD-ROM drives and titles are not interchangeable.

The following are some terms describing computer requirements, which you may find on title packages:

- "IBM-compatible": This term may be used to describe computers capable of using the DOS operating system (see below).
- "PC": PC (Personal Computer) usually refers to the most common type of microcomputer, those capable of running DOS. This is synonymous with "IBM-compatible." Approximately 90% of all microcomputers sold are PCs.
- "Macintosh (Mac)": These are computers made by Apple Computer, or by one of several companies licensed by Apple.
- "Power Mac/Power PC": This is a more recent type of computer that has been developed to be used both as a PC and as a Macintosh.

A computer is often identified by that which acts as its "brain" or instruction center, its "processor." A CD-ROM title's requirements list may also state a processor type rather than a computer type, for example, "486" rather than "PC." Common types of processors for PCs are: 286, 386, 486, and Pentium. Common types of processors for Macs include the Motorola 68000 series and Power PC chips. The higher the number, the faster the processor. (Current CD-ROMs are unlikely to run on a slower processor, such as a 286.)

Every CD-ROM title will run more smoothly on a faster computer processor (486 versus 386, for example). On less powerful computers, a CD-ROM title may run, but only slowly. The sound may be choppy or broken up. The screens may refresh or repaint very slowly. This can be a significant problem if the CD-ROM is an action game in which the player has to react quickly to on-screen events; but it may be negligible in other CD-ROM titles and even games like those in which the player thinks for a few moments before making a move, such as chess.

OPERATING SYSTEM

In addition to the type of computer or computer processor, the operating system of the workstation must also meet the requirements for the CD-ROM title. An operating system is a set of software programs that provide central, controlling instructions to the computer.

Popular operating systems include:

- DOS: A common operating system for PCs, for which numerous CD-ROM titles have been developed. (Note: If you are using a version of DOS earlier than 6.0, you should immediately upgrade to 6.0 or later and, if possible, to Windows.)
- Windows 3.X (3.0, 3.1, and 3.11): Technically, Windows 3.X is considered to be an "operating environment" that enhances DOS. Windows,

while graphically user-friendly, still relies on DOS. To run many CD-ROM titles, it is necessary to "exit" Windows and use the CD-ROM with DOS. To run many other CD-ROM titles, you must also have Windows 3.1, as well as DOS.

- Windows 9X (Windows 95 and later versions): The newer version of Windows does much to help users play CD-ROMs, such as provide "Plug and Play" installation capabilities. It still retains ties to DOS, but users need not "exit" to DOS to run any CD-ROM titles (in fact, many Windows 95 systems are set up so that users cannot exit to DOS).
- Mac OS (Systems 6, 7, or 8): The Macintosh operating system runs on Macintoshes and Power Macs with a Power PC processor.
- OS/2: This IBM operating system provides capabilities for running some "Windows and DOS-compatible" CD-ROMs.
- UNIX or LINUX: Most commercial CD-ROMs are not compatible with UNIX (which requires a CD-ROM format called RRIP). You may encounter UNIX on computers to which you connect via modem or on networks.

If the CD-ROM title is said to be PC-compatible, you must know whether it requires DOS or Windows. If DOS, in most cases you will be able play it on a Windows 3.X workstation in a "DOS window." If you would rather not use a DOS window, then you must select a disc that is labeled as Windows compatible. If the CD-ROM title lists Windows as a requirement (not just an option), that means it may not be run in a DOS window or from DOS alone.

If the title you want requires a Macintosh, you need not be as concerned about the operating system, since it is generally easier to install CD-ROM titles on a Macintosh. Be sure that the Mac OS version is adequate, though (see below).

Whether your workstation is a Mac or a PC, the operating system is often so important to using CD-ROMs that you must know its exact version and release number. These numbers precisely identify the operating system. Often it is not enough to know, for example, that it is version 6, but you must know that it is precisely 6.0.7.

In general, the higher the number of the version, the better the operating system. This is not necessarily always true for running CD-ROM titles, though. Older CD-ROM titles may work only with earlier versions of an operating system or may work best with a specific earlier version. Rather than retain old versions of an operating system just for a single older CD-ROM title, it is better to obtain updated, newer editions of the titles to run with your current operating system.

If you do not know, offhand, what version number your operating system is, then you must find out before you try to select the best CD-ROM title. Specific details about how to determine the operating system version number are found in your computer's manuals, and some tips are provided in Chapter 7.

RANDOM ACCESS MEMORY ("RAM")

References on a CD-ROM title's packaging to a computer's "memory" almost always mean a type of memory called RAM or Random Access Memory. This is the set of microchips where programs and other data are stored temporarily while in use. CD-ROM titles tend to require large amounts of RAM, usually more than most other programs. Increasingly, 8 Mb is considered the minimum RAM to run most CD-ROM titles. (Many newer operating systems themselves require 16 Mb or more of RAM.)

If a workstation has the minimum required memory as stated on the CD-ROM title's package, and all else seems to be adequate or more than adequate, you should be able to install and run the CD-ROM title. With the minimum memory, though, you may encounter occasional pauses, slow access to information, or glitches in the sound.

HARD-DRIVE SPACE

A CD-ROM title's requirements for hard-drive space should not be confused with RAM requirements. Hard-drive storage space, where programs and information are permanently stored even when not in use, is also measured in megabytes. Hard-disk storage space usually consists of hundreds of megabytes or even several gigabytes (thousands of Mb). Some CD-ROM titles tend to use a large amount of hard-drive space, but this requirement varies considerably by title.

The total physical size of a hard-disk drive is not an important consideration when buying a CD-ROM title, only the available "free" (unused) space on the hard disk. If there isn't sufficient space at any given time, you can use several techniques to make enough room available for the title. (See Part Three for more information on the use of hard-disk space.) As your collection of CD-ROM titles grows, keep in mind that more hard-drive space will also be needed to install new titles and upgrades to titles.

MULTIMEDIA FEATURES

Multimedia CD-ROM titles make extensive use of specialized internal computer components called "interface" or "adapter cards," which are circuit boards inside the workstation. The most important cards for CD-ROM titles are the video and sound cards.

A few CD-ROM titles may require specialized adapter cards to be able to "decode" or "decompress" (in other words, "play" on the workstation) certain types of multimedia data files. Most notably, if a CD-ROM disc includes MPEG or MPEG-2 video, the workstation must have an MPEG adapter card (or "board") to decompress and then display the video rapidly and smoothly. It is possible to install an add-on card of this type so that you can play a title with these special requirements. (Later in this chapter we discuss how to determine whether you have the necessary adapter cards.) Note that multimedia adapters must be physically located in each CD-ROM workstation, even those on a network.

Most CD-ROM title discs do not require these special decoders, because the title discs either include software to perform all the decoding or they store files in formats that can easily be read by your workstation's operating system without special equipment.

Video Card

The resolution and the screen-size requirements for the workstation's video card (sometimes called the "graphics adapter") are among the most important and inflexible CD-ROM title requirements. If you believe a workstation is only just barely capable of displaying the graphics and video as stated on the title's packaging, you may not be able to run the disc at all.

Table 3.2 Display Resolutions

Name	Number of Pixels	Number of Colors
MCGA	320x200	256
VGA	320x240 or 640x480	256 or 16
SVGA	800x600 or 1024x768	256 or 16

Sound Card

If a workstation's sound card does not have all the advanced features required by the CD-ROM title, but you have "at least" an 8-bit sound card, you will be able to hear some of the sounds on most CD-ROM title discs. If music or voices are essential to the content of a disc, though, it may not be worth the risk to purchase the title without a 16-bit card. If the only reason you are interested in sound is as background music or sound effects, but you are willing to settle for less, you may be able to run the disc without any sound at all.

INPUT DEVICES

Input devices are a matter of taste more than a requirement for most CD-ROM titles. The most common input devices used with CD-ROMs are mice, keyboards, and joysticks for games. Often the only issue to consider is the number of buttons required for the input device. For example, mice come in one-, two-, and three-button models. While most CD-ROMs provide a keyboard equivalent for the missing mouse buttons, the awkwardness of the keystrokes may be a deterrent to buying a CD-ROM for which a special device is recommended.

CD-ROM DRIVE SPECIFICATIONS

One hardware requirement that cannot be ignored is the specifications of the CD-ROM drive: (1) the speed of the drive and (2) the types of discs the drive can read. CD-ROM drives are generally distinguished by their "speed," meaning primarily the speed with which information is transferred from the disc to the workstation. Speeds are usually measured in multiples of 2: dual speed (2X), quad speed (4X), 6X, 8X, 12X, 16X, and better.

The faster the speed, the better. The faster CD-ROM drives, however, are more expensive, even though most titles are incapable of exploiting the top speeds of the fastest ones. In other words, a title running on a 6X drive may not appear to run any faster than on a 4X drive, and in some cases may even run poorly. Despite claims to the contrary, almost all CD-ROM titles produced before 1995 can play adequately on many single-speed drives and certainly on double-speed drives. Triple- and quad-speed drives insure smoother replay of digital video but may not noticeably speed up anything else.

Do not ignore a title's requirement for a CD-ROM-XA or Kodak Photo CD drive, no matter how fast the workstation's CD-ROM drive is. If a title disc is not compatible with a specific CD-ROM disc format, the drive will not even recognize the disc. (Refer to "Glossary" for information about these formats). Chapter 7 discusses CD-ROM drive technology in detail.

DEVICE-DRIVER SOFTWARE

All attachments ("peripherals," including printers and CD-ROM drives) for workstations require special software programs called "driver" programs, or "device drivers." These are contained in files, often stored on the workstation's hard drive where the operating system software is installed. These are particularly important for CD-ROMs (see Chapter 7 for details).

NETWORKED CD-ROM SYSTEMS

Device drivers must reside on the hard drive associated with the network operating system or CD-ROM server. Most networked CD-ROM workstations will have CD-ROM device drivers installed on them as well, as part of the workstation's operating system, but those device-driver files will never be used unless the workstation has a CD-ROM drive physically located in it and a CD-ROM title installed on it for its stand-alone use. For example, if a workstation has a CD-ROM drive and the drive is used to install Windows 95 from a CD-ROM disc, then the CD-ROM device-driver files on the workstation's hard drive will be used.

Workstations on a network, however, must have up-to-date multimedia device drivers installed for the proper functioning of the sound card and video display.

INTERPRETING CD-ROM TITLE "REQUIREMENTS"

Each of the categories of configuration information can impact the performance of a CD-ROM title—in fact, each can make it impossible to run certain titles on a workstation. Until very recently CD-ROM titles had no uniform style of labeling.

RECOMMENDED CONFIGURATION

When acquiring CD-ROM titles for a library or school, try to avoid selecting titles with a recommended minimum configuration that exceeds or just matches the computer on which the title is going to be run. Unless the workstation's configuration exceeds the minimum requirements of a title, numerous problems will occur during the title's use.

"GREATER THAN"—"BETTER THAN"—ANYTHING "+"

When a CD-ROM title's list of requirements states that elements must be "greater than," "better than," or "+," you must be familiar with the numbering sequence in order to decide if your workstation meets the basic requirements. For example, do you know whether MCGA is better than SVGA? Do you know whether a Quadra Macintosh is better than or earlier than a Power Mac? Is a CD-ROM drive with 150 kb/s transfer rate better than or worse than one with 180 kb/s access time? Is one with a 64 k disk cache better than one with a 256 k disk cache? Is wavetable audio better than CD audio? Tables 3.1–3.3 included in this chapter should help you answer these and other questions.

Each of the items listed on a CD-ROM title's packaging as recommendation can be further understood by referring to Chapter 7, which provides details on how to determine the configuration of any workstation and how to compare specific CD-ROM title specifications with a workstation's configuration.

Table 3.3 Is Your Operating System
Earlier Than or Later Than?

DOS Operating Systems
and Intel-Compatible Chips

Version Number	Year Released	Processor Type
3.0	1984	286 or 386
4.0	1988	386
5.0	1991	386 or 486
6.0	1993	386 or higher
6.2	1994	386 or higher

Windows Operating Systems
and Intel-Compatible Chips

Version Number	Year Released	Processor Type
3.0	1990	386
3.1	1992	386 or higher
3.11	1992	386 or higher
NT	1993	486 or Pentium
Windows 95 (DOS 7.0 included)	1995	486 or Pentium

Macintosh Operating Systems
and Motorola-Compatible Chips

Version Number	Year Released	Processor Type
6.0	1988	68000 series
6.0.7	1990	68000 series
7.0	1991	68030 and 68000 series
7 Pro	1993	68030 and 68000 series
7.5	1995	Power PC

Obtaining and Maintaining Serialized CD-ROM Titles, Updates, and Supporting Software

Many CD-ROM titles of interest to libraries and schools are multi-disc titles, titles in a series, titles that are frequently reissued, and titles for which supporting software and services are available, such as via the Internet. These types of CD-ROM titles must be selected with the same considerations in mind as single-disc titles, but in addition, all of the discs and updates to each title must be taken into consideration. Never assume that because a CD-ROM title has been installed and successfully run on your institution's workstations that all subsequent discs and updates will as well. When committing to a major purchase of CD-ROM titles in a series or for which several updates are included make sure that you understand the technical requirements for discs planned to be issued in the future.

Serialized CD-ROM titles should be purchased only if the CD-ROM title vendor is committed to supporting your institution's technical environment for several years. For example, operating systems are frequently modified and upgraded to take advantage of technological advances. If the producer of a serialized CD-ROM title issues subsequent discs in a series to take advantage of these operating system changes, but your institution cannot afford to upgrade its operating system at the same time, will you be able to run the newer CD-ROM title discs in the series? Very often, each new disc in a series must be installed in the computer system (whether a stand-alone workstation or a CD-ROM network) as if it were a new title. Preferably, installation of a series title should only have to be accomplished once, with each new disc in the series automatically installed.

If content updates or subsequent discs in a series are supplied only via the Internet, your institution must be able to connect to the Internet to obtain those updates. If not, you may be able to obtain updates on diskettes through the mail. What you need to understand about this kind of update is that the changes to the title are recorded only on the hard drive where the title was first installed. At this time, commercial CD-ROM titles are not issued on a writeable medium, and so changes are not made to the CD-ROM disc.

When a CD-ROM title is issued with errors, whether in content or in program code, these types of updates are almost always issued over the Internet or on diskette. Rarely will a producer issue a new CD-ROM disc to correct errors or "bugs." If a new disc is issued, you may be required to re-install the title. If updated files are issued via the Internet or on diskette, the process is usually a simple one in which a few files are copied onto the hard drive where the title is installed.

This means that, if your library or school is interested in updating reference titles from the Internet (which is, indeed, a convenient resource), care must be taken to perform the update on a properly prepared workstation. It is recommended that a single individual be designated to perform the update function—most certainly not a patron or student. An orderly procedure and a regular schedule should be established. Records of each update should be kept. The amount of hard-drive space consumed by each update should be tracked. And, prior to performing the first update, a decision should be made at what point it would be preferable to obtain a new, updated CD-ROM disc rather than continuing to update the title on the hard drive.

In other words, as discussed in Chapter 1, there is a hidden cost to Internet updates to a CD-ROM reference title: the personnel costs and the hard-drive space. Calculate the hourly salary plus benefits of the individual performing the update. Calculate the cost of the portion of the hard drive required for the update. When these costs exceed the cost of a new CD-ROM disc, it's time to upgrade the disc.

CD-ROM COPYRIGHT AND LICENSING ISSUES

CD-ROM titles present some special considerations regarding both copyright and licensing. As software, a CD-ROM title contains digital information, a type of information which presents numerous issues not addressed by the copyright laws and which are currently under study by Congress. Also, software is never sold outright to consumers; rather it is licensed for limited use. Each of these topics is considered below.

DIGITAL COPYRIGHTS

Digital copyrights are under study by Congress because of the ease with which digital information can be copied and modified. In addition, digital information technically can't even be accessed unless it is copied from one medium (such as CD-ROM disc) to another medium (such as a workstation's memory). Numerous hardware and software techniques are being developed to combat unauthorized copying, distribution, and modification of intellectual properties. The courts are asked almost daily to consider new situations in which new digital formats are involved or new channels of presentation of digital information.

Even the concept of "fair use" of digital information is evolving, a concept which is of critical importance to libraries and schools.

Certain concepts, however, can be assumed to have remained unchanged. Plagiarism of digital information is exactly the same as plagiarism of analog or text information. The unmodified reuse of intellectual properties and claiming authorship of someone else's intellectual properties is illegal. It violates copyright, trademark, patent, and even Common Law. Users of CD-ROM titles may not illegally plagiarize the content of the discs.

Unauthorized copying of digital information for distribution is also a violation of copyright law, but what is considered "authorized" and what is considered "distribution" is less clear. For example, if a library were to copy a digital photo from an encyclopedia disc and then insert the photo into a poster for display in its lobby to notify the public of the acquisition of the title, would this be unauthorized copying? Probably not, since the CD-ROM title's license, purchased by the library, should have included provisions for public access to the disc in the library and, as a result, the poster probably falls under the license's definition of access to the disc. On the other hand, if the library purchased a single copy of a CD-ROM title and its license did not include network distribution, it would be a violation of copyright to provide public access to the title at more than one workstation in the library or library system. This would be unauthorized copying and distribution each time a user accessed the title from a network client workstation.

A wide variety of public domain information is also available on CD-ROM discs. As mentioned earlier, freeware and shareware are often distributed on disc. The minimal cost of the disc doesn't cover the copyrights or distribution rights to the disc's contents, but rather only the cost of materials, testing, overhead, shipping and handling. The digital information on such discs may be freely copied. In the case of shareware, the content may not be copied and distributed without the payment of a fee or may not be copied beyond a certain limited period of time as a trial.

As a general rule, librarians and educators should be particularly vigilant in protecting digital copyrights, especially until clear federal laws are developed. Under no circumstances would it be permissible to copy a CD-ROM title using a CD-R drive or CD-WR drive. Under no circumstances would it be permissible to copy an audio, video, or image file off a CD-ROM disc and incorporate it into any other digital presentation, videotape, or audiotape. Under no circumstances would it be permissible to transfer a database or a portion of a database off a CD-ROM disc onto a hard drive, tape, or other digital medium.

Care should be taken to insure that users (library patrons or students) don't print out excessively long text passages or massive portions of a database. Users should not have access to disk drives whereby they might copy portions of a title disk onto a removable or floppy disk.

Special care should be taken not to allow access to CD-ROM titles over the Internet, an intranet, wide-area network (WAN), or bulletin board system. Portions of a CD-ROM title should not be incorporated into library or school Web pages.

Every user of the CD-ROM system in the institution should be aware of the licensing limitations for the CD-ROM titles in its collection. CD-ROM titles licensed for use on a single workstation must be safeguarded. Inadvertent violations of an expensive CD-ROM title license can result in the rescission of the license, as well as legal penalties.

CD-ROM TITLE LICENSING OPTIONS

When acquiring a CD-ROM title, the purchaser acquires only the physical medium on which the title is published, not the content of the title. The content is licensed for use, just like other digital information and software (in fact, a CD-ROM title consists of both software and other intellectual property content).

In most cases, the price of a license gives the purchaser possession of the title disc, the packaging materials, and any associated documentation (but again, subject to copyright laws). Technically, these materials can be resold or transferred to another party, but actually only as scrap, that is, as plastic and paper. A third party would have no right to use the intellectual properties on the disc if it were resold to them. Some licenses may permit a purchaser to transfer a title to use the content under certain specific (and very limited) circumstances. As a result, it is critical that the acquisition of CD-ROM titles for public use in libraries and schools be conducted with a full understanding of the licensing limitations and options available.

Single Licenses

Most CD-ROM titles, such as those sold to consumers in retail stores and catalogs, are licensed for use by a single user on a single computer (often called a "single CPU"). This includes most popular encyclopedias and learning discs, which you are likely to be interested in. Resale or transfer of the license is generally prohibited under any circumstances, because the single-unit price of the CD-ROM title is low and considered to be fair and within the price range of individuals.

Use by a single user on a single computer is controlled in several ways. One way is by what is known as a "shrinkwrap license." The packaging in which the CD-ROM title is shipped contains a clear exterior warning that by opening the package, breaking a seal, or breaking the shrinkwrap plastic covering the box you agree to the terms of the single-use license. The legality of this license has been upheld in court repeatedly.

Another control is often built into the CD-ROM title installation program. The installation program can be designed to identify a specific computer by examining certain configuration information stored in the computer, by prompting the installer for certain information, by requiring the user to connect to an Internet Web site for registration, and by other means. A common method of identifying the single user and single computer is by requiring the installer to enter a password or code available only on a slip of paper or card in the original packaging. If the card and code are lost, reinstallation or subsequent installation on a second workstation may be impossible.

Most installation programs also copy files off the CD-ROM disc onto the hard drive of the workstation. Anyone attempting to run the title on a workstation hard drive where the title has not been previously installed will receive an error message or be unable to proceed. A few CD-ROM titles use a separate installation diskette, rather than storing the installation program on the CD-ROM where it can be reused. And, since most CD-ROM title discs are read-only and contain far too much data to copy to a single hard drive, most CD-ROM titles are only usable on a single workstation at a time.

There is one other form of protection, but it is rarely employed because it is both expensive and cumbersome. A hardware plug may be issued along with a CD-ROM title, which the purchaser must attach to the workstation where the title is going to be installed. Without the special hardware attachment, installation is prohibited.

Most single-user licenses and shrinkwrap licenses are not negotiable, are the same for all customers of a given company, are pre-printed, and are signed by neither party. It isn't necessary to be overly concerned about the terms of such licenses. Most of them follow industry standards that have stood up in court. If a dispute arises between your institution and the vendor of the license, the court generally finds in favor of the customer, because you had no choice in determining the terms of the license, so long as you have abided by the conditions of use—you have not illegally distributed the software or violated the copyrights.

Site Licenses for Software and Multi-Disc Discounts

Libraries and schools, by definition will have more than one user per CD-ROM title. You may install the title on only a single workstation, but numerous individuals will use the workstation where the title is made available. Consequently, many CD-ROM titles are available which provide for multiple users, multiple copies of the discs for multiple workstations, and distribution to multiple workstations over a network. Such licenses generally specify exactly the number of users for which the license is valid or exactly the locations where it is valid. These are called site licenses and ought not to be confused with discounted purchases of multiple copies of a CD-ROM title.

Discounted multiple copy purchases generally make use of single-user licenses. The discounts are provided only as a courtesy to public institutions. The vendor of the title may gain some economies of scale to make the discount feasible, or may even distribute the discs in less-expensive packaging or without complete documentation. Still, each disc may only be installed on a single workstation; it may not be transferred to another user; and it may not be installed on another workstation at a later date. Even when multiple copies have been purchased at full price for a library or school system, the title may not be distributed over a network to libraries and schools within the system.

When the number of copies of a title is large enough, or when it is known in advance that the title will be needed for network distribution, the license is usually a network license, or a site license. Multiple site licenses are also used in circumstances where the locations at which a title will be installed for network use or multiple-workstation use are widely distributed, such as throughout a state. Such site licenses are intended for an unlimited number of users and an unlimited number of workstations at a single location, such as a campus or administrative office. The license not only allows the installation and distribution of the title over a network but also provides an unlimited number of reinstallations. However, it generally provides technical support only to a single individual or single administrator at a site. In other words, the vendor provides assistance only to one person for each site. Technical assistance must be administered centrally.

Multi-site licenses are generally expensive and must be customized for each situation. If you are involved in the development of such a license, in most cases a lawyer's services are required. In particular, work with a lawyer licensed in your state, who can practice law in the courts of your state. All business contracts include a paragraph specifying the state whose laws apply to the contract, that is, "the governing law." This refers to the state in whose courts any dispute will be settled, not to the different statutes that may exist in different states.

Versions versus Editions

The license for a serialized CD-ROM title often includes one edition and some limited number of subsequent editions of the title, much like a magazine subscription. Periodic renewal fees for the license are required. In some cases, the license is a contract in which you must promise to pay a fee according to a predetermined schedule. In other cases the license requires advance payment for all purchased editions of the title. In all cases, when the license expires, use of the CD-ROM titles is prohibited: old editions of the title may not be used in lieu of purchasing current and future editions. In a few cases, outdated editions of the title discs must returned to the vendor.

Editions of serialized or annual titles are not the same as versions of the title or title software. All CD-ROM discs are issued with a version number. This identifies the contents of the disc for the developer of the title. Often enhancements to a title are made after its first release to the public or errors are corrected. The version number tracks each change to the title, no matter how minor or whether or not it is even apparent to the user.

When purchasing a CD-ROM title, the license is generally issued only for a single, specific version of the title. License holders are not automatically entitled to new versions. In some cases, where the quality of a version is seriously impaired by an error in content or a flaw in the software, new versions will be issued free of charge to license holders under the terms of the original license. In other cases, a new license must be purchased to obtain a disc containing the enhancements or corrections.

In many cases, enhancements are available in digital form for installation on the hard drive of the workstation where the title is installed. These usually include Internet downloads and diskettes, which may be obtained free of charge except for the cost of connect time to the Internet or the cost of the diskette's shipping and handling. See section 7.2 for further details.

LICENSING AND COPYRIGHT SUMMARY

The planning process for CD-ROM technology must include a plan for securing the copyrights of CD-ROM title copyright holders and for obtaining appropriate licenses for your needs. Copyright protections and licensing policies should include:

- A written policy on fair use of CD-ROM titles within your organization
- A means of preventing Internet access to a CD-ROM title
- A means of controlling all network access to single-user licensed material
- Controls on the use of printers available to CD-ROM workstations
- Written procedures and policies concerning the authorized installation of CD-ROM titles
- Written policies and procedures on access to technical support supplied by vendors of CD-ROM titles, where site licenses are concerned and where multiple users or the public have access to a single-user licensed CD-ROM title
- A procedure for the authorized archiving, destruction, or return of outdated CD-ROM discs for which the license has expired

When purchasing a license, be sure to consider all licensing options. In some cases a single-user license may be sufficient, in others a network or site license may be necessary. Discounts may be available, but limitations on use of individual copies could make multiple copies for single-users impractical or undesirable. When considering site licenses, always make sure that technical support from the title vendor will be available to every workstation, librarian, educator, or system administrator who may need it.

CHAPTER SUMMARY

This chapter discusses some critical considerations for the acquisition of CD-ROM titles other than quality of content. In order to be installed and run successfully on a computer system (whether a stand-alone workstation or a network of CD-ROM workstations) the technical requirements of each title must be taken into consideration. Every title is different and has different technical requirements, from the type of operating system to the speed of the CD-ROM drive.

In addition, every disc in a series of CD-ROM title discs must be evaluated separately for its technical requirements. One requirement of every CD-ROM title is a certain amount of hard drive space where title-specific files can be installed. This hard drive space is important when a CD-ROM title is planned to be updated via the Internet or from diskettes and if several titles are going to be installed on the same system.

Finally, the complexities of CD-ROM title licenses must be understood.

Not only are copyright issues involved, but also the type of access a library or school may provide to each title. Some titles are permitted to be run on a network while others are not. Some titles may be installed on several workstations while others are restricted to a single workstation.

Part Two
PRACTITIONER'S GUIDE

Part Two is intended to provide practical guidelines for librarians and educators who are responsible for the day-to-day supervision and operation of CD-ROM workstations, including installing CD-ROM titles on stand-alone workstations, caring for workstations and title collections, ensuring the continued proper operation of the workstation and of each title running on it, and providing support to users of workstations. Chapters 4–6 are written for nontechnical individuals for whom CD-ROM workstation responsibilities are subsidiary to other duties, but who have already read Part One.

Chapters 4 through 6 provide overview and background information, general guidelines for analysis and problem-resolution, and some specific instructions on how to perform common CD-ROM workstation installation and maintenance tasks. Chapter 5, "CD-ROM Workstation Maintenance and Upgrades," may also be of interest to library and school administrators who are budgeting for future equipment purchases. More detailed, advanced technical information is covered in Part Three; and Chapter 6, "Troubleshooting a Library's or School's CD-ROM Workstation," should be considered prerequisite reading for Part Three.

4. Supervising the CD-ROM Title Installation Process

This chapter discusses the installation of CD-ROM titles on a stand-alone workstation in a library or school. It also briefly discusses issues concerning installation of CD-ROM titles on a networked system, but does not explain the network-installation process in detail. CD-ROM titles should be installed on a networked system by a network system administrator, while titles may be installed on stand-alone workstations by any librarian or educator.

Installation is often the most difficult task for individuals responsible for CD-ROM workstations—a process that should be easy (and which CD-ROM title vendors claim to be easy) is often very difficult, even for the most technically skilled individuals. Nonetheless, by carefully preparing for the installation of CD-ROM titles and understanding the steps that go into an installation, you can install most CD-ROM titles successfully even if you have very little computer knowledge or experience.

Most CD-ROM titles are installed with installation programs supplied by the title producer. This chapter focuses on using such vendor-supplied installation programs. If you encounter problems during the installation, refer to Part Three for detailed instructions on how to install the title "manually," (that is without the help of the vendor's "automatic" installation program).

When installing any new CD-ROM title, you can prevent many problems and ensure success if you follow a few simple rules:

1. Plan carefully—gather all materials before you begin, and allow plenty of time for the installation.
2. Back up the system *before* making any changes to it or installing a title—critical portions of the system to back up include the operating system files and directories (or folders).
3. If a CD-ROM title installation requires any changes to the workstation's setup, make the changes one at a time; then test each change before continuing.

4. Make a backup of the new system files *after* a successful installation, before trying to enhance performance by making further changes.

THE TECHNICAL PURPOSES OF CD-ROM TITLE INSTALLATION

CD-ROM titles aren't like audio CDs—they can't simply be "played" on any workstation. Each new CD-ROM title must be individually installed. Whether or not your library's or school's workstation, computer system, or network already has one or more CD-ROM titles on it, every additional title must be set up to run properly on the equipment. Even if the new CD-ROM title is simply an upgrade or a new edition of a currently installed title, it still must be installed, usually as if the older title version did not exist.

Each CD-ROM title is unique: it contains unique information. Each model of CD-ROM drive is unique: it is constructed with special features not found in competitors' equipment. Each computer system that includes the CD-ROM drive and runs the CD-ROM title is a unique system of components from several manufacturers, running software from several software producers. In order to ensure that every CD-ROM title will function correctly on every model CD-ROM drive and every possible computer hardware and software system, it is necessary for CD-ROM title installation programs to customize title installations for each situation.

CD-ROM title installation programs serve three primary purposes: (1) determining the nature of the computer system onto which the title is being installed, (2) customizing the way the title will run on that system, and (3) setting up a means for users to access and start the title. To accomplish these ends, the installation program usually creates a new folder or directory on the workstation's hard drive, then copies a few files off the CD-ROM disc into that directory or folder, and finally may modify files already on the workstation.

CONSIDERATIONS FOR NETWORK INSTALLATIONS

When CD-ROM resources are networked, individual librarians and teachers are less likely to be required to install titles. Networked CD-ROM titles are generally installed by a technical system administrator onto the CD-ROM server from which individual workstations access the discs. If for some reason you wish to install a CD-ROM title onto an individual workstation that is part of a network system, you should contact the network system administrator before attempting to do so, since every networked workstation's operating system is configured to function in the context of the total network; you might inadvertently change the configuration of the individual workstation while installing a CD-ROM title onto it. For example, while most CD-ROM title installation programs add new files only to new directories or folders on a workstation's hard drive, in some instances they may add new files to important, existing system directories or folders or may modify system files. It's important to make such changes only with a complete understanding of their implications. Before allowing an installation program to make such changes, be sure you know how the changes will affect the network.

The remainder of this chapter provides technical details and self-help for those teachers and librarians who either must resolve installation problems on their own or who are interested in learning to do so. Others among you may choose to skip ahead to the specific installation techniques for your type of workstation (in Chapters 9–12) or refer to Chapter 6 on how to obtain technical assistance.

UNDERSTANDING CD-ROM DEVICE DRIVERS

If you encounter installation or operating difficulties with a CD-ROM title, the odds are that the problem isn't a mechanical problem (requiring repairs) or a defect in the disc or even a design flaw in the CD-ROM title. In all likelihood the problem is with so-called "device driver" files stored on the workstation's hard drive.

Perhaps the most important software for optimal performance of a CD-ROM workstation is its "device drivers." The operation of device-driver files is generally transparent to computer users. You need not know anything about them or deal with them until you attempt unsuccessfully to install a CD-ROM title. If you have a basic understanding of device drivers, you can probably solve most of the problems that may arise during the installation of a CD-ROM title disc on a stand-alone workstation—without having to call a technical support hot line, or, worse yet, without having to give up completely and discard the CD-ROM disc.

WHAT IS A DEVICE DRIVER?

CD-ROM workstations are complex multimedia computers made up of numerous individual components. Specialized software is needed to allow all of the CD-ROM drives, monitors, and sound cards from different manufacturers to function as part of a single computer system. These specialized software programs are called "device drivers." Device drivers are translators with a limited vocabulary. They speak the language of one component of a computer system. Device drivers are files that enable a computer's operating system to take control of, or "drive," the computer system's components. Among other functions, they describe that component (such as a CD-ROM drive) to the operating system (for example, DOS).

Device-driver files can be found on every computer system, regardless of type or operating system—on PCs with DOS, Windows 3.X, and Windows 9X, and on Macintoshes with Systems 6, 7, or 8.

WHEN TO UPDATE DEVICE DRIVERS

The operating system and appropriate device drivers were first installed when your library or school first acquired its CD-ROM workstation. During the useful life of a computer when it is modified, upgraded, or new software is installed on it, new device drivers may also be installed. Device drivers are sometimes installed along with a new operating system, a new piece of hardware, or, occasionally even a new CD-ROM title.

A computer may be modified or upgraded without also upgrading the device drivers, but this places new demands on the old device drivers. Eventually new device drivers, which speak the language of the new computer equipment, are needed. In some instances, simply installing a new CD-ROM title may require a new or upgraded device driver.

Device drivers may need to be upgraded when any one of the following events occurs:

- You upgrade the operating system on a workstation; for example, you move from Windows 3.1 to Windows 95 or from DOS 5.0 to DOS 6.2.
- You change or upgrade to a different piece of equipment, such as replacing a double speed CD-ROM drive with an octuple-speed ("8X") drive.
- You add new equipment, such as a scanner or sound card.
- You try to install a new CD-ROM title and discover that it requires a newer version of a device driver than is currently installed on the workstation.
- You discover that a device driver may be defective. (If you encounter such a defect when installing or running a CD-ROM title, the screen will display an error message.)

MANAGING DEVICE-DRIVER FILES

Managing the process of upgrading device drivers is difficult for everyone concerned, for the computer industry as well as its customers. *CD-ROM Technology* attempts to guide librarians and educators through this difficult process. This book helps you identify when a device-driver file may be the source of a CD-ROM problem (see Chapters 7 and 8), how to obtain a new device-driver file, and how to install it on a stand-alone workstation. As mentioned above, if a networked workstation needs new device drivers, a network system administrator should be the one to obtain and install them, in order to maintain the integrity of the network.

You can generally assume that a more recent version of a device driver exists than the one installed on any given CD-ROM workstation. You need not assume, however, that you must have each and every update. Only if one of the events listed above occurs should you consider researching the status of the device drivers on the workstation.

Current CD-ROM device-driver files are generally supplied on a diskette along with new CD-ROM drives. Different versions of the files are supplied for each operating system with which the drive must be compatible—DOS, Windows, Macintosh, etc. Every time a new version of an operating system is developed, new device drivers are also developed. If the CD-ROM manufacturer discovers errors in a device driver or makes improvements in the performance of a device driver, a new version of the device-driver file is issued. Consequently, for every computer component that requires a device driver (such as CD-ROM drives), there are several versions of the device-driver file available at any given time. Every CD-ROM workstation, though, doesn't necessarily need to have the most current version of every device driver installed on it. Device drivers usually only need to be updated when you want to run a CD-ROM title that requires a more advanced version of the device drivers.

Managers of computer systems are responsible for determining whether a new, improved version of a device driver is available or necessary. If you install new CD-ROM title discs, add a new peripheral to a workstation, or upgrade to a new operating system, you or the technical manager of your school's or library's computers should also upgrade the device drivers. Few, if any, equipment manufacturers or software vendors send out notices when updated device drivers are available. Even if they did, in a library or school system it's unlikely the notice would reach the individual responsible for managing workstations.

If you have a CD-ROM workstation with an operating system (like Windows or the Mac) that insulates users from the most common problems of device drivers, you may be able to ignore out-of-date device drivers for quite some time. For example, Windows 95 provides device-independent, universal device drivers. If a specific CD-ROM device driver is damaged or missing, Windows 95 will automatically fall back on the universal device driver. On the other hand, this kind of universal device driver cannot optimize the way in which every model CD-ROM drive runs, so a manufacturer's specific device driver may be desirable as well.

COST OF A NEW DEVICE DRIVER

In most instances device drivers are generally free or available for a nominal fee to cover the cost of materials, shipping, and handling. These programs are supplied as a part of every purchase of equipment or an operating system.

Updates are generally supplied free of charge from either the CD-ROM drive manufacturer, the computer manufacturer, or the operating system producer. For example, a Dell computer may contain a Toshiba CD-ROM drive and may be running Windows 95. A new CD-ROM device driver, in that case, could be obtained free of charge from Dell, from Toshiba, or from Microsoft.

HOW TO OBTAIN A NEW DEVICE DRIVER

When new versions of device drivers are available, they can be obtained from many different sources. Device drivers may be obtained on a diskette through the mail or electronically through e-mail, the Internet, or by modem transfer (see Appendix C for a list of some of these sources). If you wish to obtain a device driver by mail on diskette, the fastest way to do so is to call the technical support line of the CD-ROM drive manufacturer or the operating system producer. If you wish to obtain a device driver electronically, the fastest way to do so is to connect to the Internet, appropriate bulletin board service, or online service. The source from which you choose to obtain a device driver will be determined by the urgency of your need, the criticality of the problem to your mission as a librarian or educator, and the type of online services to which you have access. Read Chapter 7 for more information on how to use the Internet and online services to obtain files electronically.

The most reliable sources of information about the latest version of a device driver are equipment manufacturers and the operating system software vendor. If it is critical to you that you obtain the most current version of the device driver, contact one of them. Online services, computer user groups, and, occasionally, CD-ROM title producers are less likely to have the most current versions of the file.

Since equipment manufacturers are sometimes less consumer- and customer-service-oriented than software vendors, it may be best to begin researching new device drivers with the operating system vendor rather than the hardware manufacturer. The technical support staff of a software company is more experienced helping nontechnical consumers. See the Appendix C for a directory listing of many CD-ROM hardware and software vendors.

For example, Microsoft maintains and supplies at low cost to Windows users a collection of updated drivers for the most commonly used devices, called the "Windows Driver Library." It can be obtained by dialing in to the Microsoft bulletin board service, by connecting to the Microsoft Internet site, from the Microsoft Network ("MSN"), or by writing to Microsoft for a diskette.

To learn about the current release of all types of Apple Macintosh device drivers and system software, the best source is Apple Computer's Web site or Claris's Web site. They include downloadable copies of the latest updates and technical information. Many Apple retailers are also willing to exchange old operating system disks for updated ones with new device drivers.

It isn't advisable, however, to obtain a device driver from friends or colleagues. In rare instances, the CD-ROM device driver required by an older workstation may no longer be publicly available. Sometimes a CD-ROM drive manufacturer may no longer be in business, or the model may no longer be supported. This may be true especially for first-generation single-speed drives and some double-speed drives. Many of these old device drivers, though, can be obtained from online archives. Since device drivers are supplied at no cost, and since they may legally be freely copied (by users, not by software developers), device drivers should be obtained only as a last resort from other libraries, schools, or other interested parties who happen to have the same type of CD-ROM drive and system you do. Unless you obtain a device driver from an authorized source you may not have access to installation instructions. Furthermore, you may have difficulty determining whether the version of the device driver is the one you need. In the long run, it may be wiser and more cost-effective to upgrade the workstation hardware than to attempt to use old equipment with undocumented, unsupported device-driver files.

OVERVIEW OF DOWNLOADING DEVICE DRIVERS

Most computer companies have bulletin board services (which are not on the Internet), Internet FTP ("File Transfer Protocol") addresses, or World Wide Web sites where device drivers and other forms of technical support are available. (See section 7.2.1.1 for details.) If you are on the Internet, either FTP or the Web may be the easiest, fastest way to find out when new device drivers are available and then to obtain them by downloading. If you are not on the Internet, you can still obtain files electronically, if you have a modem and specialized communications software (as explained in section 7.2). A third option is to use an online service, such as America Online. To save the cost of a long-distance call to an out-of-state equipment manufacturer's bulletin board service, if you belong to an online service, you may be able to locate a vendor's support forum on that service to obtain and download the device driver from there.

Typically, device drivers must be downloaded in a compressed format. This saves you time and phone charges, because it takes less time to download a smaller file than a larger file. Once you have successfully downloaded the compressed file, it must be expanded, or decompressed, before you install it. It will either be automatically decompressed for you by your online service's software, or you will need to decompress it using a utility program. (The downloading and decompression processes are explained in detail in section 7.2.)

Keep the following issues in mind during this process. You may find that the file, once decompressed, expands into several separate files, including a file of documentation. You need to install it, an installation program, and often several different versions of the device driver. Allow plenty of space on the hard drive of the workstation for the decompressed files.

If you access the bulletin board, online service, or Internet site from the same workstation on which the device driver is to be installed, be careful not to overwrite existing device drivers and files. Download the files and decompress them into temporary folders or directories or onto a diskette. Then make backup copies of all old device drivers before attempting to install the new device drivers.

SUMMARY OF CD-ROM DEVICE DRIVER ISSUES

As explained above, the first step in preparing to install a CD-ROM title is to make sure that all the equipment on the workstation is functioning properly, especially the CD-ROM drive (for specifics, see Chapter 7). The second step is verify that the device-driver files on the workstation are up-to-date and properly installed.

Device-driver files affect almost every aspect of a multimedia, CD-ROM workstation. (Details on how to verify that the device drivers on a workstation are set up correctly in advance of installing a title, see Chapter 7.) If a workstation requires new device drivers, you can obtain them from hardware manufacturers, software vendors, CD-ROM title producers, users groups, and elsewhere. They can be obtained on diskette or electronically from the Internet, bulletin board services, or online services (as explained in Chapter 7).

OTHER PREPARATIONS FOR INSTALLATION

When you are ready to install a CD-ROM title on a workstation, be sure to have the following at hand: operating system manuals, CD-ROM title manual and license, and the workstation's log book. As explained in Chapter 1, the implementation phase of CD-ROM technology in a library or school must include both training and documentation for staff and users of the system. Each workstation should have a log book containing information on its hardware and software configuration, a record of installations of software and modifications to the system, and a maintenance log. You will need to have access to this information during the CD-ROM title installation process because the installation program will ask you questions about the technical set up of the workstation and about how you want the title to be installed. The log book should also include printed reports generated by the operating system with details about memory usage or the IMA's *CD-Match* disk, such as the reports discussed in Chapter 7.

Be sure to compare the technical requirements of the title you are about to install against the technical specifications of the workstation on which you wish to install it. If you notice discrepancies, it is advisable to install the title on a better-suited workstation or to obtain a replacement disc that is compatible with the workstation. While it is possible to install some titles on some workstations with less than optimum configurations, it is difficult.

BASIC STEPS IN AN INSTALLATION

In most cases, CD-ROM title installation is a simple process, with clear on-screen instructions. Most installation programs follow industry standards and are similar to all the others. After successfully installing your first CD-ROM title, other installations should seem easy. Of course, unusual situations are bound to occur. When this happens, if you understand the steps in the installation process, you should be able to resolve the problem quickly by referring to the chapters on problem-resolution, Chapters 9–12.

Here are the three primary phases in all CD-ROM title installations:

1. Hardware Setup—Set up the CD-ROM hardware first, before installing any new title. Make sure that the CD-ROM drive is properly installed and properly functioning.
2. Device-Driver Setup—Once the hardware is working, verify that all device-driver files are installed and functioning. (Refer to Chapter 7 for details.)
3. Software Installation—Install the CD-ROM title by running the vendor-supplied installation program. If the installation fails, try the techniques described in Chapter 8.

Regardless of the type of workstation or operating system, the installation process for most CD-ROM titles is generally the same. Try to follow the CD-ROM disc's installation instructions first. An installation program is often included on the disc; all you need to do is run it. The installation program usually begins by verifying that the workstation is compatible with it; then copies files to the workstation's hard drive; and finally modifies a few system files on the hard drive.

The individual responsible for installing the CD-ROM title generally has to perform several tasks. First, you must load the CD-ROM disc into the CD-ROM drive from which you plan to give your patrons or students access to it (the title disc must always be run using the same CD-ROM drive when more than one is available). In other words, during the installation process, a CD-ROM title is assigned to a specific CD-ROM drive, designated by a label or identifier: on PCs the label is a letter (D or E, for example) and on Macintoshes the label is a SCSI ID (see section 7.4.6.3 and "Glossary"). If you wish to run the CD-ROM title from a different drive, you must often de-install it from the first drive and re-install it on the second drive (many Macintosh titles are exceptions to this rule).

Then, you must run an installation program (usually located on the CD-ROM disc, although some installation programs may be located on a separate diskette). The vendor-supplied installation program is separate from the other programs that comprise the CD-ROM title. The installation program is usually run only once. Thereafter, the CD-ROM title program is run, and the installation program is archived for later use or simply ignored.

In addition, you must make decisions about the title's installation by responding to screen prompts. You may encounter problems at any point in this process. For example, you may have problems accessing the installation program on the CD-ROM disc; you may not be able to run the installation program; or you may encounter error messages during the process. Each of these situations is discussed in Chapter 18, to which you should refer if you have problems with installing a CD-ROM title.

Errors can occur at each step, of course. If the CD-ROM disc's installation program can't handle these errors for you, refer to Chapter 8. Not only does it give tips on how to resolve these problems, but it also explains how to install the CD-ROM title "manually" if all else fails.

TYPICAL INSTALLATION-PROGRAM WARNING MESSAGES

Many CD-ROM title installation programs will fail or will prompt you for input after determining there are possible deficiencies in the workstation on which you are attempting to install the title, especially if the amount of memory available is inadequate. Less often it will fail if the speed of the CD-ROM drive is too slow or the graphics adapter is incompatible or inadequate (although you still may not be able to run the title after the installation is finished). Very often, the installation program will ask you to name a new directory or folder into which you wish to install the title or specify certain settings for the audio.

Each of these is discussed briefly below, so you can make informed decisions during the installation process. If problems occur, refer to Chapter 8 for specific techniques to install troublesome titles.

DRIVE SPEED

CD-ROM drive speed is an important consideration when installing a CD-ROM title. Some CD-ROM titles require a minimum drive speed not only for playing the title, but also just for installation. Sometimes the CD-ROM's packaging labels will warn you of this. Sometimes the CD-ROM title's documentation will warn you of this. Sometimes an installation program will display a warning message about drive speed requirements. And, sometimes an installation program will actually test the speed of the CD-ROM drive before allowing the title to be installed on the workstation.

When a CD-ROM title requires a certain minimum drive speed, this is generally because the title is designed to access the disc frequently, for example, to display video scenes (sometimes called "cut scenes" or "video clips") or to play audio, such as background music or human voices. A slower CD-ROM drive may cause these media segments to run poorly or even to freeze the system. Don't try to install a CD-ROM title if the workstation's CD-ROM drive is too slow, unless you are willing to make the extra effort required to run the title (as explained in Chapter 8).

GRAPHICS ADAPTER AND MONITOR

Many installation programs require you to specify exactly the model of video graphics adapter. If you have the workstation log book close at hand, this is a simple task. If not, then respond with an industry-standard option: for example, SVGA graphics adapter. Or try each of the options presented by the installation program one at a time until one works.

CD-ROM titles that rely heavily on the use of video often are designed for certain specific types of video file formats and may require certain types of graphics processor chips on the graphics adapter in the workstation in order to function properly. For example, the most widely accepted video compression format, MPEG, cannot be displayed by certain types of graphics adapters. Often older CD-ROM titles using earlier graphics compression formats won't recognize the newer MPEG chips as valid video processor chips, so, for example, a workstation with an Intel Indio™ chip might encounter error messages when installing an older DOS CD-ROM title, even though the workstation is actually capable of displaying the video.

Sometimes this problem can be solved by installing older video device drivers. Refer to Chapter 8 for information on how to install a CD-ROM title so that the workstation uses an alternative configuration and set of device drivers just for that title.

Sound Card

Many CD-ROM titles require a specific type and model of sound card. Refer to the workstation's log book for information on the type of sound card installed in the workstation. If that information isn't available, select an industry-standard audio type, such as 16-bit or 32-bit audio or SoundBlaster™-compatible sound. Or try each of the options one at a time until you find one that works.

An installation program may also ask you for specific numerical settings associated with the sound card, including the "COM port" or "IRQ."

OTHER INTERFACE-CARD SETTINGS

Many of the most troublesome error messages during CD-ROM title installation refer to a "COM port" error or conflict in an "IRQ address." When you receive such an error message, the CD-ROM's installation program is alerting you to a conflict between certain system settings. The installation program attempted to verify the presence of a certain hardware component, but could not find it, or found something unexpected in its place. You can generally fix this simply by changing some of the interface card's settings in the operating system software's configuration files (see section 8.2.2.2).

For example, a CD-ROM installation program may read information off the hard drive or out of the computer's memory in order to identify a sound card. Then, later, the installation program may verify that information against a CD-ROM file on the hard drive or in memory and find that the two conflict. One of them is right and one is wrong. You may have to change the information files so that they accurately reflect the workstation's setup.

This type of error occurs most often in systems that have been recently upgraded and more often in PCs than Macs. Step-by-step instructions on how to edit the configuration files in order to resolve these problems are located in Chapters 9–12.

CHAPTER SUMMARY

This chapter has provided a general introduction to CD-ROM title installation. You are advised to prepare for the installation of each CD-ROM title by verifying that the workstation on which the title is to be installed meets the title's minimum requirements, that all essential files on the system have been backed up, and that you have gathered documentation (especially the workstation log book).

This chapter assumes that the CD-ROM title's installation program follows an industry-standard pattern. The installation program checks to determine the configuration of the workstation, prompts you for input about the workstation, creates a directory or folder on the workstation's hard drive, and then copies files into that directory. Installation programs may also modify some configuration files on the hard drive of the system.

The chapter lists some typical problems and warning messages that may be encountered during a typical installation. For detailed, technical assistance with problematic installations you are referred to Chapter 8.

5. CD-ROM Workstation Maintenance and Upgrades

SUPERVISING WORKSTATION MAINTENANCE AND ENHANCEMENTS

A CD-ROM workstation in a public location requires extra care to maintain its optimum performance. Not only its exterior surfaces, but also its operating system and utility software programs, hard disk, CD-ROM drives, and other internal equipment experience greater-than-normal wear and tear. This chapter identifies the components of single CD-ROM workstations, CD-ROM networks, and CD-ROM disc collections that require extraordinary care and then provides guidelines for regular maintenance procedures.

BASIC MAINTENANCE REQUIREMENTS AND TECHNIQUES

Well-designed and carefully observed maintenance and upgrade procedures take time, but not as much time as it can take to recover from CD-ROM workstation failures. Follow the recommendations in Chapter 1 to allow an adequate maintenance budget. Assign staff to regular maintenance tasks. Supervise those staff to ensure that maintenance tasks are properly performed and documented and to identify trends that may lead to system failures. Intervene in time to prevent serious problems.

Chapter 1 surveyed the proper environment in which to locate a CD-ROM workstation to prevent physical damage. No public location, though, is ever going to be hazard-free and perfect for computer equipment. Among the factors that will inevitably lead to problems are air quality, electrical factors, movement of the workstation, proximity to other movable objects, and the care taken by the users of the system.

MAINTENANCE RECORDS AND SCHEDULES

A regular schedule of daily, weekly, and monthly maintenance procedures can prevent problems. Plans should be made to replace workstation components before they completely break down. New workstations should be included in school and library budgets as discussed in Chapter 1.

Maintain a three-ring binder notebook of maintenance information for each CD-ROM workstation or network server. The binder should be kept close at hand. The binder should include a schedule of required maintenance tasks and checklists to document the performance of each. The checklist should include the name or initials of the individual who performs the task, the nature of the task performed, the date performed, and any anomalies found in the system at the time. A record of operating system information should also be available, including the precise version number, the date on which the operating system was installed or upgraded, all utility programs installed (with dates and version numbers), warranty information, phone numbers for technical support, and so on. The system specification reports explained in Chapter 7, section 7.3 should be stored in the binder, too.

Whenever you have a CD-ROM problem, you should make a note in the log book of when it occurred, what its cause was, and how it was resolved. Problems often recur, and, unless you have an exceptional memory, it is easy to forget how to solve them—this means that you have to go through the arduous process of problem-resolution all over again.

A workstation log could include the following items of information:

- Information on the processor type (CPU or ROM) and bus architecture, monitor/graphics adapter and video boards, serial and parallel ports, modem, sound card, disk drives, mouse or other input devices, and CD-ROM drive.
- Technical specifications for each component (often supplied by the manufacturer in a section of the manuals or as a separate pamphlet)
- Purchase information: date and place, warranty information if applicable
- Version numbers and names of device-driver files supplied with the equipment
- How the product was installed or configured, if options were available. For example, if the device was an internal SCSI device, was it properly terminated? What is the SCSI ID number? If a card required jumpers or the setting of an IRQ number by means of DIP switches, what settings were used during installation?
- Slots used: Computers often have several "slots" into which adapter cards can be installed. These slots often accommodate different types of adapters. Make a note of which slots, of which types, were used.

Regularly scheduled tasks should include:

- Maintenance of the CD-ROM server and each workstation
- Maintenance of each workstation's keyboard, mouse, monitor screen, diskette drive, hard drive, CD-ROM drive, power supply, and cables
- Backups of system software and files
- Running of virus-detection programs

Usage Guidelines

Especially if you can't control the way library patrons or students use the workstation, post cautionary signs near the workstation. Ask users not to bring beverages to a workstation to avoid spills on the keyboard or on surfaces on which the mouse is rolled. Where static electricity is a common problem, ask users to touch a discharge plate before touching the workstation.

During a working session (between times when the workstation is restarted) depending upon the type of computer and operating system, the memory in the computer can develop problems. This can occur because users of the workstation may not know how to shut down CD-ROM titles properly after using them; too many programs may be left running in memory; memory errors may not be resolved before a second user attempts to access information in the system. Posted guidelines should instruct users on proper CD-ROM title shut-down procedures and ask them to seek assistance if they are unsure how to close down a program before leaving the workstation.

External Care of Equipment

Physical care of the exterior surfaces of CD-ROM workstations involves the same considerations as any computer or electronic equipment: moisture and dust must be prevented from coming in contact with most parts of the equipment. Moisture and dirt must kept off the surface of CD-ROM discs so that they do not come into contact with the delicate components that make up a CD-ROM drive.

Airborne dust can clog disk drives, the power supply fan, and the keyboard. The exterior of these components should be periodically vacuumed using a small computer vacuum cleaner. Air-borne humidity is less likely to cause damage to equipment, but it can cause temporary problems, especially interfering with the sheet feeder in a laser printer.

Magnetic fields, which erase the data from most computer disks and from computer memory, do not affect CD-ROM discs, but magnetic fields should be kept away from CD-ROM workstations, in any case, since a workstation includes memory chips and (almost always) a hard drive. Heavy cleaning equipment with powerful electric motors can generate such fields. Unshielded stereo-equipment cables can generate a magnetic field. Never allow magnets, such as small "refrigerator magnets," to be placed on CD-ROM workstations. Keep magnetized paper-clip holders away from CD-ROM workstations.

Understand that each time a CD-ROM workstation is powered on and each time a user accesses a CD-ROM title, several internal components of the system are put to use—both hardware and software. The most heavily used component of the workstation is the hard drive, followed in most instances by the CD-ROM drive. Both types of drives will eventually wear out and need to be replaced. In the case of the hard drive, the surface coating of the disk is physically altered each time data is written to it, and consequently eventually deteriorates. In the case of both the hard drive and the CD-ROM drive, the moving parts that spin the discs can physically break, and the heads that locate and transfer data can become dirty, picking up dust and other particles. Regularly running a hard-disk maintenance program can help preserve the useful life of the hard drive, while using a CD-ROM drive cleaning kit can help prolong the life of the CD-ROM drive. CD-ROM laser-lens cleaning discs are available by mail order for less than $10. Keep the drive door closed to prevent dirt from entering it, and do not insert dirty discs into it. If the drive is caddie-less, wipe away any accumulation of dust in the drive tray before using it.

Electricity is the greatest danger to the internal components of the workstation. Power surges can erase volatile memory temporarily or even destroy electrical circuitry. Brownouts and power outages can cause the head on a hard drive to crash into the surface of the hard disk and thus destroy it and all the data on it. Always be sure the workstation's power supply is connected to a surge protector and line filter with a backup power supply. When a power outage occurs, shut down the workstation properly—do not attempt to continue operating on the temporary backup power supply. Make sure all staff understand proper shut-down procedures in such emergencies. When power is restored, check that surge protectors and backup power supplies are reactivated. Special procedures are required for the shutdown of networks during power outages and electrical storms. The network system manager should supply instructions for each workstation on the network.

Finally, workstations should be permanently installed and immobile. Movement is detrimental to the longevity of most computer equipment. Never move a workstation while it is powered on or in use: damage to the hard drive is likely. At all times, moving cables and cords can cause them to short out or become disconnected from the workstation. Check all cable connections regularly, including the keyboard and mouse cables.

UNDERSTANDING CD-ROM DISC MAINTENANCE

The CD-ROM title discs in your library's or school's collection are unlikely to cause maintenance problems. The discs are very durable. Most CD-ROM disc manufacturers warrant the discs they manufacture, under normal use, for ten years or longer, far beyond the expected life span of diskettes, audiotapes, and videotapes. The standard expected life span for a disc with normal to light usage is even longer than the warranty—100 years.

In addition, there's no fear of head crashes with CD-ROMs—even though a so-called "disk head" physically touches the surface of a diskette or hard disk when accessing data on it, this is not true of a CD-ROM drive and disc. In a CD-ROM drive, there is no physical contact between the drive's disc-reading device and the disc. Instead, the CD-ROM disc is read by means of a laser beam focused through a lens. In other words, you need not be concerned about over-using a CD-ROM disc and causing its surface to deteriorate.

A CD-ROM disc has a pattern of pits molded onto it. These pits represent the encoded data stored on the disc. The plastic is covered by a thin reflective coating (the silver you see on the disc), which is itself covered with a protective lacquer coating. If you scratch or damage the lacquer coating on the CD-ROM disc, the silver coating is susceptible to damage. If the reflective surface of the disc is damaged, or the pattern of pits is scratched, even through the top label surface, the laser beam may improperly read the data.

Caring for Discs

If you are responsible for physically inserting the CD-ROM disc into the drive, the disc must be placed label-side up in the drive. The silver side must be face down. Some CD-ROM drives use a shelf-like tray into which you insert the disk. Others require a disc caddie. If the CD-ROM drive requires you to use a caddie, don't attempt to insert a disc without one. Always make sure the CD-ROM drive is turned on before you try to open the drive door and insert either the disc or a disc caddie.

There is no real advantage or disadvantage to disc caddies. Caddie-type drives are sometimes easier to keep clean. They provide a storage container for CD-ROM discs as well as allow you to insert a disc into the drive.

A warped, scratched, or dirty disc will be unreadable by the CD-ROM drive and will likely damage the drive itself. Common sense dictates that you should touch only the edges of the discs, keep them out of direct sunlight and away from heat sources that may warp the disc, and keep the discs clean.

If you damage a disc, contact the manufacturer. They may be willing to replace the disc if you can prove you are honestly trying to replace a disc and not obtain a free second copy. They are not obligated to replace a disc that you damaged. Disc warranties cover only discs that are inoperable when you buy them, and even then only for a fixed time after purchase.

Cleaning Discs

If a disc becomes soiled, it may be cleaned with a lint-free cloth and cleaner like those for maintaining audio CDs. Some experts recommend that you wipe only in straight lines out from the center of the disc to the edge, rather than in a circle around the disc. Just be careful not to scratch the surface of the disc by rubbing dirt into or across it. A cloth dampened in water is also probably as safe as an alcohol-based liquid, so long as you do not insert the wet disc into the CD-ROM drive—be sure the disc is entirely dry before using it.

CD-ROM discs should not be left out in the open, unprotected from dust and other environmental hazards. In most cases, the CD-ROM drive in a public workstation should prohibit access to the drives by means of security devices, as described in Chapter 1. Not only does this prevent theft, but it prevents discs and drives from coming into contact with dust and other contaminants.

Storing Discs

In most cases, it is recommended that CD-ROM title discs (including archived copies) should not be accessible by the public. Your library's archives, though, will need a means of storing discs. Most CD-ROM discs are distributed in a plastic box called a "jewel case." Keep the disc in the jewel case when it is not in use, or store the disc in the CD-ROM drive's caddies. Numerous styles of CD-ROM disc storage cases are available, some that store the disc in the jewel case and some that do not. Not only do computer stores sell these cases, but you may also find a suitable storage system in a music CD audio store.

Some storage options include:
* stackable storage racks that hold 12 CDs in their jewel cases
* CD flip trays that hold 20 CDs with or without jewel cases
* 5.25 in disk cases that hold multiple CDs in their jewel cases, or large "floppy" disks

Cataloging Discs

How do you keep track of all the CD-ROM titles in your library, and all of the individual programs, graphics, music files, and so on that are stored on them? You need a database system to do so. Tools that might help include utilities that track the installation and removal of programs from the workstation or network system, or simple card-file programs (like HyperCard on the Mac or the Cardfile in Windows 3.X). Some multimedia authoring tools include multimedia databases for organizing large libraries of graphics and sounds, and some popular drawing programs, like CorelDraw, include indexing systems.

Workstation Cleaning and Maintenance Supplies

If something becomes lodged in a keyboard or a diskette drive, or for some reason you decide to open up the workstation, you will need a computer toolkit. Inexpensive kits are available with some very useful tools. Most useful are tiny screwdrivers (regular and Philips head), and long-handled tweezers. Some of the more oddly shaped items (which it is recommended you not try to use) are chip pullers and tools for manipulating jumpers on little legs of the chips.

Note: It is very common, and undoubtedly tempting, when problems occur to use everyday household or office items like tweezers, scissors, wrenches, and even hammers when trying to repair a workstation, remove a recalcitrant disc from a drive, or open a compartment in the equipment. Never do this. You will damage the equipment, probably irreparably. You must always use demagnetized, static-free, properly designed computer repair tools when working on a computer.

Summary of CD-ROM
Workstation Maintenance

The number of things that go wrong with a CD-ROM is probably infinite. It is certainly a function of the number of different operating systems multiplied by the number of different CD-ROM drives. Be sure you are well-prepared before making any call for technical assistance.

CD-ROM TITLE MAINTENANCE

RESTORING TITLES TO A WORKSTATION

It's inevitable that from time to time you will need to reinstall a CD-ROM title following the occurrence of an error. The reinstallation will be easier if you anticipate the necessity and maintain proper records of each installation as part of the log book.

Whenever you install a CD-ROM title, be sure to:
- Save all documentation for the title, properly catalogued and easily accessible for future reinstallations
- Return the warranty cards, so you have the right to obtain free technical support from the CD-ROM title producer
- Save the phone number for technical support and keep it handy
- Record the installation date, version number of the CD-ROM title, and any variable information, such as the name of the directory or folder on the hard drive where it was installed and any system settings used by the installation program (IRQ, DMA, drive speed settings, virtual memory, etc.)

When reinstalling a title, attempt to recreate the original installation exactly. If the original installation was working properly up to the time when the error occurred, there's no reason to change the way you installed the title.

Even if you suspect that the installation was done improperly and is the cause of the error, first try to duplicate the original installation and then verify that it was in error before trying any changes in the installation process. If you do reinstall the title differently from the original installation, be sure to record all of the changes in the log book for future reference.

If you followed the recommendations in this book, you retained a disk or tape backup of all important workstation system configuration information, both before and after the original installation of the title. Be sure to do the same in this case, making sure you don't overwrite or destroy the first archives. The copies of the configuration files prior to reinstallation may contain clues to any problems that occurred and should be made available to a technical specialist if you have problems determining what caused the errors. In some cases, you may be able to use the original archives to help you restore the system to working order or even to reinstall the CD-ROM title.

Of course, if a workstation has several titles installed on it, be especially careful not to disturb their operation by reinstalling or restoring files. Before reinstalling a title, always check the log book of installations. Look for other CD-ROM titles or programs running on the workstation that use the CD-ROM device drivers, sound-card device drivers, and monitor or graphics device drivers. Watch out for conflicts. Try not to overwrite lines in configuration files. In many PCs, installation programs add lines to the end of configuration files (including CONFIG.SYS, AUTOEXEC.BAT, and Windows .INI files); be aware that lines added toward the end of these files can have the effect of overriding commands and settings in lines preceding them in the file.

UPDATING TITLES ON A WORKSTATION

When new releases, new editions, or additional volumes of a CD-ROM title are made available, you may need to install them much like installing or reinstalling a CD-ROM title. The same quality-control mechanisms should be used in these cases. Always maintain thorough logs of system changes and title changes.

In addition, be aware that updates to titles can add new files to the hard drive on a CD-ROM workstation. Verify that there is adequate hard-drive space before installing any updates. Old files may also be overwritten during the process. Be sure to make a backup of all affected directories or folders before proceeding with such an update so that you can restore them in the event the update procedure encounters problems.

ENHANCING CD-ROM WORKSTATIONS

This section discusses ways to enhance the capabilities of a stand-alone CD-ROM workstation, either in order (1) to resolve a performance problem with a specific CD-ROM title or (2) to install and run a new CD-ROM title with requirements that exceed the workstation's configuration. Such situations are likely to occur when new CD-ROM titles are issued that are of particular interest to your library or school, but at a time in the budgetary cycle when funds aren't available to replace the workstation.

Many inexpensive software improvements can be made in most stand-alone workstations. Hardware improvements are not only more expensive but somewhat more difficult to make without the assistance of a technician. This section surveys a range of both software and hardware options. Detailed technical information on how to accomplish most of these improvements is provided in Chapter 7.

Enhancements to network CD-ROM workstations involve different issues than the ones discussed here. Many software enhancements to the individual client workstations on a LAN (local area network) will make little difference in the performance of a given CD-ROM title on that workstation. Software enhancements must be made to the CD-ROM server, under the direction of the network system manager. A few hardware enhancements to local workstations on the network may be desirable, such as upgrading to a monitor with a faster screen "refresh" rate or upgrading to better multimedia stereo speakers. Such enhancements should be carefully planned and budgeted.

Among the software enhancements discussed in this chapter are operating system upgrades, memory management programs, and disk-drive management programs (including disk caches for both hard drives and CD-ROM drives, and CD-ROM drive accelerators). Among the hardware improvements discussed are video adapters, monitors, sound cards, speakers, and headphones.

HARDWARE VERSUS SOFTWARE UPGRADES

Hardware enhancements tend to be more expensive and difficult to make than software enhancements. Many hardware enhancements also necessitate changes to the workstation's operating-system configuration. As a result, software enhancements should be attempted before hardware enhancements.

The least expensive enhancements involve the operating system running on the CD-ROM workstation; in some cases simply making changes in the way in which the operating system is configured (as explained in Chapter 8) may be sufficient. In other cases, a new operating system may be required; in most cases operating-system upgrades cost less than $100, while entirely new operating systems cost only slightly more. Some software performance-enhancement programs are available as freeware and shareware, but licenses for the most reliable commercial programs are also priced fairly inexpensively. Given the importance of these programs to the quality of a workstation's performance, the commercial programs are preferable to the freeware and shareware because of the technical support that accompanies them.

Some hardware enhancements can be added to a workstation simply by plugging in a new component. Most, however, require the installation of adapter cards inside the workstation's system unit. The older the computer, the more difficult the installation of an adapter card is. In some newer models, installation of an adapter card, such as a PCMCIA card is almost as easy as inserting a credit card into an automatic teller machine. The older the computer, the more strongly it is recommended that you have a technician install hardware upgrades.

Some enhancements require hardware upgrades, while others don't. Enhancements from 8-bit to 16-bit or 32-bit color or sound often require upgrades to the processor chips in the workstation (that is, hardware). Some types of enhancements to the computer display may require a better monitor, while some may require both a monitor and video adapter card.

Other enhancements can be made through software—sometimes small software enhancements may be sufficient to improve the performance of a CD-ROM title, while in other cases the effects of a software enhancement may be negligible. Software changes can supply additional hard-drive space by compacting the data on the drive or improving the methods with which the drive stores data. Software can improve the speed with which a computer processes information or make the allocation of memory more efficient so that it performs as if it actually had more memory. Software can speed up access to a CD-ROM drive, so that a slower-speed drive can accommodate an advanced title disc. Guidelines are provided below to help you decide where to begin.

OPERATING-SYSTEM UPGRADES

Significant improvements in the performance of any computer can be made by upgrading to a more powerful operating system, if one is available. Upgrade kits generally are free or cost significantly less than a completely new system. Be careful to obtain a set of upgrade disks, if that is what you need, and not a completely new system, since upgrades are both less expensive and can be installed more easily. Upgrading an operating system also tends to preserve old files and system configuration information, rather than overwriting them, which may occur when installing a completely new system.

If the workstation is more than three years old, the latest version of an operating system may not be compatible with the processor or other hardware components. For example, a Mac II is incapable of using Mac OS 8. In such cases, refer to Table 3.3 for information about which operating systems the workstation in question is capable of running. Older versions of operating systems are often available through one of the sources listed in Appendix C.

Operating system upgrades affect several aspects of system performance and provide a foundation for most hardware upgrades. As a result, simultaneously with upgrading a workstation's hardware, an operating system upgrade may be necessary. Among the system features affected by the operating system are memory, access to data on disks, and multimedia devices.

Upgrading PC Operating Systems

If the workstation is running a DOS-only or a DOS plus Windows 3.X system, it is recommended that it be upgraded at least to DOS 6.2. This version of DOS includes numerous programs for maintaining the system and enhancing its performance.

The decision to upgrade from Windows 3.X to Windows 9X is a little more difficult. Many CD-ROM workstations in organizations throughout the U.S. still run Windows 3.1 and most new CD-ROM titles are compatible with Windows 3.1 as well as Windows 9X. Windows 9X, to run optimally, requires substantially more RAM and hard-drive space than does Windows 3.1. While it is possible to run Windows 9X on a computer with only 8 Mb of RAM, it is highly recommended that the computer have at least 16 Mb of RAM. Windows 9X takes up at least 20 Mb of hard-drive space. Furthermore, in most cases an upgrade from Windows 3.1 to Windows 9X won't improve the performance of your existing CD-ROM library. It will, however, provide you with significant benefits for programs and CD-ROM titles designed to run under Windows 9X—a much wider range of multimedia capabilities are available for Windows 9X system. Consequently, an upgrade to Windows 9X need only be considered for new CD-ROM titles, not to improve the performance of an existing library of titles.

In addition, one of Windows 9X's most powerful features is "Plug-and-Play," which is the ability of the operating system to sense what type of new hardware has been installed and then to adjust the system configuration files to accommodate it. Unfortunately an older workstation isn't likely to be designed for Plug-and-Play. So, you may wish to wait until you buy a new workstation before upgrading to Windows 9X.

Upgrading Macintosh Operating Systems

Upgrades to the Macintosh operating system are discussed in detail in Chapter 12. Not all Macintoshes are capable of running the newer versions of the operating system, as is explained there. If the workstation is running Mac System 6, it should be upgraded to the latest version of System 7 that the computer is capable of running. In other situations, you may be forced to run an older version of the operating system, and this may limit the number of CD-ROM titles that can be installed on the workstation.

INCREASING MEMORY THROUGH RAM PERFORMANCE SOFTWARE

Software utilities are also available to enable a stand-alone workstation to use RAM more efficiently, sometimes even creating the appearance of more RAM than is actually installed. Many operating-system upgrades also include features that manage memory better than do older systems. (For information on using built-in operating-system memory-management programs, see Chapters 8 and 12.)

The hardware alternative is to have additional memory (RAM) chips installed in the workstation. This is a fairly simple process in many new computers, including those which support Windows 9X "Plug-and-Play" and those with PCMCIA slots into which compact, credit-card-sized RAM cards can be installed. Consider having a technician install RAM chips in older computer models.

HARD DRIVES AND CD-ROM DRIVE IMPROVEMENTS

Improving the hard drive on a CD-ROM workstation, as well as improving the CD-ROM drive itself, can have a substantial impact on the workstation's ability to run CD-ROM titles. Most CD-ROM titles use the workstation's hard drive as well as its CD-ROM drive. Most operating systems also use the hard drive extensively as temporary memory when running multimedia CD-ROM titles. Consequently, increasing the storage space on a hard drive can improve several aspects of a CD-ROM workstation.

Rather than installing a larger, faster hard drive or a faster CD-ROM drive, you may be able to use software to increase the storage space on a hard drive or to speed up the hard drive and CD-ROM drive.

Hard-Disk Compression Software

The workstation's hard drive plays an important role in a CD-ROM library: it stores the installation files for each CD-ROM; it may permanently store some CD-ROM data to insure that the data is readily available while the CD-ROM is in use; and it is almost always used by the application or player programs on the CD-ROM to temporarily store items from memory. As a result, the CD-ROM workstation's hard drive can quickly become full or have just barely enough space to install the latest CD-ROM titles.

The cost of storage space is steadily decreasing. Not only are high-capacity hard drives readily available for under $200, but high-capacity diskettes and drives, such as Zip drives, are available. The emerging writable DVD format also promises to make storage of massive amounts of data possible at relatively low cost. Consequently, depending on the type of computer and its ease of hardware installation, adding a new hard drive or replacing a low-capacity drive with a higher-capacity one, may be cost-effective.

If the computer is several years old, or if it doesn't include expansion slots in which to install new equipment, it may be possible to optimize the drive by means of software. It is possible to increase the capacity of a hard drive without replacing it—by means of disk compression software. This software allows you to manage space on an existing hard drive more efficiently.

Unless you are a technically advanced computer user, however, you should not compress the hard drive for purposes of using a CD-ROM drive more efficiently or for multimedia purposes. Some CD-ROM titles and other programs are not compatible with a compressed disk drive. The maintenance utilities used to backup the workstation or to perform other types of maintenance must also be compatible with the disk compression software used. The process of repairing a computer system with a compressed hard drive is more complex, as well.

Swap Files and Caches

A swap file or a cache is a temporary file created by applications and operating systems to store information for fast retrieval. The stored information includes not only data but also parts of programs that are used only infrequently. Swap files or caches are created "on the fly"; they are not permanent.

A swap file or cache is located in one of several places in the computer system: memory (RAM), the hard drive, or a computer chip installed on a component of the system, such as the CD-ROM drive. Data in RAM (which is a set of chips inside the computer) is very quickly accessed. The hard drive is accessed a little less quickly, but it is still faster than accessing data on, say, a diskette drive or CD-ROM drives. The chip built into the CD-ROM drive can more quickly store and present data to you than the drive itself can access data from a disc.

Use of swap files and caches can speed up the performance of CD-ROM titles. Software caches are available to speed up the overall processing by the computer (processor speed), to use RAM more efficiently, or to speed up access to data in RAM, a hard drive, or a CD-ROM drive. These programs are available for very low cost, especially as compared to the cost of memory upgrades or the cost of trying to keep up with the ever-increasing speeds of CD-ROM drives.

CD-ROM Accelerator Software

Some RAM-cache utilities are designed specifically to improve the performance of CD-ROM drives. Some other utility programs are designed to improve the disk cache that is built into the CD-ROM drive itself. Most good CD-ROM drives have a disk buffer chip into which data is read from the disc and temporarily stored while it is being piped to the computer. The size of the chip (its capacity in bytes) is the first determinant of its performance. A 256 k chip will store four times as much data as a 64 k chip, and consequently will significantly improve the speed with which a workstation can access the data on a title disc.

Windows 9X has built-in CD-ROM disc caching (a program called CDFS.EXE), which can help if the built-in CD-ROM drive buffer is small, say, only 64 k (refer to section 11.4.2.2 for more information).

Upgrading a CD-ROM Drive

CD-ROM drive and disc technology is rapidly changing. Hardware manufacturers continue to increase the speed of drives and the number of disc formats. Most CD-ROM drives are capable of running most CD-ROM titles. You are unlikely to require a new CD-ROM drive simply in order to install and run a specific title. If a workstation, however, has a very old CD-ROM drive, such as the first-generation external CD-ROM drives ("single-speed") or an early MPC-standard CD-ROM drive ("double-speed"), you may see substantial improvements (especially in the display of full-motion video) with a faster CD-ROM drive. Some CD-ROM installation programs may even prevent you from installing them on slower CD-ROM drives. Refer to Chapter 7 for an explanation of the features to look for in a new CD-ROM drive.

MULTIMEDIA HARDWARE OPTIONS

Most of the above-mentioned enhancements are useful only for stand-alone CD-ROM workstations, ones with a CD-ROM drive installed in them. Some enhancements to workstations on a network are also possible. Most of these involve multimedia adapter cards, which must be installed in every workstation on the network.

Audio Options

The audio options are determined by whether or not the workstation is a single-user workstation or is used to present information to a group. They are also determined by the location of the workstation, whether out in an open space where sound can disturb others or in a soundproof booth or private office.

Older workstations can be improved by upgrading the sound card installed in the system unit. Older multimedia workstations may have so-called 8-bit sound cards and can benefit greatly by upgrading to a 16-bit sound card. New sound-file compression standards may also require a hardware upgrade, such as Dolby AC-3 required for MPEG-2 and DVD (see "Glossary").

Speakers can generally be easily attached to a workstation to improve the quality of sound emitted by it or to allow the use of the workstation in front of large groups. Headphones may need to be replaced when the cords develop shorts that can create static.

Video Options

As with audio enhancements, video adapter cards may need to be upgraded to accommodate new video-compression formats and greater color depth (from 8-bit or 16-bit to 32-bit color). Large monitors can be added to a workstation to accommodate group presentations. Projector devices are available to project screen images onto a wall or movie screen, circumventing the monitor. In classrooms, "whiteboard systems" are especially useful: networked workstations can be controlled by a teacher, who "broadcasts" from one workstation to all the others or who can control the display of all workstations.

PREPARING PRINTED SUPPORT MATERIALS FOR CD-ROM WORKSTATION USERS

Quick-reference cards, job aids, and more detailed documentation both of the workstation hardware and of its CD-ROM titles should be made available to all workstation users. The easiest way to produce this documentation, when copyrights permit, is to reproduce suitable pages from vendor-supplied user's manuals. A local copy center may be able to plasticize these pages so you can attach them to the workstation with a cord or chain.

In many instances, though, you may need to design the workstation's documentation. This section provides guidelines for CD-ROM workstation documentation: search engines, printing, and menuing systems.

ASSISTING USERS WITH CD-ROM SEARCHES

CD-ROM title users frequently need help searching for information. Most CD-ROM titles employ a unique, proprietary "search engine," but most also rely on some standard computer-search principles. The documentation you provide for CD-ROM title users should include both title-specific techniques and standard computer-search techniques, such as the use of keywords, Boolean operators, and punctuation marks.

CD-ROM title search engines differ depending upon the type of information on the title disc. Textual information (including hypertext and Web pages) must be searched in most cases using one technique, while structured databases must be searched using other techniques. Some titles can only be searched by means of the title's "search engine," while others can be searched by means of separate utility programs or database programs that may reside on the hard drive of a workstation. You must provide separate instructions for each title-specific search engine, but you may supply just a single set of instructions for using utility and database programs in conjunction with several titles. For example, you should provide separate instructions on searching the *SelectPhone* CD-ROM and *Microsoft Bookshelf,* but you may supply only a single set of instructions on how to use Netscape *Navigator* to search several CD-ROM titles that include HTML documents.

When designing these materials, keep explanations short, provide numerous lists of commands and keywords, provide examples drawn from the specific titles, and consider using computer screen-prints to illustrate especially complex concepts.

Most search engines are designed to conduct one or both of two general types of searches: field searches or free-form statement searches. In a field search, the computer screen presents a series of discrete fields (they look like labeled boxes) indicating the keywords or topics available. In a free-form search, the computer screen often presents a blank line where a word, phrase, or a complete sentence must be typed according to a prescribed pattern.

Field Searches

When explaining field-search techniques, always alert the user to the fact that the more fields that are filled in, the more specific the search will be and consequently the faster the user will obtain the desired results. The fewer fields that are filled in, or the more often "don't care" or "wild card" characters and keywords are used, the longer the list of items the search engine will retrieve.

Free-form Searches

You need to provide more assistance for users of free-form search engines, such as those found on the Internet. Free-form searches are more difficult to conduct since the computer screen provides no hints about the type of information that may be available in the database. In a free-form search the user must know the rules of syntax for its searches, rather like knowing all the rules of punctuation and grammar when writing a sentence in one language or another.

Boolean Operators

Most free-form search engines recognize "Booleans." The quick-reference materials you design should provide lists of acceptable Boolean words or "operators." For example:

   & (AND)
   = (ONLY)
   > (GREATER THAN or LATER THAN)
   < (LESS THAN or BEFORE)
   <> (NOT EQUAL TO or NOT)

Explain the importance of using Booleans to speed up a search, both in terms of actual computer-processing time and in terms of the number of steps a user must complete before obtaining the desired information. Provide numerous examples.

Punctuation of a Search Statement

Explain the correct punctuation for any search statement and for filling in data in a field for each CD-ROM title.

Some search engines are case-sensitive: inform users they must use both upper and lowercase letters correctly or the system will ignore matching words that are not capitalized exactly as indicated. Some search engines allow the listing of search terms separated only by spaces, so that a list like "red blue yellow" would mean "red or blue or yellow," while some search engines would treat the words as a string or phrase. Other search engines require terms to be separated by commas, for example, "red, blue, yellow" (without the quotation marks). Some search engines require the use of parentheses to group words and phrases.

For example, the Microsoft *Bookshelf* CD-ROM requires the following punctuation of a search: use double quotes to find exact matches for a phrase. Use parentheses to group words and phrases so as to expand or limit the search. Use an asterisk at the end of a string of letters or words to indicate that the retrieved items must begin with exactly those letters or that word, but can end with any other series of letters or words.

In all cases, alert users to the fact that a failure to retrieve data at any given time, using any given technique, does not mean that no such data is available on the CD-ROM title. It merely means that they must try a different search technique.

DEMONSTRATING HOW TO PRINT

Whether a CD-ROM workstation shares a networked printer or whether it has a printer directly attached to it, printing instructions must be supplied to users.

Printing procedures differ for every CD-ROM title and every CD-ROM workstation. Include the following information on quick-reference sheets for users:

- Is there a charge for printing?
- When is printing permitted, when prohibited?
- After printing from a CD-ROM title, where can the print-out be found (if the printer isn't located adjacent to the workstation)?
- Can screen prints be made, and if so how?
- How is information printed from the CD-ROM titles that are accessible from the workstation?
- A statement of copyrights and policies at your library or school

DEMONSTRATING MENUING SYSTEMS

If a CD-ROM workstation was originally designed to provide access to only one CD-ROM title, before installing additional titles on it, consider enhancing the workstation with a shell program or menuing system. Not only do these programs make it easier for you to maintain and support, but users will find it easier to access titles. Consider supplying a quick-reference card on use of the menuing system for workstation users.

CHAPTER SUMMARY

This chapter discusses several areas of maintenance and support required for each CD-ROM workstation, whether it is part of a network or is a stand-alone unit. Attention must be paid to the physical use and care of workstations and title discs. Maintenance and cleaning must be conducted on a regular schedule, using proper equipment and supplies. Records must be kept of the hardware and software configuration of each workstation, of the maintenance work performed on the workstation, and of all changes made to a workstation's hardware and software, including its installed CD-ROM titles.

Workstations must be kept up to date in terms of both the versions of CD-ROM titles installed on them and of the operating system and utilities that control workstation performance. Inexpensive but powerful performance enhancements are available, both in the form of software and hardware. Some equipment, such as keyboards, must be replaced frequently. Some operating system software must be upgraded regularly.

Guidelines for usage of each workstation should be posted prominently. Each workstation should also be supplied with relevant quick-reference sheets and other forms of documentation covering the use of specific CD-ROM titles, the menuing or shell system on the workstation, printing, copyright restrictions, and usage tips, such as tips on computer search techniques.

6. Troubleshooting a Library's or School's CD-ROM Workstation

ESSENTIAL PREVENTATIVES AND BASIC SOLUTIONS TO CD-ROM TITLE PROBLEMS

In order to resolve problems with CD-ROM systems you have to be able to classify the problem, identify its cause, know when it is a hardware problem requiring the intervention of a technician and when it is a software problem you can resolve yourself, and whom to contact for help when you can't resolve the problem. This chapter discusses each of these issues, with reference to unique characteristics of the DOS, Windows, and Macintosh operating systems running on stand-alone workstations. This chapter also suggests specific procedures for problem-resolution and steps to take before any problems occur.

This chapter is written with nontechnical librarians and educators in mind. Read this chapter if you are responsible for overseeing CD-ROM workstations, including assisting library patrons and students with use of the system. Follow guidelines presented here both to establish troubleshooting procedures in advance of problems and to learn how to troubleshoot a CD-ROM system. Specific technical instructions for correcting the most common problems are provided in Part Three, Chapters 9 through 12.

CD-ROM PROBLEM ANALYSIS TECHNIQUES

Every library and school with CD-ROM workstations should establish procedures for troubleshooting the system and provide thorough documentation to individuals who are responsible for the workstations. Network system administrators should ensure that individuals responsible for client workstations within the network know when to contact technical support staff for

assistance and what the limits of their personal responsibilities are for maintaining and supporting each workstation and each CD-ROM title.

Of course, in order take appropriate steps, individuals must understand
the problems that are occurring—this is not a trivial task. CD-ROM workstation "managers" must know what to do when problems occur, how to shut
down a workstation, how to recover from errors, how to troubleshoot common hardware and software problems, and how to interpret error messages.

PREPARING FOR PROBLEMS

The time to address CD-ROM workstation problems is well in advance
of their occurrence. All the important files on the workstation's hard drive
should be backed up onto diskettes or computer tape so that they can be easily restored to the hard drive in the event of system failure, damaged files, or
deleted files. Follow the recommendations in this book concerning maintaining up-to-date device drivers and a written log of system changes.

In addition to the operating-system manuals, buy a good book on the
version of your workstation's operating system that includes background concepts as well as reference information. (See "Recommended Reading.")

WHAT TO DO FIRST

This section is designed to assist you in resolving problems, such as the
following:

> After successfully starting up a CD-ROM workstation, a user attempts to
> access a CD-ROM title. An error message displays, halting the CD-ROM
> title. The problem may have occurred the first time the CD-ROM title was
> accessed, or it may have occurred after the title had been running properly
> for some time. The user calls on you for help.

To resolve the problem, follow these steps:

1. Write down the error message exactly as it appears on the screen. Make
   a note of the circumstances under which the error occurred: what events
   immediately preceded the display of the message? The text of an error
   message usually states what type of error has occurred. The event
   immediately preceding the display of the message is usually the source
   of the problem.
2. Attempt to shut down and restart the system properly; the error may not
   recur.
3. If the error recurs, follow the advice in the "Troubleshooting" sections
   of Chapters 9–12 to identify the source of the error.
4. Follow the instructions in the "Most Common Problems" sections of
   Chapters 9–12 to correct the error.

5. If all else fails, restore the system configuration from the backups you prepared for just such situations, and then reinstall the CD-ROM title. This may correct earlier installation errors or repair damaged files.

6. If the problem persists, contact the CD-ROM title vendor.

If a stand-alone workstation encounters problems with a CD-ROM title, attempt to recover control of the workstation by shutting the system down and restarting it. If it is on a network, follow network administration guidelines. If the problem isn't resolved by restarting the computer and CD-ROM title, then you will need to follow the methodology presented in this chapter. Once you have eliminated common hardware problems and CD-ROM title errors ("bugs"), you must troubleshoot the operating system and attempt to correct the error.

HOW TO USE PART THREE

Each "Troubleshooting" section in Chapters 9–12 covers the following:
- Steps to take as soon as an error message is displayed
- Procedures for safely shutting down and restarting the computer
- Tips to help you pinpoint the anomaly that caused the specific error message to display

After referring to the appropriate "Troubleshooting" section, scan the list of error messages that follow in the "Most Common Problems" sections of each chapter, looking not only for identical messages but also for similar messages or messages containing similar "keywords."

The messages in each chapter in Part Three are listed in the order in which they are most likely to occur. Consequently, if several messages listed in a chapter are similar to the message you received, but none is exactly the message, you should *assume* the last message listed in the section is the *first* message you should study. On the other hand, if a message listed exactly matches the error you received, begin with it.

If possible, wait until after hours when all your patrons or students have left the premises before you do anything else. You need an uninterrupted period of time (at least one hour) to work on the problem. You should also have at hand the phone number of a technical-support specialist to call, if all else fails.

If you are unable to resolve a problem using the tips in Part Three, you will probably call the CD-ROM title producer's technical support line. The technician will be able to help you if the problem is a "bug" in the title or a "known" (previously identified) incompatibility between the title and your specific hardware configuration. Most problems arise from the workstation itself—something in the configuration files. So, don't expect miracles from a technician on a long-distance phone call. He or she may provide clues to a solution, but ultimately you may have to resolve the problem independently.

Understanding Error Messages

Error messages are important clues to the origin of a problem: sometimes error messages are comprised of text and instructions, while at other times they are simply warning symbols. Error messages can be produced by the operating system on the workstation, by application programs or utility programs running on the workstation, or by the CD-ROM title. You must be able to recognize and distinguish error messages from these different sources. It is especially important to be familiar with the format of operating-system error messages. Refer to the operating system's technical manuals for this information.

An error message is almost always a reflection of the final error in a chain of errors that has occurred. If you eliminate the problem that produced an error message late in the chain reaction, you may uncover an earlier error in the chain. Sometimes an error message may even seem to indicate a problem where there really is none: the message may actually indicate only that an error occurred, somewhere, sometime. So, you may need to make several error corrections before you can run a CD-ROM title successfully.

You can generally track down the first and most important error in a chain of errors by eliminating some possibilities and then focusing on the remainder. For example, determining exactly *when* the error occurred is critical. By watching the computer start-up process, you may spot the first error in the chain. If an error occurs after the computer has been "booted up," then watch the sequence in which programs start up or the sequence in which hardware components are activated. For example, the first error may occur after a CD-ROM title first attempts to play sound. This could provide a hint that the problem lies with the sound card and its device drivers rather than with the CD-ROM title; or perhaps the title is incompatible with the sound card's device driver.

DOS Errors and Error Messages

Assume from the moment you obtain a DOS CD-ROM title that you *will* encounter problems with it; then attempt to forestall or prevent them in advance, and have your "triage" process in place so you will be ready when they occur. DOS is a very complex operating system with very little error tolerance built in.

DOS error messages always display beside the DOS prompt. Some DOS error messages begin with a numerical code, but most are simply text messages. Remember that Windows 3.X-based workstations are also running a version of DOS: DOS errors can occur on Windows 3.X systems as well as Windows 3.X errors. Often a DOS error on a Windows 3.X workstation won't display its normal message because the DOS prompt isn't visible. At other times, the system may "return to DOS" unexpectedly from Windows in order to display a DOS error message. Refer to a *Microsoft MS-DOS User's Guide* for help with DOS error messages, or refer to Chapter 9.

WINDOWS 3.X ERRORS AND ERROR MESSAGES

Compared to DOS, Windows 3.X is easy to use—deceptively easy, and easy to disrupt. Users can introduce errors into a Windows 3.X system by inadvertently changing elements of the system configuration. It's also very difficult to protect a Windows 3.X system from intentional changes made by a knowledgeable user.

The first line of defense against Windows 3.X problems is to protect the system from the introduction of errors by users. Most library or school CD-ROM workstations running Windows 3.X should include a shell or menuing system to hide Windows from its users. Only authorized individuals (library or school staff members) with passwords should be allowed to access Windows 3.X or DOS. Besides protecting files from damage, the best preparation for Windows 3.X problems is to retain a set of good backups. Important system files for Windows 3.X include all the files ending in the file name extension .INI in the \WINDOWS and \WINDOWS\SYSTEM directories.

A Windows 3.X workstation first performs DOS tasks and then performs Windows tasks. DOS errors always precede Windows errors. The only error message you may receive when running a Windows 3.X CD-ROM title, however, may be a Windows message caused by an error that originates in DOS. Follow the advice in section 10.3 of Chapter 10 to identify the Windows 3.X error. If none of the messages listed corresponds to the message you received, it may mean that the message is a DOS rather than a Windows 3.X message. Turn to the DOS messages listed in section 9.3.

Windows 3.X error messages can be long and explicit or terse, numerical, and vague. It's often hard to tell whether the message was generated by Windows itself or by an application program, such as a CD-ROM title. Several programs may be running in memory simultaneously, and any one of them may have caused an error message. Section 10.4 primarily lists general messages, keywords, and codes that may appear in the message text, and a few specific Windows 3.X message texts. To locate information about a particular error, scan the list of messages. Remember, you may find clues and solutions under several related headings.

Many Windows error messages are displayed in a warning box with an exclamation point inside a yellow circle. Often Windows error messages require the user to click an **OK** button (which does not mean that the situation is okay, but only that the user has read the error message). Other error messages offer two options, such as **Cancel** and **Retry**. Error messages with a "GPF" code or labeled as "General Protection Fault" are produced by

Windows but actually represent a problem with the application title that is running, including problems with CD-ROM titles.

WINDOWS 9X ERRORS AND ERROR MESSAGES

Like Windows 3.X, Windows 9X is deceptively simple to use, and its error messages appear to be straightforward. Also like Windows 3.X users, Windows 9x users can introduce errors into a Windows 9X system by changing elements of the system configuration. It's very difficult to protect a Windows 9X system from a knowledgeable user (indeed, this can be said of almost any computer system): the password protection provided by Windows 9X **User Profiles**, for example, is far from adequate for this purpose. Consequently, most library or school CD-ROM workstations running Windows 9X should use a shell or menuing system to hide Windows from its users. Only authorized users with passwords should be allowed to access Windows 9X.

Besides protecting files from damage, the best preparation for Windows 9X problems is to have a set of good backups. All the important files on the workstation's hard drive should be backed up onto diskettes or computer tape so that they can be easily restored to the hard drive in the event of system failure, damaged files, or deleted files. Important system files for Windows 9X include the **Registry** and all files that are included in the emergency start-up disk created during the Windows 9X installation procedure.

One of the most common and most misleading error messages generated by Windows 9X is one that states that "the application program has performed an invalid operation" and instructs the user to contact the vendor. If this message displays while a CD-ROM title is running, then it probably means that there is an error in the CD-ROM title and its producer should be contacted. It may, however, mean that there is a problem with another application program running in the background, including programs developed by Microsoft (the "vendor" of the application and of Windows 9X). In that case you must follow the troubleshooting techniques recommended here to decide which vendor to contact.

MACINTOSH ERRORS AND ERROR MESSAGES

Though very easy to use, the Macintosh operating system is prone to "crash" and prone to suffer from memory errors. Application programs, such as CD-ROM titles, can cause these errors, without being either poorly designed or "buggy." The most common error message, in such cases, is the one that includes a cartoon bomb: when such errors occur, there is nothing you can do but restart the Mac. The error may never again recur.

Macintosh operating-system error messages may include a numerical code or an icon (such as the bomb symbol) and a text message. Most programs that run under the Macintosh operating system also produce error messages in the same format as the operating system's error messages, so it may be difficult to determine which is causing the problem. Refer to Chapter 12 for assistance.

PROBLEM ANALYSIS

If you find you can't resolve a problem on your own, you will probably contact the CD-ROM vendor's technical support "hot line." Before calling a technician, however, you must determine as best you can what the source of the problem is. If you cannot do so, it will be very difficult for a technician to help you over the phone. A technician will have to lead you, step by step, through a time-consuming analysis that may not be useful, because he or she won't be able to see what you are doing to the workstation or how the workstation is responding.

This chapter provides an overview of problem analysis for CD-ROMs. Follow the steps outlined here when trying to analyze a specific problem. As you proceed through the steps in the analysis sequence, carefully record everything that happens—be certain to write down the complete text of all error messages so that you can read them to a technician if you need help.

The basic problem-analysis method is to proceed from the general to the specific. Narrow down the possibilities. Determine whether it is a hardware or a software problem or a combination of both. Then, having determined the general category of problem, narrow down the problem to its specific source. Find out whether nothing is working properly or only one thing. Next, determine whether that "one thing" never works or works intermittently. If it works intermittently, what are the conditions that cause it to fail?

ELIMINATING POSSIBLE PROBLEMS

Begin the troubleshooting process by eliminating possibilities:

Does anything work?

No, nothing works. If that is the case, then you're probably not dealing with a problem caused by either the CD-ROM drive or CD-ROM title. Instead, the power supply or power switch may be broken, or the power source may not be turned on. If the power source is turned on, then the problem is likely to be equipment requiring repair. If, however, only the CD-ROM drive or some other component of the workstation doesn't seem to be working, then you have begun to narrow down the possibilities.

If yes, what works? By listing all the working components of the system, you eliminate most of them as the cause of the problem.

If the system works intermittently, what are the conditions of failure?

The system may work fine sometimes and not others. Or, it may cease to function after running for some period of time. List all of the functions that operate properly. List the steps in the start-up process that work. When you reach the point at which the system fails, you may have identified the cause of the problem.

Is the problem something new, something recently broken?

This is critical. If you have recently changed something in the system (perhaps while installing a new CD-ROM drive or a new CD-ROM title), you may have introduced errors into the system. Study the changes you recently made to discover the most likely cause of the problem.

Is this the first time you have tried to run a specific CD-ROM title, or to use a new CD-ROM drive or other hardware component?

If everything was working fine and then stopped when you tried something new, the new element is the source of the problem.

Can you restore the system to its prior, working condition?

Sometimes a new addition to a workstation system can also impact a previously existing piece of equipment or software. For example, when installing a new DVD drive, you may have mistakenly disconnected a cable for a CD-ROM drive. You may have loosened cables and plugs on the back of the workstation. If new software was installed, perhaps it is being loaded into memory when the workstation first starts up, and it takes up memory needed by a CD-ROM title. If you can temporarily disable the new component, try to use the old computer setup to see if it still works. If not, then you have also changed something in the old setup and that may be the problem.

DETERMINING THE TYPE OF PROBLEM

Having narrowed down the list of possible causes, you should be able next to determine the category of the problem:

Is this a hardware, software, or combination problem?

Perhaps by analyzing the system you have narrowed down the source of the problem to the CD-ROM drive—you still don't know whether the problem is with the equipment or with the device drivers.

Is there something physically wrong with the hardware (such as the CD-ROM drive)?

Are all cables and power cords firmly connected? Even though you may have checked repeatedly, re-seat all plugs and reconnect all cables, one more time. It might help to completely disconnect all cables and then reconnect them.

Are all cables connected to the correct ports and sockets? Verify that you have attached everything to the correct locations. Many connectors on computers are very similar. Not all cables are designed to prevent you from making mistakes.

Is the power source "live"? Is the wall socket functioning? Grounded? Verify that all the power sources are live. Plug in something, such as a lamp, to be sure. Even a power strip contains circuit breakers and can be shorted out, thus preventing a flow of power to your computer system.

Is the equipment plugged into a power strip, line filter, backup power source, or multiple-device switch that has to be powered up separately? If so, is that powered up? Power strips and surge protectors often have their own on/off switches.

Does the equipment have an internal "power supply" that you can, or should be able to, hear? If so, many such power supplies require an internal fan; can you hear the fan? Are there indicator lights on the equipment? Are they on? A common source of problems is the internal motor (or power supply) on computers and external peripherals, such as external CD-ROM drives. You can't always tell whether power is reaching the peripheral if its internal power switch is relatively silent or lacks indicator lights.

Have you received any unusual warning messages? Many systems perform self-tests when powered on. They report problems to you, either by displaying error messages on the screen, by flickering or flashing lights, or sometimes by beeping. Restart the workstation, and watch the screen carefully. Write down all error messages.

Using operating-system commands (such as those described in Chapters 9 through 12), can you control any feature of the hardware component? If so, you know the equipment is receiving power. You do not know, however, whether the component may have been installed improperly, for example, with the wrong switches or internal cabling. *If not,* but everything else about the equipment seems to be in working order, the problem may be a software problem (see below).

Run the diagnostics to receive a report on the computer's components. Many computer operating systems include diagnostic software that produces a report listing hardware errors. If a diagnostic report doesn't even list a component that is installed in the computer (such as a CD-ROM drive or sound card), that means the component is not functioning.

Is it a software problem?

Perform software diagnostics on memory, hard drives, and so on, which may tell you where the problem lies.

Verify that the operating system and device drivers work.

They seem to be OK. Move on to application software.

They don't seem to be OK. Do you receive any error messages when attempting to use the CD-ROM disc or drive?

You receive error messages when running the title or CD-ROM drive. Write them down and refer the Chapters 9–12. Those chapters will provide some clues as to which software program is giving you the problem. All error messages come from a specific program: if a message comes from the operating system, it may name the other program that is not functioning. If it comes from a device driver, the device driver program may be named. If it comes from the software on a specific CD-ROM, that program name may appear in the error message. Write down all error messages exactly, and note at what point in the process the message appeared. This is critical information for the technician.

SOURCES OF ASSISTANCE BEYOND THIS BOOK

USERS GROUPS AND OTHERS

Sources of help with CD-ROMs include: other users, the title producer, hardware and software vendor hot lines, title distributors, and retail stores. If you have the time and are fairly certain you know what the problem is, the least expensive source of support is other users of the CD-ROM title or computer equipment. Locate a local users group, a bulletin board service dedicated to the topic, online service forums, or Internet resources. Such individuals will generally be more willing to help you and to explain things in nontechnical language. Refer to Appendix C for a list of some of these resources.

If you have less time, but you are nonetheless fairly certain you know what the problem is, contact the specific CD-ROM title producer or the CD-ROM drive manufacturer. Such individuals will probably be able to identify the problem and solution more quickly, but they may not be able to explain things clearly or simply. If you don't know what the problem is but still need a solution quickly, begin by contacting the CD-ROM title producer. If the producer can't help you, turn to the retailer or distributor who sold you the product. Finally, as a last resort, contact the manufacturer of the workstation or CD-ROM drive (a "last resort" because hardware vendors are least likely to be able to help you with a problem related to a specific CD-ROM title).

CONTACTING A VENDOR

Deciding whether to call the CD-ROM title producer, your distributor, or the computer equipment manufacturer can be difficult. Not only is it best to know what the source of the problems is, but you also need to take into account which technical resource is most accessible and knowledgeable.

Distributors and Retailers

A distributor or retailer will probably be more accessible than a manufacturer, but also probably less knowledgeable. If, however, you know that the technical support supplied by the distributor is good, then you might call them first. If the title or equipment is still under warranty, you might want to call the retailer first to verify procedures for repairs and replacements under the terms of the warranty.

The retailer or distributor is the first line of defense if you need to return a defective disc. Any good retailer should allow you to return a clearly defective disc at any time for a replacement or refund. How do you know if the problem is a defective disc, that is, that there is a physical defect in the disc? First, examine the shiny side of the disc for bumps, imperfections, or dirt. If dirt is present, clean the disc as described in Chapter 5. If there appears to be a physical flaw in either surface of the disc, then it is defective. Bumps or scratches on either side of the disc, including the label side, can make it impossible for the CD-ROM drive to read the data on the disc. Another way to tell if the disc is defective is if you have successfully used other CD-ROM discs on the workstation before, but the workstation will simply not even recognize the presence of this disc. In other words, if the workstation doesn't allow you to select the CD-ROM drive as an active drive on the system when the disc is properly inserted into the drive, then the disc is at fault. Or, if you are normally able to view the contents of a CD-ROM disc just like any other disk on the workstation, but you cannot view the contents of a specific disc, then the disc is defective.

Title Producers

On the other hand, you may choose to contact the CD-ROM title producer first because that company has an easily accessible bulletin board system, fax-back system, or large customer service department. When dealing directly with the producer, you are likely to receive the best technical information. You are also likely to be required to prove you are a licensed owner of their products and to understand rather complex technical details.

Technical Support Hot Lines

Technical support lines for computer companies sometimes require pay-as-you-go fees. With some products you receive a few weeks' or months' assistance via a "free" phone number, either an 800 number or a standard toll number. After that period, you may be required to pay for the call by dialing a 900 number or by supplying a credit card number to which the time they spend helping you can be charged. You need to be aware that even some 800 number calls aren't toll free and can be charged back to your phone number. Always ask as soon as you reach a technical support line whether you are being charged for the call.

Sometimes the hardest part of obtaining technical support is just finding a phone number. Many hardware companies do not support the public directly, but rather provide services through distributors, retailers, and third-party technical support. Look first in Appendix C or look in the product's manuals for the number. You can also locate most hardware companies through the standard business directories, such as Hoover's directories. A hardware manufacturer who is unwilling to be contacted easily by end-users of its products can always be contacted through its business headquarters—dial the receptionist and ask for technical support.

Preparing to Make the Call

Registration, License, and Warranty Numbers. Always fill out and mail in the registration and warranty cards for all CD-ROM titles and equipment, since this is what entitles you to receive technical help and updates to the product. You need not fill in all the demographic information requested, although it is a good idea for later reference to list when and where you bought the item. When you call for technical support, you may be required to provide the registration or warranty numbers found on the card.

Retain a copy of the registration, license, or warranty numbers for all CD-ROM titles and computer equipment in a location near the computer. For example, write the information on the inside cover of the technical manual provided with the product, or staple a copy of the registration form inside the front cover of the manual. File all registration, license, and warranty information. Most importantly, make sure you record the phone number and addresses of both the product manufacturer's business offices and technical support lines.

Gathering Hardware Technical Information. When seeking technical support, it will be essential for you to know the technical specifications of the workstation hardware and be able to describe them to the technician. (Refer to Chapter 7 for details on how to find out what kind of hardware you have.)

Gathering Software Technical Information. When calling a CD-ROM title producer's technical support line, the single most important item of information to have at hand is the version number of the CD-ROM title. Assuming you store the CD-ROM disc inside the original jewel case in which it came, the inside slipcover will probably state the copyright date. This, however, is not the version number of the software. A CD-ROM may be copyrighted in one year and not shipped to resellers until the following year. More than one version of the CD-ROM may be distributed within a given year.

The disc itself may have some version information or other identifying information on the label. Most often, the version number for the CD-ROM title is displayed while you are running the CD-ROM itself. DOS CD-ROMs may list the version on a title screen or under a menu item. Windows CD-ROMs likely have an **About** menu item that lists the version. Mac CD-ROMs generally display the version in the **Get Info** menu window.

You may also need to tell a technician that you obtained a disc as part of a package with other discs, especially when the discs are distributed by a CD-ROM drive manufacturer or a computer manufacturer. The label printed on the disc will note, for example, that the disc was produced by Packard Bell for distribution with Packard Bell computers. This indicates that the hardware manufacturer (rather than the CD-ROM title producer) may be responsible for support of that version of the CD-ROM.

Making the Call

You are ready to place a call if (1) you have the technical specifications of the workstation available, (2) you have proof that you are entitled to technical support from a given source in the form of a registration or warranty number, and (3) you have tried to determine the source of the problem. Be prepared to provide this information to the technician.

If possible, make the call from a phone near the workstation. Restart the workstation or CD-ROM title until you reach the problem with the error message displayed, then make the call. The technician will ask you to do this, if you haven't done so.

Don't be distressed if you receive a busy signal. It may mean that you are not the only person who is having this problem. This can be a good thing, because it means the technician—when you reach him or her—will already likely know about the problem and how to fix it. (It's never fun to be the first person to find a bug in a program.) Of course, the busy signal could also mean that there are only a few technicians available to answer your call, and you will have to be persistent if you wish to get through.

Don't be distressed if you reach a voice mail system or a recorded message when calling for technical support. Sometimes the voice mail system can play back to you brief answers to the most frequently asked questions. This may be the quickest means to a solution of a problem. Usually such systems are available 24 hours a day, seven days a week.

A very useful innovation in customer support is the fax-back system. In these systems you generally call a technical support line first and hear a recording. You select a technical document or a catalog of information by punching phone keys and supplying your own fax number. If you don't have access to a stand-alone fax machine, you may have a fax/modem that will allow the workstation to answer the phone and receive the fax. The fax is sent to you and is stored as a bitmapped graphic image on the workstation. You can read the fax on the workstation's screen or print it out. A fax-back system tends to reduce your long-distance charges for technical support related to common problems.

Anticipating Questions

As soon as you reach a technician, expect to be asked the following questions:

1. "What product and what version number of the product are you calling about?" You may need to be transferred to a specialist.
2. "Are you a registered user or is the product under warranty?" You may need to prove you own a license to the software, have purchased a support agreement, or that the product is still under warranty.
3. "What's the problem, or how can I help you?" This is the toughest question to answer. Many times, if you just knew what the problem was, you wouldn't even need to talk to a technician. This is where your efforts at troubleshooting will help you. State as briefly as possible what you think the problem is. For example, "I just bought the CD-ROM and installed it. The installation seemed to go OK, but when I tried to start using the disc, nothing happened, not even an error message."

Take detailed notes throughout the conversation. You may need to try several different things in order to resolve the problem. At first, you can expect that the technician will assume that you are experiencing one of the more common problems. You will be asked whether you had everything turned on, whether the disc was in the drive, and so on. Don't be offended.

If the technician suggests that you try something and then call back, be sure to get the technician's name (at least the first name) and extension or direct phone number. You don't want to have to go through the whole process of explanation again with a new technician when you call back.

In addition, it is often useful for a technician to see a print-out of the workstation's configuration or software setup. For a Mac, this means printing a directory listing of the System Folder and Extensions folder. For a DOS PC, this means printing a copy of the AUTOEXEC.BAT and CONFIG.SYS files. For a Windows system, it means including not only the AUTOEXEC.BAT and CONFIG.SYS files, but also the SYSTEM.INI and WIN.INI files, among others. This information can be mailed or faxed to the technician via your fax/modem. Be sure to get the fax number and address to which these items should be sent. Or, if the company or technician has an e-mail address and you have access to Internet, the file can be attached to an e-mail message and transferred instantly.

Asking the Right Questions

If you begin to sense during the conversation that your problem is new or unique, or to feel that you have already tried everything the technician is suggesting, ask, "Would you like me to explain what I have tried so far?"

Asking questions of a computer technician is both an art and a skill. You are unlikely even to be "speaking the same language" as the technician. The following are some useful questions to ask of a technician.

"Should this be happening?"

This question is important. It may be that the product in question is supposed to be doing whatever it is doing, which you think is a problem; for example, the screen may be flashing or the computer may be making a noise. The technician can tell you why it is doing "that."

"Has anyone else reported this problem?"

If the answer is "yes," you can relax a little. The technician may already know how to solve your problem without further research.

"Is this disc (or equipment) the most current version?"

If the answer is "no," you should request information about obtaining the latest version. Newer versions may fix the problem for you.

"Is there a patch or update file available? Online or by e-mail?"

If the answer is "yes," you will be able to obtain the updated file quickly.

"Has this CD-ROM title been tested with my type of computer? Are other people successfully using this product?"

If the workstation is an "off" brand or a particularly unique system, the CD-ROM may not have been tested for use on the system. CD-ROM title producers try to test for the most commonly used systems and configurations, but cannot test on all possible models and brands.

"Can I call you back personally if I still have problems?"

The answer should be "yes." If the answer is "no," find out why not. If it is because of company policy, ask to be transferred to a supervisor so that you can insist on a name or number to contact in the event you need to call back.

"Is there a users group, bulletin board, online service, or other public source of support in addition to you?"

This book has provided several reasons why you should try to find a strong support group for your use of CD-ROMs.

Use the following questions when the technician seems to have run out of possible solutions:

"What are the most common problems people have with your product?"

The technician may not want to tell you about problems other people have had, since it may seem as if the product is defective. On the other hand, if he or she is willing to share this information, it can provide you with valuable clues to your problem.

"How can I return this if it is defective or I need a different version?"

Needless to say, the easiest problems to fix are physical defects in products that are still under warranty: you simply return them. But, if the warranty has expired (for equipment), it may not be easy to find a repair center without the technician's help. In addition, most CD-ROM titles are warranted against physical defects only for a brief period after purchase. You are expected to find the defect soon after purchase. If that is not possible, a good customer-service-oriented company will generally let you return the disc to them for a replacement.

"What am I doing wrong, or what have I done that sounds unusual to you?"

This is a last-resort question. If you have tried to provide diagnostic information and listened to the technician's suggestions, but nothing seems to work, you have to open the discussion up in this way.

CHAPTER SUMMARY

This chapter provides guidelines for nontechnical individuals who find themselves in the position of having to troubleshoot a CD-ROM workstation. Problems are bound to occur with workstations throughout the work day: CD-ROM title users will frequently request assistance, even with a properly configured and maintained system.

When problems occur, the error message must be noted and the workstation must be returned to a working state as quickly as possible. Then, an orderly troubleshooting process should be conducted when there are no disturbances. Walk through the checklist of issues supplied in this chapter. Then, refer to Part Three for specific instructions on how to solve problems related to DOS, Windows, or the Macintosh operating systems. Finally, if the problem can't be solved with reference to this book, gather up all the warranty and license information for the workstation and the CD-ROM title, and contact one of the sources of technical support recommended here.

Part Three
TECHNICAL
GUIDE

Part Three of *CD-ROM Technology* provides technical reference information and step-by-step instructions on performing CD-ROM workstation maintenance. It is designed for individuals who must work with the operating system and other software components of the library's or school's CD-ROM systems, not just with CD-ROM titles.

Part Three is not intended to be comprehensive with regard to computer operating systems, software, or hardware, but rather only to provide details on procedures discussed in Parts One and Two. These procedures include analyzing a computer to determine its technical configuration; configuring or modifying components of a CD-ROM workstation's operating system; downloading, decompressing, and installing device-driver files; installing CD-ROM titles with or without a vendor-supplied installation program; system performance-tuning; and troubleshooting CD-ROM workstations.

To use Part Three, you should have basic computer skills and a willingness to learn about technical details; you need not be a technical expert. Part Three is also intended as a guide to information about older operating systems and as a starting point for CD-ROM problem-resolution by expert network-system administrators and technical-support staff of multi-location institutions.

Chapter 7, "Preparing to Install CD-ROM Titles," provides instructions on how to perform tasks discussed in Chapter 4, "Supervising the CD-ROM Title Installation Process." A librarian or educator who has read Chapter 4 and needs further assistance with the device-driver files on a workstation, or with determining whether a given title is compatible with a workstation before installing it, should refer to Chapter 7.

Chapter 8, "Installing CD-ROM Titles," provides instructions on how to install CD-ROM titles on several different types of workstations. A librarian or educator who has difficulty installing a title should refer to Chapter 8 for possible alternatives to the vendor-supplied installation program.

125

Chapters 9–12 provide solutions to the most frequently encountered CD-ROM problems, including tuning operating systems to enhance the performance of CD-ROM titles, techniques for identifying the source of CD-ROM title problems and error messages, and solutions to typical problems. You need only refer to the chapter that discusses the relevant operating system.

Multimedia is a complex field. No single book can hope to cover all its aspects. The information in Part Three is intended only to highlight the most common problems with CD-ROM technology and their solutions. Readers are urged to consult "Recommended Reading" for more detailed information on the topics covered here.

Note on Section Numbering. Each section in Chapters 7 through 12 is numbered for purposes of cross-reference. Each section number begins with the chapter number: in Chapter 7 all section numbers begin with 7, for example (7.1).

7. Preparing to Install CD-ROM Titles

7.1 THE KEY TO SUCCESSFUL TITLE INSTALLATION

Preparation is the key to successful CD-ROM title installation. This chapter covers specific techniques for preparing a CD-ROM workstation for the installation of CD-ROM titles. The workstation must include the minimum required hardware for every CD-ROM title chosen to run on it; the workstation's operating system must be configured correctly; and the workstation must have the necessary device-driver files installed. Each of these topics is discussed in this chapter.

7.2 HOW TO DOWNLOAD SOFTWARE FOR A CD-ROM WORKSTATION

In order to prepare a workstation for CD-ROM titles, and frequently after titles have been installed, you may need to obtain updates and other files by downloading them from another computer. This section explains the downloading process.

Downloading software from an online source requires a computer that is either on a network or that has a modem with access to a phone line. This need not necessarily be the CD-ROM workstation on which the downloaded software ultimately will be used: files can be downloaded to one workstation and then transferred to another workstation.

Files can only be downloaded onto a diskette or hard drive, not a CD-ROM disc or CD-ROM drive. Consequently, it is necessary to ensure that sufficient unused disk space is available before beginning the downloading process. Insufficient disk space can result in an incomplete transfer of data from one computer to another. Downloading too much data onto a workstation's hard drive can also result in damage to the receiving computer system. When too much data is copied onto a hard drive, many operating systems erroneously record the data onto critical parts of the drive. This is especially common on older Macintosh systems and DOS systems. When this happens, the drive is said to have key components "overwritten," usually the file allocation table (or "FAT"). When the file allocation table or other fundamental segments of a hard drive are overwritten by excess data, the hard drive becomes unusable.

Note: In the following sections, the material downloaded from one computer to another is referred to as a "file." A computer file is any set of data: it may be a text file (such as instructions or a newsletter) or an executable program file (such as a file with a name ending in .EXE or .COM), or a database file.

7.2.1 OVERVIEW OF THE PROCESS

The steps in the downloading process include:
1. Connecting the workstation to the computer system from which you wish to obtain the file (including text files, data files, graphics, and programs)
2. Navigating through the online system to locate the file
3. Obtaining information about the file
4. Initiating the download process by selecting the file, specifying the type of download, and indicating where the file should be stored on the receiving computer
5. Waiting for the file transfer to take place
6. Verifying that the transfer was successful
7. Decompressing the file
8. And, if the file was a device-driver file or other executable program, installing it

Files may be downloaded from several sources: the Internet (including several different types of sites), bulletin boards, and online services. The Internet provides three facilities for obtaining files: World Wide Web sites, FTP sites, and newsgroups. Each of these Internet facilities is explained below. Bulletin boards are private computer systems that can be accessed via modem or the Internet, usually for a fee or with password permission, such as sources of information about technical support provided by hardware manufacturers. Online services are for-fee services accessible via modem or the Internet, such as America Online, which combine features of the Internet and bulletin boards. This section (7.2) provides tips on the downloading process. For detailed information on how to connect to the Internet, to a bulletin board, or to an online service, refer to one of the books listed in "Recommended Reading" or to the technical support staff of the service.

Having successfully connected to the online file source (step 1 above) and located the software you wish to download (step 2 above), also locate information about the file(s) you wish to download. Critical information includes:

- the file-compression format
- how to decompress the file
- the size of the compressed file
- estimated time to download the file

The time estimate can help you schedule the session—for example, you may wish to walk away from the computer and work on something else while a large file is being downloaded. The size of the file is also critical information, because you must check after downloading and disconnecting from the online file source to make sure that you have received a complete file. It's very easy to be accidentally disconnected from an online source during a file transfer; when that happens, you may receive an incomplete file but not realize it until you try unsuccessfully to use the file. If you find that the size of the file you received isn't as large as you expected, an error may have occurred. Download the file again.

7.2.1.1 Downloading from the Internet

The Internet includes sources of several types of information that may be useful to librarians and teachers who manage CD-ROM workstations, including a range of resources from CD-ROM title reviews to update files for CD-ROM titles. World Wide Web sites are public postings on the Internet of information covering various topics; a "Web site" is comprised of pages of hypertext (see "Glossary") with links to related pages at other Web sites, and which often include files that can be downloaded. File Transfer Protocol ("FTP") sites are Internet sites where files are stored in one of several formats (excluding hypertext) for public distribution; you can both download files from an FTP site and upload your own files for distribution. Newsgroups are online forums where you can post and read messages of interest to you in specific subject areas, including CD-ROMs; newsgroups can provide valuable tips on device drivers and where to obtain the latest versions.

World Wide Web Sites. If your library or school has access to the World Wide Web, begin your search for files there. Refer to Appendix C for Web addresses (also called Universal Resource Locators or "URLs") that are likely to have what you need. Once you've located a Web page from which a file may be downloaded, the process is as simple as pointing and clicking with a mouse. Be sure to follow the instructions displayed on the screen; steps may vary by Web page and according to the Web browser software you use.

To access a World Wide Web site using your Internet Web browser software, type its URL, such as:

http://www.microsoft.com

When the Web page displays, look for information about how to download the files available and how to install them. These types of instructions can often be printed using your Web browser software or can be saved to a file on the hard disk to print later. To download a file from a Web site, follow all instructions on the screen. Both of the two most popular Web browsers (Microsoft's *Internet Explorer* and Netscape's *Navigator*) work generally like this:

1. Using the mouse, click on an on-screen button to initiate the download.
2. A warning message may display asking your permission to continue; or asking you to type the name you wish to assign to the file for storage on the receiving computer's hard drive; or asking you to select a folder in which to store the file.
3. The downloading process will begin, and a "progress thermometer" or other indicator of the percentage of the file which has been transferred is displayed.
4. The process can take several minutes or even hours, depending upon the speed of the modem or Internet connection in use and the size of the file.

FTP Sites. FTP sites are Internet locations where public and private information is stored. Some FTP sites can be accessed via an Internet Web browser. Some FTP sites must be accessed by means of specialized FTP software. Check with your local network administrator (if you have one) or your local Internet Service Provider ("ISP") if you have questions about obtaining and using FTP software.

Anyone can "ftp" to a public site and sign on as "anonymous" (that is the universal, generic user name and password for FTP sites). To reach an FTP site, type an FTP address using your Internet connection software. For example, type:

ftp://microsoft.com

to access the Microsoft FTP site. (Note: An FTP site's address never includes the letters "www," as does a Web site, since "www" stands for World Wide Web.) Having accessed the FTP site, follow the on-screen instructions to access the directory or folder in which a desired file is stored. Select the file from the directory listing, and then initiate the download. The specific commands and steps vary slightly depending on the FTP software program you use.

To use many FTP access programs, you must know a few FTP commands. (When using some FTP programs—and some Telnet programs, such as the ones used to access many online card catalogs—you will find that you are using features of the UNIX operating system. See the "Glossary" for more information about UNIX.) If you are familiar with DOS, FTP commands will seem familiar. Below are a few FTP commands that may be helpful when downloading a file from an FTP site:

Command Word	Function
cd XXXXXXXX	*change to or access a directory*
dir	*list files in a directory*
get XXXXXXXX	*download a file*
quit	*leave after downloading*

The X's in the above table represent variable file names. Note that you must use lowercase, because upper- and lowercase letters mean different things to the UNIX systems that host FTP sites.

The secret to successfully downloading an Internet file from an FTP site is to specify correctly whether the file should be treated as a text file or as a graphics file or as a program. Programs and graphics are binary; text is ASCII (see "Glossary"). To download a text file, at the prompt type:

ascii

To download a graphics file or a program, type:

binary

Files at an FTP site with names ending in .Z are compressed and must be decompressed before you can use them. (See section 7.2.2 below for information on decompressing files.) Some such compressed files will be automatically decompressed by the FTP program used to download them. In other instances, you may need a UUDECODING program (available from most Internet providers and online services). A UUENCODED file is a binary file that has been converted to a text file for Internet distribution. If a file you wish to download is labeled as UUENCODED, be sure to look for all the associated parts of the original file so that you can download them all. Once downloaded, use the UUENCODER to recompile the pieces and convert the file to its proper binary format. Refer to the UUENCODER's documentation for assistance with this process.

Newsgroups. While Web sites provide both information and files to download, FTP sites provide only files to download, and newsgroups provide only information, not files. Newsgroups are an excellent source of information about where to obtain software to download, as well as general information on a wide range of topics, including CD-ROMs. To access a newsgroup, you need newsreader software, which is generally available from your ISP or online service. Refer to the newsreader program's documentation for instructions on how to download information from a specific newsgroup.

Be sure to obtain a file called a FAQ, which stands for "Frequently Asked Questions," about the newsgroup. Look for a copy of DRIVERSFAQ.TXT, for example, in popular CD-ROM newsgroups, for information on device drivers. FAQs are filled with useful information about updates, bugs, problems, and enhancements to CD-ROMs. The Massachusetts Institute of Technology (MIT) maintains a list of newsgroup FAQs at ftp://rtfm.mit.edu (this is an FTP site—see above).

7.2.1.2 *Downloading from Bulletin Boards and Online Services*

The Internet may not be easily accessible from your library or school. Direct connections to the Internet are available only in certain locations (though the number is growing steadily). It may be necessary for you to use a modem and phone line to connect to the Internet in order to download files, or you may need to connect to either a bulletin-board service ("BBS") or online service, such as America Online (through which you can also access the Internet). This section explains how to download files from a BBS or online service.

Bulletin Board Services ("BBS") and online services (such as America Online) are conceptually similar. To access files to download from either a BBS or an online service you need a modem and communications software. To use a modem to dial into a BBS, you need a general purpose communications program. For example, Macintosh users might use *MacTerminal*, while DOS users might use *CrossTalk*. These programs allow you to dial the BBS's phone number and connect to it. To dial into an online service (America Online) you need a dialer program supplied by the service. Once connected to the online service, you navigate using point-and-click menus. Follow on-screen instruction to download a file from an online service.

Unlike the newer online services, a BBS may be character-based, not graphical (its screens display only text characters, not graphics). For example, you might dial into a CD-ROM drive manufacturer's support bulletin board. After reaching the BBS, a text-only menu of options will display. Because this kind of character-based interface can be intimidating, this section describes the BBS downloading process in detail.

These are typical steps in the process of downloading a file from a BBS:
1. After connecting and accessing the main menu, select an option by typing a number and pressing the Enter key.
2. Navigate through a series of menus to find a list of files to download.
3. Select an item number from the list to indicate which file you wish to download.
4. If the system displays information about how long it will take to download the file, or instructions about de-compressing and installing the file, write it down immediately. Often these instructions are supplied only once.
5. From the menu choose a "modem protocol" supported by your computer's communications program. The protocols include Kermit, Xmodem, Zmodem, and others. (Refer to the communications program manual for a list of supported protocols.)
6. Specify whether you wish to download the file as a program (binary) or a text (ASCII) file. Select "program" or "binary" when downloading a device-driver file or any other compressed file.

7. Initiate the download process from within your communications program by providing a name under which to store the compressed device-driver file on your computer's hard drive (it doesn't need to be the same as the name used by the BBS).

8. Watch the messages that appear on the computer screen. When the file has been completely downloaded, you need to sign off the BBS by typing "BYE" or another exit command. If you don't do this, you may not fully disconnect from the system and could prevent others from dialing in.

9. Be sure to "hang up" the phone, so as not to incur unnecessary phone charges. (Most communications programs provide a command for hanging up the phone.)

10. Exit from the communications program and turn off the modem.

7.2.2 DECOMPRESSING FILES

Most files are stored online in a compressed form to save storage space and reduce the amount of time required for downloading. After downloading a compressed file, you must decompress it in order to use it. There are many different file compression formats: the file-name extension (usually a period followed by three letters) indicates the type of format used to compress the file.

This section provides an overview of how to decompress several types of compressed files. Some compressed files are automatically decompressed by the Web browser or FTP software used to download them. Some compressed files are "self-running" or "self executing," which means that you must type the name of the file to decompress ("expand" or "explode") it. For example, to decompress a downloaded self-running file named UPDATE.EXE, you need to "run" the file: either type the word UPDATE at the command-line prompt, or click on it (just as you would run a CD-ROM title or other application program).

If a downloaded, compressed file isn't self-running, then you must decompress it using a copy of the appropriate decompression application software, among the most popular of which are *PKZip* and *StuffIt*. A compressed file's file-name extension (such as .ZIP or .STF) indicates the decompression software required. File names ending in .ZIP require *PKZip* and file names ending in .STF or .SEA require *StuffIt*. Always be sure to find out what type of decompression software is needed for a file before downloading it. Most popular decompression programs are available as freeware or shareware from online services, ISPs, and Internet sites.

Many online services and Web browsers provide an automatic decompression utility. The process of downloading from an online service or with a Web browser varies depending upon the service to which you subscribe. Refer to the service's online help for more information.

7.2.3 INSTALLING A DOWNLOADED FILE

After obtaining and decompressing a file from an online source, you must install it, just as you would any other software or a CD-ROM title. Installing downloaded software generally includes the following steps:

1. Copy the decompressed file(s) to an appropriate directory or folder on a hard drive or diskette.
2. If you downloaded the software onto a diskette or a hard drive other than the CD-ROM workstation where the file is ultimately needed, you must transfer the files from the temporary disk to the workstation. Be sure to test all downloaded files for viruses before transferring them to a workstation or before attempting to install them.
3. Run an installation program.

Specific information on how to install device-driver files is found in section 7.5 below.

7.3 DETERMINING A WORKSTATION'S CAPABILITIES

This section explains in detail how to determine the capabilities of a stand-alone CD-ROM workstation's hardware and operating system software. When choosing titles for a library or school, as explained in Chapter 3, you must know a great deal about the individual workstation's multimedia components. This information is often difficult to obtain, yet it is essential that a stand-alone CD-ROM workstation meets the technical requirements of each and every CD-ROM title chosen to run on it.

Networked CD-ROM workstations ("clients") are less problematic than stand-alone workstations for the purpose of installing CD-ROM titles. The CD-ROM server is the computer that must meet the specifications of each CD-ROM title, while the individual clients may be less powerful than the server. A networked CD-ROM workstation must, in most cases, have only an adequate sound adapter card, an adequate graphics adapter and monitor, and sufficient memory to display the CD-ROM title, but it can often rely on the server to meet many of the CD-ROM title's software requirements.

It's not uncommon to have a CD-ROM workstation for which there is no documentation of its hardware components. Few computers display on their exterior surfaces sufficient information about the equipment installed internally. Without opening the system-unit case and examining the interior of the workstation (which may not be helpful anyway), it's possible to analyze the system using software utilities, as explained in this section. As explained in Chapter 3, the following aspects of a workstation must meet the minimum requirements for each CD-ROM title installed: processor chip, operating system, memory, hard-drive space, CD-ROM drive speed and format, graphics adapter resolution, and sound file formats.

7.3.1 SOFTWARE TOOLS TO
ANALYZE THE WORKSTATION

Software utilities can interrogate a computer's memory to find answers to various questions when the computer's specifications are unknown. These utilities are sometimes included in an operating system. If not, or for a more sophisticated report on configuration details, you can obtain freeware or shareware utilities from an online service or buy commercial utilities, for example, *QuickTime Test Kit* for both Windows and the Mac, from Quantum Leap, which tests the speed and capacity of your multimedia system. This program evaluates the speed of the CD-ROM drive and other features of the system to verify that a computer is configured properly to run QuickTime or Video for Windows movies.

The Interactive Multimedia Association (IMA) distributes a free software program called *CD Match* that helps you evaluate whether a computer can play any given CD-ROM title. The *CD Match* program prints out a list of the computer's configuration to compare with the uniform-industry-requirements labels on CD-ROM title packages. This program can be downloaded off the Internet or obtained on diskette from several software vendors. Refer to Appendix C for locations from which to obtain a copy of *CD Match*.

7.3.2 PC ANALYSIS SOFTWARE

This section provides specific techniques for determining the technical specifications of a PC running DOS or a version of Windows. See section 7.3.3 below for information on the Macintosh operating system.

7.3.2.1 Identifying the DOS Version

To determine the version number of DOS running on a PC (including the DOS version on a Windows 3.X system), use the VER command. At the DOS prompt, type VER, and press the Enter key:

C:> VER

MS-DOS Version 6.20

The version number will be displayed for you, as shown.

7.3.2.2 DOS 5.0 and Earlier—
CHKDSK for Hard-Disk Space and Conventional Memory

If your PC is running DOS 5.0 or an earlier version, the best tool built into the operating system to assist you with the task of determining your computer's configuration is CHKDSK (a command that stands for "check disk"). Refer to a *Microsoft MS-DOS User's Guide* for more information on CHKDSK.

(Warning: If you are running a version of DOS before 5.0, it is strongly recommended that you upgrade to DOS 6.2. DOS 5.0 has many more features than DOS 4.2, but also includes some bugs and limitations. DOS 6.0 is likewise much more powerful than 5.0, but contains bugs not found in DOS 6.1. DOS 6.2 has the greatest power and fewest problems.)

CHKDSK is a DOS command that displays information about the amount of so-called "conventional" memory available in the workstation, as well as the amount of available, or "free," hard-drive space, both of which are critical to the installation of CD-ROM titles. To obtain this information, run the CHKDSK command from the DOS prompt in the root directory (C:\). If you are running Windows 3.X, you must exit from Windows in order to run this command. If you try to run it from the DOS prompt window, you will receive an error message. To run the program, simply type CHKDSK, and then press the Enter key:

C:> CHKDSK

The screen will display the following information:

XXX,XXX,XXX bytes total disk space   *(size of the hard drive)*
   XX,XXX,XXX bytes in X hidden files   *(these are system files)*
      XXX,XXX bytes in XXX directories   *(number of sub-directories)*
XXX,XXX,XXX bytes in X,XXX user files   *(total files on the drive)*
   XX,XXX,XXX bytes available on disk   *(free disk space)*
… (various other information)
      XXX,XXX total bytes memory
      XXX,XXX bytes free

In the example screen report, the "total bytes memory" indicates the available conventional memory (for a definition, refer to the "Glossary"; for more about conventional memory, see section 8.2.3 on installing CD-ROM titles on a DOS system). The "bytes available on disk" indicates the free hard-drive space.

Notice that the total RAM is not listed, only the amount of conventional memory available to run an application program like a CD-ROM title ("total bytes memory"). If a CD-ROM title requires a certain minimum conventional memory, but a workstation has less than the minimum "free," refer to Chapter 8, for information on how to make more conventional memory available. If the amount of free hard-drive space seems to be insufficient, remove some unnecessary files in order to make more space available.

While CHKDSK can help you evaluate whether a workstation's configuration is capable of running a certain CD-ROM title, it does not tell you everything, such as how much RAM is installed (this is not the same thing as conventional memory; see the "Glossary"). Other utilities described below can determine the total amount of RAM installed in a workstation.

7.3.2.3 DOS 5.0 and Later—MEM for RAM

If you have DOS 5.0 or a later version of DOS, you can use the MEM command in addition to CHKDSK. MEM has the advantage of telling you how much RAM is available, as well as how much conventional memory. (It also lists expanded memory, as opposed to extended memory, which some older DOS CD-ROMs may require.)

As with CHKDSK, you must be at the DOS prompt (with Windows shut down) in order to run the MEM command. Simply type MEM at the DOS prompt, and press the Enter key:

C:> MEM

The following information will display:

Memory Type	Total	=	Used	+	Free
------------	------		----		----
Conventional	640K		66K		574K
Upper	111K		68K		43K
Reserved	384K		384K		0K
Extended(XMS)	7,057K		1,245K		5,812K
------------	------		----		----
Total memory	8,192K		1,763K		6,429K
Total under 1 MB	751K		134K		617K
Largest executable program size					574K

To determine how much RAM is installed in the workstation, examine the "Total" column on the line listing "Total memory." The example above lists 8 Mb RAM (round the number down). To determine the amount of conventional memory available, look at the line labeled "Largest executable program size." This should be equal to or greater than the amount of conventional memory required by the CD-ROM title. (Note: On all DOS systems, MEM will always list the "Total" "Conventional" memory installed as 640 k.) As mentioned above, don't be too concerned if the available or free conventional memory seems inadequate. Section 8.2.3 explains how to recover enough memory to run most CD-ROM titles.

7.3.2.4 DOS 6.1 or Later—MSD for a Detailed Analysis

Versions of DOS beginning with 6.1 include a diagnostic program called MSD.EXE, which can produce a printed or on-screen report of most of the configuration details of a workstation. For Windows 3.X users, it will also print out copies of the SYSTEM.INI and WIN.INI files.

MSD.EXE must be run from the DOS prompt (with Windows shut down). Simply type MSD at the DOS prompt, and press the Enter key:

C:> MSD

A menu will display, showing the most important aspects of the workstation. Refer to the online "Help" menu for instructions on how to print a copy of the complete, detailed report, either to a printer or to a file.

The MSD report contains most of the information you need to make an intelligent purchase of a CD-ROM title. Make a note of everything listed on the screen. To obtain additional details, either click with a mouse on the menu item of interest or type the highlighted letter. This detailed information can be extremely helpful when installing CD-ROM titles: it can tell you the names of the CD-ROM drive device drivers or sound card device drivers, for example. It also provides invaluable information about IRQs.

7.3.2.5 Third-Party Utilities for DOS

Among the most well-known and longest-lived diagnostic utilities for DOS are the *Norton Utilities* from Symantec. Many other fine programs are available, as well. Most of them demand a certain level of computer expertise of their users, however. For nontechnical computer users, the built-in DOS programs described above are probably more useful.

7.3.2.6 CDSPEED for DOS and Windows

Microsoft distributes a programmer's utility called CDSPEED that tests a CD-ROM drive for MPC compatibility. This program is available on Microsoft's *Developers Network* CD-ROM disc and elsewhere. The program must be run from the DOS prompt and with Windows shut down. The program produces a report on the drive speed, seek time, CD-ROM drive mode compatibility, and other technical specifications.

7.3.2.7 Identifying the Windows Version

To find out the specific version of Window 3.X (either 3.0 or 3.1) running on a workstation, simply access the **Help** menu from the **Program Manager**. Select **About Program Manager**. The Windows version number will be displayed.

To determine the specific version of Windows 9X, open the **Control Panel**. From the Help menu, select **About Windows**. Be aware that there are several versions of Windows 95, including beta versions, the first release version, and an OEM hardware-vendor version, each with slightly different features.

7.3.2.8 Windows 3.X Tools

Windows 3.X provides two ways to determine information about a workstation, **Windows Setup** and the **Control Panel**. These applets have some limitations, though. First, it is possible—indeed, easy—for an inexperienced user to make inappropriate changes in these programs, which can later mislead you, if not incapacitate the workstation. Second, these applets report only on the way in which the operating-system software and memory are being used in the workstation, not on the computer hardware and its capabilities. For example, if a workstation has a video card capable of displaying SVGA resolution screens, the workstation may be set up to use only VGA resolution screens—this is an error in the way Windows is installed on the workstation, not a limitation of the computer hardware itself.

Windows Setup. To access **Windows Setup**, from the **Program Manager**:

1. Select the **Main** program group icon.
2. From the **Main** program group, double-click on the **Windows Setup** icon. The **Windows Setup** window tells you what type of graphics, or video, the workstation is using, the type of keyboard, the type of mouse, and whether the workstation is on a network.

Control Panel. To access the **Control Panel**, from the **Program Manager**:

1. Select the **Main** program group icon.
2. From the **Main** program group, double-click on the **Control Panel** icon. The **Control Panel** displays a group of applets, including **Ports**, **Printers**, **386 Enhanced**, and **Drivers**, which may be of use.
3. Double-click on each one to view configuration information.

The **Ports** applet tells you how many COM ports are available on your computer (that is, modem ports). The **Printers** applet shows how many printer device drivers are installed (even if there are no printers currently attached to them). The **Drivers** applet tells you which multimedia device drivers are installed.

The **386 Enhanced** applet tells you how Windows is using memory on a given workstation. This can be misleading if not considered in conjunction with one of the DOS diagnostics listed above. Windows creates and uses "virtual" memory on the hard drive, rather than physical memory (that is, chips). So, for example, even if a workstation has 8 Mb RAM, Windows may create a virtual memory area on its hard drive of almost any size desired.

Much more useful than either the **Windows Setup** or **Control Panel** applets is a freeware program, available from many online services, called *Winfo.* (See Appendix C.) It tells everything you need to know, even the version number of the workstation's graphics video-display device driver.

7.3.2.9 *Windows 16-bit versus 32-bit Software*

Windows 3.X is designed for so-called "16-bit" application programs, while Windows 9X is capable of running not only 16-bit applications but also

32-bit applications. The number of "bits" refers to the way the operating system and application software handle program code, in chunks sized 16-bit or 32-bit. Some DOS applications may be 32-bit applications, but no Windows 3.X applications may be. If a CD-ROM title requires a 32-bit operating system, be sure to note its operating-system requirements carefully before attempting to install it on a workstation in your library or school.

7.3.2.10 Windows 9X Analysis

In Windows 9X, the **Control Panel** provides detailed information about a workstation's hardware and configuration.
1. Using the **Start** button, select **Settings**.
2. Select the **Control Panel**.
3. Select **System**.
4. Click the **General** tab for information about the type of processor (or "CPU") and amount of RAM installed.
5. Click the **Performance** tab for information about graphics capabilities.

7.3.3 MAC ANALYSIS TOOLS

To determine whether a Macintosh is capable of running a CD-ROM title, you need to know four things: (1) the sequence of Macintosh models so that you can decide whether a workstation's model is "later than" or "better than" the minimum required, (2) the System version number, (3) the amount of RAM, and (4) the available hard-drive space.

Refer to Table 3.1 for the sequence of Macintosh models.

Some information is available through **About the Finder** if you have System 6 or **About This Macintosh** if you have System 7:
1. With the desktop displayed, highlight the hard-drive icon.
2. Next select either **About the Finder** or **About This Macintosh** from the **Apple** menu. A window will display showing the total available RAM and the System version number. You need at least System 6.0.7 or System 7 to run most CD-ROM titles.

To determine a Macintosh's monitor's resolution, use the **Control Panel**. Select **Monitors**. Click the **Options** button (or, in some versions of the system, press the **Option** key and the **Options** button simultaneously) to see a list of available monitor resolutions and types. (Of course, if the Mac has a black-and-white monitor, such as on a Mac Classic, it may not have a **Monitors Control Panel**.)

To verify the amount of hard-disk space available, with the desktop displayed:
1. Double-click the hard-drive icon to open it and display the contents.
2. Select **View**.

3. Select **By Icon** or **By Small Icon**. The hard-drive space being used and the available space are listed at the top of the window. If you have System 7, you may change the **View** in the **Control Panels** so that this information is always displayed in all folder headers.

7.3.3.1 Desk Accessories

Numerous freeware and shareware utilities are available to help you diagnose a Macintosh system's configuration. Some of these can be installed as Desk Accessories or Apple menu items. One such Desk Accessory is *Tattletale*, which is available on many online services. Refer to Appendix C for an address from which to obtain it.

7.4 CD-ROM DRIVE SPECIFICATIONS

This section discusses CD-ROM drive technology, in order to help you assess whether your workstation's CD-ROM drive is capable of running a given CD-ROM title.

7.4.1 CD-ROM DRIVE TERMINOLOGY

The following characteristics distinguish various CD-ROM drives: speed, access time, data transfer rate, read-ahead disk cache, and controller or interface type. The most important is "speed." If the workstation doesn't have a CD-ROM drive fast enough to accommodate the CD-ROM title, you may need to replace the drive with a faster one. This will most often be the case if the drive is a first-generation "single-speed" drive or an MPC double-speed drive. Most "quad-speed" drives are capable of running most CD-ROM titles. Some more recent multimedia titles with full-screen video may require faster speeds.

7.4.1.1 Drive Speed

The speed of the drive is the rate at which the disc spins in the drive, expressed as "single-speed," "double-speed," "triple-speed," "quad-speed," and "6X speed," and so on. Many older CD-ROM titles are optimized for double-speed drives. An upgrade to a quad-speed drive may not improve an older title's performance on a computer. As drives continue to improve, their speeds may exceed the requirements of CD-ROM titles. Most CD-ROM titles only require a drive with a speed fast enough to deliver CD-audio and full-motion video smoothly and realistically in real-time. Data access need not exceed the speed of a CD-ROM title's requirements.

All CD-ROM drives, even single-speed drives, spin discs at a variable rate depending on where the data is on the disc. This allows all areas of the disc to pass over the drive's laser read-head at a constant rate—the disc spins faster if the data is near the outer edge of the disc. The original "single speed" of a CD-ROM drive was designed to play back CD-audio in real-time—this required the ability to output data at a rate of 150 kilobytes per second (k/s). (Compare this with the speed of a typical hard drive: 2 Mb to 5 Mb per second.) Although the speed of the spin varied while the audio track was played, the rate of data transfer never varied from 150 k/s.

Data, however, needs to be output from the drive more rapidly than real-time audio. So, drives that could locate data at 300 k/s were developed (two times 150), hence the term "double-speed" drives. A triple-speed drive can locate data at speeds up to 450 k/s. Quad-speed drives can locate data at speeds of up to 600 k/s, and so on. The speed, then, is the rate at which the drive can output data by increasing the spin rate of a disc.

7.4.1.2 Data Transfer Rate

The term "transfer rate" is just another way to describe the speed of output from the drive. The transfer rate is the number of kilobytes per second that it takes for a drive to output data to a workstation.

7.4.1.3 Access Rate or Seek Time

The terms "access rate" and "seek time" mean the speed with which the CD-ROM drive's laser read-head finds and reads the area of the disc where the sought data resides. It is a function of the spin rate and the speed at which the read-head can locate a specific point on the disc.

The access rate or seek time is measured in milliseconds (ms). The lower the number of milliseconds, the faster the drive. For example a quad-speed drive may have a transfer rate of 600 k/s and a seek time of 250 ms. If a different quad-speed drive has a seek time of only 200 ms, then its total data-transfer rate will be greater than 600 k/s, perhaps 632 k/s.

You can use the access or seek time as a way to distinguish between the quality of two quad-speed drives. If the cost is significantly more for the slightly faster drive, however, it isn't necessarily going to provide sufficiently superior speed to justify the extra cost.

7.4.1.4 Disk Cache or Disk Buffer Size

"Disk cache" or "disk buffer" size can have a significant impact on the performance of the CD-ROM drive. This cache is a computer chip in the CD-ROM drive where data is temporarily stored before the drive transfers it to the workstation's memory. The disk cache provides a conduit between the computer and the CD-ROM drive. The larger it is, the more data it can store, and the faster the drive's performance will be. It's as if the cache is a pipe, and the wider or larger the pipe, the more data can be piped through it. A disk cache or buffer is measured in terms of the number of kilobytes (k) it can process, so the larger the number of k in the disk cache, the better the drive.

7.4.2 DRIVE CONTROLLER OR INTERFACE TYPES

A CD-ROM drive can be attached to a CD-ROM workstation via one of two general types of controller cards, either IDE-type or SCSI-type (pronounced "skuzzy"). PCs often use IDE interfaces, while Macs often use SCSI interfaces. SCSI (Small Computer System Interface) interfaces are becoming more popular for both sorts of computers, and new, enhanced interface types are continually being developed. Advanced IDE interfaces are labeled E-IDE (for Enhanced IDE) and advanced SCSI interfaces are labeled SCSI II (or 2).

Both types of interface cards are installed inside the workstation, whether the CD-ROM drive for which they are intended is an internal or an external drive. Both types of adapters also establish ports or connectors on the back of the workstation to which external peripherals may be attached. An internal IDE or E-IDE adapter provides a port or connector that looks a lot like the connectors for other types of peripherals (a short, flat "socket" with two rows of pins or holes). A SCSI card provides a connector that may look a lot like a parallel port for a printer or may be a long flat connector.

An IDE-type interface can generally be used for only one external device at a time. As a result, attaching an external CD-ROM drive to an IDE or E-IDE interface card is simply a matter of attaching a cable from the PC to the drive. SCSI adapters, though, allow you to attach multiple devices. So, attaching a SCSI device takes a few additional steps. See section 7.4.6.3 to learn more about SCSI connections.

The type of hardware interface used by a CD-ROM drive is *not* a particularly important consideration when installing a CD-ROM title. Few, if any, CD-ROM titles require a specific type of hardware interface between a computer and a CD-ROM drive. It is possible, however, that during the CD-ROM title installation process or when first running a CD-ROM title, you may receive an error message that implies a problem with the way your CD-ROM drive's interface is physically installed. If you have used the CD-ROM drive previously with success, then the problem is most likely in the title's installation program rather than the drive's interface. Still, you may encounter installation error messages that require you to modify the interface card's "settings."

If you encounter this type of error every time you try to install CD-ROM titles or other software, then the workstation's equipment may in fact be installed improperly. The workstation probably needs changes to jumpers, DIP switch settings, or internal cabling. There could even be something seriously wrong with the equipment, including a bad chip on the adapter card.

7.4.3 INTERNAL VS. EXTERNAL DRIVES

The speed and performance of a CD-ROM drive are not determined by whether the drive is internal or external to the workstation. Nor does the length of cables—internal or external—having anything to do with the speed of the drive. The speed of both an internal and an external CD-ROM drive depends on the size of the disk cache, the access rate, and the spin rate of the drive; these form the pipe through which the data travels, not the cables.

It is true that there is a limit to the length of cables. At a certain length, computer cables can become ineffective, but when the difference in length is less than a foot, there is no discernible degradation in the data access.

There is no technical advantage to an internal drive versus an external drive. An external drive is easier to transport when necessary, and easier to have serviced when necessary. For example, a malfunctioning external drive can be serviced without otherwise disturbing a workstation. Devices are also available to connect an external CD-ROM drive to a workstation through a parallel port (where the printer is usually connected) without having to install an adapter card inside the computer. In such cases, you may actually be able to install an external CD-ROM drive without the help of a technician. Internal drives, though, have some advantages. An internal drive may be slightly less expensive. An internal drive uses the computer's built-in power source, while an external drives may also require a separate power source. Of course, most CD-ROM network jukeboxes, stackers, and towers are external drives.

7.4.4 DRIVE COMPATIBILITY WITH DISC FORMATS

The workstation's CD-ROM drive must be compatible with the CD-ROM title's disc format. CD-ROM formats are sets of industry standards for organizing the information on the CD-ROM disc. Because each set of standards is issued to the industry in a book with a different-colored cover, each format is often referred to by the color of the book's cover. "Red Book" standard is basic CD-audio format; "Yellow Book" is CD-ROM; "Green Book" is CD-I, and so on. In addition, Yellow Book format was issued with several extensions or enhancements, so you will also encounter references to "High Sierra" format (which was actually the first CD-ROM format put into use) and "ISO 9660," which is a later, but very similar, format.

Here are a few of the available formats:

- Red Book—CD audio, music CDs
- High Sierra—a type of CD-ROM data disc
- ISO 9660—Yellow Book CD-ROM data disc
- CD-ROM-XA—a "bridge" format that accommodates both data and sound files; also the same as Kodak Photo CD
- CD-I—CD-Interactive (Green Book), features 16 audio tracks, plus data
- CD-Plus—Blue Book standard discs that play music on both stereo systems and computers, and that display graphics when played on a computer
- Photo CD—Kodak CD-ROM-XA format for images
- MMCD—Sony CD-ROM format, a Yellow Book format using DOS and MCGA graphics
- DVD—a video CD format, sometimes called "digital versatile disc" in order to stress its capacity to store massive amounts of all types of digital information
- Mac HFS—Macintosh Hierarchical File Structure (data in folders)
- CD-R—Recordable CD; CD-ROM drives allowing a user to save data one time to a writable CD-ROM disc
- WORM—Write Once Read Many, similar to CD-R

Refer to the "Glossary" for more detail on each format.

The only way to be sure a CD-ROM drive will be able to read a given disc format in advance of installing a title is to retain the drive's documentation listing its specifications. Compare the compatible formats listed in the drive's documentation with the compatible formats listed for the CD-ROM title. Keep in mind that few CD-ROM drives are capable of reading all possible CD-ROM formats. (Note that the format has nothing to do with the diameter of the CD-ROM disc; a larger-sized CD-ROM drive tray or caddie does not necessarily accept or read a smaller-sized disc, even if the format is compatible.)

A final concern about drive types and disc formats is compatibility between PCs and Macintoshes. Some CD-ROM drives can be used on both PCs and Macintoshes (as can many other types of peripherals). The relative ease of using a single CD-ROM drive on two different types of workstations depends entirely upon the design of the drive. In some cases, all that may be necessary to accomplish a transfer from one type of workstation to another is to change the cable, while in others the CD-ROM drive itself may need to have special adapters built into it for both types of computers (usually at extra cost). Furthermore, just because the CD-ROM drive can be moved between a PC and a Mac doesn't mean that a collection of DOS or Windows discs can be installed on the Mac, or vice versa. Some hybrid CD-ROM discs do, in fact, contain information for both PCs and Macs (on different tracks and in different formats), but not all discs. Read the CD-ROM title's packaging and marketing literature to determine whether a title disc is readable by both types of CD-ROM drives and computers or whether you must buy separate versions of the title for different workstations.

A CD-ROM network eliminates many of the problems involved in using both PC and Macintosh CD-ROM titles. It is possible to configure a network that will give all workstations on the network access to several different disc formats, regardless of the operating system of the individual workstations.

7.4.5 CD-ROM DRIVE
INSTALLATION RECOMMENDATIONS

If your library or school has no technical staff available to install CD-ROM drives in workstations, consider paying a technician to install internal CD-ROM equipment for you. Whether you choose an external drive that requires an internal adapter card or an internal CD-ROM drive, the installation process is difficult and potentially hazardous, both to you and to your computer, if you don't know what you are doing. In addition, after the equipment is physically installed correctly, device-driver software must also be installed. (Section 7.5 explains device-driver installation.) Professional installation will add from $30 to $75 to the total cost of the drive, but you will be assured of having a working drive and workstation in the end.

The installation of some CD-ROM drives in some types of workstations can, of course, be quite simple to accomplish. Many newer models of computers are specifically designed to make installation of new equipment easy. Such computers have "bays" that are designed so that drives can simply be slipped into place; cables and connectors are easily accessible and simple to attach. (Chapter 1 explains the advantages to purchasing such types of workstations for your library or school.) Older computers, however, often require disassembly of the system unit, detachment of several cables and adapter cards, and sometimes also the removal or "jumping" of chips. In almost all cases, a physical cable connection must be established between not only the CD-ROM drive and the motherboard of the computer, but also between the CD-ROM drive and the sound card. If the workstation in question is an older workstation, it is highly recommended that you obtain technical assistance when installing a new CD-ROM drive.

7.4.6 OPERATING A CD-ROM DRIVE

Once a CD-ROM drive is installed (whether the drive is an external or an internal drive), it must be functioning properly before you can install a CD-ROM title on the workstation. All of the following must function properly: the power source, external knobs and controls (such as a volume control knob), and exterior jacks and connectors for multimedia equipment. Be sure to test each of these prior to installing a new CD-ROM title.

7.4.6.1 *Exterior Controls and Connections*

Most CD-ROM drives and their interface cards provide several connectors, jacks, knobs. When connecting an external CD-ROM drive to the computer, you must identify the connectors on the computer and drive, attach the cables properly, and often attach other power cords and various wires. This means that you must be familiar with the type of interface card the drive in the workstation uses and how to make the right connections.

External CD-ROM drives, jukeboxes, towers, and stackers require proper cabling and proper connections. Cables between an external CD-ROM drive and the workstation must meets the specifications of the interface card in the computer. A SCSI cable cannot be used for an IDE interface or vice versa. A SCSI II cable cannot be used for a SCSI interface. (The same cable, however, can be used for both IDE and E-IDE interfaces.)

It is also possible to obtain an external adapter to convert a PC's parallel port to SCSI, for example, Trantor's Mini-SCSI Adapter and H45 Technology's Quick SCSI Connector. These small adapters, costing under $100, are extremely easy to install and use. They consist of a small palm-sized plug that is attached to the parallel port on the back of a PC. (Note: These are available only for PCs. A Macintosh does not need one since SCSI adapters are standard equipment on all Macs.)

7.4.6.2 *IDE and E-IDE Connections*

PCs often use IDE or E-IDE connections for the CD-ROM drive. These types of connections, also called interfaces, are dedicated to the single CD-ROM drive (SCSI adapters can be used to connect several different peripherals). The operating system of the workstation locates each IDE or E-IDE device by means of the communications port to which it is connected. The ports are numbered (rather than the devices, which are numbered when SCSI connection are involved). (Note: There are two types of communications ports, serial and parallel. On PCs serial ports are labeled COM1, COM2, and so on. Parallel ports are labeled LPT1, LPT2, and so on.)

7.4.6.3 *SCSI Connections*

SCSI connectors are quite common on both PC and Mac external CD-ROM drives. It is easy to attach multiple SCSI devices to a single SCSI card on a workstation, including external hard drives, CD-ROM drives, and backup systems.

Each SCSI device is assigned a number from 0 to 7 to identify it. The devices can then be chained together in any sequence, because the operating system in the workstation can locate or identify each device by its SCSI ID (identification) number.

SCSI devices are typically set to ID 3 at the factory. SCSI IDs 0, 1, and 2 are reserved for bootable devices, such as the computer's processor or ROM and the internal hard drives. Even if there is no SCSI device numbered 0, 1, or 2 on the workstation, an external CD-ROM drive's SCSI ID may be set to ID 3, since the ID is a name for the device, not its sequence in any chain. The sequence is not important. The important thing is not to duplicate ID numbers on the same system.

Each workstation can have only one device named SCSI ID 3. If you plan to move an external CD-ROM drive between two workstations, be sure to select an ID number that is unused on both systems, so as not to create a conflict between devices when the drive is attached to one of the workstations.

Changing SCSI ID Settings: Every SCSI device has a hardware switch for selecting a SCSI ID number. Usually, the switch is clearly visible somewhere on the back of the device. On Macintosh-compatible SCSI devices, such as CD-ROM drives, the switch is often an easy-to-use rotary "thumb wheel" switch.

On some older devices, the switch is a DIP-style switch. DIP switches are a series of tiny switches that must be toggled up or down to match a pattern supplied in the hardware device's documentation. To toggle the switches, use the point of a ball-point pen or a pencil.

If there is no external means of selecting or setting the SCSI ID, that means the drive has an internal, factory-set switch, probably set to ID 3. If that is not acceptable for the workstation in question, you may need to have a technician make a change in the SCSI ID for you.

Each SCSI chain, whether it consists of one device or several, must be terminated at the physical beginning and ending of the chain. Internal SCSI devices (such as the first hard drive in the chain) are usually terminated at the factory. If you add an external SCSI device, however, then the additional device must also be properly terminated. Some external CD-ROM drives are also terminated at the factory.

Other external CD-ROM drives must be physically terminated when they are installed in a workstation. This is usually a simple matter of putting a small plug-like device on one of the connectors on the back of the CD-ROM drive. When you add a device to an existing SCSI chain, either (a) add the new device to an intermediate position in the chain, or (b) remember to move the terminator plug to the drive if it is the last device in the chain. Most SCSI devices, including CD-ROM drives, have two long, flat connectors on the back. It doesn't matter which one of these is terminated. Remember, unlike IDE connectors (ports with specific ID numbers), the connectors on a SCSI device are not numbered—the device is.

7.4.6.4 Cable Basics

Although a cable looks like a simple wire or cord, it's actually a specially designed item of computer equipment. The cable that connects an external CD-ROM drive to the workstation is a specialized cable, consisting of the correct number of wires and pins, with the correct plugs on either end. If you ever have to obtain a replacement cable, keep in mind:
- the number of pins required in the plugs at both ends of the cable and
- which of the plugs is male and which is female.

(Females are "in-ies" and males are "out-ies.") Be certain that you know how many pins are required for both ends of the cable—the ends may differ. Always refer to the CD-ROM drive's technical documentation before purchasing a new cable. Do not simply rely on a vague description on the cable's packaging, such as "SCSI cable for IBM XT/AT/PS2." (This applies to both PCs and Macintoshes.)

All cables are very fragile and ought not to be manipulated often: try to keep all cables away out of the reach of workstation users. All cables also seem to be made so that they have to be twisted in order to be connected to the drive and computer: this contributes to frequent shorts in CD-ROM drive cables. If a CD-ROM drive fails after several weeks or months of operation, replace the cable, since a short in it may be the cause of the problem. There is no other way to determine whether a problem is caused by a short in a cable.

Jacks: The back of an external CD-ROM drive's outer casing presents not only interface cable connectors but also audio jacks of the kind found on stereo systems. The back of a workstation, where the sound card is installed, may also have a variety of different types of audio jacks. In order for these jacks to be operative, however, and to play all types of CD-ROM sounds, the workstation's CD-ROM drive and sound card must be properly connected to one another. If not, only certain types of sounds will play through the workstation's speakers, or digital audio may only be heard through the headphones or speakers attached to the headphone jack on the front of the CD-ROM drive. Ideally, all sound should be funneled through the sound card by means of properly installed connections between the sound card and the CD-ROM drive interface card. Then, all of the jacks on the workstation can be used for stereo speakers, headphones, and other audio equipment.

If a sound card and CD-ROM drive are not connected and transmitting sound through the sound card and computer speakers, you need to make a physical connection between the drive and the sound card's "line-in" jack. If the drive is an older internal CD-ROM drive that has an output jack, use a stereo cable to connect the CD-ROM drive's output jack on the back of the computer to the sound card's input jack on the back of the computer. (The output jacks generally require an RCA stereo plug, while the input jacks generally require a male "mini-plug." Cables with such connectors are widely available, at Radio Shack and other music and electronic equipment stores.) If an older-model internal drive has no output jack, then you may be able to connect the headphone jack on the front of the drive to the line-in jack on the sound card (wrapping the stereo cable around the computer).

Volume Controls: The volume control dial on the front of the CD-ROM drive controls only the volume of sound produced by the headphones or speakers attached to the front of the drive. The volume of any sound generated by the sound card in the computer is controlled by both the software and the volume control knobs on the external speakers.

7.4.7 SUMMARY OF CD-ROM DRIVE PREPARATIONS FOR INSTALLATION

Make sure that the workstation's CD-ROM drive is installed properly before installing any CD-ROM title disc. Ensure that power is reaching the CD-ROM drive when the drive is turned on. If the workstation has an external CD-ROM drive, also make sure that:
1. The cabling is correctly attached to both the drive and the workstation
2. The correct type of cable is used
3. There are no conflicts between interface card settings or SCSI ID numbers.

If the external CD-ROM drive is a SCSI device with a clearly visible ID switch, you should be able to change the ID as necessary. If the drive doesn't have an external switch, seek the assistance of a factory-authorized technician. Verify that sound can be heard through all speakers and headphones (see sections 9.4.3.3, 10.4.5.4, and 12.4.4.2 for specific techniques to test sound).

7.5 DEVICE DRIVERS

Having installed a CD-ROM drive, added a CD-ROM drive to a workstation, or upgraded a CD-ROM drive, it's often necessary to upgrade the software that controls the CD-ROM drive as well. This software is the CD-ROM device-driver software. Most multimedia devices (monitors, sound cards) require up-to-date device-driver files, as explained in Chapter 3. This section explains how to install a new device driver, with particular attention to CD-ROM drive device drivers.

The process of device-driver installation varies slightly by device type and operating system. In general, however, the process is simply to copy the file to the required location on the CD-ROM workstation's hard drive. In addition, you may also need to modify a few system information files so that the computer's operating system is properly notified of the existence of the new device driver. General guidelines for the operating systems covered in this book are provided below. When you obtain a new device driver, it will be accompanied by precise instructions on how to install it (such as a README file)—if not, call its supplier and obtain those instructions. For example, if you download a Toshiba-manufactured CD-ROM drive's device driver, the device-driver file should be accompanied by a text file containing installation instructions and perhaps an installation program, as well. If not, contact Toshiba for that missing information.

Warning! Always make a backup copy of all old device drivers and device-driver directories or folders on the workstation's hard drive before attempting to upgrade its device drivers. You may need to return to an earlier version at a later time. Remember to record updates to device drivers in the workstation's log book.

7.5.1 DOS DEVICE-DRIVER INSTALLATION

Unless the device-driver manufacturer supplies an easy-to-use, menu-driven installation program, you need an intermediate-level understanding of DOS in order to install the drivers. The instructions below assume that you are familiar with the DOS file system and DOS naming conventions and know how to edit the CONFIG.SYS and AUTOEXEC.BAT files.

DOS device-driver installation is a two-step process. First, the device-driver files must be copied to the hard drive of the CD-ROM workstation. Second, changes may need to be made to CONFIG.SYS and AUTOEXEC.BAT to accommodate the new drivers.

Take special care when updating old device drivers with new device drivers having the same name. Retain a backup copy of the old file, if you copy the new file over an old file in the same subdirectory. You may find old device drivers (files with names ending in .SYS) in the root directory, in the DOS directory, or in any subdirectory, such as ones created specifically for storing device drivers.

In most cases, device drivers may be copied to any location on the hard drive. Often device-driver subdirectories are named \DRIVER, \BIN, or \DEVICE. If the manufacturer recommends a specific directory for the device driver, you should use that directory, even if it isn't mandatory, if for no other reason than to simplify maintenance of the files.

Once the device drivers are copied to the designated directory, you may need to add lines to, or change lines in, CONFIG.SYS and AUTOEXEC.BAT so that the new device driver will be loaded into memory when you restart the PC. Follow the manufacturer's instructions carefully. Be certain that you use the complete path name of the new file, indicating the location of the file in the correct subdirectory. For example, if the device-driver file is stored in C:\BIN, then any references to it in any configuration file must begin with the path name C:\BIN. For example, the complete path name of a file named NECCD.SYS would be C:\BIN\NECCD.SYS.

If you place the new file in a different subdirectory, be sure the configuration files (CONFIG.SYS and AUTOEXEC.BAT) do not continue to search for the file name in the old directory—in other words, change the complete path name in both files.

7.5.1.1 MSCDEX.EXE for DOS and Windows 3.X

In addition to the CD-ROM drive's unique device drivers (files ending in .SYS), your PC must have a compatible version of Microsoft's CD-ROM extensions software, called MSCDEX.EXE. This file is usually stored in the DOS directory, but may be placed anywhere on the hard drive. If you are running Windows, it may be stored in one of the Windows directories or in the DOS directory. If you must update MSCDEX.EXE, follow these steps:

1. Test that the CD-ROM drive is working: Change to the CD-ROM drive by typing the drive letter, such as D: If you receive an error message, this means either that you typed the wrong letter or that the CD-ROM device drivers are not properly installed.

2. Next, after you have changed to the drive, type DIR to see a listing of files or directories on the CD-ROM disc. If you receive an error message, it means (a) that there is no CD-ROM disc in the drive, (b) the disc does not contain recognizable data files (try a different disc), (c) the drive isn't working (check to see if it is turned on), or (d) the device drivers may not be properly installed. In other words, a drive-specific device driver must be loaded into memory by means of the CONFIG.SYS file (see above), and requires that MSCDEX.EXE be run by means of the AUTOEXEC.BAT file (see step 3 below).

3. Now, check to see that the AUTOEXEC.BAT file contains the necessary line, such as:

    \mscdex.exe /d:mscd001 /m:15 /l:s

    The first "word" on the line in the example above is the complete path name of the MSCDEX.EXE file. In this case, it is located in the root directory on the C: drive. If it were in the DOS directory, it would have to be listed as C:\DOS\MSCDEX.EXE. The second "word" assigns a name to the device; this is usually the letters MSCD and three digits, beginning with zero, such as 000 or 001. This name must be identical to the name used in the CONFIG.SYS (see step 4 below). The third "word" assigns a number of memory blocks to the device driver; this number is usually 10 or 15. The final "word" assigns a letter to the CD-ROM drive. In this example the drive is letter S. The letter may be any letter from D through Z, as long as the letter is not being used by another drive on the workstation. Otherwise, there is no significance to the letter chosen. Technically, a letter that occurs later in the alphabet takes up a little bit more memory than one closer to the beginning.

4. Check to see that the CONFIG.SYS file contains the necessary line for the specific CD-ROM drive's device driver:

device=c:\sbprocd.sys /d:mscd001

The line above is an example of what should appear in the CON-FIG.SYS. The first "word" tells DOS where to find the device driver and what it is named. In this case, the device driver is located in the root directory of the C: drive and is called SBPROCD.SYS. The second "word" indicates which hardware device is being controlled by the device driver, in this case it is MSCD001 (see step 3 above). (The CD-ROM drive's device drivers will probably have different names than the ones in the example.)

More than One CD-ROM Drive. It is possible to use MSCDEX.EXE in DOS or Windows 3.X to configure a system with multiple CD-ROM drives. If your library's or school's CD-ROMs are accessed over a network or if a workstation has a stacker device or multiple CD-ROM drives, this situation applies. Each drive must be specified in both the AUTOEXEC.BAT and CONFIG.SYS files, as parameters (or "words") in the required lines. In the AUTOEXEC.BAT file, the command statement for MSCDEX.EXE must include a parameter naming each drive, such as /D:CDROM1 and /D:CDROM2, as shown in the example below. Then, the CONFIG.SYS file must include separate lines with the device drivers for each CD-ROM drive, even if the device drivers are from different manufacturers and have different names, such as DEVICE=SBPROCD.SYS and DEVICE=NECCD.SYS. A specific example follows. AUTOEXEC.BAT lines might include:

c:\mscdex.exe /d:cdrom1 /d:cdrom2 /m:15 /l:s

CONFIG.SYS lines might include:

device=c:\sbprocd.sys /d:cdrom1

device=c:\neccd.sys /d:cdrom2

Note that the AUTOEXEC.BAT file sets the drive letter to S. This means that the first CD-ROM drive will be S, while the second drive will assume the next letter and become T.

Follow the instructions in the manufacturer's documentation for stackers and jukeboxes. Even though the device may appear to be a single unit or single drive into which discs are inserted automatically, it may consist of several different "logical" or "virtual" CD-ROM drives, each of which must be identified in the AUTOEXEC.BAT and CONFIG.SYS files. If so, when installing individual CD-ROM titles, you will need to install the title on a specific drive designated by a specific letter.

7.5.2 WINDOWS 3.X DEVICE DRIVER INSTALLATION

Windows 3.X requires not only MSCDEX.EXE for the CD-ROM drive (as explained above), but also Windows device drivers (files with names ending in .DRV) for several multimedia devices. If you need to update CD-ROM device drivers, first follow the instructions above to install the correct version of MSCDEX.EXE. Then, you will need to install the Windows device drivers, as explained below. Of course, most manufacturers of Windows multimedia devices supply easy-to-use setup programs for their devices. You are unlikely to have to install Windows device drivers "manually," as described here. This information is supplied primarily so that you understand the process and can make modifications to the setup if you wish to enhance the device's performance or to resolve occasional problems.

Note: You may also need to update DOS device drivers (as explained above) if you wish to run DOS CD-ROM titles in a DOS window.

Installing the Windows device drivers requires using two Windows applets, both of which are found in the **Main** program group: **Windows Setup** and **Control Panel**. If you are updating an old device driver, rather than installing a totally new device, you must first use these applications to remove the device driver from the system. (Removing a device driver does not actually delete any files from the hard drive; it merely removes them from the Windows system so that you can install new device drivers.)

Windows Setup within the **Main** program group allows you to change the primary settings that were created when you first installed Windows by running the SETUP.EXE program. You use the **Setup** applet to install new monitors, printers, keyboards, and mouse devices.

Note: Some hardware manufacturers provide their own device-driver installation programs (in place of **Windows Setup**), which follow slightly different steps than this.

Before you begin, the device-driver files must either have been copied to the workstation's hard drive (into the \WINDOWS\SYSTEM directory) or be available on a diskette (such as the original Windows installation disks or a hardware manufacturer's OEM ["Original Equipment Manufacturer"] disk). Throughout the update process, follow the on-screen instructions and refer to your Windows manual.

You will be prompted to select the name of a device driver or to indicate that you wish to use an OEM device driver. **Windows Setup** looks for the device-driver files in the \WINDOWS\SYSTEM directory. If **Windows Setup** cannot find the files, you will see a message, such as "Installing a Driver Not Supplied with Windows."

After copying the device-driver file to the hard drive from a diskette or locating it on the hard drive, **Windows Setup** (and alternative vendor installer programs) modifies the SYSTEM.INI and other .INI files. At this point, you must restart Windows in order for the changes to take effect.

Some device drivers may be installed or modified after they have been installed by using the **Control Panel** applet. For the most part, the **Control Panel** is for installing and configuring multimedia devices, such as sound and

MIDI. Like the **Windows Setup** device-driver files, these also must reside on the hard drive or on a floppy diskette supplied by a hardware manufacturer. Follow the on-screen instructions to complete the installation.

Remember that the essential device driver in Windows, as it is in DOS, is MSCDEX.EXE. Any errors in the way it is installed in the CONFIG.SYS and AUTOEXEC.BAT files, or incompatibilities with different versions of DOS, Windows, and other device drivers, will also affect Windows' use of the CD-ROM drive on your system.

7.5.3 WINDOWS 9X DEVICE DRIVER INSTALLATION

Windows 9X includes numerous multimedia device drivers and automatically installs them for you, by means of its Plug-and-Play feature. It also greatly simplifies the situation by providing universal device drivers. However, many peripherals need more-specialized device drivers than those for optimal performance.

Use the **Control Panel** to examine the device drivers that are installed in the workstation. To reach the **Control Panel**, either double-click **My Computer** and then double-click the **Control Panel** icon; or select the **Start** menu from the **Task** bar, followed by the **Settings** menu, and then the **Control Panel**.

Double-click the **System** icon and then the **Device Manager** tab. This **Property** sheet shows all installed device drivers and the interface (adapter) cards to which they relate. Close the **Device Manager** and **System** windows to return to the **Control Panel**.

Next, double-click the **Multimedia** icon. The **Multimedia** icon provides information about the Audio, Video, MIDI, and CD Music drivers and settings. Select the **Advanced** tab to see a detailed list of multimedia device drivers. To expand the tree of items listed, double-click the plus sign next to the name of a device. Especially interesting are the Video and Audio "Compression Codecs," which represent the types of compressed video and audio files a workstation is capable of using. Return to the **Control Panel** window.

To install a new Windows 9X device driver, open the **Control Panel** and select **Add New Hardware**. The **Wizard** will lead you through the process.

The process for changing and updating device drivers varies slightly depending upon the different **Property** sheet windows for the device driver you are attempting to change. Remember first to remove the old, out-dated driver before attempting to add an updated driver. Use the **Add/Remove Programs** applet in the **Control Panel** to remove the old driver and add the new driver. (Note: Removing a device driver only removes the driver from the system's configuration; it does not delete any files from the hard drive, so that you can reinstall it later.) When you obtain a new device driver, the manufacturer will supply an installation diskette and program. Insert the diskette in the A: drive. Click the **Install** button. The **Add/Remove Programs** applet will guide you through the installation process.

If this does not result in a properly set up device driver, you may need to modify the **Properties** sheet for the hardware device.

1. First, double-click the **System** icon in the **Control Panel**.
2. Select the **Device Manager** tab.
3. Double-click the name of the hardware device in the tree structure, for example, CD-ROM drive.
4. Then double-click the name of the specific device driver whose properties you wish to change.

Windows 9X provides so many options and so many different ways to accomplish the same task that you may find it necessary to keep careful notes when making changes to the system. Write down the **Property** sheet settings for the device driver before making any changes. Also write down the settings you have changed. Then, if you find you have made a mistake you can easily restore the system to the original settings, or you can more easily determine any additional changes to make.

7.5.4 MAC SYSTEM 6 DEVICE DRIVER INSTALLATION

Most Macintosh System 6 device-driver files are installed simply by placing them in the **System Folder**. This is true whether the device drivers are **INITs**, **Cdevs**, or **Desk Accessories**. To install any of these types of device drivers, the first step is to copy them or move them into the **System Folder**.

If the device driver is a **Desk Accessory**, after copying the file into the **System Folder**, use the **Font/DA Mover** application to install it in the System. Refer to your manual for details about using the **Font/DA Mover**. In most instances, the **Font/DA Mover** icon can be found in the **System Folder**. Simply double-click the icon. Display the System 6 file in one half of the window, and then display the list of device-driver files in the other. Select the **Desk Accessories** to be installed, and then click the **Copy** button.

If the device driver is a **Cdev** (control device) or an **INIT** (initialization file), it will automatically show up in the **Control Panel** when you restart the computer. Select the **Control Panel** from the **Apple** menu. Scroll down until the icon for the device driver appears. Then click on it to access and adjust the settings as necessary.

7.5.5 MAC SYSTEM 7 DEVICE DRIVER INSTALLATION

Most device drivers are automatically installed by the Installer program supplied along with the hardware device. The Installer program decompresses the files on the Installer disk and copies them into the appropriate folders on the Macintosh's hard drive. Device drivers typically go into the **Extensions**

Folder inside the **System Folder**. (You do not need the **Font/DA Mover** as in System 6.) If you must manually install the device drivers, all you need to do is move or copy the device driver files into the **Extensions Folder**.

If at any time during the installation process you receive an error message, such as "Extension files must be placed into the Extensions Folder," simply click OK. The message can mean any one of several things, including that you have tried to place them in the **System Folder**, but not in the **Extensions Folder**. When done, simply verify that the files have been stored in the **Extensions Folder**.

7.5.6 INSTALLING DVD DEVICE DRIVERS

If you upgrade a workstation from standard CD-ROM to DVD-plus-CD-ROM you will need to install DVD device drivers, as well as CD-ROM device drivers. Some older operating systems simply may not work with DVD device drivers at all. Before attempting to upgrade from CD-ROM to DVD, you need to understand that the two are not the same. Just because the discs are both the same size physically does not mean that they are the same. The physical drives are different, and completely different sets of device drivers are needed.

7.6 CHAPTER SUMMARY

This chapter covers a wide range of technical topics relating to steps that must be taken before a CD-ROM title can be successfully installed on a workstation. The chapter covered ways to determine the technical specifications of a CD-ROM workstation so that titles can be selected that are compatible with it, technical aspects of CD-ROM drives which can have an impact on the performance of a CD-ROM title running on the drive, installation of device drivers, and how to download software off online services.

8. Installing CD-ROM Titles

8.1 INTRODUCTION TO ADVANCED TITLE INSTALLATION TECHNIQUES

This chapter supplements the information in Chapter 6 about the CD-ROM title installation process and provides several techniques for installing titles when vendor-supplied installation programs fail. Augment the instructions in this chapter with information from operating-system and computer manuals, technical reference books listed in "Recommended Reading," and CD-ROM title documentation.

The chapter is divided into sections about DOS, Windows 3.X, Windows 9X, and Macintosh titles. To install Windows titles it may be necessary not only to refer to section 8.2 in this chapter but also to Chapter 9 on DOS.

In order to benefit from the information in this chapter, a reader need not be a technical expert in the operating system under which a CD-ROM title runs. You should, however, be familiar with the fundamental concepts and most frequently used commands and concepts in the operating system. Be sure to read Part Two, Chapter 6, for recommendations about installation procedures before you attempt to install a CD-ROM title.

The information in this chapter is intended for librarians and teachers who are responsible for the installation of CD-ROM titles on stand-alone workstations. The information is relevant to workstations with either one or several dedicated CD-ROM drives, but not necessarily to networked CD-ROMs.

8.2 INSTALLATION OF DOS TITLES

Until recently most CD-ROM titles were designed specifically for DOS. Even now that advanced versions of Windows are available, many graphics-intensive CD-ROM games and multimedia titles are still designed for DOS. Many CD-ROM titles run in a DOS window under Windows 3.X and Windows 9X. So, despite technological advances, DOS installations are still quite common. DOS installations can also be quite difficult, because each installation of a DOS CD-ROM title must be customized for each PC workstation.

This section covers installing DOS CD-ROM titles in several different ways: vendor-supplied installation programs, manual installation, and reconfiguring the workstation with a menu.

8.2.1 VERIFYING THAT THE CD-ROM DRIVE WORKS

Note: Throughout this section, reference is made to the "DOS prompt." In examples, the DOS prompt is shown as a capital letter, followed by a colon and a "greater than" sign, for example, C:>. This assumes that your CD-ROM workstation is set up to display the DOS prompt in this format. For information on the DOS prompt, refer to the *Microsoft MS-DOS User's Guide.* When duplicating the examples at a workstation, never type the characters C:>. Type only the commands that follow the DOS prompt. The simulated DOS prompt is shown in examples only to illustrate the position on the screen in which commands should be typed.

Before installing a CD-ROM title, always verify that the CD-ROM drive is working:

1. Make sure the CD-ROM drive is turned on. A light should display on the front of the drive.
2. Insert a CD-ROM disc (such as the CD-ROM title you plan to install) into the drive, label side up.
3. Having started up the workstation, at the DOS prompt, type the letter designating the CD-ROM drive, followed by a colon, and press the Enter key. For example, if your CD-ROM drive is drive D, at the DOS prompt type:

C:> D:

As long as no error message displays and the letter used by the prompt changes (in the above example, to D:>), this indicates the CD-ROM drive is installed properly and powered on. If not, refer to sections 9.3 and 8.3.1.1.

Next, verify that the CD-ROM title disc is readable. Type the following "directory listing" command at the DOS prompt, and then press Enter:

C:> DIR

A list of directories and files on the CD-ROM disc should display. If so, the workstation is prepared to install the CD-ROM title. If you receive an error message, make sure there is a disc in the drive. (Note: A CD audio disc will not provide a listing; you must insert a CD-ROM title in the drive.)

8.2.2 VENDOR-SUPPLIED INSTALLATION PROGRAMS

Most vendor installation programs follow a similar pattern. You begin by inserting a diskette into a drive or the CD-ROM disc into the CD-ROM drive. Then, at the DOS prompt, type a command to run the installation program found on the diskette or the disc. (Most installation programs are named

INSTALL.EXE.) If the installation program is on a diskette in the A: drive, at the DOS prompt, type the following, and press Enter:

A:> INSTALL

If the installation program is on the CD-ROM disc (and assuming the CD-ROM drive is D), type the following, and press Enter:

D:> INSTALL

Assuming the CD-ROM title is compatible with the workstation's configuration, the vendor-supplied installation program should make the installation process quite simple. Most installation programs perform the following tasks for you:

1. Check the system configuration to verify that it is compatible.
2. Present installation options on a menu, often concerning the use of the hard drive or the type of audio desired when running the title.
3. Modify the AUTOEXEC.BAT and CONFIG.SYS files and create a batch file to run the title.
4. If even one component of the workstation doesn't meet the CD-ROM title's requirements, the installation program may "abort" or "terminate" without installing the title.

Below are some of the events that may occur during an installation.

8.2.2.1 Verifying Compatibility

In most cases, vendor installation programs terminate the installation process if they detect that a workstation isn't completely compatible with the CD-ROM title, even when, in fact, some of a CD-ROM title's requirements can be ignored. For example, it's often possible to run a title intended for a 486/SX processor on a 386 processor, and the speed of the CD-ROM drive is also sometimes irrelevant.

Other requirements, however, cannot be ignored, such as the amount of free hard-drive space or the resolution of the monitor. If an installation program determines that a workstation has insufficient storage space on the hard drive, more space must be made available by backing up and then deleting unnecessary files. If an installation program determines that a monitor's resolution is insufficient, little can be done to complete the installation unless the problem stems from the graphics device drivers. For example, if you are certain that the monitor and graphics card in the workstation are capable of displaying the resolution required by the CD-ROM title, but an installation program fails to recognize the fact, then you probably need a higher-resolution graphics device-driver file. Contact the manufacturer to obtain the latest device driver and instructions on how to install it (see section 7.5).

8.2.2.2 IRQ Interrupts and Address Conflicts

Error messages concerning "I/O addresses," "IRQs," and "DMAs" are common during DOS title installations. These errors indicate that there is a conflict between two components of the workstation. (Such conflicts can occur for several reasons. One component may have been installed before the other, but both were set up to use resources intended for only one device, for example. If such a message appears while you are installing a CD-ROM title, the installation program probably has encountered a conflict between the sound card and some other peripheral, perhaps a modem or a scanner.

The number assignments for one of the conflicting devices must be changed. Refer to the workstation's log book to find the "IRQ" numbers and "I/O addresses" assigned to the sound card and to manufacturers' equipment manuals for information on how to change them. Some settings can be changed easily through software; others must be changed by adjusting physical switches on the adapter cards involved. If the manuals don't specify which settings are acceptable, it means that it is irrelevant what numbers are assigned to a sound card; it is simply a matter of changing the number to any other number. In some cases, though, the IRQ or I/O address can only be set to specific numbers. If the error involves a "memory address," such as 220H or some other combination of digits and letters (a hexadecimal number), you may be required to specify only numbers within a certain range or to exclude numbers within a certain range. Contact the manufacturer of the hardware device and device driver for a list of acceptable settings if you need assistance changing an IRQ or I/O address.

8.2.2.3 Choosing between Hard Drive and CD-ROM Storage

Typically, sound files, image files, or critical program codes are copied to the hard drive by vendor installation programs. Files that are copied to the hard drive run faster and are more easily accessible than if they must be accessed from the CD-ROM each time they are required. On the other hand, these files can be quite large, requiring a lot of hard-drive space, and must be manually deleted when the CD-ROM title is no longer used. If a CD-ROM title's installation program allows you to decide whether certain files should be copied from the CD-ROM drive to the hard drive, the decision will impact the performance of the CD-ROM title. Choose hard-drive installation to optimize performance, but choose to leave files on the CD-ROM disc if hard-drive space is at a premium.

8.2.2.4 Planning for Deinstalling

All CD-ROM title installations result in numerous changes to the files and directories on the hard drive of the workstation. As a result, deinstalling a CD-ROM title can be difficult: simply deleting the batch file that runs the title isn't enough. Plan ahead for deinstallation by backing up the system thoroughly before installing a CD-ROM title. Keep a record of all changes made to the hard drive and to the AUTOEXEC.BAT and CONFIG.SYS files by the installation program. After deleting the CD-ROM title's directory and the files it contains, be sure to clean up the AUTOEXEC.BAT and CON-FIG.SYS files either by deleting the lines that apply only to the title or by "remarking" the lines using the REM command at the beginning of the lines. It's also recommended that you acquire and use a deinstallation utility program, such as *Uninstall-It!* or *Remove-It.*

8.2.3 MANUAL INSTALLATION OF DOS TITLES

If a vendor installation program fails to install a title, or if it terminates before installing the title, it is possible to install a DOS title manually (that is, if the workstation has the appropriate hardware). You can create a customized configuration of the operating system and software to run the CD-ROM title. When a workstation is dedicated to running only a single title, the workstation can be reconfigured just for that title, and no others. This section explains how to do this.

When a workstation will be running several CD-ROM titles, though, you must set up special configurations for each title and then allow users to access the titles from a configuration menu. Many shell programs and menuing systems are available to help you do this. You need not use a shell or menu system: You can create a DOS configuration menu. The following section tells you how to do this.

8.2.3.1 Modifying a Workstation's Configuration

Two kinds of changes to the start-up files on the hard drive must be made in order to manually install a CD-ROM title: (1) delete lines containing information not necessary for successful operation of the specific CD-ROM title, and (2) add instructions to produce a more efficient use of conventional memory. (Refer to the "Glossary" for definitions of these terms.)

To decide which lines to delete from the AUTOEXEC.BAT and CON-FIG.SYS, if any, refer to Tables 8.1 and 8.2. In most cases, very few lines are really necessary to most start-up files and are included only for rather esoteric performance reasons. To free up conventional memory, all that's necessary is to insert a word at the beginning of a few lines in the start-up files.

(Remember, making these changes alters the workstation's normal operations.)

Note: While it is possible to edit the files with any text editor (not a word processor), it is recommended that you use DOS EDIT.

Table 8.1 Lines for a DOS CD-ROM CONFIG.SYS

Unnecessary Lines		
BREAK=	**COUNTRY=**	**INSTALL=**
NUMLOCK=	**REM**	**SET=**
SHELL=	**SWITCHES=**	**VERIFY=**
MENUITEM=	**SUBMENU=**	**MENUDEFAULT=**
MENUCOLOR=	**INCLUDE=**	**FCBS=**
DEVICE=	**DEVICE=**	**DEVICE=**
ANSI.SYS	**DBLSPACE.SYS**	**DISPLAY.SYS**
DEVICE=	**DEVICE=**	**DEVICE=**
DRIVER.SYS	**EGA.SYS**	**INTERLINK.EXE**
DEVICE=	**DEVICE=**	
POWER.EXE	**RAMDRIVE.EXE**	

Necessary Lines		
DEVICEHIGH=	**DOS=**	
FILES=	**BUFFERS=**	**LASTDRIVE=**

Table 8.2: Lines in a DOS CD-ROM AUTOEXEC.BAT

Unnecessary Lines		
MODE	**ECHO**	
SET	**DOSKEY**	**VSAFE**
FASTOPEN	**SUBST**	**APPEND**
DBLSPACE		

Necessary Lines

PROMPT
PATH
SMARTDRV.EXE
MSCDEX.EXE
• programs required by your audio card
• the program that runs your mouse in the DOS environment

Both files contain several lines of instructions. You must decide which lines or parts of lines are unnecessary for running the CD-ROM title and then delete them. By deleting the unnecessary instructions, you free up parts of the workstation's conventional memory so that there will be enough available memory to run the title. Refer to Tables 8.1 and 8.2 above showing the command words or instructions you are likely to find in both files. Compare the lines in both files against the tables, to identify lines you may delete.

Note: If you are afraid you will delete the wrong lines, "remark" them instead of deleting them: Insert the letters REM and a blank space at the very beginning of any line you wish to temporarily disable. If later you find that you need the line after all, simply delete the letters REM and the extra blank to enable the command.

If you simply cannot decide whether it is going to be useful to delete any lines, don't. Do, however, add the lines and words recommended below.

Most CONFIG.SYS files contain the following lines near the beginning. If your CONFIG.SYS does not contain these lines, add them at the very beginning of the file:

DEVICE=HIMEM.SYS
DOS=UMB,HIGH
DEVICE=EMM386.EXE (followed by various parameters)

Check the CD-ROM title's installation manual. The manual may suggest what additional parameters (various letters and numbers) to add to the DEVICE=EMM386.EXE line. If so, type the line exactly as the manual indicates. If not, after DEVICE=EMM386.EXE add a space and the letters NOEMS so that the line reads as follows:

DEVICE=EMM386.EXE NOEMS

If other lines in CONFIG.SYS begin with the word DEVICE, change the word to DEVICEHIGH. For example, if the CONFIG.SYS file contains a line like the following:

DEVICE=C:\MOUSE\MOUSE.SYS

change it to:

DEVICEHIGH=C:\MOUSE\MOUSE.SYS

The AUTOEXEC.BAT file runs certain programs automatically when the workstation is turned on; you may insert the word LOADHIGH or the abbreviation LH in front of these lines (refer to the *Microsoft MS-DOS User's Guide* for further help). Most programs (file names ending in the extensions .EXE and .COM) can be run using LH. For example, if the AUTOEXEC.BAT file contains a line like the following:

C:\MOUSE\MOUSE.COM

change it to:

LH C:\MOUSE\MOUSE.COM

or change it to:

LOADHIGH C:\MOUSE\MOUSE.COM

Warning: Do not insert LOADHIGH or LH in front of a line containing MSCDEX.EXE.

The CONFIG.SYS and AUTOEXEC.BAT files must include instructions to run the workstation's CD-ROM drive, and if the CD-ROM title requires them, the sound card, and mouse, as well. CD-ROM device-driver instruction lines must appear in both files. (Granted, it isn't always easy to determine which lines relate to the CD-ROM drive and sound card.) Do not delete the lines needed by the CD-ROM drive and sound card device drivers. Refer to Chapter 7 for details.

As an example, here is a CONFIG.SYS file that has been successfully used to run a DOS CD-ROM title on a 486-based PC:

```
DEVICE=C:\HIMEM.SYS
DEVICE=C:\EMM386.EXE RAM
BUFFERS=30,0
FILES=30
DOS=UMB
LASTDRIVE=F
FCBS=4,0
DOS=HIGH
DEVICEHIGH /L:1,12048 =C:\DOS\SETVER.EXE
DEVICEHIGH /L:1,11328 =C:\SBPRO\DRV\SBPCD.SYS
    /D:MSCD001 /P:220
```

The following is an example AUTOEXEC.BAT that was created for use with the above CONFIG.SYS:

```
@ECHO OFF
PROMPT $P$G
PATH C:\;C:\DOS;C:\XXX-CD
C:\SBPRO\SBP-SET /M:12 /VOC:12 /CD:12 /FM:12
C:\SBPRO\DRV\MSCDEX.EXE /V /D:MSCD001 /M:15
LH /L:0;1,16400 /S C:\WINDOWS\SMARTDRV.EXE 1024 512
C:\WINDOWS\MOUSE
C:\SBPRO\SBFMDRV.COM
C:
CD XXX-CD
RUN
```

Some of the lines in the examples above could also have been deleted if more conventional memory were needed. (Keep in mind, these files are unlikely to work on your workstation. The files are provided here only as examples.)

Most CONFIG.SYS and AUTOEXEC.BAT files used on CD-ROM work-stations are long and complex. When you create a new configuration, you are attempting to reduce the length of the files to the bare minimum required for running the hardware components needed by the specific CD-ROM title. The "bare minimum" may turn out to be quite long, as in the above examples. You may only be able to remove a few lines, such as ones related to the use of a printer or to eliminate Windows-specific information.

On the other hand, you could also end up with something as minimal as the following CONFIG.SYS:

DEVICE=C:\HIMEM.SYS
DEVICE=C:\EMM386.SYS
DOS=UMB, HIGH
FILES=30
BUFFERS=30
DEVICEHIGH=C:\NECCD.SYS /D:MSCD001 /P:220

Your AUTOEXEC.BAT could be as simple as this:

PATH C:;C:\DOS
LH MSCDEX.EXE /D:MSCD001 /M:15

Testing the Results: After you have copied and edited the CONFIG.SYS and AUTOEXEC.BAT files, reboot (restart) the computer. The workstation will then restart using the new configuration you created. Carefully watch the messages that flash by on the screen. If you see any messages indicating that something was "not found" or "not loaded," you may have made a mistake or deleted one or more needed lines. Edit the files again, correcting or adding one line at a time, and testing after each addition.

Be certain that the path names identifying device drivers, such as HIMEM.SYS, and programs, such as SETVER.EXE, are correct and complete.

Once everything seems fine when you reboot the workstation and the DOS prompt displays, verify that there is enough conventional memory and that there is enough hard-drive space for the CD-ROM title. (Refer to Chapter 9 for more details on how to do this, or follow the instructions below.)

1. At the DOS prompt , type DIR /W, and press Enter, to display the contents of the C drive.

2. Underneath the list of files and directories there will appear a line showing how much space is available. For example, the following might display:

```
PROMIX.EXE    SASBID.DLL      SBPAUX.DRV
SETUP1.EXE    IDEAWZRD.INI    VISUALBA.GRP
SAT10-21.TXT  WINSOCK.DLL
```

312 file(s)   11,579,218 bytes
37,335,040 bytes free

C:\TMP>

In the example above, the phrase "37,335,040 bytes free" indicates there are 37 Mb available on the hard drive. Compare the available free space with the CD-ROM title's requirements. If there is insufficient space, delete some files or programs from the hard drive. (Be careful; back up everything first). Even if the CD-ROM title itself doesn't seem to be taking up much space when it's first installed, it is possible that the title will eventually use more space. It may use the hard drive while it is running or may create files as the title is played. Don't risk running out of disk space in the middle of an activity.

3. Check the amount of memory available. At the DOS prompt, type MEM and press Enter (note: the MEM command isn't available in all DOS versions). The MEM command displays detailed information about how memory is being used on the workstation. Look for the line that lists "largest executable program size." The number listed must be at least as great as the conventional memory requirements of the CD-ROM title. In the example below, a CD-ROM title that required at least 580 k would *not* run:

Memory Type	Total=	Used +	Free
Conventional	640K	66K	574K
Upper	111K	68K	43K
Reserved	384K	384K	0K
Extended (XMS)	7,057K	1,245K	5,812K
Total memory	8,192K	1,763K	6,429K
Total under 1 MB	751K	134K	617K
Largest executable program size			574K

4. Follow the instructions in the CD-ROM title's manual to start the title.

Even though you are certain the workstation has enough RAM to run the title, you may still receive the "insufficient memory message" when trying to start the title. If so, the fault lies with the CONFIG.SYS and AUTOEXEC.BAT files. You must continue to edit them as explained above. Use DEVICEHIGH in CONFIG.SYS and LOADHIGH in AUTOEXEC.BAT to make sure that all the RAM in the workstation is used efficiently. Also continue to pare down the two files until they contain the bare minimum required to run the workstation. Repeat the steps above until the CD-ROM runs.

What to Do If the Test Fails. Begin by verifying that the CD-ROM drive and its device drivers are properly installed. Second, verify that the sound card's device drivers are properly installed. If you have DOS 6.0 or later, use the program called MEMMAKER.EXE to optimize the configuration as explained below. (If you have an earlier version of DOS, now may be the time to upgrade to DOS, preferably 6.2 or later.)

By beginning with the CD-ROM drive as discussed here, you will be able to narrow the problem down and determine if the sound card is, in fact, the source of the problem. If the CD-ROM drive is functioning properly, try to run a simple DOS program, demo, or sample (such as ones that are frequently supplied with a sound card) to verify that the card works. If you can hear sound when running the demo program, then you know the problem isn't in the sound card but is present in the way memory is being managed by the workstation. You will need to further change the AUTOEXEC.BAT and CON-FIG.SYS files used to start up the workstation.

8.2.3.2 Using MemMaker.EXE

DOS 6.0 (and later) includes a program called MEMMAKER.EXE, which diagnoses the way a workstation's conventional memory is being used and then automatically adjusts the CONFIG.SYS and AUTOEXEC.BAT files to make more conventional memory available to the CD-ROM titles and other programs (in other words, MEMMAKER.EXE edits the files for you). To do this, MemMaker inserts and modifies the DEVICEHIGH command in the CON-FIG.SYS, and it inserts the LOADHIGH command in the AUTOEXEC.BAT file. This causes device drivers to run in RAM, not in the limited conventional memory of the workstation. The *Microsoft MS-DOS User's Guide* and online DOS HELP both contain more details on the use of MemMaker.

The following instructions assume you wish to run DOS-only CD-ROM titles, not Windows titles. You will begin by using MemMaker to adjust the AUTOEXEC.BAT and CONFIG.SYS files on the hard drive using the simplest approach, "Express Setup." If that doesn't free up enough conventional memory to run the title, you will use "Custom Setup."

Before you begin to work on the hard drive, copy both files into backup files, named AUTOEXEC.BCK and CONFIG.BCK, so that you can restore them if you are unhappy with the results of the MemMaker program.

Note: If you usually run Windows but want to run the CD-ROM title from DOS only, the next thing you must do is "remark" the line containing the WIN command in the AUTOEXEC.BAT file. Type REM followed by a blank space in front of the WIN statement in the AUTOEXEC.BAT file. This is necessary because MemMaker configures memory differently for Windows. For example, if the last line in the AUTOEXEC.BAT file is:

WIN

change it to:
REM WIN

To start MemMaker, at the DOS prompt of the hard drive's root directory (usually C:>), type the following command, and press the Enter Key:
C:> MEMMAKER

There are two ways to run MemMaker. When you type the MemMaker command at the DOS prompt, you will be asked to choose between "Express Setup" and "Custom Setup." Begin with "Express Setup," which automates the process. The MemMaker program will ask if you have any programs that require expanded memory, such as older DOS CD-ROM titles. Check to see whether the CD-ROM title in question uses expanded ("EMS"), rather than extended ("XMS"), memory. If you are uncertain, select "No" (expanded memory). Also note that MemMaker requires different responses for a DOS-only and a Windows system. (Remember: You should not have a WIN command in your AUTOEXEC.BAT file when running MemMaker at this time.)

From time to time during this process, MemMaker restarts the workstation while configuring memory and prompts you to answer a series of questions. Follow all on-screen instructions. Eventually MemMaker will tell you to press Enter to restart the workstation again: watch carefully for any error messages that display. Write them down. When MemMaker asks whether the system is working properly, respond "Yes" or "No," depending on whether or not error messages displayed at any time. If you respond "No," MemMaker will lead you through a troubleshooting process. You may also need to re-run MemMaker, this time using "Custom Setup" instead of "Express Setup."

When done, MemMaker will tell you how much conventional memory is now available for running the CD-ROM title. If you believe enough conventional memory has been freed-up, try to install and run the CD-ROM title. When you have finished running "Express Setup" on the hard drive's start-up files, use a text editor (such as DOS EDIT) to examine the CONFIG.SYS and AUTOEXEC.BAT files. You will notice that MemMaker made many changes in them.

If "Express Setup" doesn't work, run MemMaker again, this time using "Custom Setup." Respond to all questions as you did before, but also make use of the "Advanced Options." Refer to Table 8.3 for recommendations about setting the "Advanced Options." Follow all on-screen instructions. Re-run MemMaker until the CD-ROM title runs satisfactorily. Eventually MemMaker will have prepared your CONFIG.SYS and AUTOEXEC.BAT files for the most efficient use of both conventional and upper memory. The CD-ROM title should then run fine.

Table 8.3: MemMaker Advanced Options

1. Specify which drivers and TSRs to include in optimization?
   NO: usually best; includes all drivers and TSRs
   Yes: only if problems occurred when starting the computer with MemMaker

2. Scan upper memory area aggressively?
   YES: usually best, will check more memory addresses
   No: only if problems occurred when starting the computer with Mem-Maker

3. Optimize upper memory for use with Windows?
   NO: if you are running Windows programs under Windows or only DOS and not Windows
   Yes: only if you are running DOS programs under Windows (see also the section in this guide on creating a PIF)

4. Use monochrome region (B000-BFFF) for running programs?
   YES: if you have an older PC with only VGA or EGA, not SVGA, to free more memory
   No: if you have an MPC 2 compliant computer, SVGA, or a monochrome (not gray scale) monitor

5. Keep current EMM386 memory exclusions and inclusions?
   YES: usually best
   No: if problems occurred when starting the computer with Mem-Maker; if No causes problems, try again with Yes

6. Move extended BIOS Data Area from conventional to upper memory?
   YES: usually best
   No: if you have tried everything else, as a last resort say No.

8.2.3.3 DOS 6.X Multiconfiguration Boot Menus

If you have DOS 6.0 or later, and if you are fairly proficient with DOS, you can develop different start-up configurations for different CD-ROM titles. So, if you have several CD-ROM titles that require different AUTOEXEC.BAT files and CONFIG.SYS files, and you frequently use different ones, then it may be worth the effort to create a start-up menu. Details on how to create the menu are found in the *Microsoft MS-DOS User's Guide.* Below is a brief overview.

To use multiple configurations on a workstation, you must divide its CONFIG.SYS file into blocks with unique names. These names will appear as items on a start-up menu. The user will select the appropriate menu item, such as "ENCARTA."

In the AUTOEXEC.BAT file use GOTO statements to jump or "branch" to labels with the same names as the blocks in the CONFIG.SYS file. (This feature has always been available to DOS batch files. The blocks in CON-FIG.SYS are the new feature in DOS 6.0.) If you are familiar with GOTO and batch files in DOS, you will be able to create multiple configurations.

8.2.3.4 Using Other Software Utilities

DOS titles can be difficult to install. As a consequence several inexpensive utilities have been developed to help install and run them. Many are designed for game CD-ROMs, but can be equally effective for any multimedia DOS titles. You can identify such programs by skimming through the most recent DOS and PC gaming magazines.

8.2.4 DOS TITLE SUMMARY

Be sure to test each CD-ROM title you plan to run on a workstation before turning it over to users. If you can view the complete introductory sequence of a title and then start to run it, your workstation's users will probably have no problems with it either. Some titles may skip the introduction section. If the workstation still doesn't have enough memory or there are other problems, then the title appears to run normally. Problems may not show up until many hours later. So, be sure you can view the introduction to any CD-ROM title you install. If the workstation freezes or loses sound later, first refer to Chapter 9, then contact the CD-ROM title producer for help.

The installation of DOS CD-ROM titles often requires modification of a workstation's operating-system configuration files, especially the AUTO-EXEC.BAT and CONFIG.SYS files. If a vendor installation program fails, first attempt to reconfigure the system by simplifying the files. Then use MEMMAKER.EXE to adjust the configuration. If you are running more than one title on the workstation, install a shell or menuing system or create a DOS configuration menu.

8.3 INSTALLATION OF WINDOWS 3.X TITLES

In order to install a Windows 3.X CD-ROM title, the following are necessary: (1) the CD-ROM drive must be functioning properly; and (2) both DOS and Windows 3.X must be properly set up to run CD-ROM titles.

Most Windows 3.X CD-ROM title discs include an installation program named either INSTALL.EXE or SETUP.EXE. To install the CD-ROM title, the vendor-supplied installation program must be run from within Windows 3.X. The installation program automatically verifies that the workstation meets the title's requirements, creates a directory on the computer's hard drive, copies files from the CD-ROM disc to the hard drive, and may also modify

Windows files, such as the SYSTEM.INI file. Finally, the installation program creates a **program group** for the CD-ROM title and an icon from which users can access the title from the Windows **Program Manager**.

Unfortunately, not all installation programs are well-designed or easy to use. In addition, since every CD-ROM workstation is different, no CD-ROM title's installation program is capable of anticipating the requirements of every workstation. As a result, problems are bound to occur during some installations. This section provides guidelines for resolving installation problems with Windows 3.X CD-ROM titles. This section also explains how to install a DOS CD-ROM title in a DOS window. For further details about DOS titles, refer to section 8.2 above.

8.3.1 INITIAL STEPS

Before attempting to install a Windows 3.X title, verify that the CD-ROM drive onto which the title is about to be installed is fully functional. Second, verify that the workstation's operating system is properly configured to run CD-ROMs.

8.3.1.1 Verifying that the CD-ROM Drive Works

The first step in the installation process must be to make sure the CD-ROM drive operates properly once a disc is inserted, as follows:

1. Confirm that the CD-ROM drive is powered on.
2. From the Windows 3.X **Main** program group, select the **File Manager**.
3. In the **File Manager** window, confirm that an icon for the CD-ROM drive is displayed. If the CD-ROM icon isn't visible, refer to section 8.2.1 for instructions on how to correct the problem.
4. Insert a CD-ROM title disc into the drive, label side up. Do not use an audio CD for this purpose.
5. Test the drive by selecting the CD-ROM drive icon. A list of files or directories should display on one side of the screen, showing the data files on the CD-ROM disc. If nothing displays, or if an error message results, there may be a problem with either the disc or the drive. Insert a different disc in the drive and repeat this step. If changing the disc doesn't solve the problem, refer to section 8.2.1.

In most cases, a CD-ROM title disc with data on track 1 should be used to test the functionality of the CD-ROM drive. If for some reason you must test a drive with an audio CD (for example, to test the drive before you acquire your first CD-ROM title), you won't be able to examine the audio disc with the **File Manager**, because audio CDs have no data on track 1. You can test the CD-ROM drive with an audio CD, however, using the **Multimedia Player** applet in the **Accessories** program group. (Refer to section 10.4.5 for more information.)

8.3.1.2 Is MSCDEX Installed?

If you are unable to confirm that the CD-ROM drive is functioning properly, the problem could be either a hardware or a software problem. Refer to Chapter 4 for assistance.

If you suspect a software problem, the most likely source is the MSCDEX.EXE device-driver file (discussed in detail in section 7.5.1.1). Shut down Windows, return to the DOS prompt, and follow the steps listed in section 8.2.1 to ensure proper functioning of the CD-ROM drive in DOS. Then, return to this chapter to continue with the Windows CD-ROM title installation.

8.3.2 TYPES OF WINDOWS 3.X INSTALLATIONS

Once the CD-ROM drive is working properly, CD-ROM titles can be installed in one of several ways: (1) in a Windows 3.X window, (2) in a DOS window, or (3) in DOS only. In all three cases, if the CD-ROM workstation also has a menuing system or shell program, after installing the CD-ROM title in Windows, it may also need to be installed in the menuing system or shell program (refer to the shell vendor's documentation for instructions).

If the disc requires Windows and will not run in DOS alone, then the easiest way to install a CD-ROM title is to use the vendor-supplied installation program. This process will create an icon in a **program group** in the **Program Manager** and may also install certain "player" files or "runtime" files on the hard drive.

If the title can run either in Windows or in DOS, you may have an option to install it as a Windows program (which means to create an icon and run the program under Windows in a re-sizable window that can be active while you are running other programs) or in a DOS window from an icon. If you choose the DOS window option, the installation program not only will create an icon in a **program group** but will probably also supply a **PIF** ("Program Information File," see below) to enhance its performance.

Or, you may be able to circumvent Windows altogether and run the title as if it were an ordinary DOS title (in other words, exit from Windows and install the title as explained in section 8.2).

If when using the title you encounter performance problems (especially memory errors), you may wish to reinstall the title using a different option. Generally, begin with Windows installation. If that seems inadequate, reinstall it to run in a DOS Window with a PIF. Finally if all else fails run it from DOS alone.

8.3.3 WINDOWS 3.X MEMORY MANAGEMENT ISSUES

Windows is a memory management program. In most cases, a Windows-installed CD-ROM title should run with few or no memory management problems. Windows frees up the memory each program or CD-ROM title needs and allows your workstation to "simulate" memory it may not really have. Sometimes, however, depending upon the workstation's configuration and the way in which the CD-ROM title is designed, Windows may actually seem to slow down or degrade the performance of the title. If you encounter memory errors while running a Windows title, refer to Chapter 10. There are several possible causes and solutions, from insufficient hard-drive space to the way Windows is installed on the workstation.

You could also try closing and exiting from other applications before attempting to run a CD-ROM title when you encounter memory errors. When you run any program under Windows 3.X and then exit from that program in order to free up memory before running another program, such as a CD-ROM title, however, you may not actually be freeing up memory. If the first application program does not properly shut itself down and politely free up memory for programs that follow, Windows 3.X can't release the memory itself. So don't be surprised if you find that a CD-ROM title runs properly one day, and the next day produces an "out of memory" error. When that happens, simply restart Windows.

You may be able to improve the performance of a CD-ROM title by first optimizing the way memory is used by DOS. See section 8.2.3.2 on the MEM-MAKER.EXE utility. Run the MemMaker program and respond "Yes" to all questions regarding Windows. Use the "Custom Setup" technique (described in detail in section 8.2.3.2) and the "Advanced Options." Answer "Yes" to question 3 (see Table 8.3). This instructs MemMaker to use the memory area called "upper memory" or "UMB" (see "Glossary") and can be very useful for systems with 2 to 4 Mb RAM.

8.3.4 VENDOR-SUPPLIED INSTALLATION PROGRAMS

It is important to back up several files on the workstation's hard drive before you run the vendor installation program (SETUP.EXE or INSTALL-.EXE), because the installation program will probably make changes to them. If you have problems with a workstation later, you will be able to return to the original working version of these files: AUTOEXEC.BAT, CONFIG.SYS, SYSTEM.INI, and WIN.INI. (See the *Microsoft MS-DOS User's Guide* and *Microsoft Windows 3.X User's Guide* for backup instructions.)

In addition, a well-behaved installation program will create a new directory on the hard drive and install new files only into that new directory. Many installation programs, however, will also add new files to the \WINDOWS and \WINDOWS\SYSTEM directories. There is nothing you can do about this (see below for information on deinstalling). At times, a program will even overwrite files that are already in those directories. If designed properly, the installation program should notify you that it is overwriting older files and updating the directory with newer versions. Some installation programs will not—you are helpless against problems this can cause when you try to run other CD-ROM titles, which may require the versions of the files previously installed on the workstation. If you encounter an error message following an installation that indicates a problem with a device driver (.DRV file) or a .DLL (dynamic link library), the vendor-supplied installation program could be the problem. Keep a complete backup of your Windows directory and all its subdirectories as originally installed on the system, so that in an emergency you can restore it to its pristine condition.

You may also purchase one of a number of third-party utility programs that will help you install as well as deinstall programs. These utilities keep track of the versions of Windows files on the hard drive, log them in and out, track, and help back up and restore files.

8.3.4.1 Running the Installation Program

In order to install a Windows CD-ROM title, you must insert the CD-ROM disc into the drive first (label side up). Next, in the **Program Manager**, select the **File** menu. From the **File** menu, select **Run**.

You will be running the installation program, which is normally located on the CD-ROM disc. It is almost always called SETUP.EXE, but may be called INSTALL.EXE. If you know the letter designation of the CD-ROM drive, for example, D, then simply type: D:\SETUP or D:\INSTALL in the box provided. Then click **OK**.

If you do not know the drive letter and the exact name of the installation program, use the **Browse** button to browse through the drives and directories until you locate the proper file. To browse, first select the CD-ROM drive from the pull-down list. When the list of files on the CD-ROM disc displays, select SETUP.EXE or INSTALL.EXE, as appropriate. Then, when the complete name of the program is displayed in the **Run** box, click **OK**.

Note: The **Run** box may contain either SETUP or SETUP.EXE or INSTALL or INSTALL.EXE. The .EXE extension on the file name is optional.

8.3.4.2 Creating the Desktop Icon

Occasionally an installation program may not create an icon in the **Program Manager**. For example, it may install the icon in the wrong **program group**. If you find the icon out of place, simply drag it out of the erroneous **program group** to the proper **program group**. If the installation program fails to create an icon, you can also create an icon yourself using the **File** menu.

It is also possible that an older installation program may not create an icon because you are expected to use the **File Run** option to run an executable file directly off the disc (an .EXE file). If so, you should create an icon for your users' convenience.

Keep in mind, though, that any desktop icon for a CD-ROM title will not function unless the CD-ROM disc is inserted into the drive. The icon simply provides a shortcut means of running a title.

If you have to reinstall a CD-ROM title, you may end up with more than one identical icon. This will not cause technical problems, but you may delete any of the extra icons if you wish.

8.3.4.3 Planning for Deinstalling

In time, you will undoubtedly want to de-install the CD-ROM title and all its associated files. This is far from an easy task, since many different files may have been placed on the hard drive during installation, and since your CONFIG.SYS, AUTOEXEC.BAT, and .INI files may have been modified by the title's installation program. One solution is to invest in a deinstallation or uninstaller program for Windows. These are widely available as freeware, shareware, and low-cost third-party utilities; for example, Microhelp's *UnInstaller* costs less than $40.

Table 8.4 PIF Recommended Settings

PIF Sheet Items	Settings	
Video Memory	High Graphics	
Memory Requirements	KB Required 580	KB Desired 640
EMS Memory	KB Required 1000	KB Limit 1024
XMS Memory	KB Required 3000	KB Limit 4000
Display Usage	Full Screen	
Execution	N/A	

PIF Advanced Options		
Advanced Sheet Items	Settings	
Background Priority	50	
Foreground Priority	100	
Memory Options	EMS Memory	XMS Memory
	Locked	Locked
	Uses High Memory	Lock Application
	Area	Memory
Display Options	High Graphics	

8.3.5 INSTALLING A CD-ROM
TITLE IN A DOS WINDOW

Windows allows you to install DOS CD-ROMs without modifying your CONFIG.SYS and AUTOEXEC.BAT files or requiring a new batch file. The key to running a DOS CD-ROM title from Windows is creating a PIF ("Program Information File") for the title. Table 8.4 shows recommended PIF settings for a typical DOS CD-ROM title; you may refer to the table and skip the following instructions, if you are familiar with the **PIF Editor**.

8.3.5.1 Verifying the Configuration Is Suitable

Before beginning, you need to know how the workstation is configured. To benefit from the information in this section, you should have a basic understanding of DOS commands, of the AUTOEXEC.BAT and CONFIG.SYS files, and how to examine the contents and modify the contents of those two files.

First, confirm that DOS device drivers are properly installed for the computer hardware required by the CD-ROM title, including the mouse or joystick, CD-ROM drive, sound Card, graphics adapter, and memory managers. (Refer to Chapter 7 for details on device drivers.)

Verify that you also have a version of the necessary Windows device drivers installed: Click on the Windows **Control Panel** in the **Main** program group. Then click on the **Drivers** icon to see a list of the joystick and audio device drivers installed in Windows. Use **Windows Setup** to check the graphics adapter driver.

Also make sure there is a **386 Enhanced** icon in the **Control Panel** (a chip symbol). This verifies that the workstation is running Windows in 386 enhanced mode, which is necessary for multitasking and running DOS titles in a resizable window. If not, shut down Windows and restart it at the DOS prompt by typing WIN /3. The /3 will force Windows into 386 enhanced mode. You may also modify the AUTOEXEC.BAT so that it contains the line WIN /3.

If the **386 Enhanced** icon fails to appear in the **Control Panel** despite your starting Windows with the /3 switch, the workstation may not have enough memory. (Refer to Chapter 7, section 7.3.2.8 to determine how much RAM is installed in the workstation.)

If the workstation has only 2 Mb RAM, you may have problems running Windows in 386 enhanced mode. 386 enhanced mode requires at least 1 Mb of free extended memory (XMS). By loading device drivers and other programs into high memory (using LOADHIGH and DEVICEHIGH in the AUTOEXEC.BAT and CONFIG.SYS files), you may have reduced the amount of XMS available for Windows. Running the MemMaker program may reconfigure memory to free up 1 Mb RAM for Windows. (Refer to section 8.2.3.2.)

Next, make sure the mouse program appears in the CONFIG.SYS file or in the AUTOEXEC.BAT before the WIN command does. Unless the mouse program starts up before Windows, you will not be able to use the mouse while using the DOS CD-ROM title. Windows usually manages the mouse, but it cannot control the mouse for a DOS CD-ROM title running in a DOS window. (You may also need to include statements in the start-up files to run a sound card's device drivers. If you later have problems with the sound, verify that the DOS device drivers appear in the AUTOEXEC.BAT before the WIN /3 line.)

When preparing to create a PIF, leave the CONFIG.SYS unchanged. One reason it's worth trying to run a DOS title from Windows rather than DOS is to avoid having to modify the CONFIG.SYS—a complicated and time-consuming process at best.

8.3.5.2 Creating a Program Group and Item

Older CD-ROM titles written specifically for DOS are unlikely to include a Windows installation program. Before you run the title in Windows, be sure you can run it from the DOS prompt according to the instructions supplied by the title producer. Once the title is installed and can be run from DOS, you will create a Windows icon and a PIF for the title.

If the title's installation program has a Windows option, it may automatically create the icon and PIF for you. You may skip the following instructions. If later you find that the CD-ROM title fails to run properly, you can adjust the PIF settings according to the instructions below.

You are now ready to create the CD-ROM's **Program-Manager program group** and **program item**.

1. From the **Program Manager**'s **File** menu select **New**. Click on **Program Group**, then click **OK**.
2. In the **Description** field, type the label you wish to appear under the group icon in the **Program Manager** (for example, "DOS CD-ROMs").
3. Leave the next line blank.
4. Click **OK**.
   Now, create the program item and icon.
1. When the **program group** window opens, from the **File** menu select **New**.
2. Select **program item**.
3. As before, in the **Description** field, type the label you wish to appear in the item window, such as the name of the specific CD-ROM title.
4. In the **Command Line** field, type the exact path name and file name of the batch file or program you wish to run from within Windows. Include the extension. For example, if the CD-ROM is started from a batch file, type its name and .BAT. If the batch file were named DISCS.BAT,

that is what you should enter in the **Command Line** field. If the CD-ROM is started from an .EXE or .COM file, include .EXE or .COM with the name.

5. The **Working Directory** field is very important. You must type the complete path name of the directory in which the CD-ROM program looks for files and other executable programs. This is usually the directory in which the start-up batch file or program resides. If you receive a "File Not Found" error later when running the title, the source of the problem could be here.

6. Now click **OK**.

7. Try to run the CD-ROM title by clicking on the icon. It may work to your satisfaction. However, the odds are that you will receive the message "Insufficient memory" or a similar message and be returned to Windows. If so, you must create a PIF, to ensure there is enough memory available.

8.3.5.3 Creating a PIF for a DOS CD-ROM Title

A PIF is a "Program Information File" that contains information about a specific DOS program, such as a DOS CD-ROM title. Windows uses information in the file to run batch files or DOS programs. To create a PIF for a CD-ROM title:

1. Locate the **PIF Editor** in the **Main** program group. To start, click on the **PIF Editor** icon. A blank PIF worksheet will display.

2. In order not to overwrite an existing PIF, first select **File** and **Save As**. In the **file name** field, type the name of the program or batch file you will be running from Windows, ending in .PIF, however, rather than .EXE or .BAT. For example, type DISCS.PIF instead of DISCS.BAT.

You are now ready to select the PIF settings for your title. These settings primarily allow you to specify memory management options, so Windows can properly allocate memory for the CD-ROM title. As a general rule, Windows should allocate as much memory to the title as possible—in fact, the title should be allowed to dominate the computer so long as it is running.

If you already have a PIF (such as one supplied with another title), you may be able to reuse that. Select **File**, open the existing PIF, and then select the file and **Save As** with a new, appropriate (see above) name. If the CD-ROM doesn't work properly when run from the Windows **Program Manager**, you should then modify the PIF.

PIF Editor Basic Settings. The first screen in the PIF worksheet presents the basic options. To select an option, click on the radio button next to it, or click to place an X in a box. In addition to filling in the name of the PIF as you did above:

1. Fill in the **Window Title** field with the label that appears under the icon in the **Program Manager**.

2. Skip **Optional Parameters** and **Start Up Directory**. The working directory you specified in the **Program Manager**'s **program item** always overrides whatever you may enter here as the **Startup Directory**. Therefore, it may prevent some confusion if you simply skip the **Start Up Directory field**. The **Optional Parameters** field is for listing any switches or parameters that may be allowed or required by the title's command line (that is, characters or letters typed after the program name at the DOS prompt)—you are unlikely to need it. For example, if a title provides a command line switch to turn off sound, such as /N, you could enter /N here. Each time you run the title, sound would be turned off.

3. Click the **Video Memory** radio button labeled **High Graphics**.

4. Next select **Memory Requirements** settings. These vary little from title to title and PC to PC. Check the CD-ROM title's packaging or installation instruction manual for the memory settings you need. The documentation will state the total RAM needed in megabytes. In addition, the CD-ROM documentation will state an amount of conventional memory needed in kilobytes. This number will probably be between 480 and 640 k (that's the most conventional memory any PC has). For example, the instructions could state that you must have at least 580 k "free" or "conventional" memory. Some documentation may also refer to EMS or XMS memory. There may or may not be any EMS in the workstation, but if it has more than 1 Mb RAM, it definitely has XMS. (See below if your title requires expanded memory [EMS].)

5. The first line in the **Memory Requirements** section refers to conventional memory in kilobytes. Next to **KB Required** type the number from the title's manual for free or conventional memory, for example, 580. Note that this is a lower limit.

6. Next to **KB Desired** type -1. This indicates that you want the CD-ROM to have access to the maximum amount of conventional memory that Windows can free up.

7. Next to **EMS Memory KB Required**, type 1000 (which stands for 1 megabyte). This tells Windows to treat the first megabyte of EMS (if you have it) as available.

8. Next to **KB Desired**, type the actual amount of RAM in the workstation. If it has 4 Mb of RAM, type 4000. If it has 8 Mb, type 8000 and so on. If the workstation has no EMS, Windows will ignore this.

9. Next to **XMS Memory KB Required**, type a number equal to 1000 less than the total amount of RAM in the workstation. For example, if it has 4 Mb RAM, type 3000.

10. Next to **KB Desired**, type the total amount of RAM as you did above for EMS. If you have 4 Mb, type 4000.

11. Once you have filled in the memory requirements, select the following settings: **Full Screen** for **Display Usage**, **Exclusive** for **Execution**, and **Close Window on Exit**.

You are now ready for the **Advanced Options** screen of the PIF.

PIF Editor Advanced Settings. Click on **Advanced**. This screen of the worksheet further ensures that no other programs will be able to compete for system resources with the CD-ROM title. The screen also provides settings to speed up the display of graphics and other operations:

1. First, make sure there is no X in the **Multitasking Options** area beside **Detect Idle Time**. If this option has been selected, deselect it.

2. In the **Memory Options** area, select all boxes so that there are four Xs—next to **EMS Memory Locked**. **XMS Memory Locked, Uses High Memory Area**, and **Lock Application Memory**.

3. In the **Display Options** area, select **High Graphics** on the **Monitor Ports** line.

4. Select **Retain Video Memory**. Leave everything else blank.

5. Now, click **OK**.

6. From the **File Menu** select Save. (You have already named the file if you followed the instructions above.)

7. Test running the CD-ROM by clicking on the **program item** icon in the **Program Manager**. If you receive the "insufficient memory" error message, return to the **Memory Requirements** section of the first screen of the PIF worksheet. Change **KB Required** to -1 (just as **KB Desired** is already -1). If that does not resolve the problem, you may be forced to install the title in DOS alone. It could be that the workstation doesn't have enough memory to run the title, in any case. You might also try to change the **Advanced** memory options in the PIF. Deselect all of them and test the results; then deselect each of the four options one at a time and test the results.

There is one other possible source of problems, the SYSTEM.INI file's **[386enh] section.** Settings in that file may override PIF settings. Unfortunately, it requires considerable technical skill to determine how to change the SYSTEM.INI settings. A list of those settings is available in Microsoft's *Windows Resources Kit.*

If your PIF worksheets look like those in Table 8.4, you ought to be able to run most CD-ROM titles that do not require advanced graphics capabilities.

8.3.6 FINE-TUNING .INI FILES

Windows 3.X relies heavily on a number of files ending in the file name extension .INI, located in the \WINDOWS directory. These include

SYSTEM.INI, WIN.INI, and often .INI files for individual programs (such as CD-ROM titles) that have been installed on the workstation at one time or another. (When you remove a program from the hard drive and delete its **program item** or **group**, the .INI files remain as they were, cluttering up the Windows directory. Finding and removing these is one purpose of un-installer program utilities.)

Adding and modifying .INI files to enable a program to operate correctly, or to optimize its performance, requires a high degree of technical skill; every program requires different lines in the .INI files. It is not a task to be assumed lightly. Unfortunately, when you call a technical support line for installation help, from time to time they may instruct you to edit an .INI file.

It is a good idea to be prepared to work with .INI files at such times. Be sure to "associate" the .INI file name extension with your favorite text editor, such as **Notepad.** Then, you can simply double-click the .INI file name in the **File Manager** to open it.

The following are the steps you need to go through to open, read, and edit an .INI file. Once the file is ready to edit, you should rely on the advice of the technician as to what changes to make.

If you are in the middle of running the installation program, you can briefly return to the **Program Manager** by pressing the Alt key and the Tab key simultaneously and then pressing Tab again and again until you see the words "Program Manager" in the window. Release both keys, to temporarily return to the **Program Manager** without exiting from other programs on the computer. If you have not associated .INI files in the workstation's system with **Notepad,** follow the steps below. If you have, simply double-click the file name in the **File Manager**; then you may skip the following instructions:

1. Double-click the **Accessories program group** icon to open the **Accessories** window.
2. Double click the **Notepad** icon. **Notepad** is a "text editor" suitable for editing .INI files. You should not use a regular word processor for this purpose.
3. From **Notepad**'s **File** menu, select **Open**.
4. Make sure the list of files that displays is in the \WINDOWS directory, and, if not, change to the \WINDOWS directory. In the **File Name** box, change *.TXT to *.INI, and click **OK**. Scroll through the list of .INI files until you find the name of the file you wish to edit, such as SYSTEM.INI.
5. Select that file: either double-click the name, or highlight the name so that it shows up in the **File Name** box; or type the file name in the **File Name** box, and then click **OK**. The .INI file will open.
6. You can edit it just as you would any file in a word processor.
7. When you are done, be sure to select the **File** menu and **Save** before

you exit from **Notepad** or the changes won't be effective. Also, you will need to completely shut down Windows and restart it in order for the changes in the INI file to take effect.

If for any reason you cannot use **Notepad** to edit the .INI file, you can use Windows **Write**, which is also found in the **Accessories** program group. You must be careful to use **Save As** rather than **Save**, however, after making changes. Be sure to **Save As** *.TXT, not as a Windows **Write** or other word-processor file. The .INI file must be in plain, unformatted, text format. Most word-processor files are not plain text; they include hidden formatting codes, which would make the .INI file unusable by Windows.

To return to the program you were running before you had to modify the .INI file, use the Alt-Tab combination again.

If your DOS CD-ROM title requires expanded memory (EMS), refer to Chapter 9 for information on properly specifying EMS in CONFIG.SYS and AUTOEXEC.BAT, using EMM386.EXE. In particular, the driver EMM386 should not exclude EMS: change the line in the CONFIG.SYS file to remove the word NOEMS. Also, examine the **[386enh] section** in the SYSTEM.INI file for a line reading:

NoEMMDriver = yes

This turns off EMS as well. Insert a semicolon (;) in front of that line to disable it.

Since few programs require EMS, you may need to use an optional start-up menu when you run this title, so that your other applications are not affected by these changes. (The SYSTEM.INI change suggested above should not affect the normal operation of Windows, however.)

8.3.7 WINDOWS 3.X TITLE SUMMARY

This section has explained how to install a Windows 3.X CD-ROM title using the vendor-supplied program. It also explained how to install a DOS CD-ROM title so that it can be run from within Windows, using a PIF. It also covered the use of **Notepad** to edit .INI files needed to run many DOS CD-ROM titles.

8.4 INSTALLATION OF WINDOWS 9X TITLES

Windows 9X is designed to simplify CD-ROM use. As a result, many Windows 9X users probably do not expect to need help installing CD-ROM titles. Any newly acquired workstation is likely to have Windows 9X already installed on it and be prepared to run CD-ROM multimedia titles.

You may need help installing Windows 9X titles, however, if you:

- Upgraded your computer to Windows 9X from Windows 3.1
- Are an experienced DOS user or user of an operating system other than Windows 9X
- Wish to install a DOS or Windows 3.1 title on a Windows 9X system

Windows 9X is designed to accommodate "legacy" CD-ROM discs in a collection, such as old DOS and Windows 3.1 titles. Unfortunately, the old installation programs for those discs did not anticipate the development of Windows 9X. They display messages and on-screen instructions suitable for DOS and Windows 3.1, not Windows 9X (for example, "Creating Program Group and icon ..."). When you install an older CD-ROM title on a Windows 9X system, you may need to refer to this section.

8.4.1 OVERVIEW OF WINDOWS 9X CD-ROMS

Microsoft Windows 9X is intended to eliminate many of the most common problems encountered by users of CD-ROM technology. Whether this admirable goal is, in fact, realized depends mainly on the developers of CD-ROM titles, not on Microsoft. Title producers have their own agenda with regard to the benefits of Windows 9X—they are interested in the added power of the operating system and the design freedom it gives them. Whether or not their CD-ROM titles are easy to install, run, optimize, and de-install is up to them more than it is up to Windows 9X. So don't be surprised if you find it difficult to install any given CD-ROM title, even ones designed for Windows 9X.

One goal of Windows 9X is to reduce the device-driver problems you encountered with other operating systems by providing universal device drivers. Windows 9X is much smarter about starting up and running the best available device drivers than were Windows 3.X or DOS. Nonetheless, hardware manufacturers are still responsible for producing Windows 9X standard device drivers, and you are responsible for obtaining upgrades as they are developed. Refer to section 7.5 for information on obtaining device drivers.

8.4.1.1 Windows 9X CD-ROM Features

The definitions below cover some aspects of Windows 9X that differ substantially from DOS and Windows 3.X:

CDFS.EXE. CDFS.EXE replaces MSCDEX.EXE (the Windows 3.X and DOS CD-ROM device driver explained earlier). It runs in 32-bit protected mode, as opposed to 16-bit unprotected mode, which simply means that it is less prone to errors, less likely to hang up your system, and more powerful. Unlike MSCDEX.EXE, it does not take up space in conventional memory (so you need not use MemMaker to adjust conventional memory for it to function properly).

VCACHE.EXE. Instead of SMARTDRV.EXE, Windows 9X uses a disk-caching program called VCACHE.EXE, which works with CD-ROM drives as well as hard drives. This means you will need fewer third-party utilities to optimize a workstation's CD-ROM drive. The configuration still includes SMARTDRV.EXE, however, to aid in running Windows 3.X CD-ROM titles and other programs.

Miniport. Windows 9X includes a SCSI port driver, called "miniport," to simplify the installation of new SCSI devices, such as an external CD-ROM drive.

AutoSetup. CD-ROM title developers can take advantage of the **Auto-Setup** feature to make it easier for you to install their programs. To install a CD-ROM title, if the title producer has designed the installation program properly, all you need to do is use an applet called **Add/Remove Programs**.

AutoRun. Sometimes called "spin and grin" or "AutoPlay," **AutoRun** automatically starts up some CD-ROM titles as soon as you insert the disc into the drive and close the door. This is a wonderful feature especially for children's titles. When you insert a data disc into the drive, Windows 9X searches for a file called AUTORUN.INF in the CD-ROM's root directory. If there is no such file on the disc, then you must run the CD-ROM title from a shortcut (explained below).

Plug and Play ("PnP"). This term refers to Windows 9X's ability to detect the presence of various hardware components in a workstation. It makes it easier for you to upgrade the workstation, requiring you to make fewer adjustments to the system software when you install new hardware. The Windows **Control Panel (System Properties)** dialog box shows the hardware devices in a workstation and many of the port addresses as well, if the hardware is properly installed and PnP compliant.

Small "Footprint." Very little software is actually copied to the workstation's hard drive when you install a Windows 9X CD-ROM title. Instead, Windows 9X reads data directly from the CD-ROM disc more efficiently than did Windows 3.X or DOS. This means that when installing a title you will not need to decide whether to use hard-drive space in order to optimize performance of the title, as you did with DOS and Windows 3.X.

Windows 9X Device Drivers. Windows 9X also provides a wide range of device drivers for multimedia devices. These are found in the **Multimedia Properties** sheet. Among the device drivers are the **CD Audio Device, MIDI Sequencer Device, Motion Video Device, Pioneer LaserDisc, VISCA VCR Device,** and **Wave Audio Device.**

Windows 9X also includes Video for Windows for video compression and decompression support. Windows 3.X users had to install this separately each time they installed a new CD-ROM title that required it.

8.4.2 SEVERAL WAYS TO INSTALL AND RUN CD-ROM TITLES

You can run CD-ROM titles under Windows 9X in six modes: (1) Windows 9X programs in Windows 9X, (2) Windows 3.X programs in a Windows 9X window, (3) DOS programs in a Windows 9X window, (4) DOS programs in Windows 9X Full Screen Mode, (5) DOS programs in a Windows 9X DOS window, or "DOS Mode," and (6) as DOS programs under DOS. Each of these modes is explained below.

If you have Windows 9X titles or Windows 3.X titles, you should run them in Windows 9X mode. It is only older DOS CD-ROM titles that require one of the other modes. Installing some Windows 3.X titles may also produce some surprising error messages.

Before you install a CD-ROM title under Windows 9X, verify that disk-caching is properly set up on the workstation. To do this:

1. Double-click the **System** icon in the **Control Panel** window.
2. Then select the **Performance** tab.
3. Click the **Advanced** settings' **File System** button.
4. Select the **Hard Drive** tab, and then move the "Read-ahead optimization" slide to any position you wish. The higher the number, the larger the disk cache will be.
5. Select the **CD-ROM** tab, and set "Optimize access pattern for" to the speed of your CD-ROM drive.
6. Click **Apply**, then **OK**, and then **Close**.
7. When prompted to restart the computer, click **Yes** and allow Windows 9X to restart.

8.4.2.1 Vendor-Supplied Installation Programs

In Windows 9X, the vendor-supplied installation programs work one of two ways: they either use "AutoRun" to automatically start up the title as soon as it is properly inserted into the CD-ROM drive, or they allow you to use the **Add/Remove Program** applet in the **Control Panel**.

In either case, if there is an INSTALL.EXE or SETUP.EXE program on the disc, you may use the Windows 9X **Control Panel** applet called **Add/ Remove Programs** for installation. The applet automatically searches the A drive, the B drive, and the CD-ROM drive for any programs named SETUP.EXE or INSTALL.EXE and then runs them. You just click the **Install** button. What happens next depends upon the design of the installation program. Windows 9X also aids in the de-installation process—if the application is a true Windows 9X application, the application's name appears in the **Add/Remove Programs' Uninstall** window.

Windows 9X installation programs do not need to modify a workstation's CONFIG.SYS, AUTOEXEC.BAT, SYSTEM.INI, or other files. This makes it much more convenient, since you no longer have to keep track of changes made by intrusive vendor-supplied installation programs (as you did for Windows 3.X). In addition, most Windows 9X device drivers are only loaded into memory temporarily by the CD-ROM title programs when you are using the title, not each time you start up the PC. This makes it easier to play many different titles on the same workstation.

The only problem is that you must rely on the vendor to write a polite, user-friendly installation program. There is no guarantee that the program will not modify important system files or otherwise make it difficult for you to de-install the title when done. Most vendor installation programs should also leave a shortcut on the desktop so that you can start the CD-ROM title easily. If there is no disc in the CD-ROM drive when you click the shortcut, you ought to receive a warning message.

Creating a Shortcut. If a title's installation program fails to create a short-cut automatically, you may do so yourself. One way is as follows:

1. Locate and launch the **Windows Explorer** window.
2. Double-click the plus sign beside the hard-drive icon.
3. Highlight the name of the program that runs the CD-ROM title, on the righthand side of the screen.
4. Select the **File** menu from the **Windows Explorer** window's menu bar at the top of the screen.
5. Select **Create Shortcut**. If you would also like the shortcut to appear somewhere else on the **desktop** or on a menu, click on the **shortcut** with the right mouse button and drag it to a new location.

8.4.2.2 Running Windows 3.X
CD-ROMs under Windows 9X

CD-ROMs designed to run under Windows 3.X should run well under Windows 9X.

You can install Windows 3.X CD-ROMs from the **Add/Remove Programs** applet, as explained above. Try that first: Windows 9X may even be able to create a shortcut for you automatically.

Or you can run the installation program from the **Start** button. To install a Windows 3.1 program from the **Start** button, do as follows:

1. Insert the CD-ROM disc in the drive, label side up.
2. Click the **Start** button.
3. Select **Run**.
4. Click **Browse**, and locate the installation program on the CD-ROM disc (similar to the way you would have if you were still in Windows 3.1).
5. When the installation program name (such as SETUP.EXE) is listed in the **File** name box, press **Enter** or click **Open**.
6. The same name should now appear in the **Open** box on the **Run** window. Click **OK**.

7. The installation program will begin—follow the instructions that display, just as if you were using Windows 3.1.

Windows 9X normally handles the installation well. In many cases it will even use the vendor-supplied Windows 3.X icon to create a shortcut and place the **shortcut** in a folder on the **Programs** menu (rather than in a **program group**). If no shortcut is created, refer to the instructions above on how to create a **shortcut** for the CD-ROM title.

The installation program for a Windows 3.X disc may also be a little confusing, since the screen prompts and instructions may refer to elements in Windows 3.X that no longer exist in Windows 9X, such as **program groups** and **items**. Miscellaneous error messages may display during the process as well. Such error messages, which are generated by the installation program, need not mean anything. Write them down so that you can refer to them later if you have problems running the CD-ROM title, but otherwise don't be too concerned about them.

Windows automatically sets up the **Properties** to run a title in a standard Windows 9X window. Some older programs may display all the features of a Windows 9X window, while others may only display one or two features—the **Close** box on the menu bar, for example. As a result, Windows 3.1 titles seem to be a type of hybrid application, but you should still be able to use Alt-Tab to change from one active application to another. These application programs draw some of their on-screen elements directly from the Windows environment rather than from within their own program code. Such elements include title bars, menu bars, and some other aspects of window design. So, don't be surprised if a CD-ROM title's on-screen interface looks a little different under Windows 9X than under Windows 3.X.

8.4.2.3 Running DOS Titles under Windows 9X

As a general rule, first try to install a DOS CD-ROM title as if it were a Windows 3.X title (see above; use the **Start** button and **Run** window). Let Windows 9X establish what seems to be the best set of **Properties** and the mode for the title. If that fails to produce acceptable results for you, next modify the **Properties** sheets for the title. Change from full-screen mode to DOS mode as a third option. Install the title under DOS alone only as a last resort. The instructions below follow this general methodology.

System Resource Report. Print a "System Resource Report" before you begin. This report shows the details of a workstation's hardware and configuration. This information will assist you both as you respond to the DOS installation program's prompts, and also if you need to adjust the **Properties** after installation. To print the report:

1. Click **Start**.
2. Select **Settings**.

3. Select **Control Panel**.
4. Double-click the **System** icon.
5. Select the **Device Manager** tab.
6. Click **Print**.
7. Select **All devices and system summary**.
8. Click **OK**.

Note: Keep a current copy of this report handy when you buy new CD-ROM titles or install new hardware.

8.4.2.4 Full-Screen Mode

Windows 9X **Properties** sheets are similar to PIFs in Windows 3.X. They provide settings to control each program running on your system. If installing a DOS CD-ROM title using the standard properties (as described above for Windows 3.X titles) does not produce adequate results, you will need to modify the **Properties** sheets to optimize full-screen mode for the title.

To access the **Properties** sheets once the DOS title has been installed and a shortcut has been created:

1. In the **Windows Explorer** window, click the right mouse button on the **shortcut**.
2. Select **Properties**.

To optimize full-screen mode for a CD-ROM title:

1. Select the **Screen** tab. If any settings are displayed, this means that Windows automatically set the program to run in full-screen mode.
2. You may try changing the type of window: your options are a normal full-screen, or a Windows 9X window that is either minimized or maximized. A normal window prevents you from using Alt-Tab to alternate between active programs and windows. A maximized or minimized window may allow you to use Alt-Tab.
3. Select the **Memory** tab. If the program is in full-screen mode, you will be allowed to modify the way memory is managed by Windows 9X when running the title. (Refer to Chapter 10 on installing DOS titles under Windows 3.X for an explanation of the purpose of the various memory settings.) The principal difference between DOS and Windows 9X memory usage is that you may assign the maximum amount of "conventional" memory to your CD-ROM title on this screen, without being concerned that your computer's configuration may not allow it. For example, if you had difficulty freeing up 570 k of conventional memory to install a title under DOS, you may enter 570 in the **Conventional** memory box on this screen. If the CD-ROM title also requires extra RAM, for example 4 Mb or 8 Mb, then be sure to check the box next to **Uses HMA**. Other settings should be set to **Auto** unless you have previously tested this and found it not to work.

4. Select the **Program** tab.

5. Click **Advanced**. While using full-screen mode, you may wish to experiment with the box next to **Suggest MS-DOS mode as necessary**. Try either adding or deleting the check mark: this toggles a setting allowing Windows 9X to determine whether or not to switch out of full-screen mode and into DOS mode. You will know that the title is running in DOS mode if the computer restarts when you double-click the **shortcut**.

6. Finally, select the **Misc**(ellaneous) tab. If the title is set up for full-screen mode, then you can also change the following **Properties** to optimize performance:

   • Deactivate the **Allow screen saver** option under **Foreground**
   • Activate the **Always suspend** option under **Background**
   • Slide the **Idle sensitivity** bar to **Low**

Now, try to run the CD-ROM title. If you find that the sound or the video clips are rough, modify the **Properties**, especially the **Memory** tab settings.

8.4.2.5 Disabling Disk-Caching

If a DOS installation program or the CD-ROM's documentation indicates that disk-caching should be disabled, or that the CD-ROM title includes its own disk-caching software, you may need to turn off disk-caching on your Windows 9X system temporarily, while running the title. To do this:

1. Double-click the **System** icon in the **Control Panel** window.

2. Then select the **Performance** tab.

3. Click the **Advanced** settings **File System** button.

4. On the **Hard Drive** tab, slide the **Read-ahead optimization** button to **None**.

5. On the CD-ROM tab, set **Optimize access pattern for None**.

6. Click **Apply**, then **OK**, and then **Close**.

7. When prompted to restart the computer, click **Yes** and allow Windows 9X to restart.

8.4.2.6 Running DOS CD-ROM Titles in MS-DOS Mode

Some DOS CD-ROM titles simply will not run under Windows 3.X and may not run in full-screen mode under Windows 9X. They may, however, run in a DOS window using DOS mode. This means that Windows 9X must temporarily shut down and restart using different device drivers and configuration files before running the program—it is a little like running the program from the DOS prompt. One advantage to using DOS mode over booting up from an older version of DOS is the speed with which you can restart Windows 9X when you are ready to do so.

To change a shortcut so that the CD-ROM title runs in DOS mode, you must modify the **Properties** sheets:

1. Select the title's **shortcut**, and click once with the right mouse button to display the menu.
2. Select **Properties**.
3. Select the **Program** tab and **Advanced Properties**.
4. Assuming that you have tested the title in full-screen mode, next disable the settings found under the **Screen** and **Memory** tabs, by selecting **MS-DOS mode** on this **Properties** sheet.
5. By checking the box before **Warn before entering MS-DOS mode**, you will always receive a dialog box message after clicking on the title's **shortcut**. This gives you a chance to save files before the system shuts down other programs that may be running.
6. It is also recommended that you first try **Use current MS-DOS configuration** by checking that box, before you try the second option (explained below). This setting causes the system to restart with the CONFIG.SYS and AUTOEXEC.BAT files established when Windows 9X was installed. These startup files are less likely to cause problems running the DOS title than did the older DOS startup files. Of course, if the title still does not run properly, you can always change this setting.
7. Finally, be sure to click **OK** to save all the changes to the **Properties** sheets.

When you double-click the CD-ROM title's **shortcut**, Windows 9X will warn you to shut down any other programs that are running. Then the workstation will restart using the current version of CONFIG.SYS and AUTOEXEC.BAT. Next, the DOS CD-ROM title will play. When you exit from the title, Windows 9X will restart.

If the standard settings in DOS mode do not prove to be satisfactory, you can modify the **Properties** for the **shortcut** to create a CONFIG.SYS and AUTOEXEC.BAT specifically to run the CD-ROM title. Follow the steps above to access the **Programs Advanced** settings sheet. Select **Specify a new MS-DOS configuration**. Now, write your new CONFIG.SYS and AUTOEXEC.-BAT commands in the boxes below. You may also copy the lines from old versions of the files, or from the current startup files, and then paste them into these boxes from the **Clipboard**. For example, start the **Notepad** accessory (or another editor); open an old file; select and copy the lines; then return to the **Properties** sheet and paste the lines. When Windows 9X reboots the workstation using these new startup files, it gives the DOS title complete access to the workstation's hardware; no other programs will be using system resources; all other applications are shut down.

Warning: Do not leave a blank line at the end of either file, in particular the AUTOEXEC.BAT, or else, when Windows 9X restarts, you may find yourself paused at the DOS prompt. If so, just type the usual DOS command to start your program.

This technique also allows you to use third-party memory manager programs by running them from the new start-up files, so that you can try to free up the precise amount of memory you want.

8.4.2.7 Circumventing Windows 9X to Run a Title

As a last resort, if a DOS CD-ROM title simply refuses to run in any Windows 9X mode, you can start up the workstation from DOS (Windows 9X DOS, version 7.0) or even an old DOS version. Although you may not simply shut down Windows 9X and return to DOS as you did with Windows 3.X, there are three ways to do this: (1) restart the computer from a separate boot disk in the A drive, (2) press F8 while booting from the hard drive to start Windows 9X DOS, or (3) press F4 while booting from the hard drive to start the old version of DOS.

Boot Disk. The only way to completely circumvent Windows 9X is using a separate boot (or start-up) disk (see section 9.3.7 for information on how to do this).

It's impractical, even if it is technically possible, to reboot a public CD-ROM workstation using only DOS and not Windows 9X. In most instances this would mean giving considerable control of the workstation to users, which could result in serious damage to the software running on the workstation. If you need to reboot a Windows 9X workstation with a version of DOS, refer to Chapter 11, section 11.3.3 for instructions.

8.4.3 Windows 9X Summary

Windows 9X gives you more options for running CD-ROMs than any other operating system. It allows you to use your existing CD-ROM library so that you need not invest in a whole new set of discs along with a whole new operating system. Unfortunately, you are provided with very little documentation about running older CD-ROMs. The best advice is to install as many older CD-ROM titles as you can using the standard Windows 9X features, since the operating system is powerful and will eliminate many problems you once may have encountered. Still, keep this guide handy. With a little time and patience you can install even DOS-based CD-ROM titles.

8.5 INSTALLATION OF MACINTOSH TITLES

The following information focuses on installing CD-ROM titles on most Macintosh workstations. While the process is fairly simple and straight-forward, a few tips may be helpful for people who have older Macintoshes, older CD-ROM drives, or older discs. Also, understanding SCSI connections is very important in the Macintosh environment. Older models of Macs are likely to require an external CD-ROM drive using a SCSI connection. Therefore, this section provides details on SCSI setups that are not covered in the earlier topics (see section 7.4.6.3).

8.5.1 OVERVIEW OF MAC ISSUES AND FEATURES

If you have a Mac with an internal CD-ROM drive, the operating-system software installed on the computer includes everything you need to make a CD-ROM drive fully functional. You will need to be concerned about the compatibility of CD-ROM titles with the workstation only if you upgrade to a new version of the system software. You may not even need to read the remainder of this section. Instead, if you encounter problems during installation of a title, refer to Chapter 12.

Even if you have a Mac with an external CD-ROM drive, you are unlikely to encounter problems when installing a new CD-ROM title. Problems tend to occur because of incompatibilities only if you are running System 6 and wish to use a new CD-ROM disc, such as a disc that requires a new version of *QuickTime* or the latest version of 32-bit *QuickDraw*.

If you have problems or need to install new device drivers or system files in order to run a new CD-ROM disc, refer to Chapter 7.

Macintosh SCSI connections also involve a few more issues than do most other SCSI devices. So, if you have an external CD-ROM drive, the following information relates to your system. The remainder of this section also covers details on how to install new system files, how to run a vendor-supplied "Installer" program, how to plan for deinstalling a title, information on specific CD-ROM device drivers required for System 6 and System 7, and some tips for overcoming the occasional installation problem.

8.5.2 CONNECTING AN EXTERNAL CD-ROM DRIVE TO A MAC WITH A SCSI CONNECTOR

All external CD-ROM drives connect to the SCSI adapter connector on the back of the Mac (see Chapter 7, section 7.4.6.3). On most Macs, the SCSI connector is marked with the SCSI symbol and looks similar to a female, 25-pin connector. The other end of the SCSI cable is a long, flat, typical SCSI adapter. This cable is called a "system" SCSI cable and is used only to connect the first SCSI device in a chain to the computer. A few models of Macs, such as Powerbooks, may require a different-looking cable that attaches to a small square connector on the computer's back, called an "HDI-30 SCSI cable." There is also a third type of SCSI cable, called a "peripheral" cable, which is used to connect two external SCSI devices in a chain. Do not try to use any other types of cables—you can damage both the computer and the peripheral device itself.

In most cases, you also need a SCSI terminator, which you place on either the top or bottom SCSI connector on the CD-ROM drive. It doesn't matter which one you terminate. All Apple Computer–manufactured external CD-ROM drives require a terminator; a few third-party-manufactured drives are terminated internally at the factory.

Remember that each device in a SCSI chain must be identified by a different number. All Macintosh internal hard drives are set to ID 0. The computer itself is considered to be ID 7. That leaves ID numbers 1 to 6 for external devices.

If you need to know the ID number for an internally set device:

1. Start up the Mac with the CD-ROM drive also powered on.
2. Highlight the drive icon on the **desktop**.
3. Pull down the **File** menu.
4. Select **Get Info**. The SCSI ID of the device is displayed in the **Get Info** window.

If the Mac doesn't have an internal hard drive (like many older Mac Plus, Mac II, and even some Powerbook models), then there is no internal device with a SCSI terminator. This can complicate the installation of more than one external SCSI device, such as a hard drive plus a CD-ROM drive. Both of these devices need to be terminated. Remember that both the first and last SCSI devices in a chain must be terminated.

You also need a power cable and external power source for the drive. Do not attempt to rely upon the power from the computer to power on an external device; this can result in damage to the computer.

Remember, when starting up the Mac workstation, always turn on all external SCSI devices before you turn on the computer. Also, the last device in the chain must be turned on, even if you do not plan to use it.

Before installing the CD-ROM device drivers on the Mac's hard drive, first turn on the external CD-ROM drive and restart the Mac. If you attempt to start the Mac with the drive not powered on, you may not be able to boot up from the hard drive: you may receive an error message in the form of an X-ed out disk icon, or you may see nothing but a blank screen.

8.5.3 INSTALLING CD-ROM
SOFTWARE AND DEVICE DRIVERS

Whether you are running System 6 or System 7, installation of the CD-ROM drive software and device drivers that come packaged with the drive is similar. You will be supplied with one or two installation disks. Insert the first disk in one of the Mac's disk drives, open the folder, and double click on the

Installer program icon or similarly named icon. Make sure that you follow the on-screen instructions to install the software in the correct **System Folder**, if you have more than one disk drive or more than one **Startup** disk. For example, the main Installer screen should display a picture of the icon for the hard drive that is the **Startup** drive on the workstation. Use the **Switch Disk** button if the wrong drive is displayed to switch to the **Startup** hard drive where the proper **System Folder** is found.

The installation program will verify that you have a compatible version of the system software for the software being installed. You will probably need a compatible version of *QuickTime* and *QuickDraw* in your **System Folder** or **Extensions Folder** as well.

8.5.3.1 *System 6 Files and Device Drivers*

Older CD-ROM titles (such as those developed for System 6) require only the following files to be included in the **System Folder**:
- Apple CD-ROM file extension
- Apple Photo CD
- High Sierra File Access
- ISO 9660 File Access
- CD Remote—a CD audio player program, under the Apple menu

If you encounter any problems installing or running a CD-ROM title, always check first to make sure that these files are present.

Note, however, that System 6 is incapable of handling many types of multimedia CD-ROM titles.

In addition, some CD-ROM drive extensions, once installed, place an **AppleCD Speed Switch** in the **Control Panel**. Older CD-ROM discs, which are optimized for single-speed drives, may not run well on a double-speed or faster drive. If this is the case, use the **Speed Switch** to slow down the faster drive.

8.5.3.2 *System 7 Files and Device Drivers*

When you install a new Mac CD-ROM drive or system software, the installation program automatically installs several extension files in the **System Extensions** folder (some titles may only verify their existence). If the files already exist or older versions exist on the workstation, you will have the option not to install the newer versions, although there is no reason to avoid it. System 7 installations include the following files:
- Apple CD-ROM system extension
- Apple Photo CD Access
- Audio CD Access
- High Sierra File Access

- ISO 9660 File Access
- Apple CD Audio Player—a CD audio player program, under the Apple menu
- *QuickTime* and 32-bit *QuickDraw* (for video)
- *QuickTime* Musical Instruments
- Foreign File Access
- *QuickTime* Power Plug (for Power Macs)

If you encounter any problems installing or running a CD-ROM title, always check first to make sure that these files are present.

8.5.4 VENDOR-SUPPLIED INSTALLATION PROGRAMS

In most cases Macintosh CD-ROM titles do not have to be "installed" on the hard drive of a Mac. Instead, they run entirely off the CD-ROM disc. In a few cases, a CD-ROM title may need to install some of its files on the hard drive. When this is true, the vendor generally supplies an installation or setup program. This program often verifies that all the necessary system files and extensions are present in the **System Folder** or **Extensions Folder**. Then the Installer decompresses the CD-ROM title's files and copies them to the hard drive.

Be sure to read "Read Me" files that come with the title disc or to print them out. This may be the only documentation you have of the changes the installation program made to your system. It may also list last minute changes that require you to modify or update files in the **System Folder**.

8.5.5 PLANNING FOR DEINSTALLING

It can be difficult to completely deinstall a CD-ROM title from a hard drive, since many different files may have been placed on the hard drive. You probably have no record of all of the changes made by the CD-ROM's installation program. If so, you may wish to invest in a de-installation or un-installer program for the Mac. These are widely available as freeware, shareware, and low-cost third-party utilities.

Alternatively, print out a copy of the **System Folder** and the **Extensions Folder** (System 7), from **Date View**, so that the date and size of all the files are listed, before installing the CD-ROM title. Then, after installing the software, print another copy and compare the two. Any files with different dates have been updated by the CD-ROM Installer. You can either restore the original version of the files or continue to operate with the replacements. You can also remove any unwanted or unnecessary files after you have finished with the CD-ROM disc.

8.5.6 Increasing Macintosh Memory

Regardless of which system version is running on the workstation, a common problem when attempting to run a CD-ROM title for the first time is insufficient memory.

To determine the amount of memory required by a CD-ROM title, look at the **Get Info** window.
1. Highlight the icon representing the application program on the CD-ROM disc.
2. Pull down the **File** menu and select **Get Info**. The window will display a **Suggested Memory Size**, which is the CD-ROM title producer's recommended amount of memory.

To increase the actual amount of memory available to the CD-ROM title, type a larger number in the **Available Memory Size** (System 6) or **Minimum size** (System 7) box.

To determine the amount of memory currently being used, under the **Apple** menu in System 6 check **About the Finder** and in System 7 check **About This Macintosh**. Restart the computer for the new memory setting to take effect.

This technique actually requires that "contiguous" memory be retained for the CD-ROM title. Contiguous memory means one complete chunk of memory rather than bits and pieces that add up to the total. Because the order in which you start up applications (in System 6 when running **MultiFinder** or in System 7) on the Mac determines which applications really gain access to complete chunks of memory, you may still have problems if you try to run the CD-ROM title after you have run (or while you are running) other programs. If so, simply restart the workstation, but this time immediately start up the CD-ROM title first.

Another cause of insufficient memory is the amount of memory a Mac uses for the system file, any **INITs** that are installed as soon as you turn on the Mac, the number of **Control Panel** devices **(Cdevs)**, and the number of **Desk Accessories**. Short of removing all these programs from your computer, to free memory the first step is to prevent the **INITs** from being "loaded" into memory when you start the Mac. To do this, simply press the Shift key while starting the system. You will notice that none of the **INITs'** icons display on the screen.

If this doesn't solve the problem, try temporarily hiding other system programs from the system upon start-up. For example, create a folder called "Temp" inside the **System Folder**; move all unnecessary files into that Temp folder where the system will ignore them upon start-up.

Alternatives include using a separate start-up diskette (as described in Chapter 12) with a system file in which fewer fonts and other system programs have been installed. (Keep in mind that workstation users ought not to be given access to the start-up disk.) Look at the size of the system file on the Mac's hard drive. The system file can consume the same amount of memory as it does hard-drive space (before you even have a chance to run your CD-ROM title); so any amount you can reduce the size of the system file on the hard drive is memory you may free up as well.

8.5.7 MACINTOSH SUMMARY

The process of installing a CD-ROM title on a Macintosh often consists of one step: clicking on an icon. On the other hand, depending on whether the workstation runs System 6 or System 7 and the title requirements, you can encounter a number of frustrating problems. The key to success is making sure that the **System Folder** is properly set up and at system start-up that you control the amount of memory available to run the title.

8.6 CHAPTER SUMMARY

This chapter discussed techniques for installing CD-ROM titles on stand-alone workstations. Most installation problems stem from memory allocation or device-driver files. Help with such problems an be found in Chapters 9 through 12.

9. How to Solve Many Common DOS Problems

9.1 INTRODUCTION TO THIS CHAPTER

9.1.1 WHEN TO CONSULT THIS CHAPTER

This chapter provides specific steps to take when you encounter problems with DOS CD-ROM titles or with CD-ROM workstations running DOS, including CD-ROM titles running in a DOS window in the Windows 3.X or Windows 9X environments.

It isn't always self-evident when a CD-ROM title is running in a DOS window, especially if the workstation is controlled by a menuing system (see "Glossary"). So, if you have either Windows 3.X or 9X, be sure to find out before problems occur whether any CD-ROM titles have been installed to run in a DOS window (this information should be included in the workstation's records or log book, as discussed in Chapter 5). If you encounter a problem with a Windows 3.X or Windows 9X CD-ROM title, refer first to Chapters 10 and 11, respectively, and then refer to this chapter for supplemental or background information.

9.1.2 WHEN TO SEEK OUTSIDE HELP

This chapter is written under the assumption that you are either interested in resolving DOS CD-ROM problems yourself or that you have no other choice. If you work within a system of libraries or schools where technical support staff is available, you should consult them first before attempting to resolve DOS problems on your own. Not only will it save you time, but it will also prevent you from inadvertently introducing new problems into the CD-ROM network or workstation.

9.1.3 HOW MUCH MUST YOU KNOW ABOUT DOS?

DOS isn't a particularly "user-friendly" operating system. It has survived for years on many computers, however, because once it is set up and running, it is highly reliable. If your library or school owns older DOS computers, it is probably because they have functioned error-free for many years—at least until you tried to install a new software application or CD-ROM title on them. When something new is introduced into a DOS operating system environment, a lot can go wrong, and it can take a solid understanding of DOS to fix it.

The scope of this chapter, regrettably, is insufficient to provide you with all the background information you may need to troubleshoot a DOS computer system and CD-ROM title. This chapter is written to assist you if you understand the following aspects of DOS:

- Disk and file structure (the root directory, directories, subdirectories, and file-naming conventions)
- The concept of a path and "path name" or complete "file name"
- Commands for traversing the file structure, locating specific files, and copying, "renaming," saving, and deleting files
- Commands for opening and editing text files
- Commands for preparing, maintaining, and formatting disks
- The concept and basic functions of a batch file (such as AUTO-EXEC.BAT) and a configuration file (such as CONFIG.SYS), especially how to write and modify them

If you are unfamiliar with any of the above, please obtain and study a basic DOS text or manual, or seek the assistance of a colleague who already has this background.

The instructions in this chapter depend on your prior knowledge of the above concepts. Even if you are familiar with DOS, the tips and techniques in this chapter will be easier to understand and more powerful if you supplement the discussion with additional reading. For example, if a tip refers to a computer concept, such as "memory," supplement the instructions with reading more about DOS memory. If a tip refers to a specific DOS command, such as "CHKDSK," refer to a DOS manual for details on its purpose, how to use the command, and its options. Refer to "Recommended Reading" in the back of this book for a list of good DOS guides.

9.2 *Improving DOS Performance*

The DOS operating system includes several programs that can be used to improve the overall performance of a workstation, the performance of the CD-ROM drive, or the performance of individual titles. Refer to a *Microsoft MS-DOS User's Guide* for detailed instructions on how to use these programs. Most of these programs are loaded into memory during system start-up if they are included in the AUTOEXEC.BAT or CONFIG.SYS files.

FASTOPEN.EXE is provided in most versions of DOS to enhance the performance of older PCs, such as 286 systems. It helps DOS locate and open files on a hard drive (but not a CD-ROM drive). If a CD-ROM title accesses the hard drive frequently, this program may be useful. Do not, however, use FASTOPEN on a 386 or later computer. Other programs are provided for that purpose.

Older systems with extended memory can also use HIMEM.SYS effectively to free up conventional memory. Many older PCs have only conven-tional and expanded memory, not extended memory, so it's useless to run HI-MEM. SYS on such a computer.

If you are running a version of DOS prior to 5.0, you probably don't have the SMARTDRV.EXE program. In its place, use RAMDRIVE.SYS to improve the speed of your system's access to data. RAMDRIVE.SYS is a disk-caching system, which temporarily stores data in RAM rather than on a disk drive. If SMARTDRV.EXE is available, use it instead of RAMDRIVE.SYS.

If you have older programs running under a newer version of DOS on a 386 or later processor, you may need to "emulate" expanded memory. Note: this is expanded, not extended, memory. If an older DOS program requires expanded memory (such as some CD-ROM titles), use the program called EMM386.EXE.

9.3 DOS TROUBLESHOOTING

Follow the troubleshooting procedures below to pinpoint errors.

Errors often halt the operation of either the CD-ROM title, the operating system, or the entire computer. Some errors even result in permanent changes to files on a workstation's hard drive, and, as a result, introduce flaws into the system, which may cause additional problems later. You need to be able to restart the computer properly and restore it to the state in which it operated before you attempted to install the CD-ROM title or before the error occurred. You can accomplish this either by identifying all the problems with the computer and then fixing them, or by "restoring the system" to its previous "configuration" (see the "Glossary" and Chapter 5 for explanations of these terms).

If you choose to restore the system, you will regain full use of the workstation, but you won't have solved the CD-ROM title's problems. The error will probably continue to occur each time a patron or student tries to run the CD-ROM title. While identifying and fixing all the problems is more difficult, in the process of correcting the problems you will probably uncover the reasons the error occurred and will be able to resolve them so that the CD-ROM title can be used as it was intended. Only you can say whether the effort required to fix the problem is worthwhile.

The following topics cover ways to restart a DOS workstation after an error occurs, techniques for identifying DOS problems, ways to modify a DOS configuration, and how to exit from Windows 3.X to DOS. The techniques listed here won't solve the CD-ROM title problem, but they will help you isolate the problem.

9.3.1 THE POWER SWITCH

The power switch on a PC should only be used as a last resort. It is highly recommended that you secure the power supply so that unauthorized users can't turn the computer off and on.

After powering off the computer, always wait a few seconds before turning the computer on again to allow the power supply's fan to stop completely. Restarting the computer before the fan has stopped can cause damage to the power supply. In addition, because the power switch itself is one of the few moving parts on a computer, overuse causes it to wear out. Always use a power strip with a separate on-off switch to control the PC's power in order to protect the switch. Furthermore, if you power off the computer while a DOS CD-ROM title is running, you may damage any files stored on the hard drive that are open or currently in use.

9.3.2 THE RESET BUTTON

In an emergency when you must restart the computer, use the reset button (which is usually located on the front of the system unit) instead of the power switch or power strip. The reset button not only restarts DOS, it completely resets memory without straining the power switch or fan. Of course, you may still damage files or lose data by pressing the reset button while files are open and in use. Like the power switch, the reset button should be secured out of the reach of patrons and students (this is one of the reasons that it is recommended in Chapter 1 that the complete system unit be locked inside a protective cabinet).

After restarting the computer with the reset button, you should test to make sure everything is running properly. Check the menuing system or "shell" system. Check each of the CD-ROM titles installed on the computer. Try to complete the task that caused the error message: for example, try to reinstall or run the CD-ROM title.

9.3.3 "SOFT BOOT"

Less drastic than using the reset button is pressing the Ctrl-Alt-Del key combination. This is sometimes called a "soft boot" (meaning a software start), a "warm boot," or even a "hot reboot." This key combination restarts DOS, but it may not correct memory errors or reset all memory addresses (that is, temporary data storage areas in memory). In other words, there are instances in which a "soft boot" does not completely restart or properly restart the system.

If a soft boot fails to restore full functionality to the system, next try the reset button to completely restart the system. Then, as a last resort, completely shut down all equipment (including peripherals), wait a few seconds, and then power on the system normally.

9.3.4 BIOS SELF-TEST OR POST (POWER ON SYSTEM TEST)

Most newer models of computers run a self-test upon start-up, before DOS starts. The ROM chips in the computer, sometimes called the ROM BIOS (see "Glossary"), run through a quick check of the hardware components that make up the system.

If you need to know how the computer is configured (for example, what types of drives are installed or what the monitor's resolution is), you can pause the self-test process immediately after starting the computer and examine a list of system equipment. To do this, after you start the computer, notice that messages display indicating that you may press a key, such as the Shift key or Alt-Shift key combination, in order to view and change the system setup.

If you have tried both the reset button and a "soft boot" to no avail, completely power off and then restart the computer. Viewing the system setup screens may help you debug problems, such as problems with CD-ROM drives. Having this information available when speaking to a technician may be helpful. It is not recommended that you make any changes to these settings. Follow the instructions that appear on the screen to pause the system and examine its setup. Make note of the information for use by a technician, then continue with the start-up process. Do not turn the computer off before you have completed the start-up process and the DOS prompt is displayed.

9.3.5 "MANUAL" START-UP—F5

While attempting to determine the source of an error message, you may begin to suspect that the problem is in one of the two important DOS start-up files (AUTOEXEC.BAT and CONFIG.SYS). For example, the installation program for the CD-ROM title may have modified one of these files, or an existing line in one of these files may conflict with the requirements of a certain CD-ROM title.

With DOS 6.0 and later, you can start-up the computer by overriding the instructions contained in these two files, using the F5 key. The *Microsoft MS-DOS User's Guide* calls this "manual" start-up. Instead of starting up using the instructions in the AUTOEXEC.BAT and CONFIG.SYS files, the system is forced to start up using only the few instructions available to it in the COM-MAND.COM file.

Pressing F5 allows you to bypass both the CONFIG.SYS and AUTO-EXEC.BAT files with a bare minimum of conventional memory. You can then try running a specific program to determine if it is causing problems, with assurance that nothing else is running in memory at the same time. You can also test each of the lines in the AUTOEXEC.BAT file to see whether it contains statements that are causing problems.

First, be sure the root directory of the hard drive contains the file called COMMAND.COM, since F5 works only in such a case. The workstation must have this file stored somewhere on its hard drive in order to function, but sometimes the file is located in a subdirectory, rather than the root directory. If this is the case, copy the file to the root directory before using the "manual" start-up technique. (Refer to a *Microsoft MS-DOS User's Guide* for details, the scope of which is beyond this guide). As soon as you start the computer and see the message "Starting MS-DOS," immediately press the F5 key (or press and hold the Shift key). When the DOS prompt appears, try running the program you suspect is causing the problem, to observe what happens.

Instead of testing a program, you can use F5 to start up DOS while testing each line in the AUTOEXEC.BAT file to determine if one of the lines is the source of the problem. After pressing F5 and waiting for the DOS prompt, type each command from the AUTOEXEC.BAT file, one at a time, on the command line at the DOS prompt. Carefully read the messages that display as you press the Enter key following each command. Any error messages that display should be written down, as they are clear indications of problems with a workstation's start-up files.

9.3.6 "INTERACTIVE" START-UP—F8

Also beginning with DOS 6.0, you can start up DOS and the workstation while viewing each line in both the CONFIG.SYS file and the AUTOEXEC.BAT file, as they are executed. You are prompted to decide to skip or execute each line in the files, one at a time. As with "manual" F5 start-up (section 9.3.5 above), turn on the computer and wait until you see the message "Starting MS-DOS." Then press the F8 key. The system will prompt you ("Yes or No?") to allow it to continue to start up using the commands in the start-up files. Read the messages that display after each command line in the files displays. Write down all error codes or messages, especially ones that indicate that files or devices are missing. This is a common source of problems: such files may either truly be missing or their complete "path names" may be incorrectly listed in the AUTOEXEC.BAT or CONFIG.SYS files. If a CD-ROM title's installation program alters either the CONFIG.SYS or

AUTOEXEC.BAT file, it may erroneously insert a "file name" without including its complete path. As a result, DOS won't be able to find that file when it's starting up and will display an error message to the effect that the file is missing or not found. Always verify the complete path names of files used by the CONFIG.SYS and AUTOEXEC.BAT file. Insert the correct, complete path in front of the file name to correct the problem. (Refer to a *Microsoft MS-DOS User's Guide* for more information on the proper syntax for a complete path and file name.)

9.3.7 A DEBUGGING TOOL—A BOOTABLE DISKETTE

It is also a good idea to have a bootable diskette handy in the event of system problems. If you install a CD-ROM title by making changes to the AUTOEXEC.BAT or CONFIG.SYS files or other system files on the hard drive, in emergencies you may need to start up from the A drive, using a simple, but workable, configuration.

9.3.7.1 Creating a Bootable DOS Diskette

In order to install a CD-ROM title, you may need to create a diskette with everything the workstation needs to start up using the A drive, instead of the C drive (which is probably the source of the title's problems):

1. Obtain a blank diskette.
2. Turn on the workstation. (If Windows automatically starts up at the same time, wait until all activity appears to have stopped. When the top of the screen is labeled **Program Manager** select **File** and then select **Exit Windows**. Follow the on-screen instructions to leave Windows and return to DOS.)
3. The DOS prompt will display; it should look something like this: C:> You are now ready to create the boot disk. Insert the blank disk into the A drive. At the DOS prompt, type the following, and then press Enter:

   C:>   **FORMAT A:/S**
4. Follow the on-screen instructions. When asked to enter a volume label, just press the Enter key (you don't need a volume label). Next, "change" to the A drive. Type the letter A and a colon (A:), and then press Enter.
5. The DOS prompt should look something like this: A:> Now, copy the CONFIG.SYS and AUTOEXEC.BAT files from the C drive to the disk in the A drive. Type the following, and then press Enter:

   A:>   **COPY C:\CONFIG.SYS**
6. When done, type the following and then press Enter:

   A:>   **COPY C:\AUTOEXEC.BAT**

You now have a bootable disk (system start-up disk) with three files on it: COMMAND.COM, AUTOEXEC.BAT, and CONFIG.SYS. (The COMMAND.COM file was placed there automatically when you formatted the disk with the /S switch.)

9.3.8 MODIFYING A WORK- STATION'S DOS CONFIGURATION

In order to install a CD-ROM title or to improve its performance, you may need to make changes to the configuration files on the hard drive of a CD-ROM workstation, specifically to AUTOEXEC.BAT and CONFIG.SYS files. Here's how to do that.

First you must know how to open and edit these files. They are located in the root directory of the start-up hard drive. You must have a text-editor application available to make changes in them. In this book it is assumed that you use the DOS EDIT program for this purpose. The EDIT program is included as part of DOS and is available in the DOS directory. To open a file with EDIT, at the DOS prompt type:

C:>   EDIT AUTOEXEC.BAT

If you follow the EDIT command with a file name, EDIT will start up and open the file. You will then be able to make plain text changes to the file (changes that do not include hidden formatting codes).

If your intention is to delete some commands from an AUTOEXEC.BAT or CONFIG.SYS file, it may be advisable instead simply to temporarily deactivate the commands. To do this, simply add the REM command word to the beginning of a line containing a command or statement you wish to deactivate. (This is sometimes also called "remarking" the line.)

9.3.9 REINSTALLING A CD-ROM TITLE

If you're unable to determine the source of the problem or to resolve the problem quickly, in some cases you can correct the problem by reinstalling the CD-ROM title. For example, if you have successfully used the CD-ROM title for some time before the error occurred, reinstallation may be the best solution. First, run the CD-ROM installation program as if you had never installed the title. This may overwrite any old, damaged, or incorrectly configured files on the hard drive. It may also allow you to correct any installation errors that occurred during the first installation but which weren't initially apparent. If reinstallation doesn't solve the problem, restore the AUTOEXEC.BAT and CONFIG.SYS files from backups made prior to the first installation of the title (to eliminate any subsequent errors in those files), and then try reinstalling the CD-ROM title.

9.3.10 EXITING TO DOS FROM WINDOWS 3.X

In a few instances, you may need to restart ("reboot") the Windows work-station in DOS:

- To open a DOS window, double-click on the **MS-DOS Prompt** icon in the **Main** program group.
- To exit from Windows to DOS, pull down the **Program Manager**'s **File** menu and then select **Exit Windows**.
- To restart the computer in DOS (instead of Windows), use a "boot disk," such as is described in section 9.3.7.

Refer to a *Microsoft Windows User's Guide* for specific instructions. If you have never used a DOS window or have never used DOS commands after exiting from Windows, please seek the assistance of a colleague who has more experience with DOS.

9.4 THE MOST COMMON DOS PROBLEMS

The following lists the most common error messages, with explanations and troubleshooting tips. They are listed in the order in which they are most likely to occur. Remember, you need a good working knowledge of DOS to benefit from most of the information presented below. Keep your DOS manual at hand for quick reference.

9.4.1 PROBLEMS UPON SYSTEM START-UP

9.4.1.1 "Incorrect DOS Version"

(Note: A Windows system may also encounter this problem upon start-up.)

This error is most often caused by a conflict between a DOS version and an old version of the file named MSCDEX.EXE. This conflict is most likely to show up if you upgrade from DOS 4.01 to a later version of DOS, or if you install an older model CD-ROM drive in a newer system. If you have DOS 5.0 or later, you must also have MSCDEX.EXE version 2.2 or later. In addition, if you have a version of MSCDEX.EXE earlier than 2.21 (including version 2.2), your AUTOEXEC.BAT file must contain the SETVER statement.

To determine the version number of MSCDEX.EXE (after it has been loaded and is running in memory), you may run the device-driver program at the DOS prompt to view the version number that displays. Type the following at the DOS prompt, and press the Enter key:

C:>   MSCDEX

Assuming that the MSCDEX.EXE driver is not loaded in memory or that typing MSCDEX as shown above doesn't work, check the documentation that came with the CD-ROM drive and software, especially the README file, for the version number of the MSCDEX.EXE file.

If you have determined that the version of MSCDEX.EXE is too early (before 2.2) or you cannot tell what the version number is, check the CONFIG.SYS file for a line containing SETVER or SETVER.EXE. If there is none, you must add the line to the CONFIG.SYS file in order for MSCDEX.EXE to be usable on the workstation. Add the following line to the CONFIG.SYS file:

DEVICEHIGH=C:\DOS\SETVER.EXE

Warning: This line must appear in the CONFIG.SYS file before the line on which the CD-ROM drive's device driver is loaded. To identify the line containing the device driver, look for an abbreviation of the manufacturer's name; for example, a SoundBlaster Pro device driver is often named SBPCD.SYS and is found on a line that includes the text string /D:MSCD001.

9.4.1.2 *"Invalid Device" or "Device Not Loaded"*

This error means that either MSCDEX or the CD-ROM drive's device driver was not loaded into memory when the computer started up. The cause may be (1) that the versions are incompatible with the workstation's DOS version (see above) or (2) there is an error in the CONFIG.SYS or AUTOEXEC.BAT file. If it is the second problem, review both files carefully, checking the syntax of the CD-ROM device statements and the accuracy of all paths and file names.

You do not need to run the VER command to add the MSCDEX.EXE to the version table, however, since it is contained in it by default (see the *Microsoft MS-DOS User's Guide* for details on the version table).

If DOS refuses to recognize and load MSCDEX.EXE after these changes, it's possible that MSCDEX.EXE may be loaded into high memory rather than in conventional memory. Remove LH or LOADHIGH and DEVICEHIGH from the associated device driver statements in the CONFIG.SYS and AUTOEXEC.BAT files.

9.4.1.3 *"Not Enough Drive Letters"* *or "Invalid Drive Specification"*

Error messages concerning the letters used to designate drives on the workstation have several possible causes and corrections. To analyze this problem, you need to understand a few facts about how these letters are assigned to physical disk drives on the system, including the CD-ROM drive.

All versions of DOS (and Windows 3.X) label the drives on the workstation automatically each time you start up the system. The "floppy" diskette drives are assigned the letters A and B (if there are two diskette drives). The first hard drive is assigned the letter C and the second hard drive D. After that, all drives and partitions are labeled in sequence with the remaining letters of the alphabet. If your AUTOEXEC.BAT or CONFIG.SYS files contain commands that create RAM drives, then those "virtual" drives receive the next set of letters after the hard drives.

The only exceptions to the rule that DOS assigns drive letters automatically are device drivers. A device driver, such as the CD-ROM device driver, may specify any letter it wishes to have assigned to its physical device. So, for example, a device driver could specify the letter Z to designate the CD-ROM drive on the workstation, even when it has only one diskette drive (A) and one hard drive (C). Or, a device driver could specify that the CD-ROM drive should be designated drive D: even though the workstation has two internal hard drives.

If you receive an error message related to the letter used to designate the CD-ROM drive, it is probably caused by a recent change in the drive designations on the system (such as changes made when adding a new CD-ROM drive) or by an installation program that may have automatically changed the drive designation improperly. For example, if the error message suggests that you have run out of letters of the alphabet, check to see whether a device driver that uses Z has been loaded into memory during the start-up procedure (in either CONFIG.SYS or AUTOEXEC.BAT where you find a line containing the characters =Z). If the statement that loads your CD-ROM's device driver occurs in the start-up files after the statement using Z, then you need to change the letter Z to something more reasonable, like E, F, or even L.

If the error message suggests that the drive letter is invalid, then check to see whether there is a conflict between drives. Two drives cannot use the same letter. The letters A, B, and C are reserved for diskette drives and hard drives.

On the other hand, if a device driver specifies that a certain letter must be assigned to a certain nonexistent physical device, you may also receive an error message. This could mean that a physical device has become disconnected from the workstation (check all the cable connections), or the power may not be turned on to an external device, such as an external CD-ROM drive.

9.4.1.4 "IRQ" or "Interrupt" or "Address Conflicts" (at system start-up)

See Chapter 8, section 8.2.2.3 for an explanation of this error and possible solutions.

9.4.2 PROBLEMS DURING TITLE
INSTALLATION OR WHEN FIRST RUNNING A TITLE

9.4.2.1 "CDR-101" Errors

This error message is similar to "wrong disc." It means that the device is not being recognized by DOS. It may indicate a compatibility problem with hardware components or discs. Try a different disc. If the problem persists, shut down all software programs and then, methodically, restart each program one at a time until you locate the cause of the error.

9.4.2.2 "CDR-103" Errors

This error indicates that the CD-ROM drive cannot recognize the format of the disc in the drive. Verify that the disc is of the correct type for the workstation.

9.4.2.3 "Insufficient Memory"

Reread Chapter 8: you may need to modify your CONFIG.SYS and AUTOEXEC.BAT files. This error is the most common of all CD-ROM error messages. Many sections of this book are intended to help you avoid this problem. The error can be caused by insufficient total RAM, insufficient conventional memory, insufficient hard disk space, or temporary memory-use errors.

If the problem is truly that more RAM is needed, you may be able to use a software RAM enhancer or you may simply need to have more RAM installed in the workstation.

If the problem is that more free conventional memory is needed, refer to the DOS CD-ROM title installation section 8.2 for information on how to free up enough conventional memory to run a title.

If the title uses hard disk space as a temporary memory "swap file," then the problem could be that the hard disk is filled.

If you are using a RAM disk-caching program (for example, if RAM-DRIVE.SYS is included in the CONFIG.SYS file) you may need to disable it—RAM drives use precious memory and are intended to improve the performance of hard disk drives, not CD-ROM drives. A CD-ROM workstation probably should not be configured to use RAMDRIVE.SYS. Below are a few other things to try in the meantime.

Solution 1: Turn off the sound or use "simpler" sounds: many CD-ROM titles can be installed without the more sophisticated sounds, which require that a device driver be loaded into memory for the workstation's sound card. This takes up memory that you may need just to run the basic elements of the program. "Simpler sounds" include CD audio and the workstation's speaker sounds, such as those using SPEAKER.SYS.

Solution 2: Select a lower graphics resolution. If during the installation process, you are prompted to run the title either in VGA or SVGA, select VGA. In SVGA resolution, the title may need additional device drivers loaded into memory, or the CD-ROM software may use more memory in SVGA mode.

Solution 3: Reboot with a new configuration (different CONFIG.SYS and AUTOEXEC.BAT files on a bootable diskette; see Chapter 9 for instructions).

Solution 4: If you encounter this error message after a patron or student has been using the CD-ROM title for some period of time during a single session at the workstation, simply restarting the workstation may clear memory and reset the configuration. If that doesn't work, try reinstalling the title with a new, more efficient configuration. Refer to Chapter 8 in this guide for installation tips.

9.4.2.4 *"SHARE Violation" or "Not a Network Drive"*

You may encounter error messages related to the DOS SHARE program or errors that refer to network drives, even when the CD-ROM drive isn't on a network. Such error messages can result from the fact that DOS treats a CD-ROM drive as if it were a network drive, in other words, a read-only drive. Such an error message usually means that there is something wrong with the program you are running. The program is either attempting to open a file on the CD-ROM disc that is already open and in use on the workstation, or the program is attempting to write to the CD-ROM drive. Try to close down all the programs running on the workstation, including TSRs (see "Glossary"), and restart the workstation properly. The problem should go away.

If the problem recurs, check your CONFIG.SYS and AUTOEXEC.BAT files. They may have identified a hard drive as a CD-ROM drive (see "Invalid Drive Specification", section 9.4.1.2 above), or the files may include some other syntax error involving drive names.

9.4.2.5 *"Insufficient Disk Space"*

The solution to this error is either to remove unwanted files from the hard drive or to improve the performance of the drive. (Keep in mind, however, that most public CD-ROM workstations aren't set up for individual users to save files, including bookmarks. The real problem may be that the CD-ROM title running on the workstation when the problem occurred wasn't designed to be used in a library or school.)

Solution 1—CHKDSK /F: Check to see how much free space is available on the hard disk. Two commands can be used to tell you quickly how much disk space is available on the hard drive: DIR and CHKDSK. Refer to section 7.3.2.2 for additional details.

While DIR can tell you how much space is available on the hard disk and how much is being used, CHKDSK is more sophisticated and can help free up unused (or poorly used) space, as follows:

1. Type the command CHKDSK /F, and then press the Enter key. The screen will display a number of statistics followed by:

    X lost allocation units found in X chains.

    Convert lost chains to files (Y/N)?

2. Respond Y, for Yes.

3. Then type the command below exactly as shown, and press the Enter key:

    C:>   DIR FILE*.*

A list of one or more files named FILE0000.CHK, FILE0001.CHK, etc., will display. These files contain unnecessary data. Simply delete the files. This will often free up a substantial amount of hard-drive space.

Solution 2—Defragmenting the Disk: A seriously fragmented disk requires defragmentation. (See "Glossary" for a definition of fragmentation.)

When a hard disk is first used, the computer can store large chunks of information on it in contiguous sections. Over time, however, the available space becomes more and more filled. When some of the information is deleted, gaps are left where additional information is then stored. A single file may actually be stored in widely scattered blocks all over a hard-disk drive. This is called fragmentation.

As the disk becomes fragmented, it becomes more difficult for the computer to locate information on the drive. If you have DOS 5.0 or earlier, in order to defragment (reorganize) a hard drive you must use a third-party utility or completely reformat the hard drive. Popular programs to accomplish this include *Norton Utilities* and *Disk Optimizer.* (The time and expense of this is probably not worth it—instead upgrade to DOS 6.22 so that you can easily defragment the drive.)

If you have DOS 6.0 or later, you can also check to see if the physical surface of the hard drive is beginning to degrade and find unused parts of the disk with the SCANDISK command. Refer to the *Microsoft MS-DOS User's Guide* for instructions on using SCANDISK.

If you have DOS 6.1 or later, you can defragment your hard disk with the DEFRAG command. While this can be a long process, it may be necessary in order to install the CD-ROM title.

If you have access to none of these programs, but you must defragment a hard disk, you must completely reformat the hard drive. This process will wipe out everything currently on the hard disk. It is unwise to reformat a hard drive yourself unless you have done it before and have a very good means of backing up the data on it before you do it. You must back up everything on the hard drive, either onto diskettes or some other medium, such as an external hard drive, a removable cartridge system, or a tape backup system. Even if technical support staff at your library or school is available to reformat the drive for you, the technician may make you responsible for the backup and then for restoring the files to the hard drive after it has been reformatted.

Since a DOS upgrade to 6.2 will cost only about $50, this is a better option. Alternatively, buy a utility program, many of which can be purchased for less than $50.

Windows 3.X Users: You must exit from Windows in order to use CHKDSK, SCANDISK, or DEFRAG. They will not run even in a DOS window under Windows.

Windows 9X Users: Before reformatting a hard disk or running a defragmentation program, be certain you check on the program's compatibility with Windows 9X and any older versions of Windows and DOS still installed on the drive. This is especially important if you use long file names.

9.4.3 PERFORMANCE PROBLEMS

9.4.3.1 "The wrong disc is in the CD-ROM drive ..."

This message generally means that the system requires you to insert a different CD-ROM disc into a specific CD-ROM drive. If you believe that you have inserted "the right" disc, there is a compatibility problem. The CD-ROM title, the DOS version, and the CD-ROM drive must all use compatible versions of the CD-ROM device drivers. The message may also mean that the drive itself may not meet MPC standards (see "Glossary"), perhaps because it is a very old CD-ROM drive. Try to use a different disc in the drive, just to be sure that the "right" disc has data on it in a readable format. If that does not work, verify that the drive is functioning (see Chapter 8 for details).

9.4.3.2 System Freezes or Hangs

This problem can be caused by almost anything ranging from a power surge on the electric circuit to a program bug in the CD-ROM title. There is nothing to do but restart the system. Watch to see if the system hangs repeatedly at the same place in the CD-ROM title each time you use it, or whether it occurs only sporadically and unpredictably. If it always happens at the same place, report the error to the CD-ROM producer—it is a bug for which they may have a patch (that is, a correction you can copy onto the workstation's hard drive).

The problem may be caused by conflicts between the CD-ROM drive and sound-card device drivers. Try running one device driver at a time in conventional memory, to see which one is causing the problem. To do this, use the interactive start-up techniques (F8) described above in section 9.3.6, skipping all but one device driver each time you start up. Then, run the CD-ROM title to see what happens. For example, complete the interactive start-up process (section 9.3.6) once, skipping the line in which the sound-card device driver is loaded, and then run the title.

Some system hang-ups are caused by conflicting programs, such as DBL-SPACE.BIN: Some DOS CD-ROM titles conflict with the DBLSPACE.BIN file used by the DOS disk compression program, called *DoubleSpace*. To work around this problem, if you are using *DoubleSpace* to compress the hard drive, try booting (starting) the computer from the "uncompressed host drive" using the interactive start-up technique (F8) described in section 9.3.6. (Refer to the *Microsoft MS-DOS User's Guide* for information on DBLSPACE.BIN.) To determine which drive is the host drive on a system running *DoubleSpace,* at the DOS prompt type either DRVSPACE /LIST (for DOS 6.22) or DBL-SPACE /LIST for earlier DOS versions.

Another source of problems can be CD-ROM device drivers that do not load into high memory under any circumstances. They must run in conventional memory. (Some versions of the CD-ROM device driver FDCD.SYS are like this.) Refer to the device driver's documentation to check. Do not use the LH, LOADHIGH, or DEVICEHIGH statements in CONFIG.SYS and AUTOEXEC.BAT with such device drivers. To see whether you have attempted to load devices into high memory when they do not belong there, try configuring the workstation with nothing loaded high: create a boot disk with a CONFIG.SYS and AUTOEXEC.BAT from which all DEVICEHIGH and LOAD-HIGH statements have been removed.

Note: MSCDEX.EXE must never be loaded high.

9.4.3.3 Poor Sound Quality

Refer to the manual that came with your sound card. Look for information on controlling popping and pausing, or look for information on buffering. Some sound cards' device drivers create temporary buffers. You can often improve the quality of the sound by changing the buffer size or by modifying one of the system start-up files (CONFIG.SYS and AUTOEXEC.BAT). This is also often listed in the sound card's manual in the index under "smoothing." A slower computer may need a larger buffer. This is usually a disk-based buffer, not a memory-based buffer, so you should not need to worry about using up scarce memory while increasing the buffer size. You may also need to include the statement BUFFERS=30 (or a larger number) in the CONFIG.SYS file, to increase the DOS memory buffer.

Remember that your speakers may also produce pops, static, and hissing. A short in a cable can also produce these noises. Even humidity can interfere with electronic and audio equipment.

Sound distortion can be caused by setting a volume control too high. Try reducing the volume, either through software or hardware volume controls.

In a few cases, if the sound card and the video card are installed in adjacent slots in the workstation, the two may interfere with each other. It is not recommended that you attempt to move adapter cards from one slot to another to correct this. Have a technician resolve the problem.

Finally, if the sound card does not support "wavetable sound," but does support MIDI, you may need to install CD-ROM titles to rely on a simplified MIDI version of some sounds. Short of upgrading the sound card, there is little else you can do. If a title's installation program gives you the option of using CD audio rather than digital wavetable sound, select CD-audio quality sounds. The title may run more slowly, or access sounds more slowly, but you will receive the full benefit of CD audio quality sound.

9.5 CHAPTER SUMMARY

This chapter recommends that you only attempt to resolve problems with DOS CD-ROM titles if you have a good understanding of DOS itself. Always allow plenty of uninterrupted time for resolving such problems, since DOS problems can be difficult to analyze, let alone resolve.

Begin the process of DOS CD-ROM problem-resolution by identifying the real source of the problem. Use the troubleshooting techniques recommended in this chapter, such as restarting the computer in one of several ways, restoring a backup copy of the system, or reinstalling the CD-ROM title that caused the problem.

Finally, review the list of error messages in this chapter to find the one most similar to the error message displayed by the CD-ROM title. Follow the instructions provided to analyze and resolve the problem.

10. How to Solve Many Common Windows 3.X Problems

10.1 INTRODUCTION TO THIS CHAPTER

10.1.1 WHEN TO CONSULT THIS CHAPTER

This chapter provides specific steps to take when you encounter problems with Windows 3.X CD-ROM titles or with CD-ROM workstations running Windows 3.X. This chapter does not include information about Windows for Workgroups or Windows NT. Since many CD-ROM networks are Windows NT–based, the information in this chapter is applicable to stand-alone workstations rather than networked workstations.

Most of this chapter explains how to respond to specific error messages. A few tips are also provided for improving the quality of performance of a CD-ROM title or a CD-ROM workstation. Since many Windows 3.X problems stem from the DOS configuration of the workstation, you may also need to refer to Chapter 9 for Windows 3.X solutions.

10.1.2 WHEN TO SEEK OUTSIDE HELP

This chapter assumes that you are responsible for maintaining a stand-alone CD-ROM workstation running Windows 3.X. Many Windows problems are easy to resolve, while others require technical skill and experience. If you work within a system of libraries or schools where technical support staff is available, the technical staff should provide you with a set of guidelines concerning when to consult with them and when to attempt to resolve problems on your own. Your technical support staff may prefer that you leave Windows 3.X problem-resolution to them.

Problems with Windows for Workgroups and Windows NT may appear to be similar to problems with Windows 3.X. Since these are networked systems, however, it is recommended that you consult with your technical or network system administrator before attempting to troubleshoot those systems.

10.1.3 WHAT MUST YOU KNOW ABOUT WINDOWS 3.X?

While Windows 3.X is powerful and simplifies numerous complex operations, problems are bound to occur, especially with CD-ROMs. Windows provides only a few tools designed specifically for multimedia CD-ROMs, and the *Microsoft Windows User's Guide* lacks many critical technical details for CD-ROM title users. In addition, Windows 3.X relies heavily on DOS, and problems can occur at the DOS level, which affect the operation of Windows.

In order to benefit from the information in this chapter, you should be familiar with the following Windows 3.X concepts:

- Using the Program Manager, File Manager, and program groups
- Using **Notepad** to examine, create, and edit a text file, such as CONFIG.SYS, AUTOEXEC.BAT, PROGMAN.INI, and SYSTEM.INI
- All of the DOS concepts listed in Chapter 9, section 9.1.3, especially the use of file names, path names, and directories (including the root directory and subdirectories)
- Understand the DOS PROMPT command: the examples in this chapter often indicate that commands and statements must be typed at the DOS prompt. The DOS prompt is usually shown as C:>. In some cases, a slightly different DOS prompt is shown to indicate that the command must be typed while a specific directory is the "current" directory.

If you are unfamiliar with any of the above concepts, please obtain and study a basic Windows text or manual (see "Recommended Reading"), or seek the assistance of a colleague who already has this background.

10.2 IMPROVING WINDOWS 3.X PERFORMANCE

Windows 3.X includes several means of performance tuning: these include **Windows Setup**, the **Control Panel**, and some of the DOS programs discussed in Chapter 9, section 9.2. **Windows Setup** is used to install Windows 3.X and to deinstall or reinstall system applications and device drivers. If you encounter problems with the performance of a Windows 3.X workstation, running **Windows Setup** may help: some of the tips in this chapter make use of **Windows Setup**. The **Control Panel** provides several applets for performance-tuning and problem-resolution (also as discussed in this chapter).

Some DOS programs must also be used correctly in the AUTOEXEC.BAT and CONFIG.SYS files on a Windows 3.X workstation. If you are running a version of Windows 3.X, you are likely to have a 386 or faster computer. In such a case, you don't need either EMM386.EXE (except to run a few older DOS programs) or FASTOPEN.EXE (see section 9.2). With a 386 system you only need to run EMM386.EXE when using a DOS window to run a DOS-based CD-ROM title that specifically requires expanded memory. However, you should use HIMEM.SYS and SMARTDRV.EXE on a 386-based Windows 3.X workstation. HIMEM.SYS frees conventional memory, into which many CD-ROM title programs are loaded, and SMARTDRV.EXE is a disk-caching program that can speed up access to the hard drive. When you douse EMM386.EXE, add the NOEMS switch, to exploit this program's memory-management features that are not related to expanded memory.

For versions of Windows 3.X running under a DOS version earlier than 6.22, SMARTDRV.EXE works only to improve the performance of nonnetworked hard drives, and not on CD-ROM drives at all. However, beginning with DOS 6.22, SMARTDRV.EXE can also be used to set up a CD-ROM disc cache to improve the speed with which a Windows system accesses data on the CD-ROM disc. See *Microsoft MS-DOS User's Guide* (version 6.22) or *Microsoft Windows User's Guide* for information on how to do this. In the AUTOEXEC.BAT file, on the line for SMARTDRV.EXE (which must follow the MSCDEX.EXE statement), specify the CD-ROM drive as the disk that needs to be cached by including the drive letter followed by a plus sign, for example:

SMARTDRV D+

A note about SMARTDRV.EXE: You may find both SMARTDRV.EXE and SMARTDRV.SYS in your DOS or Windows directories. The .EXE program is the one you will most likely use—add it to the AUTOEXEC.BAT file. The .SYS program is loaded into memory via the CONFIG.SYS file and is used only rarely by systems with a disk-drive controller that requires a technique called "double-buffering." Do not use SMARTDRV.SYS unless the documentation for a CD-ROM or other disk drive requires it.

10.3 WINDOWS 3.X TROUBLESHOOTING

Windows 3.X runs "on top of" DOS. Consequently, troubleshooting Windows 3.X involves DOS as well as Windows. Often, Windows 3.X may seem to freeze, while DOS continues to function properly. This does not necessarily indicate that the problem is entirely within Windows and not in DOS. This section explains how to troubleshoot Windows 3.X and how to determine whether DOS may also be at fault.

An error message (as discussed in this chapter) is a warning about a specific problem that is issued by Windows. (If you receive a DOS error message, refer to Chapter 9. If you receive an error message from the CD-ROM title, refer to its user manual.) The standard Windows 3.X error message is presented in a small warning box with an exclamation point inside a yellow circle. In addition to information about the error, the warning box generally instructs the user to press the Enter key or to click on an OK button in order to remove the warning from the screen. (See Chapter 6 for more information about interpreting error messages.)

Some Windows 3.X error messages prompt the user to select either an "Ignore" or "Exit" button. Always select the "Ignore" option first: when the error isn't significant, selecting the "Ignore" button should cause the CD-ROM title to resume its normal operation. If selecting the "Ignore" button produces no results, it means the error is significant: in such a case there is no choice other than to select "Exit," which usually terminates the operation of the CD-ROM title. Refer to sections 9.3 and 10.3.3 for information on how best to restart the CD-ROM title following a significant error.

This section provides the following information:

- How to safely shut down Windows 3.X when an error occurs
- How to determine which one of several programs running in memory may have caused a problem
- Several different ways to restart Windows 3.X to help pinpoint the source of a problem
- How to determine whether the problem may be caused by something external to Windows, such as DOS or the CD-ROM hardware

Follow the troubleshooting procedures below to pinpoint errors. Please also read section 9.3 for information on the correct way to power off and restart a PC, whether it's running Windows 3.X or another operating system. When resolving Windows 3.X problems, you may also need to refer to the information in Chapter 9 for additional advice. Section 9.3 explains how to determine whether an error was caused by DOS; how to shut down the computer and restart it safely; and how to test the commands stored on the hard drive in the AUTOEXEC.BAT and CONFIG.SYS files using "manual" and "interactive" start-up techniques. DOS problems must be solved before any Windows problems can be solved.

10.3.1 HOW TO RUN DOS ON A WINDOWS 3.X WORKSTATION

To resolve problems in DOS, if you are using Windows 3.X, you must either open a DOS window or exit to DOS from Windows. In a few instances, you may need to restart ("reboot") the computer in DOS:

- To open a DOS window, double-click on the **MS-DOS Prompt** icon in the **Main** program group.
- To exit from Windows to DOS, pull down the **Program Manager**'s **File** menu and then select **Exit Windows**.
- To restart the computer in DOS (instead of Windows), use a "boot disk," as described in section 9.3.7.

Refer to a *Microsoft Windows User's Guide* for specific instructions. If you have never used a DOS window or have never used DOS commands after exiting from Windows, please seek the assistance of a colleague who has more experience with DOS.

10.3.2 EXITING TO DOS BEFORE TURNING OFF THE SYSTEM

Always exit from Windows 3.X before turning off the computer. If you turn off the computer while Windows 3.X is running you risk an improper shutdown. You may damage files by leaving them open or in use.

To shut down properly:

1. Exit from all programs in Windows, such as any CD-ROM titles.
2. Return to the **Program Manager** window.
3. Select the **File** menu.
4. Select **Exit Windows**.
5. When prompted, click **OK**. If you have failed to close all application windows, before exiting from Windows you will be instructed to return and shut down all programs that are running.

Only when the DOS prompt displays is it safe to turn off the power to the computer.

10.3.3 WINDOWS SHUT DOWN OPTIONS

If you encounter a problem while in Windows 3.X, you may have to press the Ctrl-Alt-Del key combination ("soft boot") if no other options are available.

After you press Ctrl-Alt-Del, if the current application (such as a CD-ROM title) is still active (even if it seems to be doing nothing), Windows 3.X will prompt you to press the space bar to return to the program and wait for the problem to resolve itself. You may, however, press Ctrl-Alt-Del a second time to restart the computer, just as if you were at the DOS prompt. Windows 3.X will warn you that you could lose data in this process. You're most likely to lose data stored temporarily in the **clipboard** or data which was being modified when the error occurred. You are not likely to lose data that you previously saved to disk.

If the CD-ROM title has "hung" (that is, stopped responding to Windows 3.X), when you press Ctrl-Alt-Del Windows alerts you to the fact that the program has stopped functioning. The message also informs you that you may wish to return to the program and wait in hopes that the program may eventually respond. If you fear data may otherwise be lost, try this option. Waiting more than two or three minutes is probably useless, unless you notice that the hard drive is being accessed (you will hear the drive spinning and see the drive light flashing). Never shut down Windows 3.X or turn off the workstation while the hard drive is in use. If the drive continues to spin, it indicates a serious problem—press the Reset button on the workstation.

10.3.4 DETERMINING WHEN A PROBLEM IS A CD-ROM DRIVE PROBLEM OR DOS PROBLEM

You must decide whether the problem is a CD-ROM drive problem rather than a problem with the CD-ROM title. That means you must verify that the CD-ROM drive works properly with other CD-ROM titles in Windows 3.X. That's fairly simple: Attempt to run a different CD-ROM title in Windows 3.X. If another title works properly, then the problem is specific to the first CD-ROM title and not a problem with the drive.

If no CD-ROM titles function in Windows 3.X, you must decide whether the problem originates in Windows 3.X or in DOS. Refer to section 8.3.1.1 to verify that Windows 3.X is properly set up to recognize a CD-ROM drive. If so, then verify that the CD-ROM drive is accessible from DOS, as explained in Chapter 8, section 8.2.1. To test whether the CD-ROM drive works in DOS, first exit from Windows 3.X as explained in section 9.3.10.

If a list displays, then the CD-ROM drive is working fine in DOS. The problem must, therefore, be in Windows 3.X. If no list displays and yet you are certain there is a CD-ROM disc in the drive being tested, refer to the "DOS Troubleshooting" section 9.3.

10.3.5 EXAMINING A PIF FOR ERRORS

A CD-ROM title designed for DOS requires a properly configured PIF ("Program Information File") to run in Windows 3.X. Always verify that DOS CD-ROM titles run properly in DOS before you attempt to run them in Windows 3.X. Refer to Chapter 8, section 8.2 for information on installing DOS CD-ROM titles, and refer to section 8.3.5 for information on installing DOS CD-ROM titles to run under Windows 3.X.

Check whether PIF settings are being overridden either by: (1) the **Program Manager** program item that runs the DOS CD-ROM title or (2) the SYSTEM.INI files **[386enh] section.** See section 8.3.5.3 for details.

10.3.6 POSSIBLE PROBLEMS WITH WINDOWS 3.X SETUP

In addition to the DOS setup (especially CONFIG.SYS and AUTO-EXEC.BAT) a key consideration is the Windows 3.X setup. Some Windows 3.X settings are managed by the CONFIG.SYS and AUTOEXEC.BAT. These include (optionally) the mode in which Windows 3.X starts up, the location and size of the \TEMP directory, and the use of the SMARTDRV.EXE disk-caching program. Others, however, depend on the **Windows Setup** program and various applets in the **Control Panel**.

Many Windows 3.X settings can only be changed via the **Control Panel**. Other settings can also be changed by editing the Windows 3.X .INI files in the \WINDOWS\SYSTEM directory. Many application installer programs (including many CD-ROM title installation programs) make changes to the .INI files. The settings in files such as SYSTEM.INI, WIN.INI, and CONTROL.INI can have a significant impact on the performance of CD-ROM titles. Refer to Chapter 8, section 8.3 for details.

Read the *Microsoft Windows 3.X User's Guide* for information on the use of the **Control Panel** and **Windows Setup**. Become familiar with the DOS EDIT program so that you can make changes to CONFIG.SYS and AUTOEXEC.BAT. Learn to use **Notepad** to examine and (if necessary) edit the Windows 3.X .INI files. Many of the solutions in section 10.4 below require you to work with these files and applets.

10.3.7 ALT-TAB ("MULTI-TASKING" OR "TASK-SWITCHING")

The standard keystrokes for switching between active programs are the Alt key followed by the Tab key. Sometimes you can recover from a system hang-up or even from a General Protection Fault error (GPF code error; section 10.4.6) by switching briefly to another active program.

1. Hold down the Alt key, and then press the Tab key repeatedly to display the names of active programs.
2. If no other application than the current CD-ROM title is running, the only other program name displayed will be the Windows 3.X **Program Manager**. When you release the Alt-Tab keys, the other program whose name is displayed will become the active window. (You may notice that the hard-drive light flashes as you do so.)
3. Now, press the Alt-Tab key combination again until you return to the CD-ROM title. The problem may have cleared up. If so, it's probably wise to exit from all applications (including the CD-ROM title), exit from Windows 3.X, and restart Windows 3.X before continuing.

This task-switching function is only possible when Windows 3.X is in 386-enhanced mode. If you are unable to use the Alt-Tab keystroke combination, check the **Control Panel** to verify that you are running Windows in 386-enhanced mode and that multi-tasking is enabled. Look for the **386 Enhanced** chip icon in the **Control Panel**. Look for an X in the **Desktop**'s "Applications Fast 'Alt-Tab' Switching" box.

10.3.8 USING A SIMPLE BOOT DISKETTE

If all other techniques fail to help you diagnose the problem, create a bootable diskette for the Windows 3.X workstation, which uses the bare minimum configuration required to run Windows 3.X. Refer to Chapter 9, section 9.3.7, for details on how to create such a diskette. Exclude from all start-up files on the diskette the words LH, LOADHIGH, or DEVICEHIGH in order to troubleshoot the CD-ROM drive. Then, add one command or statement at a time to the start-up files on the diskette until the system *fails*. At that point you have identified the command or statement in the start-up file that is the source of the problem.

In addition to the start-up commands in the configuration files required by DOS, Windows 3.X needs several additional lines. The AUTOEXEC.BAT file must contain the complete path to both DOS and Windows 3.X. Include the following line in the AUTOEXEC.BAT:

SET TEMP=C:\WINDOWS\[PATH]

The CONFIG.SYS file should include the following two lines:

DEVICE=HIMEM.SYS
STACKS=9,256

10.3.9 STARTING WINDOWS 3.X

The WIN statement in the AUTOEXEC.BAT file starts up Windows 3.X. The statement may also include "switches" or "parameters" to force Windows 3.X into different modes, or ways, of operation, including standard mode and 386-enhanced mode. It may be useful to change the mode in order to improve the performance of CD-ROM titles.

Running Windows 3.X in 386-enhanced mode is likely to conflict with older CD-ROM device drivers. If you are unable to resolve a CD-ROM problem using the techniques described elsewhere in this chapter, try running Windows 3.X in standard mode and then testing the CD-ROM drive.

To run in standard mode, start Windows 3.X at the DOS prompt or in the AUTOEXEC.BAT file with WIN /S. (The statement WIN/ 3 starts Windows 3.X in 386-enhanced mode.) If you find the CD-ROM drive works only in standard mode, this means that you need to obtain an upgraded CD-ROM device driver either from Microsoft or the drive manufacturer (see Chapter 7 for details on device drivers).

Refer to a *Microsoft Windows User's Guide* for other ways to start up Windows. For example, it may also help to prevent Windows 3.X from using upper memory blocks (UMB) while running the CD-ROM title. In some cases (such as when a workstation uses EMM386.EXE or another upper-memory manager) you must control the way Windows 3.X uses upper memory. Try starting Windows 3.X with the WIN /D:X mode command, or add the following so-called "exclude statement" to the **[386enh] section** of the SYSTEM.INI file:

EmmExclude=A000-EFFF

If you aren't certain whether a device driver is conflicting with upper memory, examine a "boot log." To create a printable file that logs the Windows 3.X start-up process and flags any device drivers that couldn't be loaded into memory, start Windows 3.X with the following command switch:

WIN/B

This creates a file during Windows 3.X start-up called \WINDOWS\ BOOTLOG.TXT. Examine the contents of the file. If the BOOTLOG.TXT file lists a device driver as having not been loaded, then you must use the exclude statement in the SYSTEM.INI file, as explained above. If a device driver still cannot be loaded, even after using the exclude statement, it means that a new device driver is needed.

10.3.10 WINDOWS 3.0 PROBLEMS

Windows 3.0 is more likely than Windows 3.1 to have problems with CD-ROM drives. If you have Windows 3.0, it is strongly recommended that you upgrade to 3.1. This will cost little but provide tremendous benefits. (If the workstation has at least 8 Mb RAM and a 486 processor, consider upgrading to Windows 9X.)

10.4 THE MOST COMMON WINDOWS 3.X PROBLEMS

The following discusses some common error messages and other problems that are likely to occur with CD-ROM titles running under Windows 3.X.

10.4.1 PROBLEMS UPON SYSTEM START-UP

10.4.1.1 *"CD-ROM Drive Not Recognized"*

Examine the CD-ROM drive using the Windows **File Manager.** If the **File Manager** window does not display an icon for the workstation's CD-ROM drive next to the icon representing the hard drive, then Windows 3.X is not recognizing the presence of the CD-ROM drive in the workstation. (This assumes that the workstation in question isn't on a network, but has at least one CD-ROM drive physically installed in it.) Verify that the drive is receiving power and is properly connected to the computer: cables connecting internal CD-ROM drives may have become disconnected, or cords and cables connecting external CD-ROM drives may have come loose or be broken.

If that isn't the problem, verify that DOS recognizes the drive. Refer to section 8.2.1 above for instructions on how to do this.

If you don't receive an error message when testing the drive in DOS, then the problem is in Windows 3.X. Check to see whether the MSCDEX.EXE statement *follows* the WIN statement in AUTOEXEC.BAT. If so, this is the problem. MSCDEX.EXE must *precede* the WIN statement in the AUTOEXEC.BAT file. (Note: An easy way to examine the AUTOEXEC.BAT file while in Windows 3.X is to open the file using the **Notepad** applet in the **Accessories** group.)

10.4.1.2 "Device not Found" or "Incorrect DOS Version"

This message indicates a conflict between versions of MSCDEX.EXE and DOS, even when the workstation is running Windows 3.X. If you upgrade to a new version of DOS 6.2 or later, upgrade from Windows 3.1 to Windows for Workgroups or an OEM version of Windows 3.11, or from a computer manufacturer's special version of Windows 3.X to Windows 3.1 from Microsoft, the MSCDEX.EXE file is automatically upgraded simultaneously to version 2.3. Some CD-ROM device drivers, however, do not respond properly to MSCDEX.EXE version 2.3, preferring 2.1 or 2.2. To correct the problem: (1) contact the maker of the device driver for an update that is compatible with MSCDEX.EXE version 2.3; (2) restore version 2.2. Refer to sections 8.2.3.1 and 9.4.1.1 for information on using the line DEVICE=SETVER, in the CONFIG.SYS file in such cases.

Keep in mind that if the operating system on the workstation has been upgraded at any time, there may be multiple versions of MSCDEX.EXE on its hard drive. Be sure that the AUTOEXEC.BAT file is running the proper version: the complete path name used in the AUTOEXEC.BAT file must be correct. For example, you may have version 2.2 in the Windows 3.X directory, but the AUTOEXEC.BAT file is running version 2.1 from the root directory (C:\MSCDEX.EXE rather than C:\WINDOWS\MSCDEX.EXE).

If you are running MSCDEX.EXE 2.2 or *later*, you may also need to remove the following line from the SYSTEM.INI file in the Windows 3.X directory:

DEVICE=LANMAN10.386

If you are running MSCDEX.EXE 2.2 or *earlier*, you may need to add the above line to the SYSTEM.INI.

Note: Windows 3.0 in enhanced mode requires MSCDEX.EXE 2.0 or earlier. If the workstation has Windows 3.0, check to see whether the AUTOEXEC.BAT file contains the following line: WIN /3. If so, verify the version number of MSCDEX.EXE (see section 9.4.1 for instructions).

10.4.2 PROBLEMS DURING TITLE INSTALLATION

10.4.2.1 "IRQ" or "Interrupt" or "Address Conflict"

If you receive an error message that refers either to an I/O port address or an IRQ, first read section 9.4.1.4. That section explains the meaning of the error messages.

Windows 3.X provides easy access to some I/O port address and IRQ information in the **Control Panel** applet. For example, the **Control Panel's Ports** window lists the "Base I/O Port Addresses" and "IRQs" for up to four serial devices (such as a modem, a joystick, a special mouse, etc.). If more than one serial device driver has been set to use a single ID number, the workstation will encounter conflicts. Check to see whether the active serial ports are already using IDs that are also assigned to a newly installed device. Then change the settings for one of the devices.

To examine the **Base I/O Address** and **IRQ** for each serial COM port:

1. From the **Main** program group, select **Control Panel**.
2. From the **Control Panel**, select **Ports**.
3. From the **Ports** window, select a COM port, such as COM1. Then, click the **Setting** button.
4. From the **Settings for COM1** window, click the **Advanced** button.
5. The **Advanced Settings** for COM1 window displays the current **Base I/O port Address** and **IRQ** for the COM port. Notice that you can display a list of possible settings for each.
6. Carefully write down these numbers. Compare them with information you have about the other devices, especially those that require an IRQ.

As a general rule, some IRQs are used by standard components of a PC, and so are inappropriate to use when installing new equipment. These include 0 (the timer), 1 (keyboard), 3 and 4 (COM ports), 6 (diskette drive), 7 (LPT1, a parallel printer), 8 (clock), 13 (math coprocessor), and 14 (hard drive). IRQ 5 is often used by a sound card, although it can also serve as LPT2 when a computer has two parallel printers (a rare occurrence). IRQs 2 and 9 work in tandem and are programmable (that is, directly accessible via software programs). IRQs 10–12 and 15 are generally available for you to use.

10.4.2.2 "Insufficient Memory to Run the Application"

This is probably the most common error message encountered when running Windows 3.X CD-ROM titles. It can have several different causes.

First, the workstation may need more RAM. If so, additional RAM chips must be installed.

Second, the workstation may simply need more free conventional memory. (See section 9.4.2.3 on DOS memory for ways to free up conventional memory.) In most cases, though, Windows takes care of this automatically. If not, the AUTOEXEC.BAT or CONFIG.SYS files on the workstation may be at fault. They may not contain the best set up to run Windows.

Other common causes of an "insufficient memory" Windows 3.X error message include having insufficient hard-disk space, having insufficient "contiguous" hard-disk space, and having Windows 3.X "Virtual Memory" set too low.

Windows 3.X uses hard-drive space as temporary memory. While running some CD-ROM titles, Windows 3.X will "swap" parts of the program out of RAM and onto the hard drive so as to temporarily free up RAM for other tasks. To cure these Windows 3.X "temporary memory" problems, modify: (1) total free hard-drive space, (2) total **Permanent Virtual Memory** settings, or (3) total free, contiguous hard-drive space.

Solution 1—Total Hard-Drive Space: If the workstation's hard drive is fairly old or heavily used, it is likely that either (1) the disk is filled or (2) the disk is "fragmented" (see the "Glossary"). Examine the total amount of free or unused space available on the hard drive (refer to section 9.4.2.5). If the hard drive has little or no remaining free space, simply delete unnecessary files and temporarily remove items you can safely back up and restore later. Unnecessary files may include temporary files created by Windows 3.X, such as any files in the \TEMP directory, the WIN386.SWP file in the \WINDOWS directory, and any files that begin with the tilde (~) symbol. Use the **File Manager** to find and delete these files. Temporary files using the tilde are usually listed at the beginning of the **File Manager**'s directory listing when it is sorted by file name (not by date or size). (Refer to your *Microsoft Windows User's Guide* for help on using the **File Manager** to delete files from the hard drive.)

Solution 2—Virtual Memory: Check the amount of **Permanent Virtual Memory** set up for Windows 3.X. To do this:

1. Open the **Main** program group window.
2. Then, double-click on the **Control Panel** to open its window.
3. Double-click on the **386 Enhanced** icon (a computer chip) to open the applet.
4. Click the **Virtual Memory** button. In the box that displays, note whether the **Type** is listed as **Permanent**, and note the **Size** in kilobytes. If the **Type** is **Temporary** or **None**, you must change it to **Permanent.** If the **Size** specified exceeds the total free space on the hard drive, either decrease the **Size** setting here or increase the amount of free hard-drive space. See Solution 1 above for instructions on how to determine the amount of unused hard-drive space.

To change **Virtual Memory** from **Temporary** to **Permanent**, first follow the steps above (steps 1–4) to access the **Virtual Memory** setting, then:

1. In the **Virtual Memory** window, click the **Virtual Memory** button.
2. Then click the **Change** button.
3. In the **New Settings** box, click and hold the downward-pointing arrow to the right of the **Type** box to display a list of three options: **Temporary**, **Permanent**, and **None**.
4. Select **Permanent**.

To increase or decrease the size of **Virtual Memory**:

1. In the **New Settings** box, type a number in kilobytes. Notice that Windows 3.X displays recommendations for you based on the amount of

free hard-drive space. It also displays a **Maximum Size** based upon
the amount of contiguous (not fragmented) disk space.

2. You may accept the **Recommended Size** by typing that number, or type
a smaller amount of space in the **New Size** box. Just be sure to enter
a size that is at least equal to the minimum RAM required by your CD-
ROM title. For example, if the CD-ROM title requires 4 Mb and the
workstation has 4 Mb RAM, you must specify at least 4 Mb of **Virtual Memory** for Windows 3.X. (See Chapter 3 for instructions on how
to find out how much RAM is required by the CD-ROM title.)

Less frequently, the SMARTDRV.EXE program may be the source of
insufficient memory errors. You may need to reduce the size of the memory
cache SMARTDRV.EXE creates by changing a line in the AUTOEXEC.BAT
file. (Refer to your *Microsoft Windows User's Guide* for details.) SMART-
DRV.EXE improves the performance of disk drives on the workstation by
using memory temporarily for storage purposes. Reducing the size of the disk
cache may degrade the speed of access to disk drives, but may also free memory needed to run the CD-ROM title. If reducing the size of the disk cache
doesn't help, you might also try to use an older version of SMARTDRV.EXE,
which is smaller, such a version borrowed from an older version of DOS or
Windows 3.X. You could also remove the SMARTDRV.EXE line from the
AUTOEXEC.BAT file, or disable the line by placing a colon (:) at the beginning of the line.

Solution 3—Contiguous Hard-Drive Space: If it appears that the workstation has enough hard-drive space, but the error message persists, it may
mean that the hard disk is "fragmented," and therefore has insufficient contiguous (side-by-side) free space. If so, don't worry; the physical disk isn't broken or damaged: the data files on the disk have become scattered all over the
disk instead of stored neatly in adjoining sectors. The solution is to defragment the disk as explained in section 9.4.2.5. To determine whether disk fragmentation is the problem, follow the instructions below to attempt to modify
or increase the amount of hard-disk space allocated to **Permanent Virtual
Memory**. If you cannot do so, an error message will alert you to the fragmentation problem. If you can increase **Permanent Virtual Memory**, then the
memory problem will have been solved when you make the change, and you
need not defragment the hard drive unless you wish to do so for other reasons.

10.4.3 PROBLEMS DURING TITLE INSTALLATION OR WHEN INCREASING VIRTUAL MEMORY

10.4.3.1 *"Corrupt Swap File"*

This error message usually occurs either during the initial installation
of a CD-ROM title or when increasing the amount of virtual memory avail-

able to Windows 3.1. (See section 10.4.2.2 above for information on increasing virtual memory.)

The so-called "swap file" referred to in the message is actually two temporary files Windows creates when it is using virtual memory. These files can be damaged by other programs or by the normal process of fragmentation of the disk. When you defragment the disk, the swap-file problem will usually be corrected. (See section 9.4.2.5 for information on defragmenting a hard disk.) If not, you may manually delete these swap files; then, using the **386 Enhanced** applet, create new swap files for Windows:

1. To delete swap files, you must first locate them. They are "hidden" files. Exit from Windows 3.X to DOS (do not try to perform this step from the DOS prompt). (Refer to section 10.3 for instructions on exiting to DOS). Exit from Windows 3.X to its default current directory, the Windows 3.X directory (or change to the \WINDOWS directory), where the first of the swap files can be found.

2. Then, to reveal the first of the two hidden swap files, type the following at the DOS prompt, and press Enter:

    C:\WINDOWS>   ATTRIB -r -s -h SPART.PAR

3. Verify the presence of the file: type the following, and press Enter:

    C:\WINDOWS>   DIR SPART.PAR

4. If the file does not exist, skip to step 5. To delete the file (SPART.PAR), type:

    C:\WINDOWS>   DEL SPART.PAR

5. The second file is in the root directory of the hard drive on which Windows 3.X resides, usually C. Now, to change to the root directory of the hard drive, type:

    C:\WINDOWS>   CD C:

6. In the root directory, type:

    C:>   ATTRIB -r -s -h 386SPART.PAR

7. To verify the presence of the file, type:

    C:>   DIR 386SPART.PAR

8. If the file does not exist, skip to step 9. To delete the second file, type:

    C:>   DEL 386SPART.PAR

9. Type WIN/3 to restart Windows. Now find the **386 Enhanced** applet in the **Control Panel** and set the virtual memory (as explained above in section 10.4.2.2).

Finally, restart Windows 3.X again before running the CD-ROM title.

10.4.3.2 "The free disk space on drive C is fragmented. If you have a disk-compaction utility, you should use it to compact this drive."

This message often occurs when you are in the process of changing or setting virtual memory, as described above in section 10.4.2.2. Recognize that this message does not mean you should compress the hard drive, for example, using the *DoubleSpace* program: The message means that you must defragment the disk if you wish to make use of the amount of **Permanent Virtual Memory** you have attempted to set up.

The Windows 3.X **386 Enhanced** applet may also refuse to allow you to select **Permanent Virtual Memory** (rather than **Temporary** or **None**) because the amount of contiguous, free hard-drive space available on the workstation is insufficient. At such times, you have no choice but to defragment the hard drive if you wish to run a CD-ROM title requiring that amount of memory.

Refer to the section 9.4.2.5 above for information on how to correct disk-fragmentation problems.

10.4.4 PROBLEMS WHILE RUNNING A TITLE

10.4.4.1 *"Wrong Disk in CD-ROM Drive"*

Aside from the possibility that, in fact, the wrong disc is in the drive, this message often indicates that the CD-ROM drive does not meet MPC specifications. (See also "Glossary" and Chapter 3.) In other words, you have obtained a CD-ROM title that can't be run on that CD-ROM drive—the disc is incompatible with the drive. Read Chapter 3 for more information on compatibility.

10.4.4.2 *No Mouse Cursor*

This problem occurs most often with DOS CD-ROM titles running under Windows 3.X. Windows 3.X applications require a mouse device-driver file named MOUSE.DRV, which is located in the \WINDOWS directory. The mouse driver, like all device drivers, must be properly installed for Windows 3.X CD-ROM titles. Use the **Windows Setup** applet to install a new mouse. Then use the **Control Panel**'s **Mouse** applet to adjust the mouse speed.

DOS CD-ROM titles, however, use either MOUSE.SYS or MOUSE.COM (or similar .SYS or .COM files), which are not installed by **Windows Setup**. When running a DOS CD-ROM title under Windows 3.X, the workstation temporarily simulates a DOS system in which the Windows MOUSE.DRV is not available. You must ensure that a DOS mouse driver is available to the CD-ROM title. The best way to do so is to add the following line to the CONFIG.SYS file:

DEVICEHIGH=C:\MOUSE.SYS

Place the line near the end (or at the very end) of the CONFIG.SYS file. Be sure to include the complete path name of the mouse driver file (it may not necessarily reside in the root directory of the C drive, as shown in the example above). Be aware that the mouse driver file might also have a different name than that used in the example above, but it will be a file name ending in .SYS, for example, MSMOUSE.SYS or LMOUSE.SYS.

A second solution is to modify the batch file that runs the CD-ROM title instead of modifying the CONFIG.SYS file. Include the following line anywhere in the batch file, but before the statement that actually starts the title:

LOADHIGH C:\MOUSE.COM

As in the CONFIG.SYS file, you must include the complete path of the mouse driver file and the correct name of the file. To function in a batch file, the file name must end in .COM or .EXE. Use this solution only if memory is very scarce on the workstation. Loading the mouse driver with the CONFIG.SYS file is preferable because it ensures that the mouse driver is always available to DOS CD-ROM titles.

10.4.4.3 System Freezes or Hangs

See section 9.4.3. If the techniques described there don't work, check to see if the workstation uses an SVGA video device driver or an upper memory manager, such EMM386.EXE (examine the AUTOEXEC.BAT and CONFIG.SYS files for their presence). If the CD-ROM workstation uses either of these types of device drivers, it may help to add the following line to the SYSTEM.INI file under the heading **[386enh]**:

EmmExclude=A000-EFFF

Be sure to capitalize the string exactly as shown.

10.4.5 MULTIMEDIA PROBLEMS

10.4.5.1 Problems with MCICDA.DRV

If an error message refers to MCICDA.DRV, especially when running a multimedia CD-ROM title, there may be a conflict between the Windows 3.1 version of MCICDA.DRV (which is installed as part of Windows 3.1) and some older CD-ROM or audio device drivers. You need to contact the manufacturer of the CD-ROM drive or sound card for an updated device driver. (Refer to Chapter 7 for details.)

Also check the **Control Panel**'s **Drivers** applet to make sure that MCICDA.DRV has been installed (see section 10.4.5.3 below for instructions).

10.4.5.2 Problems with MIDI Files

Assuming the sound card in the CD-ROM workstation supports the MIDI format, is properly installed, and functions properly under DOS, then the problem may be occurring because the MIDI device driver isn't installed properly in Windows 3.X or because the **MIDI Mapper** applet isn't set up properly.

First check the sound card's documentation to determine which of the optional MIDI setups the sound card requires. Most SoundBlaster compatible sound cards (MPC 1 and MPC 2 standards) function properly using the **General MIDI Setup** option.

Windows 3.X requires that the MIDI device driver be installed in the **Control Panel**'s **Drivers** applet, and then, that it be set up using the **MIDI Mapper** applet.

To verify that the MIDI Mapper is set up correctly:

1. From the **Control Panel**, select **MIDI Mapper**.
2. Select **Show Setups**.
3. In the **Name** field, use the pull-down menu to select **General MIDI**.
4. Click on the **Edit** button.

If you receive an error message stating that the MIDI setup selected isn't installed, then you need to reinstall it from the original Windows installation disks, or you need to create a new **MIDI Mapper** based upon the key-map information provided in the documentation for the MIDI device attached to the workstation.

10.4.5.3 Problems with "Music"

If a CD-ROM title displays an error message stating that there is a problem with "music" devices, the MCICDA.DRV device (for CD audio discs) isn't properly installed or is missing. See section 10.4.5.1 above.

First, verify that MCICDA.DRV file is present in the \WINDOWS\SYSTEM directory. Then, verify that it is listed in the **Control Panel**'s **Drivers** applet, as "MCI CD Audio Player" or "MCI Redbook Audio." To verify that the necessary Windows 3.X sound drivers are installed in Windows 3.X:

1. Open the **Control Panel** (in the **Main** program group).
2. Double-click the **Drivers** applet icon. A list of device drivers will display. This list must include either "MCI CD Audio Player" or "MCI Redbook Audio."

If neither "MCI CD Audio Player" nor "MCI Redbook Audio" is present on the hard drive or they aren't installed in the **Control Panel,** you must install them.

To install the driver, you must have a copy of the files either stored on the hard drive or on the original Windows 3.X installation diskettes:

1. Click the **Add** button in the **Drivers** window, and follow the instructions that appear on the screen.
2. If Windows 3.X cannot find the file in the \WINDOWS\SYSTEM directory, it will prompt you to insert a diskette in the A drive. (In most cases, this means one of the original Windows 3.X installation disks.) Insert the diskette into the A drive.
3. Follow the on-screen instructions to locate and select MCICDA.DRV.

In a few rare cases you may also need to edit the SYSTEM.INI file and insert a line in it to install the device. If so, add the following line to the end of the **[boot] section** of the SYSTEM.INI file:

drivers=mmsystem.dll

The driver file must be located in the \WINDOWS\SYSTEM subdirectory in order for the SYSTEM.INI file to function properly. It cannot be in a different directory and then accessed through a path name.

There may also be an error in the MPLAYER.INI, which is located in the \WINDOWS directory. If you suspect that MPLAYER.INI is at fault because you've eliminated all other possibilities and the error message persists, try deleting this file and then playing an audio CD using the **Media Player** applet.

10.4.5.4 No Sound

Assuming that there are no hardware problems (the CD-ROM drive and sound card must be properly connected to play both CD audio and digital audio) and that you can hear sound when running a CD-ROM title under DOS, then the problem must be in the way Windows 3.X sound device drivers are installed.

Verify that the necessary Windows 3.X sound drivers are installed in Windows 3.X:

1. Open the **Control Panel** (in the **Main** program group).
2. Double-click the **Drivers** applet icon. A list of device drivers will display. This list must include drivers for MIDI, .WAV, .AVI (movie sound), and CD audio.
3. If any one of the drivers is missing, you must install it.

See above, section 10.4.5.3, for details on installing a multimedia device driver.

10.4.5.5 Problems with Video for Windows

Windows 3.X CD-ROM titles often contain video clips in the AVI file format (see "Glossary"). If video clips on a title disc do not play smoothly, you may be able to improve their playback using the **Media Player** applet, which is found in the **Accessories** group, and the **Drivers** applet in the **Control Panel**. Before attempting to do so, examine a directory listing of the files on the CD-ROM disc to verify that files ending in the file-name extension .AVI are, in fact, present on the disc. (If not, the problem may be hardware-related; for example, the video or graphics adapter may require repair or replacement.)

First, select a test file:

1. Open the **Media Player** applet in the **Accessories** group.

2. From the **Device** menu, select **Video for Windows**.
3. From the **File** menu, select one of the .AVI files on the CD-ROM title disc.
4. Play the file to verify that it exhibits the performance problem. If the .AVI file you selected appears to display smoothly, then the video problem probably can't be solved by this method. The problem may be hardware-related or the video clips in question may not be .AVI files but, rather, some other file format.

Now, use the **Drivers** applet in the **Control Panel** to modify the way Windows 3.X displays the .AVI files on the CD-ROM title disc:

1. In the **Video Mode** area of the **Drivers** applet window, choose either **Window** (for quarter-screen display) or **Full Screen**. (Quarter-screen display will probably produce the best results.)
2. Select or deselect **Zoom by 2**, to double the size to half-screen or retain the actual frame size (quarter-screen). (Retaining the actual frame size will probably produce the best results.)
3. Select or deselect **Skip video frame if behind**. (Try both options to decide which works best with the CD-ROM title.)

Increasing the size of the displayed image may slow down the playback and cause fuzziness in the images; reducing the size can improve performance. Skipping video frames will degrade the smoothness of the playback but will speed up the overall playback of the video clip.

10.4.6 GENERAL PROTECTION FAULT (GPF) ERROR MESSAGES

GPF errors are extremely common error messages. In most cases, there is nothing you can do to prevent them from occurring. To resume normal operation of a CD-ROM workstation following a GPF error message, shut down Windows 3.X properly (see section 9.3.10), and restart the computer.

You may wish to report this error to the CD-ROM title producer since it probably indicates a bug in the title's software. If so, write down the exact wording of the error message, make a note of the circumstances under which it occurred, and contact the title producer's technical support staff.

Note: You *must* restart Windows 3.X after a GPF error. Even if the computer returns immediately to the **Program Manager** after you respond to the error message's prompt, you must exit from and restart Windows in order to refresh the memory that has been "invaded" by the faulty program. You may find that you have to reboot the workstation in order to resume normal operation of Windows 3.X. If you don't restart Windows 3.X following a GPF error, you are likely to encounter additional errors while running the CD-ROM title.

Occasionally, corrupted or outdated device drivers may cause a GPF error. Contact the vendor of the hardware device for an updated device driver. (Refer to Chapters 3 and 7 for information on device drivers.)

10.5 CHAPTER SUMMARY

This chapter provided solutions to problems with Windows 3.X CD-ROM titles running on stand-alone workstations (in other words, workstations not on a network). Problems that can be corrected using Windows 3.X applets and utilities are discussed in detail. Problems that require adjustments to the AUTOEXEC.BAT or CONFIG.SYS files or that require the use of DOS commands are also covered, but the reader is referred to Chapter 10 for details.

Windows 3.X is designed to be much easier to use than DOS, but it has only a few features to support multimedia applications, such as CD-ROM titles. As a result, many CD-ROM title producers continue to develop titles for DOS rather than for Windows 3.X, and your library or school may need to run these titles, either in DOS or in a DOS window under Windows 3.X. If so, you need to use both Windows and DOS problem-resolution techniques.

11. How to Solve Many Common Windows 9X Problems

11.1 *Introduction to This Chapter*

11.1.1 When to Consult This Chapter

This chapter provides specific steps to take when you encounter problems with Windows 9X CD-ROM titles, Windows 3.X or DOS titles running under Windows 9X, or with CD-ROM workstations running Windows 9X. This does not include information about Windows NT.

Refer to this chapter for specific instructions on resolving problems discussed in Chapters 4–8. Familiarize yourself with Chapter 4, which is an introduction to CD-ROM title installation, Chapter 5, which is an introduction to maintaining a CD-ROM workstation, and Chapter 6, which is an introduction to CD-ROM problem-resolution, before turning to this chapter.

11.1.2 When to Seek Outside Help

This chapter is designed for individuals who are responsible for a stand-alone CD-ROM workstation running Windows 9X. Many Windows 9X problems are easy to resolve, while others require technical skill and experience. If you work within a system of libraries or schools where technical support staff is available, the technical staff should provide you with a set of guidelines concerning when to consult with them and when to attempt to resolve problems on your own. Your technical support staff may prefer that you leave Windows 9X problem-resolution to them.

If you are unable to find a solution in this chapter to the problems you are encountering, follow the recommendations in Chapter 6 concerning obtaining outside technical advice.

11.1.3 HOW MUCH MUST YOU KNOW ABOUT WINDOWS 9X?

In most cases, using Windows 9X requires few technical skills—the operating system is designed for ease of use and for supporting multimedia applications, such as CD-ROM titles. This is particularly true if Windows 9X is the only operating system ever to have been installed on a workstation. If the CD-ROM workstation for which you are responsible was purchased with Windows 9X already installed, you aren't likely to encounter very many CD-ROM problems; you are more likely to encounter problems when installing DOS or Windows 3.X titles on the workstation. In such situations, you will need some familiarity with both DOS and Windows 3.X, in addition to basic Windows 9X, to resolve the problem.

If the workstation for which you are responsible originally had either DOS or Windows 3.X installed on it, and it has since been upgraded to Windows 9X, you will encounter a greater number of significant problems when running CD-ROM titles. In such cases you should acquire the *Microsoft Windows 9X Resource Kit* and the *Microsoft Windows 9X User's Guide*, in addition to the *Introducing Microsoft Windows 95* booklet that accompanies the upgrade disks.

In order to benefit the most from the information in this chapter, you need to have access to a good reference book on Windows 9X and to know the following aspects of Windows 9X:

- how to use the **My Computer** window, the **Control Panel**, and the **Windows Explorer**
- how to name, rename, copy, delete, and move files from one folder to another
- how to examine the **Properties** sheets for the system, **shortcuts**, files, and programs
- how to run (or "execute") a program
- if you upgraded from Windows 3.X to Windows 9X, you must know how to use Windows 3.X as explained in Chapter 10

If you are unfamiliar with any of the above concepts, please obtain and study a basic Windows 9X text or manual (see "Recommended Reading"), or seek the assistance of a colleague who already has this background.

11.2 IMPROVING WINDOWS 9X PERFORMANCE

Windows 9X provides several means of general performance-tuning including the **Control Panel** and **Properties** sheets for hardware and software, as explained in this chapter. Windows 9X is a very complex system, however, and it can take quite a long time to master it. As a result, it is wise for even the most technically savvy Windows 9X user to acquire and install a third-party utility program, such as *Disk First Aid*.

If a workstation once had Windows 3.X or DOS installed on it, then the choices made when the system was upgraded to Windows 9X can also have a significant impact on the performance-tuning process. When you do decide to upgrade to Windows 9X, you should consider carefully how you will do so. Microsoft allows you to retain a copy of Windows 3.1 and DOS on the hard drive on which you install Windows 95. You will need to be able to this if you have an existing library of DOS CD-ROM titles.

You may also find that some utility programs can help you with the upgrade process, such as *Remov-It II Windows 95 Upgrade Assistant* from Vertisoft and *CleanUp Coach*. These utilities help you to migrate previously installed CD-ROM titles to the new Windows 9X environment. They also help in both the installation and deinstallation of titles that were not designed to take advantage of the Windows 9X **Add/Remove Programs** applet.

Unlike DOS and Windows 3.X, the AUTOEXEC.BAT and CONFIG.SYS files on a Windows 9X system cannot be modified to improve performance of Windows 9X CD-ROM titles—most of the system configuration aspects set up by those two files are overwritten by Windows 9X after it starts up. As you will learn below, however, it is sometimes necessary to modify the two configuration files to improve the performance of a DOS or Windows 3.X title.

11.3 WINDOWS 9X TROUBLESHOOTING

This chapter focuses on Windows 9X, but not on Windows CD-ROM titles designed exclusively for Windows 9X, of which there are currently only a few. Most CD-ROM titles sold as "Windows 9X compatible" are capable of being installed and run under not only Windows 9X, but also Windows 3.X. Consequently, many of the problems you will encounter when installing or running titles such as these don't actually involve Windows 9X technical issues, but, rather, Windows 3.X technical issues or even, sometimes, DOS technical issues.

If you suspect that a problem with a Windows 9X CD-ROM title is related to either Windows 3.X or DOS, refer to Chapters 9 and 10 for instructions. When you receive an error message from a CD-ROM title, use the following general troubleshooting techniques to attempt to determine the source and exact nature of the problem. In many cases the solution to a Windows 9X error is identical to that for a Windows 3.X error—turn to Chapter 10 for details on these types of errors.

You may also encounter problems when running a DOS title, under Windows 9X, such as a CD-ROM title that simply cannot be installed to run properly under Windows 9X in a DOS window. In such cases, you may need to revert temporarily to the version of DOS that was running on the workstation before you installed Windows 9X. Keep in mind that you can only do so if you retained that old version of DOS on the hard drive when you installed Windows 9X. (Windows 9X includes a special version of DOS, which is very different from DOS 6.22 or earlier.)

When you receive an error message while installing or running a Windows 9X CD-ROM title, or when a general, unspecified problem occurs (for example, the sound is garbled or the system freezes up), the first thing to do is recover from the problem, regain control of the computer, and restart the computer to return it to normal operation. Then, determine exactly what caused the problem so that you can fix it. When you have determined what caused the problem, refer to section 11.4 for solutions.

It is very common to receive error messages from Windows 9X stating that the current or active program has performed an illegal operation, and recommending that you contact the vendor of the software. If you receive such an error message while running a CD-ROM title, that means you should contact the CD-ROM title producer. You need to be aware that even Microsoft programs can generate this kind of error.

11.3.1 SHUTTING THE ACTIVE WINDOW

If possible, close the CD-ROM title window according to the normal exit procedures. These procedures may vary by title, but as with most Windows 9X applications you should be able to click on the X in the upper righthand corner of the window. If there is no X or no title bar on the window, this is an indication that the title may have been designed either for Windows 3.X or DOS.

If the window can't be closed (for example, the title seems to be hung up or a disk-drive light keeps flashing but nothing else is happening), press the **Alt-Tab** key combination to activate a different window, such as the **My Computer** folder. (Note: **Alt-Tab** allows you to switch between tasks in Windows 9X just as in Windows 3.X. If you are unfamiliar with this technique, refer to section 10.3.7 for details.) Sometimes, just the act of cycling through the active windows will "catch the attention" of the computer, end the problem that's disrupting the CD-ROM title, and allow you to exit from the title.

If not, attempt to use the **Start** button to shut down Windows 9X and the workstation properly. Wait a few seconds for the fan that cools the power supply to stop, and then restart the system. Return to the CD-ROM title window (if it still appears to be active), and try to exit from it normally. In most cases, during the shut-down process, Windows 9X will shut down any programs that are "misbehaving." Once the title has stopped running, you can begin the process of pinpointing the problem, using one of the techniques below.

11.3.2 ESC—TO VIEW START-UP MESSAGES

The first step in pinpointing a problem is to determine whether the problem arises from the operating system's configuration. Restart the workstation, but press the **Esc** key while the Windows 9X "loading" message is displayed; pressing **Esc** reveals the lines in the CONFIG.SYS and AUTOEXEC.BAT files as they are being executed (Windows 95 retains these two start-up files from the older DOS environment). These are DOS commands, any one of which may be causing the error. Make a note of any messages that display as each line in these files is executed. Some of these messages may be related to the problem with the CD-ROM title. These error messages, generated by DOS, are clues to the problem. Refer to Chapter 9 for detailed information about many of the DOS error messages that may display.

11.3.3 F4—REVERTING TO AN EARLIER DOS VERSION

If you suspect that the CD-ROM title's problems originate from DOS (rather than Windows 9X) or from the way in which a CD-ROM drive is installed, running DOS and troubleshooting the errors using DOS may be helpful. If you installed Windows 9X so that the workstation's old DOS version was retained on the hard drive, pressing F4 halts Windows 9X and instead starts up the computer using that old version of DOS. (Turn to Chapter 9, section 9.3, for DOS troubleshooting tips.) In order for Windows 9X to allow you to restart the computer using an earlier version of DOS (for example 6.2), you must have installed Windows 9X without destroying the old operating system.

The first step is to edit a Windows 9X file called MSDOS.SYS. Use the **Windows Explorer** to search the hard drive for a directory containing the old DOS files. MSDOS.SYS is usually in the root directory of the hard drive:

1. Highlight MSDOS.SYS in the **Windows Explorer** window.
2. Select the **View** menu.
3. Select **Options**.
4. Select **Show all files**. MSDOS.SYS is a hidden file with a read-only attribute, which you must remove.
5. Close the **View** menu, and then select the **File** menu and **Properties** (or right click on the icon).
6. In the area at the bottom of the screen, remove the check marks in front of **Read only** and **Hidden**.
7. Click **OK**.

Now, edit MSDOS.SYS:

1. Open the file with an editor, such as **Wordpad**.
2. In a section of the file beneath **[Options]**, insert the following line:
   BootMulti=1

3. Save the file.
4. Close **Wordpad**.

Now you may attempt to restart the computer. As soon as a message displays, such as "Starting MS-DOS" or "Starting Windows 9X," press F4. The computer will restart with the old DOS version and display the DOS prompt without starting up Windows. Try running any DOS CD-ROM titles, just as you did before installing Windows 9X, to determine whether the problem with a DOS CD-ROM is in the DOS configuration.

11.3.4 F8—CONFIGURATION MENU

If the DOS configuration is the source of a problem, restart the workstation using the configuration menu, by pressing F8 during start-up. (Using the configuration menu may require advanced Windows 9X skills.) In most cases, you should first choose option 5 to step through each line in the CONFIG.SYS and AUTOEXEC.BAT files, so that you can accept or skip items that may be causing problems with the CD-ROM title. Obtain a copy of a thorough technical reference, such as the *Microsoft Windows 95 Resource Kit*, for more information.

11.3.5 REBOOTING FROM A START-UP DISKETTE

You should prepare a start-up diskette for each CD-ROM workstation. If the workstation runs Windows 9X, you should have an emergency boot diskette, which is created by running a program included in Windows 9X's installation kit. This diskette will include only a portion of the Windows 9X operating system (and may only allow you to start up the version of DOS included in the Windows 9X system, so some of the techniques suggested above may not be operative). Once the workstation is booted up using this diskette, follow the instructions in the *Microsoft Windows 9X User's Guide* to troubleshoot the system.

If you upgraded to Windows 9X from an earlier version of DOS or Windows, then you should also keep a start-up disk with the older version of DOS on it. Keep in mind, however, that your computer will probably have to run entirely from the diskette after you boot up from it, because during installation Windows 9X overwrites, relocates, or renames many of the old DOS programs and device drivers. What this means is that an old boot disk designed to circumvent Windows 3.X may not include all of the files needed to boot the computer after Windows 9X has been installed. The complete path names referred to in the CONFIG.SYS and AUTOEXEC.BAT files probably have changed. So, you will need to add all necessary files to the boot disk and change all path names to "point" DOS to the files on the A drive. For example, look at both the AUTOEXEC.BAT and CONFIG.SYS files on an old

bootable diskette; identify any complete path names beginning with C. Verify that all files are still, in fact, present on the hard drive in the directories
specified in the old start-up files and that they are still the same versions of
the files. Files may have been moved out of C:\DOS or C:\WINDOWS to
other directories. In Windows 9X, COMMAND.COM is in the Windows directory, for example, not the root directory. During Windows 9X installation, if
you were not careful to preserve older system files, including COM-
MAND.COM, you may have allowed them to be overwritten or moved into
other directories where you will have difficulty locating them. Newer versions of files may have replaced system files—if you attempt to run the system from the old bootable diskette, you may receive the dreaded "Incorrect
DOS version" error message and others.

This is critical—a boot diskette that worked fine when you used Windows 3.1 and DOS 5.0 or 6.2 will not work after you install Windows 9X. You
must create a new, stand-alone, self-contained system start-up disk. All device
drivers must either be on the boot diskette or located in a directory on the
hard drive where you carefully saved them during the Windows 9X installation process. Be aware also that old DOS start-up files may not work if the
installation of Windows 9X moved MSCDEX.EXE to a different subdirectory than before.

If technical support staff for your library or school installed Windows
9X on the workstation for which you are responsible, or if the workstation
was purchased with Windows 9X, the old boot diskettes for CD-ROMs will
not work with the new system. Some files on the hard drive may be difficult
to locate after the installation of Windows 9X, because they have a "hidden"
attribute. Refer to the operating system's manual or online Help for information on how to remove hidden and read-only attributes from files you must
identify and modify.

11.3.6 EXAMINE THE PROPERTIES
OF THE MULTIMEDIA DEVICES

The settings for **Properties** of various components of the workstation
can be the source of problems, as well as providing clues to problems and
their solutions. Examining these settings is easy. Unfortunately, interpreting
the settings and correcting errors in the **Property** settings can be difficult. If
you don't feel comfortable modifying **Properties** settings, just examine the
Properties windows and then be prepared to supply the information to the
CD-ROM title's technical support when you call them for help.

To examine the multimedia **Properties**:
1. Open the **My Computer** window.
2. Open the **Control Panel** window. The **Control Panel** contains both the
   System icon and the **Multimedia** icon, both of which you should examine.

3. Open the **Multimedia** window by clicking on the icon. Each of the **Multimedia** tabs can be selected to display settings information that relates to the system configuration and CD-ROM drive.

4. In the **Multimedia** window, select the **Advanced** tab. A list of device names displays. Click on a plus sign in front of a device name to expand the list to include more details.

5. Click on a device name to select it.

6. Click on the **Properties** button to display a window of information about the selected device. The information may need to be changed to accommodate the operation of the CD-ROM title. Have this information at hand when seeking technical assistance.

7. Return to the **Control Panel** and select the **System** icon. Select each of the tabs, items in the lists of system components, and **Properties** sheets as described above for **Multimedia**.

11.3.7 TROUBLESHOOTING SOFTWARE TOOLS

A number of good software tools are available to help solve Windows 9X problems. It is highly recommended that you obtain one. A list of such tools and their manufacturers appears in Appendix C. Such programs perform several valuable services, including virus-protection, tracking installed programs and assisting with deinstallation, identifying hardware problems, and helping you maintain up-to-date device driver files. Some even connect you automatically to the Internet for the latest software updates.

11.4 THE MOST COMMON WINDOWS 9X PROBLEMS

Many CD-ROM title problems relate to Windows 3.1, as explained above. Refer to Chapter 7 for solutions if the list of errors below doesn't include the error you need to solve. Many other problems arise from the way in which Windows 9X was installed on the CD-ROM workstation, especially if it was upgraded from Windows 3.1. In those cases, be prepared to make changes in the **Control Panel** and **System** (possibly with the aid of a good technical reference book, such as one listed in the "Recommended Reading").

11.4.1 INSTALLATION PROBLEMS

11.4.1.1 Incompatible or Outdated Device Drivers

Incompatible and outdated device drivers (see Chapter 7 for information on device drivers) are very common on Windows 9X systems. Windows 9X does an excellent job of providing universal device drivers (that is, device drivers that are fairly generic), but with so many different CD-ROM drive manufacturers, sound-card manufacturers, and computer manufacturers, it is inevitable that some equipment won't function properly using the Windows 9X universal device drivers. To further complicate matters, many computer manufacturers who ship their new computers from the factory with Windows 9X installed aren't very conscientious about providing good Windows 9X device drivers—many computers are shipped with Windows 3.X device drivers installed on Windows 9X systems. You are also likely to encounter device driver problems when running older titles designed for DOS or Windows 3.X under Windows 9X.

In many cases, a device driver may not have been properly installed when Windows 9X was installed, because Windows could not recognize it (it probably is not a **Plug and Play** compliant device driver). This means you must either obtain an updated device driver from the CD-ROM drive manufacturer, or you may need to run your CD-ROM titles using an old version of DOS (see Chapter 9 for instructions on how to create a DOS bootable diskette for a CD-ROM title).

You will probably receive an error message about the outdated device driver when installing the CD-ROM title or when you first try to run a newly installed CD-ROM title. Be sure to write down the exact message. Refer to Chapter 9 for help interpreting the DOS error message and identifying which one of the device drivers on the workstation may be the problem. (Read Chapter 7 to learn how to obtain an updated device driver you need.)

11.4.1.2 *"Unable to Create Directory"*
and Other File and Folder Name Problems

During installation of a CD-ROM title and when attempting to save a "bookmark" file, you may receive an error message that seems to indicate that the program was unable to create the file or the directory or folder in which the file was going to be saved. Sometimes the error message may state that a file or folder doesn't exist when you know for a fact it does. Most of the time these errors simply indicate that you did not type a valid file, folder, or directory name, or that the system is looking in the wrong subdirectory for the file, folder or directory name. You may need to browse through the directories on the hard drive for the correct name. Remember that no files, folders, or directories can be created and saved on the CD-ROM drive or disc (so don't try to use drive D when you should be using drive C, for example).

Another common problem with Windows 9X is that it recognizes "long file names," while many CD-ROM title programs do not (because they are written with Windows 3.X in mind). Try naming the file, folder, or directory using the Windows 3.X conventions: no file name may be longer than eight characters followed by a period and a three-letter extension (xxxxxxxx.xxx). Names may not include spaces.

11.4.1.3 Paths to Old Device-Driver Files

Windows 9X systems are generally safe from problems caused by "losing track" of files on the hard drive. There are occasions, though, when even Windows 9X may not be able to find a file, such as a device-driver file. In Windows 3.X and DOS this problem is known as a **path** problem. This problem most often occurs on computers that once ran Windows 3.X or DOS and onto which Windows 9X has recently been installed. If you purchased the workstation with Windows 9X already installed, this problem does not apply to you.

When Windows 9X is first installed on a computer, it generally moves the files in the Windows 3.X and DOS directories to new directories, and then replaces them with new files. If the installation process retained the old files on the hard drive, they may now reside in new directories. Any batch files or old programs that require a specific complete **path name** in order to locate files may no longer function. This is often the case for batch files used to run a CD-ROM title, including batch files for which there is now a Windows 9X **shortcut**, or old Windows .INI files that may still be in use by a batch file. Edit the batch files or .INI files to indicate the new location of the old device drivers.

11.4.2 PERFORMANCE PROBLEMS

11.4.2.1 Drive Speed Switch

Windows 9X allows you to optimize a workstation for the speed of its CD-ROM drive. CD-ROM titles designed for optimum performance on drives of a certain speed may not perform well on faster drives. Clues to such problems include choppy video or audio. Set the drive speed in the **Control Panel**.

11.4.2.2 Disk-Caching

The CD-ROM drive is automatically cached by Windows 9X: this means that Windows controls the flow of data from the disc in the drive automatically. Some CD-ROM titles designed specifically for DOS include their own disk-caching routines that may conflict with Windows 9X. If you are running a DOS CD-ROM title that provides disk-caching, or if you are instructed not to use disk-caching with a title for any other reason, you can change the **Control Panel** temporarily. Turn off the built-in Windows 9X disk cache (note:

Microsoft discourages this unless you are specifically instructed to do so by the technical support for the specific CD-ROM title):

1. From the **Control Panel**, select the **System** icon.
2. In the **System** window, select the **Performance** tab.
3. Click the **File System** button.
4. Select the **Troubleshooting** tab.
5. Put a check mark in the box in front of **Disable Write-Behind Caching For All Drives**.
6. When done with the CD-ROM title, be sure to remove the check mark from the box in order to restore the computer to normal operation.

11.4.2.3 Video Resolutions

Unlike Windows 3.X, which defaults to a video resolution of 640x480 and 16 colors, Windows 9X defaults to 800x600 and 256 colors. An older Windows CD-ROM title may perform more slowly when Windows 9X is in the higher resolution. Try temporarily modifying the resolution while running the title.

1. Open the **Control Panel** window (it's located in **My Computer**).
2. Select **Display**.
3. Select **Settings**.
4. Select **Change Display Type**.
5. Select **Change** beside **Adapter Type**.
6. Select a lower resolution device driver, such as one that is 640x480.
7. Save all changes by clicking on **OK**.
8. In Windows 95, you must next restart the computer in order to change the video resolution. Later versions of Windows 9X allow you to change the video resolution whenever necessary.

11.4.2.4 Distorted or Fuzzy Sound

Refer to Chapter 5 for tips on how to improve sound quality by upgrading computer hardware. If fine-tuning the equipment doesn't resolve the problem, make sure that the sound card's **DMA** setting in Windows 9X is set to 7, as follows:

1. Open the **Control Panel** (in the **My Computer** window).
2. Select the **Device Manager**.
3. Select the **Sound, Video, and Game Controllers**.
4. Select **Properties**.
5. Select the **Resources** tab. Make sure that the **No Auto Settings** box is checked.
6. Scroll to the list of DMAs. Click to change to DMA 7, if it isn't already set to 7.

7. Examine the **Conflict Information** to verify that no other devices are using DMA 7. If there are, keep in mind that two devices can't share the same DMA setting. You will either have to leave the current DMA setting for the sound card unchanged (and possibly endure poor sound quality when running the CD-ROM title), or you will need to refer to the documentation for the other devices that are using DMA 7 to determine whether it's safe to change those devices' DMA settings to some number other than 7.

8. Click **OK** and close the windows.

Also, if you installed Windows 9X to replace Windows 3.1 on a system with the SoundBlaster sound card, make sure you aren't using Windows 3.1 SoundBlaster 16 device drivers. If so, you need to replace the device driver files (see Chapter 7 for instructions).

11.4.2.5 No Shortcuts

A Windows 3.X title may be automatically installed by Windows 9X without creating a **shortcut**. A missing **shortcut** doesn't mean anything is seriously wrong with the installation. It just means that users may have to click the **Start** button and **Run** in order to play the CD-ROM title. It can often be difficult to locate the correct file for this purpose when using the **Browse** button: sometimes the files are hidden in subdirectories or have odd names. It is much easier to have a **shortcut** for each CD-ROM title.

11.4.2.6 "Out of Memory" or "Out of Resource" Errors

If you run several Windows 3.X applications simultaneously under Windows 9X, it is possible to run out of a type of memory often called "system resources." CD-ROM titles written for earlier versions of Windows are not designed to take full advantage of Windows 9X's 32-bit memory management features. When you close and exit from an older CD-ROM title, the title may still have possession of some memory "real estate." The only way to completely clear memory is to reboot the computer after closing a Windows 3.X application, such as a CD-ROM title. So, shut down all the programs you are running; then shut down Windows, and reboot the computer to restart Windows 9X before you run the CD-ROM title.

11.4.2.7 SMARTDrive and .INI File Problems

The SMARTDRV.EXE program and configuration files with names ending in .INI are important to the proper functioning of Windows 3.X CD-ROM titles. When a CD-ROM title running under Windows 9X causes an error message to display that includes a reference to one of these, refer to Chapter 10 for advice.

11.5 CHAPTER SUMMARY

This chapter describes several Windows 9X troubleshooting techniques. In addition, it explains how to solve many of the most common errors encountered when running CD-ROM titles under Windows 9X. Special attention is paid to two types of CD-ROM titles that frequently cause problems: titles labeled as "Windows 9X compatible" but which were actually designed for Windows 3.X and Windows 3.X titles running under Windows 9X. Since DOS CD-ROM titles can be installed in several different ways (see Chapter 8), in order to resolve problems with DOS CD-ROM titles you must first know which of the many ways it was installed. Then, refer to Chapter 9, section 9.2, for further information on changing the installation.

12. How to Solve Many Common Macintosh Problems

12.1 INTRODUCTION TO THIS CHAPTER

12.1.1 WHEN TO CONSULT THIS CHAPTER

This chapter discusses problems commonly encountered with Systems 6, 7, and (to some extent) 8 on Macintosh CD-ROM workstations. The chapter assumes that most Macintosh CD-ROM workstations are stand-alone units, not part of an AppleTalk network or other network. If the workstation is networked, refer to the network system administrator for assistance. If the workstation is on an AppleTalk network but has its own CD-ROM drives, then the information in this chapter may apply.

Running CD-ROM titles on a Mac is very similar to running other types of applications. The two most common problems are memory errors and lack of hard-disk space. Memory errors are somewhat unpredictable and whimsical, often stemming from conflicts between the CD-ROM title's software and other programs in memory, such as **INITs** in System 6. **INITs** are notoriously impolite about sharing memory with other programs. Hard-drive space can also cause unexpected problems. When there is only limited space on the drive, you may encounter problems while using a CD-ROM title, for example, if the program on the CD-ROM disc temporarily stores data on the hard disk. Important system files can be overwritten and cause a system crash, without warning, when there is insufficient hard-drive space. Macintosh system software files also have a tendency to become corrupted by use; this includes extensions, as well as the **System File** itself. Reinstalling these files may solve the problem.

12.1.2 WHEN TO SEEK OUTSIDE HELP

This chapter assumes that you are either interested in resolving Macintosh CD-ROM problems yourself or that you have no other choice. Many

Mac problems are easy to resolve, while others require technical skill and experience. If you work within a system of libraries or schools where technical support staff is available, the technical staff should provide you with a set of guidelines concerning when to consult with them and when to attempt to resolve problems on your own.

Refer to Chapter 4 for an introduction to installing CD-ROM titles and to Chapter 8, section 8.5, for specific information on installing Macintosh titles. Read Chapter 6 for an overview of the troubleshooting process before attempting to follow the instructions in this chapter.

12.1.3 HOW MUCH MUST YOU KNOW ABOUT THE MACINTOSH OPERATING SYSTEM?

The Macintosh operating system is generally very easy to use. When problems occur, however, the way in which the Mac operating system ("OS") insulates itself from its users can pose a few problems: it is sometimes difficult to determine the source of problems and then to modify aspects of the inner workings of the system.

In order to benefit from the information in this chapter, you should be familiar with the following Macintosh System 6 concepts:
- Folders, files, and directory listings in various "views"
- The **System Folder** and its contents
- The **Apple Menu** and how to add to and remove applets from it, including how to use the **Font/DA Mover** applet
- The **Finder** and **Multifinder**

You should be familiar with the following System 7 and System 8 concepts:
- Folders, files, aliases, and directory listings in various "views"
- The **System Folder** and the **Extensions Folder** and their contents
- The **Control Panels**
- The **Apple Menu** and how to add to and remove applets from it

12.2 IMPROVING MACINTOSH PERFORMANCE

Macintosh processor chips have become more powerful with time. Older Macs run noticeably slower than newer Macs. In most cases, however, it isn't possible to upgrade the processor chip on a Macintosh without resorting to a factory-authorized technician: most early Macs were not built to allow users to modify the hardware or even to open the Macintosh's case. Changing the processor chip in a Mac may even invalidate the warranty (if any remains), and, therefore, isn't often done.

The speed of a Mac will certainly be improved by adding to the amount of RAM available, and it is easier to increase the amount of RAM in many Mac models than it is to upgrade the processor. You can also free existing memory by unloading programs from memory while running a CD-ROM title (as explained section 12.4.3.3).

In System 7, the Mac operating system provides several software caches (a RAM drive, a disk cache, and virtual memory), which are located under the **Apple Menu Control Panel**'s **Memory** applet. The RAM disk is intended to speed up access to data by temporarily storing frequently used data in a virtual hard drive created in RAM (memory). When memory is scarce, however, the RAM disk will slow down overall performance of the system, and so it is generally recommended that you keep RAM disk-caching turned off. Changing the amount of memory allocated to the cache may improve performance (for example, if you use a smaller-sized RAM disk cache). In any case, keep in mind that you must restart the Mac after changing the RAM disk cache in order for it to take effect.

Mac applications have always been prone to memory errors that produce charming, but disturbing, little bomb icons and memory-error messages that can only be banished by restarting the computer. There is nothing you can do to a Mac CD-ROM workstation to avoid these types of problems.

A good way to improve the performance of any Mac is to upgrade its operating system to a more recent version. Versions of System 7 make numerous improvements in the capabilities of the Mac (as compared to System 6), not the least of which is the ability to run several programs simultaneously. System 7 also introduced *QuickTime* and other multimedia device drivers. Note that *QuickTime* (a video device driver and file format) requires the 32-bit upgrade to *QuickDraw*.

On the down side, System 7 takes up more memory than does System 6— some Macs may not even have enough memory for System 7. Many older Macs are, as a result, still running quite happily under versions of System 6. In addition, each new minor (interim) release of System 7 increases the amount of memory required. As a result, a Mac may be able to run System 7.0.1, but not System 7.5. Still, if your Mac has at least 2 Mb of memory, you should consider upgrading at least to System 7.1, because of the features included and its compatibility with so many multimedia device drivers.

To upgrade to System 7.5, your Mac must have at least 8 Mb of RAM and at least a 68020 processor (see Table 3.1 in for the hierarchy of Macintosh models). If you do not install *PowerTalk* (a network enhancement tool) or *QuickDraw GX* (for enhanced printing, graphics, and desktop publishing), 4 Mb is sufficient even on a Mac Plus. On a PowerPC processor, System 7.5 requires 16 Mb for the complete installation, and 8 Mb without *PowerTalk* or *QuickDraw GX*.

The PowerMac operating system, with its ability to run PC software, is of course only available for PowerMac models, which have a completely different processing chip (the Power PC chip) from the Mac. You cannot upgrade a system from System 6 or System 7 to the PowerMac.

12.3 MACINTOSH TROUBLESHOOTING

This section provides the following information:
- How to safely shut down the Mac when an error occurs
- How to determine which one of several programs running in memory may have caused a problem
- Several different ways to restart the Mac to help pinpoint the source of a problem
- How to determine whether the problem may be caused by something other than the Macintosh operating system

12.3.1 WARRANTIES

Some models of Macintoshes are not designed to be opened up, upgraded, or worked on except by Apple-authorized technicians. You may invalidate its warranty if you attempt to repair such a Macintosh yourself. Be sure you know whether or not you may open the Macintosh's case, or whether you must have an authorized technician perform all repairs and maintenance.

12.3.2 POWER ON SELF-TEST (POST)

When a Macintosh is turned on, it performs a self-test of its hardware components. First it checks memory, then the **SCSI Manager**, then the **Sound Manager**, and finally the mouse cursor. If any problems are detected, it will immediately alert you.

12.3.3 RESET AND INTERRUPT BUTTONS

Never turn off a Mac and then quickly turn it back on. Doing so can damage the power switch and fan inside the Mac. If you ever do have to turn off the Mac, always wait for the system to stop making any fan noises. Count off a few seconds before turning the Mac back on.

The oddly shaped pieces of plastic on the side of many Macs are the programmer's reset and interrupt buttons. The button furthest back is the interrupt button. If you encounter an error message, pressing the interrupt button may cause the program to display a code to help you assess the source of the error. Pressing the interrupt button does not clear out memory and will not help you get started again. The button toward the front is the reset button. It allows you to restart without resorting to the power switch. First press the interrupt button and write down any error code that displays (to supply to technical support staff). Then press the reset button to restart the Mac.

Some Mac models, including the Powerbook, have two small holes on the back of the computer that serve as the reset and interrupt buttons.

12.3.4 STRAIGHTENED PAPER CLIP

The tiny hole in the front of the CD-ROM drive, like that in the front of each floppy drive on a Mac, allows you to insert a straightened paper clip to eject a disk that has become stuck in the drive when the power shuts off. Always be sure to turn off the Mac and the CD-ROM drive before attempting this. (As recommended in Chapter 1, keep the CD-ROM drive and, if possible, also the diskette drive out of the reach of the public so that they cannot insert anything into these emergency access holes.)

12.3.5 SPACE BAR

Beginning with System 7.5, if you hold down the space bar while the Mac is starting up, the System 7.5 **Extensions Manager** will display. This allows you to enable or disable system **Extensions**, which may be the source of problems.

12.3.6 START-UP DISKETTE

Always keep a start-up diskette handy for troubleshooting purposes. Most original sets of system installation disks include a *Disk Tools* disk, which can be used to start up the Mac without the hard drive. If you do not have such a diskette, you can create a start-up disk as follows:

1. Initialize a disk.
2. Place a copy of the **System Folder**, containing the **System File**, **Finder** file, **Startup Device** file, and CD-ROM **Extensions** on the diskette. (Some systems may require additional files, such as the **Extensions Folder**; see your Apple manuals for details.)
3. With the diskette in the drive, restart the Mac. Hold down the Option, Shift, and Delete keys to cause it to start up from the diskette drive. If the drive ejects the disk, immediately push it back in. This should cause the Mac to use the **System File**s on the second diskette to start up.
4. Under the **Apple Menu**, select the **Control Panel** and then **Startup Device** (this changes only the new **Startup** diskette's system). If two or more disks are shown, highlight the diskette icon. Close the window.
5. From the **Special** menu, select **Set Startup Device**. Select **Finder Only**

under **Upon Startup, automatically open**. (This assumes System 6. The **Set Startup Device** option is not present in System 7 or 8.)

6. Power off the Mac. Attach the external CD-ROM drive, if necessary, and turn it on.

7. With the diskette in the drive, restart the Mac. This time it should start up without your having to hold down the Option, Shift, and Delete keys.

Note: If you ever need to know which device is the designated **Startup** device, select the **Control Panels** from the **Apple Menu**. The current start-up device is listed. In addition, most original copies of Mac system installation disks include a *Disk Tools* disk, which can be used as a **Startup Disk** in an emergency.

12.3.7 REBUILDING THE DESKTOP

From time to time, the Mac may become confused about how to display icons and folders on the **desktop**. You should rebuild the **desktop** occasionally to prevent this. You might also try rebuilding the **desktop** if you encounter problems that you cannot resolve by other means. To rebuild the **desktop**, restart the Mac while holding down the Option key and the Apple symbol key at the same time. The computer will restart and ask you if you wish to rebuild the **desktop**. Respond "Yes." Depending upon how many folders and disks are present on the **desktop**, the process may take up to several minutes.

12.3.8 LOOSE CONNECTIONS

It is easy for a SCSI cable (such as the cable connecting a CD-ROM drive to a Mac) to become loosened. Always re-seat the cable in the connectors when problems occur, just to be certain the cables aren't the source of the problems.

12.4 THE MOST COMMON MACINTOSH PROBLEMS

System 6, 7, and 8 tend to have similar problems. The list below features System 6 and System 7 errors, rather than System 8 errors, because System 8 is far less popular than System 7 since it requires 16 Mb of RAM and most older Macs have only 1 Mb or 2 Mb.

12.4.1 SYSTEM START-UP PROBLEMS

12.4.1.1 X-ed Out Icon

This indicates that you have tried to start up the computer without a valid **System File** or valid **StartUp Disk** (see section 12.3.6). You may have forgotten to turn on the CD-ROM drive before starting up the computer. It could also mean that you specified a different **Startup Disk** in the **Control Panel** than the expected or usual one.

12.4.1.2 *Failure to Turn on CD-ROM Drive First*

If you do not see an icon on the **desktop** for the CD-ROM drive or disc, it may be that the computer was turned on before the CD-ROM drive was turned on. The CD-ROM drive must be turned on first. Also, always shut down the system first, and then the CD-ROM drive, so that the drive can eject any discs before the power is shut off.

12.4.1.3 *"Wrong Startup Disk"*

If you have specified that the CD-ROM drive is the usual **Startup** disk (see section 10.3.6), and then you try to start up the computer from the hard drive instead, this may confuse the system. Or, if you change the **Startup Disk** to anything other than the hard drive and restart without that other disk being present, you will receive this error message.

12.4.2 INSTALLATION PROBLEMS

12.4.2.1 *Drive Ejects Disc*

Check to make sure that you inserted the CD-ROM disc properly, with the label side up. If that does not solve the problem, check to make sure that the SCSI chain is properly terminated at both ends (see sections 7.4.6.3 and 12.4.5). Perhaps you need to add a terminator plug to an external CD-ROM drive.

12.4.2.2 *"Wrong File Format"*

This error means either that you have tried to access a CD-ROM disc that cannot be read by the CD-ROM drive, or that the Mac's system doesn't contain the necessary extension files to recognize the file format. Verify that the disc is a Macintosh compatible format or audio CD. Then verify that the **System Folder** (System 6) or **Extensions Folder** (System 7) contains the necessary files. See section 8.5.3 for a list of required files.

The earliest Macintosh CD-ROM titles used a format called High Sierra. This was later replaced by ISO 9660. Your system must include a High Sierra device driver if you are using such an older disc.

Acceptable formats for a Mac CD-ROM drive generally include Mac HFS, CD audio, ISO 9660, and High Sierra. Other "formats" like Kodak

Photo CD and *QuickTime* video are software, not disc, formats: they will not cause this problem. If, however, the system lacks a Photo CD, *QuickTime*, or *QuickDraw* extension file, you will receive an error message.

12.4.2.3 Extension File Problems

Multimedia and CD-ROMs require several extension files to operate properly. Apple supplies most of these along with the system software that comes with the Macintosh or the CD-ROM drive. Some CD-ROM titles may also supply their own "third-party" **Extensions**. If you receive an error message indicating a problem with an extension file (stored on the hard drive, in the **Extensions Folder** within the **System Folder**), verify that the file exists and is in the **System Folder** (System 6) or the **Extensions** folder (System 7, not in the **System Folder**). Reinstall or replace the files if they are located in the correct folder but still seem to produce errors. If you have System 7.5, use the **Extensions Manager** to troubleshoot the problem. Either restart the computer while holding down the space bar in order to access the **Extensions Manager**; or select the **Extensions Manager** from the **Apple Menu**'s **Control Panels**. Once the **Extensions Manager** window is displayed, select **System 7.5 Only** from the **Sets** button. This will disable any third-party **Extensions** that may be causing the problem. If the error message does not display after you have disabled the third-party **Extensions**, then you know they are the source of the problem. Contact the vendor for support. If the error message persists, then you know that the Apple extension files are corrupted (replace them) or that you need to contact Apple for support.

12.4.2.4 "The desktop file
couldn't be created on the disk ... "

The CD-ROM disc is ejected and the above error message displays when the Mac does not recognize the CD-ROM disc as a read-only disk. In other words, it does not recognize that it is a CD-ROM and thinks it is a damaged diskette. This occurs when a disc is in a format that requires a different version of the system or additional extension files that are not installed on the workstation. It may also happen if the CD-ROM drive is an older type of drive that is not compatible with the format of the disc. You either need a newer drive to play the title, or you need to upgrade your system software.

12.4.3 PROBLEMS WHEN FIRST RUNNING A TITLE

12.4.3.1 Bus and Address Error Messages

If you have System 6, these messages consist of cryptic numerical error codes and a bomb icon. If you have System 7, these messages generally also include a text description of the error. In either case, the error is probably a programmer's mistake (that is, a "bug" in the CD-ROM title), not yours; there is little you can do, except to restart the computer. You may wish to notify the CD-ROM title producer of the error, as well.

The following error codes are programmer mistakes inherent in the software (such as the CD-ROM title) you are running (contact the CD-ROM producer to complain about the problem): 01 through 09, 10 through 13, 15 through 17, 26, 27, 30, and 31.

Some errors may result from insufficient memory to run the CD-ROM title. In order to prevent these errors, you may be able to restart the system and run the CD-ROM title alone, without running any other programs at the same time. These errors include: ID=25 Memory Full Error, ID=26 Bad Program Launch (this will generally occur as soon as you try to run the program), ID=28 Stack Ran into Heap.

The following error messages may represent a damaged **System File**: 15, 16, 26, 27, 30, and 31. You may need to replace the **System File** in the **System Folder**. Copy it from the original system diskettes.

12.4.3.2 *Unable to Open a Disc Icon*

If the CD-ROM drive is currently playing an audio CD disc track, you may not be able to open any other disc icons until it has finished. Stop the playback using the audio CD player software and try again.

If the disc is a Kodak Photo CD disc, check to make sure that both the *QuickTime* and *Photo CD* extension files are present in the **Extensions** folder inside the **System Folder** for System 7. System 6 does not automatically include either of these and may not allow you to play Photo CDs.

12.4.3.3 *"Insufficient Memory"*

In System 6, use the Apple menu's **About the Finder** window for information about the amount of memory in use and available. In System 7, use the Apple menu's **About This Macintosh** window. The window tells you the total amount of memory installed in the computer, shows the amount of memory used by the **system** itself, and shows the largest available ("free") contiguous memory block (not the total free memory) that is unused. This is a critical distinction—contiguous memory is not a matter of the hardware but of the order in which you started up the programs on the Mac. To free up a larger block of contiguous memory, restart the computer and then start your CD-ROM title first, before other programs. Alternatively, restart using a smaller **System File**, fewer **INITs**, and fewer **Cdevs** or turning off the **Multifinder** in System 6.

If the problem is caused by too many **INITs**, you can temporarily hide the **INITs** from the **system** as it restarts or temporarily disable them. To hide **INITs**, simply remove them from the **System Folder**. For example, create a **Temp Init** folder anywhere on the **desktop**, even inside the **System Folder**; drag all the **INIT** icons into the temporary folder to hide them from the **system**. Then restart the computer. You will notice that the usual display of **INIT** icons along the bottom of the screen does not occur, indicating that the **INITs** are not being loaded into memory where they would take up precious space. Alternatively, instead of hiding the **INITs**, just hold down the Shift key while restarting the computer. Again, the **INITs** will not be loaded.

You can also free up memory by deinstalling fonts and **desk accessories** that appear on the **Apple Menu**. The number of options that displays when you pull down the **Apple Menu** depends on how many you have installed— it is not standard. In System 6, it is necessary to use the **Font DA/Mover** applet to install and deinstall items on the **Apple Menu** and fonts. In System 7, you simply remove them from the **System Folder**.

Insufficient memory errors can occur even when there is enough memory available to run a program if the desired amount of memory is not properly specified in the **Get Info** window for the program. To change this, highlight the program icon, pull down the **File** menu and select **Get Info**. Change the **Memory** listed to a higher number. This is the amount of memory the Mac will set aside for running the program. Then restart the system and the program.

12.4.3.4 *"Not enough Finder memory to work with the disk"*

This is a System 6 message meaning that the disc contains a lot of separate files. You need to change the memory settings for the **Finder**, as a result. Use the **Get Info** window. Set the **Application Memory Size** to 210. Then restart the Mac.

12.4.3.5 *"This is not a Macintosh disk, initialize?"*

Assuming that this error is referring to the disc in the CD-ROM drive, you may have inserted a disc upside down or the disc is in a format that is not readable by the drive. *Do not* respond **Yes** to this prompt. You cannot "initialize" a CD-ROM disc. Replace the disc with a Macintosh compatible CD-ROM disc.

This message can also occur if you are running System 7, but the **Extensions Folder** within the **System Folder** does not contain the *Foreign File Access* or other necessary device drivers. Check to make sure that it is present. If not, reinstall them from the disks that accompanied the Macintosh or CD-ROM drive.

12.4.4 PERFORMANCE PROBLEMS

12.4.4.1 System Freezes or Hangs

This is very common with Macintoshes. It is generally caused by insufficient memory, insufficient hard-drive space, or a memory conflict caused by poorly designed software running on the computer. Push the restart button on the side of the computer to restart and try again.

12.4.4.2 Poor Sound Quality

The computer's speakers may produce pops, static, and hissing. A short in a cable can also produce these noises. Even humidity can interfere with electronic and audio equipment.

Sound distortion can be caused by setting a volume control too high. Try reducing the volume, using software and hardware volume controls.

12.4.4.3 Power Jolts

If you receive an "unhappy" Mac icon, you have a serious hardware error. These errors are often caused by shorts in the circuitry. You can cause these shorts in many ways. One way is to connect and disconnect external hardware, like the CD-ROM drive, while both the peripheral and the computer are powered on. Always completely turn off all equipment before plugging components into each other.

12.4.4.4 Poor Playback of a Disc on a Fast Drive

If the disc is old, such as one developed for single-speed drives, you must optimize the playback by slowing down the drive temporarily. Go to the **Control Panel**. Use the **CD-ROM Speed Switch** and change the setting.

12.4.5 SCSI PROBLEMS

12.4.5.1 General SCSI Problems

Many problems are caused by improperly setting up SCSI devices and SCSI chains. Some Macintosh computers (such as some Power Macs and Powerbooks) have unusual SCSI options and requirements. Using System 7.5 and SCSI Manager 4.3 software, you may be able to extend a SCSI chain beyond seven devices per system. There is also a unique black SCSI terminator for use with some Mac IIfx systems. In addition, if you use a Powerbook as a hard disk in a SCSI chain connected to another Mac, the Powerbook must be the last device in the chain and must be in so-called "SCSI disk mode." So, be sure to read the manuals for the specific workstation to ensure that the SCSI chain is properly configured.

12.4.5.2 *"No SCSI device found"*

One possible, but rare, cause of this error is the length of the cables between the computer and the items in the SCSI chain. There is a physical maximum length of twenty feet for SCSI cables. Many computer cables over ten feet long may not work properly or data may be lost.

More often, the SCSI device (probably the external CD-ROM drive) is not turned on, the cable is loose, or the device drivers were not loaded when you turned on the Mac. Carefully shut down the system. Verify that everything is properly installed. Then restart the system.

12.4.5.3 *"Incorrectly terminated SCSI device"*

Make sure (if the CD-ROM drive is the only external device) that an external CD-ROM drive has a terminator plug covering one SCSI port and the cable is connected to the other. If you have more than one device in the chain, make sure that both are not terminated.

12.4.5.4 *SCSI 2 Versus SCSI 1 Cables*

If the cable is not shorted out and everything else appears to be working normally, but you still cannot get the Macintosh to recognize the external CD-ROM drive, the problem may be the type of cable. The cable may be an older SCSI cable that is not compatible with the SCSI 2 standard device. You may need an upgraded cable.

12.4.5.5 *"Bootable device that has a SCSI ID other than 0 or 1 or 2"*

The workstation may not respond properly if you try to set the **StartUp Device** to a drive numbered SCSI ID 3 or later. In most cases, you must start the Mac up from a hard drive or from a diskette in the drive and then run the CD-ROM title on another SCSI device. The internal hard drive on the workstation is usually SCSI 0.

12.4.5.6 *"Wrong SCSI ID" or "Conflicting SCSI ID"*

Remember that each SCSI device must have a different ID in order for the system to recognize it. Internal hard drives or other internal devices may already be named ID 0, 1, or 2. ID 7 is reserved for the computer itself. Most external devices are set to ID 3 at the factory. If you have several SCSI devices attached to the workstation, they are said to be in a chain, and each one must have a different ID number. The last external SCSI device must also be terminated with a terminator plug in order for the system to recognize all of the devices.

System 6 allows you to use numbers 0 to 7 as valid SCSI ID numbers. The sequence begins with 0, because many Macs running System 6 do not have internal hard drives; so they should use ID 0 for an external hard drive. If there is an internal hard drive, it is ID 0, the first in the chain. If you have System 6 and an internal hard drive, do not try to use 0 for an external CD-ROM drive.

System 7 reserves SCSI ID number 0 for the internal hard drive on the Mac. You may use numbers 1 through 6 for the SCSI ID. ID 7 is reserved for the computer itself.

12.4.5.7 *Shorted Out SCSI Cable*

If a cable is damaged, everything will seem to be set up fine on the Macintosh, but it still won't recognize the presence of the CD-ROM drive. SCSI cables are susceptible to shorting out. When you buy one cable, always buy a backup. Having a backup as a substitute is crucial for checking cable problems. The cables break because you have to twist them to plug them in and because they are liable to be bent often.

12.5 CHAPTER SUMMARY

This chapter discusses Macintosh Systems 6, 7, and (to some extent) 8. It covers troubleshooting techniques that are especially useful for older models of Macintoshes with limited RAM. It also lists common errors and their solutions, including SCSI errors: unlike PC-based workstations, Mac-based workstations often have external CD-ROM drives connected via SCSI connectors, making them particularly prone to this type of error.

Appendix A:
Optical Disc and
Related Technologies
for Libraries and Schools

OPTICAL DISC TECHNOLOGIES

CD-ROM is only one of several forms of optical disc. Optical discs are simply plastic discs of various diameters with various types of coatings on which recordings are made. The information recorded on the disc is read by means of a laser beam that bounces off the surface of the disc (hence "optical"). Most optical discs record digital information, for example, CD-ROM and DVD; 12-inch laserdiscs record analog information.

This appendix briefly surveys several optical disc technologies that may be found in libraries and schools today. Laserdisc is the oldest of these technologies, while DVD is the newest and is, therefore, still undergoing change.

LASERDISC

Laserdiscs may be the most familiar of the optical disc formats used in libraries and schools, in a form generally referred to as "IVI." "IVI" stands for "Interactive Video Disc," a term synonymous with "laserdisc." Laserdiscs are widely available as an alternative to videotape, especially for archival quality films. In addition, many education and training applications are available as laserdiscs, and many public kiosks also make use of laserdisc as a storage medium because it is highly durable.

Technically, IVI is only one type of application of laserdisc technology: it utilizes the laserdisc standard known as CAV ("constant angular velocity"). Because of the structure of the data recorded on a CAV laserdisc, it is possible to control the disc by means of program code, allowing the user to skip video frames, to back up on the disc, and to freeze-frame. Thus, CAV discs are suitable for interactive learning and training applications.

263

A second laserdisc format, CLV ("constant linear velocity") is much like videotape in that it is designed for continuous play. Many movies are issued as CLV laserdiscs. CAV stores about thirty minutes of video per disc side, while CLV stores about one hour. CLV laserdiscs are played on laserdisc players attached to a television, while CAV laserdiscs generally require a computer as well as a player and an NTSC monitor (or television with a computer connector).

Since DVD is expected to be superior to laserdisc for both the purposes of CLV and CAV, it is unlikely that a library or school will consider adding laserdisc technology to its learning resources.

KODAK PHOTO CDS

Another optical disc standard that has been in existence for some time is Kodak Photo CD. Unlike laserdisc, however, Kodak Photo CD has not been made obsolete by a superior standard, at least not for the purposes for which it is intended. Libraries and schools with CD-ROM workstations in place may consider utilizing Kodak Photo CD because it is an inexpensive, easy-to-use means of creating personalized photographic archives.

Ordinary 35 mm print and slide film can be transferred to a Kodak Photo CD CD-ROM by authorized processing centers throughout the United States for only a few dollars more than it would cost to have them processed and printed. Once on the Photo CD disc, the images can be displayed on a computer or TV screen, captured or imported by personal computer applications, and reused in a number of creative ways.

Most recent-model CD-ROM drives are capable of reading the Photo CD discs. The drive must be either a Macintosh CD-ROM drive or a PC CD-ROM-XA drive (this includes most MPC-2 standard CD-ROM drives). Both of these types of CD-ROM drives can read the so-called "interleaved" tracks of data (photos) and sound that can be recorded on a Kodak Photo CD.

In addition, the CD-ROM drive must also be capable of reading "multisession" discs, that is, discs that have been recorded on more than once. This allows the transfer of photos to a disc in an initial session and then later the reuse of the same disc to add new photos: each transfer is called a "session." There are a few older Photo CD compatible drives capable only of reading single-session discs. And, unfortunately, many older standard CD-ROM drives do not have the capability to read any kind of interleaved discs, such as Photo CD: for example, MPC level 1 CD-ROM drives are not Photo CD compatible.

How to Put Photos on a Kodak Photo CD Disc

To create a Photo CD disc, simply mail negatives or slides to one of several processing centers in the United States. If you cannot find a Kodak Photo CD processing center in your local phone book, contact Kodak directly at the number listed in the "Directory of Resources." Kodak's World Wide Web site on the Internet also includes a screen on which you can enter your address and phone number in order to search for the closest "transfer" site.

CD-R and CD-WR

It is also becoming more feasible to create your own CD-ROMs using a personal computer. To create CD-ROMs on a workstation, the workstation needs a CD-ROM drive that can write to a CD-ROM disc, CD-ROM creation software, special device-driver files, and discs to which data can be written (remember, ordinary CD-ROM discs are read-only). An existing CD-ROM workstation in a library or school can be upgraded at moderate cost to include these components.

Two writable CD-ROM formats are available, CD-WR, which is also called WORM or "write-once-read-many" CD-ROM, and CD-R, which is rewriteable or recordable CD-ROM.

To take advantage of the new-style discs onto which data can be written easily, a workstation must have installed: (1) application software that allows users to structure the data on the disc (sometimes called "image creation," (2) software that allows the operating system to write data to a CD-ROM drive (which the operating system usually prevents from happening), and (3) a drive capable of writing to a disc.

Using CD-WR you can create a master disc from which copies can be made. With CD-R you can use CD-ROM discs as you would a hard drive for recording and archiving information.

CD-ROM Manufacturing Service Bureaus

A library or school can publish its own CD-ROMs either by creating a CD-R or CD-WR disc, or by sending data to a service bureau "for mastering," (that is, creating a master copy). Refer to "Appendix C: Directory of Resources" for a list of some CD-ROM service bureaus who can produce CD-ROM discs for you.

To produce a CD-ROM disc in this way, you will need no other special equipment than at least one workstation with suitable input devices for the data. Such devices include a flatbed scanner, a digital camera, or a microphone attached to a sound card. In addition, the workstation will need application software for each of the input devices, that is, software to create and edit graphics files acquired via the scanner or digital camera and software to create and edit audio files acquired via the microphone. (Note: it is also possible in some circumstances, where copyright allows, to copy multimedia files off CD-audio or CD-ROM discs). The details of these processes are beyond the scope of this book. Refer to "Recommended Reading" for assistance.

Having acquired the digital files, the next step is to transfer the files to a medium that can be given to the service bureau. This can be diskettes (Zip™ drive high-capacity diskettes are a good choice for this), removable optical discs, or tape.

The service bureau will provide you with a list of specifications and file-naming conventions to use when preparing the disks or tape. You may use "an authoring system" to design a user interface to be included on the CD-ROM discs; or when the service bureau returns the CD-ROM discs to you, you will need to have a search engine installed on the workstations on which you will run the CD-ROMs.

DVD

DVD ("Digital Video Disc") is a relatively new optical compact disc format that may eventually replace both videotapes and multimedia CD-ROMs. Unlike other optical disc formats (such as laserdisc and CD-I), DVD has the strong backing of the entertainment as well as the computer industry and is, therefore, likely to become an important part of home entertainment and information systems.

The DVD standard has not yet stabilized, though. Since the original industry standard (read-only DVD) was announced, two additional, competing standards have also been announced: Sony and Philips have recently backed a version of the DVD standard that would allow DVD discs to be written to, much like CD-R. Another optional standard that involves disposable discs is also being considered.

DVD MOVIES AND PLAYERS

Many technology companies and Hollywood are promoting read-only DVD players and DVD movie discs as enhancements to home entertainment systems. From the industry perspective, DVD movies have several advantages: extremely high-quality replication, compatibility with high-definition and large-screen TVs, and superior copy protection.

From the audience perspective, DVD movies can potentially provide even greater added value. For example, a DVD disc can present a movie in several versions and formats—you pick the version and screen format when playing the title. You would choose among versions with different ratings, so that, for example, a classroom of students could view a PG version of a film first released to theaters with an R rating. Toshiba, a prime promoter of the new technology, points out that you might "view the action the way the director intended" in so-called "letterbox" screen format (an aspect ratio of 4:3, the format in which movies are shown in theaters), rather than in the cropped TV format. DVD movie discs may include several sound tracks, such as English, Spanish, or French. You could choose to play the movie in your native language, or you might watch a favorite movie in a second language to hone your comprehension skills.

Movie DVDs can't be played on your library's or school's ordinary CD-ROM workstations: neither a standard CD-ROM drive nor even on a CD-I player attached to a TV. In addition, DVD disc standards vary from country to country. In North America, the DVD discs are compatible with NTSC video (standard American broadcast TV) and a type of audio called Dolby AC-3. If you purchase a disc in England, for example, it will not play on an American DVD player (but, of course, you may also encounter the same compatibility problem with videotapes).

DVD MULTIMEDIA DISCS AND DRIVES

A single DVD disc can hold up to 4.7 gigabytes of data on a single side (and double-sided discs and drives are contemplated, for a total of 8.5 gigabytes). That's the equivalent of about 12 CD-ROMs. Table C1 lists the complete specifications for both DVD discs and drives. In addition to greater storage capacity (which, in itself, opens up new creative venues for multimedia), a DVD disc has improved video and audio technology: MPEG-2 video and MPEG audio or Dolby AC-3 audio.

To play DVD discs, a workstation must have a DVD-compatible drive. An existing CD-ROM drive, even if it is a CD-ROM-XA drive or a CD Plus drive, cannot read and play DVD discs. So, you need to add a DVD drive to the system or replace the CD-ROM drive, in order to enjoy DVD. If you choose to replace a CD-ROM drive, be sure to purchase a DVD drive that is also CD-ROM-XA compatible. This may cost a little more, but unless you do so, you may find that you can no longer play your library of multimedia titles on the workstation.

When upgrading to DVD, you should also consider upgrading other elements of a workstation at the same time. The computer's monitor and sound system can significantly limit the quality of DVD video and audio. In order to enjoy the full benefits of DVD, you will likely want a very high-resolution monitor and a high-quality stereo system.

You may also need to upgrade your operating system. DVD uses a file format called UDF (Universal Disk Format), which makes it possible to store files so that they can be used on many different computer systems. If your operating system cannot read UDF files, though, it won't matter what kind of computer you have. Your operating system must be capable of reading UDF files. This requires additional, new device drivers.

Table C1: DVD Specifications

DVD Disc Specifications	
Size	5 inches (120 mm) in diameter
Storage Capacity	4.7 gigabytes/side
Image Format	MPEG-2
Audio Format for NTSC	Dolby AC-3, LPCM
Audio Format for PAL/SECAM	MPEG Audio, LPCM
No. of Audio Tracks	8 and up to 32 subtitle channels
Video Running Time	133 minutes/side
File Structure	Micro UDF or ISO-9660

DVD Drive Specifications	
Sustained Data Transfer Rate	1350 Kb/sec
Port Type	SCSI
Compatible API	TAPI
Formats	Variable: Red Book, Yellow Book, CD-ROM XA and others

Appendix B: Glossary

386 A type of Intel processor chip. It superseded the 286 chip in terms of processing speed. If a CD-ROM title requires "at least a 386 or better," that means the title requires at least a computer capable of a 386's speed and DOS 4.0 or later.

486 A type of Intel-compatible processor chip. It superseded the 386 chip in terms of processing speed. If a CD-ROM title requires "at least a 486 or better," that means the title requires at least a computer capable of a 486's speed and DOS 4.0 or later.

8-bit, 16-bit, 24-bit, 32-bit, 64-bit The number of bits of data that can be simultaneously processed by a chip or chip set.

Adapter (Card) *see* controller

ADPCM Adaptive Delta Pulse Code Modulation. A sound file compression algorithm that compresses CD-audio-quality ("Red Book") sound files into smaller files of different levels of fidelity.

Applet A small application program generally included as part of an operating system.

AppleTalk An Apple Computer, Inc. proprietary network protocol. It links peripheral devices, such as printers, to more than one Macintosh computer.

Architecture Usually, the style of circuitry on a computer's motherboard or main circuit board. *See also* bus.

ASCII American Standard Code for Information Interchange. A plain, unformatted, text-only file that can be used on any platform.

AUTOEXEC.BAT An important configuration file in DOS and Windows systems. When you boot up the system, after reading the CONFIG.SYS file, the computer looks for an AUTO-EXEC.BAT file and then automatically executes each command in it, one at a time.

AutoRun The capacity of a CD-ROM title in Windows 9X to start itself up as soon as you insert the disc into the CD-ROM drive. Also called "Autoplay."

AVI Audio-Video Interleaved, the Video for Windows file format. The file extension for a type of video file format for Windows systems.

BBS *see* Bulletin Board System

Binary In computer terms, a type of file, usually a compiled, executable program file. Especially when using a modem, you must specify whether a file is a binary or an ASCII text file. Binary also refers to a number system in which there are only two units, zero and one.

Bit The fundamental unit of computer data (a 1 or a 0, ON or OFF).

Bitmap A type of computer file that converts generally graphic information into a matrix of "bits" of data.

Bitmap font A font that consists of bitmaps for each character in the font. The characters cannot be easily enlarged or modified, but must generally be displayed and printed at a single resolution or in a single size.

Boolean Operators Named for George Boole, an English mathematician (1815–1864). The "operators" are the words AND, OR, and NOT, which you will frequently use in computer searches.

Boot To start up a computer and its operating system. The term comes from "bootstrap." By powering on the computer, you allow a small part of the operating system that is contained in the chip circuitry, in turn, to start up the rest of the operating system, as if the computer were "pulling itself up by its bootstraps."

Bridge Disc *see* CD-ROM XA

Buffer An area, usually in memory, where data is temporarily located before it is used.

Bug A programmer's error.

Bulletin Board System (BBS) A privately owned, but usually publicly accessible, computer system. Using a modem you can dial into the BBS and participate in specialized conversations and access libraries of files.

Bus The architectural elements of the motherboard in a computer that transport data to and from the main processor chip.

Byte One binary unit. Eight bits. The size of computer files is measured in bytes.

Cache Temporary storage.

Card *see* Controller

CD-audio Red Book CD format, just like the audio on your stereo music CDs.

CD-I Compact Disc Interactive. The Green Book CD-ROM format popularized by Sony and Philips. Most CD-I discs require a specialized player device to be attached to a TV.

CD-Plus The "Blue Book" standard for mixed mode CD-ROM discs, developed jointly by Sony and Philips with the support of Microsoft and Apple. This format is designed to make it easier for stereo systems to play the same discs as computers. The first track (a data track) is encoded so that a stereo CD audio player will skip it. Otherwise, there is no difference between a CD-Plus disc and a CD-ROM disc with music tracks.

CD-R CD-Recordable discs. Similar to WORM discs.

CD-ROM XA A type of bridge format between CD-ROM and CD-I. CD-ROM XA format is also used by Kodak Photo CDs. It can include both Yellow Book standard data and Red Book standard audio interleaved (woven together) for fast access.

CD-ROM Compact Disc Read Only Memory: Yellow Book standard discs that hold over 600 Mb of data in various formats.

Cdev An Apple Macintosh operating system term for a type of device driver that shows up on the Control Panel.

Chip, Chip Set Silicon-embedded circuits that look like square spiders. The chips are plugged into circuit boards by means of tiny wire jumper legs. Chips are of various types for various computer functions. These include the processors, such as an Intel Pentium or Motorola 68000 series, RAM, VRAM, and others.

Client The term for a workstation linked to a network server system. The server provides "services" to the client, such as application programs and CD-ROM drive access.

.COM A file name extension (ending) for compiled files in the DOS file and directory system. By typing the first part of such a file name (the eight letters preceding the extension), you "run" the compiled program file. For example, you might type MOUSE to run an executable program named MOUSE.COM.

COM, COM Port Communications port. *See also* Port. The COM port is used primarily by the modem on an IBM compatible computer.

CONFIG.SYS An important configuration file on a DOS or Windows computer. It is the first file read by the operating system when you power up the computer.

Configuration The way in which your computer is set up. The operating system generally has certain options for you to set and which are recorded in files on the hard drive. When the computer first starts up, it reads from these files and then proceeds according to the instructions found there. The term is also loosely used to describe the type of system you have and its peripherals.

Controller A circuit board that serves as an adapter, allowing you to connect a peripheral device to the computer. Controller cards are also sometimes called adapters or just cards. The external CD-ROM drive or your printer, for example, require such cards to be installed inside your computer.

Conventional Memory In DOS, the first 640 k of RAM on a PC. Since many CD-ROM titles must use this area of memory, you must load as many programs and device drivers, upon startup, into upper and high memory.

CPU This stands for Central Processing Unit. It is somewhat anachronistic in reference to personal computers. If you find such a reference, however, it often means the system unit (see below) or the ROM (see below).

Database A collection of information, or data. In computer terms, the data is often highly structured and accessible only through an intricate indexing scheme.

Desk Accessory A Macintosh operating system file that displays under the Apple menu.

Device Driver A small software program file that is required by the operating system of a personal computer in order to control peripherals, such as CD-ROM drives. In Macintosh terms this is called an extension file, Cdev, or INIT.

DIB (Device Independent Bitmap) A graphics file format, especially in Windows 95, that can be displayed on virtually any computer screen.

DIP Switch (Dual Inline Package Switch) Older circuit boards could be "programmed" via tiny sets of these switches.

Disc The spelling most commonly used for permanent media, such as CD-ROM discs.

Disk The spelling most commonly used for magnetic media, including diskettes (floppies) and hard drives.

Disk Cache A RAM chip, usually, that accepts and temporarily stores data that has been read off a physical disk, such as a CD-ROM disc, before the data is requested by the computer processor or application program. The disk cache enhances overall system speed. The cache is generally measured in kilobytes. The larger the cache, the faster the overall performance of the physical drive serviced by the cache.

DMA (Direct Memory Access) A type of channel used by peripherals on a computer that circumvents the central processor and thus ensures a high rate of speed for data transfer. Many sound cards use DMAs.

DOS (Disk Operating System) IBM-DOS and MS-DOS are virtually identical. If a CD-ROM title requires DOS, your PC may have either one of them.

Download To receive data from another computer. Technically, to receive data from a larger, more powerful computer onto a personal computer.

DirectDraw Windows 95 graphics adapter interface software.

DirectSound Windows 95 hi-fi sound interface software.

DirectPlay Windows 95 multi-player game interface software.

DirectInput Windows 95 joystick and advanced input device interface for game software, such as flight yokes.

.DRV The file name extension for some types of device-driver files in the DOS file and directory system.

DSP Digital Sound Processor: A type of chip on a sound card.

DVD (Digital Video Disc) An extremely high-capacity optical disc format, designed primarily for MPEG-2 digital video. A DVD disc may contain a feature-length motion picture or a multimedia title. Data on the disc must meet the industry DVD specifications: it must be encoded as MPEG-2 video and Dolby AC-3 audio (for areas of the world subscribing to NTSC TV standards) or MPEG-2 video and MPEG audio (for areas of the world subscribing to PAL or SECAM TV standards). DVD may also be used to store other types of data, but the drive used to read the data must be compatible with all the data types on the disc.

E-IDE A type of "bus," a modification of the ISA bus. This term may describe certain aspects of your computer's motherboard, which itself determines the types of additional components, or adapter cards, that may be added to it. The EISA bus is an older type of bus, which may be found in your computer if it is several years old.

EISA Extended ISA. A type of architecture for IBM compatible computers. *See also* ISA.

EMS Older versions of DOS, before 4.0, were only capable of accessing 1 Mb of RAM. The first 640 k was conventional memory. The next 256 was called expanded memory. Some DOS programs were coded specifically to access that area of memory. With later versions of DOS and greater amounts of RAM, you need an expanded memory emulation program if you continue to run these older DOS programs. EMM386.EXE is one such program.

.EXE A file extension for executable program files in the DOS file and directory system. By typing the first part of such a file name (the eight letters preceding the extension), you "run" the program. For example, you might type INSTALL to run an executable program named INSTALL.EXE.

Expanded Memory *see* EMS

Extended Memory *see* XMS

FAQ Frequently Asked Questions. Usually a file posted to an Internet newsgroup or at an FTP site. When seeking information via Internet, always look first at the FAQ to save a lot of time.

Font In computer terms (as opposed to typesetting terms), a typeface family stored in a computer file. A single font file contains plain, bold, and italic versions of the typeface family. It may also contain several sizes. An example of a font is Times Roman.

Fragmented disk, or fragmentation The status of a disk when files cannot be stored as discreet units on contiguous areas of the disk, but must be split and scattered around the disk. This happens after a disk has been reused frequently. It is a problem with the logical structure of the files and directories on the disk, not a physical problem. You can reorganize the data so that files are stored more logically. This is called "de-fragmenting the disk."

Freeware Copyrighted software that is distributed free of charge by the programmers.

FTP The Internet File Transfer Protocol. An FTP site is a storage area belonging to one of the computers on the Internet, where files can be uploaded and downloaded around the world.

Full Motion Video It depends on whom you ask. In general, when used in referring to digital video displayed on a computer, full motion is the equivalent of displaying 30 frames per second, as does American TV. However, film displays only 24 frames per second and European TV displays only 25 frames per second.

Future Domain A type of SCSI interface. This is a specific brand of SCSI adapter card and it requires a special SCSI cable. Do not attempt to use a standard SCSI cable on a Future Domain adapter or vice versa—it will short circuit your cable, card, or CD-ROM drive.

Gb (Gigabyte) 1000 Megabytes.

Gig *see* gigabyte

Gigabyte *see* Gb

Green Book *see* Red, Yellow, and Green Book

Head The device in a disk drive that accesses the data stored on the disk. In a CD-ROM drive, this is a laser beam focused through a lens.

HFS Hierarchical File Structure. The standard Macintosh file system, made up of folders and files in the folders. A CD-ROM disc may be laid out in this manner, as well, for Macintosh users.

High memory RAM in a PC above the first 1 Mb.

Hit (a database) A match between the information you are seeking in a database and the data in the database. If you are looking for all instances of a word, such as CD-ROM, each match found by the retrieval software is called a "hit."

HSF High Sierra Format. The original CD-ROM file format, superseded by ISO9660 and then the Yellow Book standards.

HTML HyperText Markup Language. A set of standard codes or tags used to develop World Wide Web pages.

HyperCard A Macintosh operating-system hypermedia development tool.

Hypermedia A style of computer program that combines primarily text materials with sounds and graphics. Objects in the file are designated as "hot links" to other files, documents, and multimedia data, such as animations, sounds, and videos.

Hypertext A style of computer program based on text material. Words are designated as "hot spots" that, when selected, link the user to other parts of a document or other documents.

Hz (abbreviation Hertz) The measurement of electrical frequency. Standard household current is 60 Hz.

IDE A standard type of connector on a computer's motherboard, into which several sorts of drives may easily be installed. Older computer drives (including hard drives and CD-ROM drives) often came with proprietary connectors that were more difficult to install because they were nonstandard.

Image Pack format A Kodak proprietary image file format. You can have any 35-mm film processed and placed onto a CD-ROM in the Image Pack format.

INIT A Macintosh operating system file that runs automatically as soon as the computer starts up, or is "initialized."

Insert Place the diskette into the diskette drive; place the CD-ROM disc into the CD-ROM drive tray and close the door; or place the CD-ROM disc into a caddie and then put the caddie into the CD-ROM drive's opening. The disc always goes in label side up. If you are putting the disc into a caddie, the disc goes in label side up and the metallic tab with the arrow on it goes first into the door.

Install To set up your computer so that it can play a CD-ROM (or other software) title. The process generally involves copying files off the CD-ROM disc to your computer's hard drive as well as making changes to various elements of your system. Installation is not as simple as inserting a disc into the CD-ROM drive, unfortunately.

Interactivity Responsiveness; a type of human-computer dialog. Using a computer, you can direct the course of action and receive feedback.

Interface In terms of computer hardware, an interface is an adapter card that allows you to attach peripheral components to your computer system. In terms of computer software, an interface is the imagery, words, and menu systems that allow you to communicate with your computer and to control it.

Internet A worldwide collection of networked locations, accessible via public points of entry. Universities, research labs, government agencies, and corporations formed the original Internet, which have since been joined by bulletin board systems and online services, so that individuals can now use the Internet for e-mail and other powerful forms of communication.

IRQ The interrupt request line ID number, or address, used by an adapter card (especially sound cards) to communicate with your computer's operating system. There are only a limited number of these available in a computer, and, consequently, there may be conflicts between devices for the use of a specific IRQ.

ISA Industry Standard Architecture, a type of "bus." This term may describe certain aspects of your computer's motherboard, which itself determines the types of additional components, or adapter cards, that may be added to it. It is in contrast to MCA, a type of bus found in IBM computers, such as the PS/2 models.

ISO9660 An older CD-ROM standard now superseded by the Yellow Book Standard. ISO stands for International Standards Organization.

Jack A plug.

Jewel Case The square plastic case in which most CD-ROMs are sold.

JPEG Joint Photographic Experts Group image file format. File names often end in .JPG.

.JPG *see* JPEG

Jumper The legs on a microchip, which connect the chip to the circuit board. You can "jump" or skip some of the connections as a means of controlling the use of the chip by the computer.

k The abbreviation for kilobyte. A kilobyte is a unit of measurement for data. One kilobyte is made up of 1000 bytes.

Kb *see* k

KHz Kilohertz

Kilobyte *see* k

Kodak Photo CD A type of CD-ROM containing images in a proprietary Kodak file format called Image Pack. Most MPC level 2 and Mac CD-ROM drives are compatible with this format.

LAN (Local Area Network) A network of linked computers sharing resources within a single location. The LAN is managed by a central server computer (either a file server or an application server, or possibly a CD-ROM server) to which one or more client workstations are attached.

Letterbox format A motion picture industry term describing the shape of the frame on the screen. In a theater,

movies are shown with an aspect ratio of 4:3, meaning the width-to-height ratio. When displayed on a TV or computer screen, the frame is usually cropped to conform to the shape of the screen, but if the 4:3 aspect ratio is preserved, then it is said to be "letterbox" shaped.

License A statement of your rights to ownership of some aspects of a CD-ROM title or other software. You generally own the material on which the program is recorded, such as the disc, but not the contents of the disc. You have only a license to use the information on the disc.

Limited warranty *see* warranty

M *see* Mb

Mb The abbreviation for megabyte, a unit of size for measuring data files. One megabyte is made up of 1000 kilobytes.

MCA (MicroChannel Architecture) An IBM proprietary type of bus that may be found on your computer's motherboard, especially if it is an older PS/2. Windows 95 Plug and Play supports some aspects of MCA computer adapters automatically; so you may find that your older IBM PC is Plug and Play compatible.

MCGA A little-used, older screen resolution of 640x200 pixels and two colors. This is sometimes used in handheld personal digital assistants and the Sony MMCD Player.

Meg *see* Mb

Megabyte *see* Mb

Megahertz *see* MHz

Memory A temporary storage area in a personal computer. Memory is made up of the chips on a circuit board.

Menuing system A type of software system that converts an otherwise difficult-to-use operating system into a system that can be accessed via menu selections.

MHz (Megahertz) The unit of measurement of sound wavelengths.

MIDI (Musical Instrument Digital Interface) A type of sound that can be synthesized (generated) by a computer's sound card through speakers or for playback and recording through external MIDI devices, including musical keyboards and Karaoke devices.

MMCD (Multimedia CD) A Sony proprietary CD-ROM format, originally using a small DOS program and MCGA graphics in a small, hand-held player device.

Mode 1 Mode 1 is a "flavor" of CD-ROM format in which the header record (a section at the beginning of the data track) contains error checking and correction codes. Because of this, mode 1 discs have slightly less room for data storage than mode 2 discs.

Mode 2 Mode 2 is a "flavor" of CD-ROM format in which the amount of space available on the disc is optimized for maximum data storage, and consequently the disc's header record lacks the error checking and correction codes of a mode 1 disc. Mode 2 discs are similar to CD-I discs.

Modem Modulation Demodulation. A computer peripheral or component that allows you to send and receive data signals over an analog phone line.

Motherboard The main circuit board in a computer. The motherboard generally contains the processor and RAM chips as well as slots for adapter cards.

MPC 1 standards An MPC 1 compatible PC must have the following:
- 386/SX
- 2 Mb RAM
- 30 Mb hard drive
- VGA display
- Two-button mouse
- 101 extended keyboard
- CD-ROM drive with CD-Audio output jack, 150 Kb/s transfer rate, no more than 1 sec seek time, MSCDEX.EXE 2.2
- 8-bit audio
- MIDI
- 1 serial port
- 1 parallel port
- MIDI I/O port

- Joystick port
- Headphone or speaker jacks

MPC 2 standards An MPC 2 compatible computer must have the following:
- 486/SX, 25 MHz
- 4 Mb RAM
- 160 Mb hard drive
- 1 3.5 inch diskette drive
- 640 x 480, 256 color VGA or SVGA display
- Two-button mouse
- 101 extended keyboard
- Double speed CD-ROM XA, multi-session drive with CD-Audio output jack, 300 Kb/s transfer rate, no more than 400 ms seek time, MSCDEX.EXE 2.2
- 16-bit audio
- MIDI
- 1 serial port
- 1 parallel port
- MIDI I/O port
- Joystick port
- Headphone or speaker jacks

MPEG (Motion Picture Experts Group video compression format) MPEG is an industry standard method of compressing video for full-motion playback on a computer screen. Video files in this format require a software run-time program or a hardware adapter card. File names often end in .MPG. MPEG-2 is a more recent standard, which has been accepted for DVD, but not for all digital media.

.MPG *see* MPEG

Multimedia In the computer industry, multimedia generally is a descriptive term for programs that incorporate audio, video, and other data.

Mixed Mode A CD-ROM format that includes both Red Book CD audio on track 2 and Yellow Book CD-ROM data on track 1.

NTSC (National Television Systems Committee) The standard set by a US commission in the early 1950s for North American television broadcast compatibility. An NTSC television displays video at a rate of 30 frames per second, and each screen is interleaved.

NuBus An Apple Computer, Inc. trademarked architecture. NuBus is a type of adapter slot on some Macintosh circuit boards.

OEM Original Equipment Manufacturer. This is usually the company that first manufactured a computer component, such as a CD-ROM drive. That company, in turn, may have sold the drive to a computer manufacturer, such as Dell or Compaq. The OEM is important to you when you are seeking an upgraded device driver for the peripheral.

Operating System The essential software for controlling your computer's hardware and peripherals. Examples are DOS, OS/2, Windows, Windows 95, Macintosh System 7, and UNIX.

OS/2 An IBM-proprietary operating system for personal computers.

Page-Turner A great book, but a poor CD-ROM title. *See* the "Introduction" to this guide.

PAL (Phase Alteration Line) The standard adopted in the 1960s for broadcast television in the United Kingdom, the Netherlands, and Germany. A PAL television displays video at a rate of 25 frames per second, interlaced. Several variations of the PAL standard are used throughout the world. Brazil uses PAL-M, France and many other European countries and former French colonies use SECAM (Sequential Couleur Avec Memoire), and there are even different types of SECAM. This proliferation of TV standards has greatly complicated international multimedia development. Keep in mind that you cannot play PAL or SECAM videotapes or DVD on players purchased and manufactured in the US.

Patch A program fix that you can install on your system without obtaining a whole new version of the CD-ROM title. It is usually a separate file from the program.

PCI (Peripheral Control Interface) A type of bus or architecture found in some Macintosh and some newer personal computers. This is of importance when you are upgrading your system. Be sure to find out what kind of architecture your computer has so that you can purchase compatible add-ons.

Pentium An Intel Corp. trademarked name for a fast processor found in IBM-compatible computers. It superseded the 486 chip.

Photo CD *see* Kodak Photo CD

PIF (Program Information File) A PIF is a Windows 3.X file that allows you to customize the way Windows runs DOS-based programs.

Pixel Picture elements. The dots of light making up a computer screen.

Platform A term used to describe a hardware plus operating system combination, which serves as the foundation for presenting software applications. You may hear discussions of the Microsoft-Intel platform, for instance, or the Macintosh platform.

Player software program *see* Runtime

Plug and Play (PnP) A hardware and software standard specified by Microsoft to make it easier to add new components to your computer system. Windows 95 automatically recognizes and sets up computer systems in which the computer's motherboard is PnP-compliant and in which the peripheral components are PnP-compliant. This means that, in general, only computer equipment manufactured after 1995 is truly Plug and Play. Microsoft can provide you with a testing program to determine whether your computer is PnP compliant.

Port The connector where external, peripheral devices "dock" with your computer. Most ports are physical plugs on the back of the system unit (see below). Each one has a name or number so that you can set up the port for special purposes and then your computer can recognize the port by the ID.

PostScript A programming language for typesetting, desktop publishing, and fonts, created by Adobe Systems.

Processor The computer chip that performs the calculations in a personal computer.

RAM Drive A virtual disk drive, created temporarily in RAM. Since RAM is faster to access than a hard drive (and certainly much faster than a CD-ROM drive or diskette drive), you can often create a temporary (virtual) drive in memory. This speeds up the access of your programs to the information. Instead of seeking the data on a disk drive, the computer has only to look as far as its own memory to find what it needs. Most RAM drives are volatile – when you turn off the computer, you lose everything stored in the RAM drive.

RAM (Random Access Memory) RAM is a type of memory chip (sometimes contained on SIMMs) for temporary storage of data.

RCA Jack A type of audio plug. It generally is used for connecting an external audio source to a computer's sound card for recording purposes.

Red, Yellow, and Green book standards Industry standards for the production of various formats of discs. Red Book sets the standards for CD audio. Yellow Book sets the standards for CD-ROM. Green Book sets the standards for CD-I. Each of these formats may be called instead by the color of the cover of the book in which the standards were first published.

Resolution The display quality of the monitor-graphics adapter combination. The resolution is measured in pixels (picture elements, or dots of light), for example, 640x480. The resolution capacity of a display system may also be designated VGA, SVGA, and so on. Each of these resolutions indicates the maximum number of colors that can be displayed by the system at a given number of pixels per screen.

Retrieval software Programs designed to quickly access information on a CD-ROM. Many CD-ROM titles are text-based databases of information, such as phone books. The titles have a menu system or other program to allow you to look up information on the disc.

ROM BIOS (ROM Binary Operating System) *see* ROM The BIOS is the minimum, built-in operating system in a personal computer.

ROM (Read Only Memory) Chips in your personal computer that contain some essential commands for your computer's operating system. You cannot store information in ROM.

Root Directory A DOS term referring to the main directory of the hard drive. All subdirectories branch off from the root directory (like an upside down tree). Most hard drives are drive C:. So, the root directory is indicated as C:\.

Runtime software program Some multimedia CD-ROM titles consist of information to be played and a program to play the information files. The runtime or player software is often copied to the hard drive of the computer. Then it can be reused by any CD-ROM title that uses the same type of information and software. Examples include QuickTime, Video for Windows, Multimedia Player, and Visual Basic's VBRUN. If a CD-ROM title requires a runtime program that you do not have, you can often obtain it free of charge from an online service or Internet ftp site.

Scalable font A font that can easily be resized because it is not a bitmapped font (see above). The font file stores each character as a resizable outline.

SCSI (Small Computer System Interface) Pronounced "skuzzy." SCSI is a type of adapter plug found on most Macintoshes and many other personal computers and equipment.

Search string The letters or key words for which you are searching in a database. If you are instructed to enter a search string while searching for information in a database, it means that you must enter a sequence of letters and characters (a "string").

Server A network computer that provides critical network services to the network and its clients. The server manages the activities of the network, allocates resources, and allows client workstations to access centrally stored files, application programs, and CD-ROM title discs, among other things.

Shareware Copyrighted software for sale at a very low cost. Many software developers sell their programs directly to the public, rather than through distributors and retailers, in order to keep prices low. The software is distributed to potential customers on a trial basis. If the trial is successful, the user is obligated to send the license fee (often less than $50) directly to the programmer.

Shell system Software that protects a computer system's critical operating system files from unauthorized use. Shell systems generally present a user-friendly, graphical interface to users from which they may select a limited number of application programs or CD-ROM titles.

Slots A narrow plug on the motherboard (main circuit board) of your computer where you may install additional components and upgrades to the system. These slots are usually capable of handling either an 8-bit or a 16-bit adapter card. When you purchase a new adapter card, be sure that you have an open, unused slot of the proper type available for installation of the card.

.SND The file name extension for Sound-format files. Many Macintosh sound files are in this format and may or may not have this file name extension (ending).

Standard Commonly accepted design principles. The computer industry designates international working committees to produce uniform design specifications for both software and hardware in an attempt to make computer components and software compatible with the widest possible range of combinations.

Storage The physical location where data is permanently saved, usually a disk. Storage of data can be temporary (in memory, for example) or permanent (on a hard drive or diskette, for example).

.SYS The file name extension for some system and device-driver files in the DOS file and directory system.

System Unit The case containing the essential components of a personal computer system. Often the system unit contains the processor, ROM chips, RAM chips, and disk drives, but other components, including the monitor and keyboard are separate.

Title A CD-ROM application program.

TSR (Terminate-Stay-Resident) TSRs are programs that usually run in DOS. After executing them in order to load them into conventional memory (generally), you can hide them and then run another program. The TSR can be instantly recalled at any time, even while the second program is active, often by pressing a designated "hot key" combination.

Type style A variation of a typeface, or font, such as plain, bold, or italic.

Typeface A named font, such as Times Roman.

TrueType A competitive technology to Postscript (see above) sponsored by Microsoft and Apple, among others. This technology provides fonts that display exactly the same on the screen of your computer as they print out.

.TXT Some text files in the DOS file and directory system are named with this ending, or file name extension. It is not a requirement, but in most cases if you see a file name that ends in .TXT the file is a text file that can be opened and read by most word-processing programs.

UDF (Universal Disk Format) A file format developed by the Optical Storage Technology Association primarily to accommodate the development of DVD discs. This file format is designed to make data files accessible independently of the hardware, software, or operating system on a computer.

UNIX A nonproprietary operating system for "small" computers, such as personal computers, engineering workstations, and server systems in a network. UNIX is the favored system for Internet servers.

Upload The process of transferring data from one computer to another (technically, from a small computer to a larger, more powerful one).

VESA (Video Electronic Standards Association) An industry association that develops standards for video graphics cards, accelerators, and monitors. Many CD-ROM titles indicate that your computer system's graphics or monitor must conform to these standards in order to be fully compatible with the CD-ROM's software. Refer to your computer's manuals to determine whether your system is VESA compliant. In addition, you may need to have certain VESA compliant software drivers installed in your system in order for the CD-ROM and your computer to perform together properly.

VLB (Video Local Bus) An addition to the ISA bus in many 486 and later computers, which improves the speed or performance of the video adapter card in the computer.

.WAV *see* Wavetable

Warranty The limited responsibility of a CD-ROM title producer or computer equipment manufacturer for the materials they produce. Each CD-ROM title you purchase is likely to have a limited warranty that permits you to exchange defective discs and other materials for a limited time following purchase. The warranty does not cover general customer satisfaction, though. Be sure to read your warranty, license, and registration information each time you purchase a CD-ROM title.

Waveform The shape of a sound wave. Some audio editing programs display graphical representations of waveforms. By modifying the shape of the waves you change the sounds.

Wavetable A synthesis technology used to reproduce lifelike sounds. The sound adapter card in an IBM-compatible multimedia computer should be capable of playing and recording wavetable sound files. These files usually end in the extension .WAV.

Web *see* World Wide Web

World Wide Web The graphic user interface of the Internet. The World Wide Web is comprised of sites throughout the world, where Internet access is available to "pages" of information and multimedia files. It is abbreviated WWW or W3.

WORM (Write Once Read Many CD-ROM disc format) WORM drives are synonymous, in most cases, with CD-R drives. These drives and discs allow a user to record a single copy of a CD-ROM disc, usually for backup and archival purposes.

XMS Extended memory in an IBM-compatible personal computer. XMS comprises the memory available over and above the first 640 k of conventional memory.

Yellow Book *see* Red, Yellow, and Green Book

Appendix C:
Directory of Resources

The information in this directory is subject to frequent change. When you need updates to this information, you can obtain addresses on the Internet's World Wide Web from the online directory at the InterNic (sponsored by the National Science Foundation and Network Solutions), http://www.internic.net/cool/WebFinder.html. Current phone numbers can be obtained from the CD-ROM directories published by Pro CD, Inc. of Marblehead, MA. For current suppliers of CD-ROM services to libraries and schools refer to the periodicals listed in Appendix D.

Searching the Internet for information related to CD-ROMs in libraries and schools should begin at the Web page for this book at:

http://www.mcfarlandpub.com

or http://homepage.interaccess.com/~icona/cdrom.html.

General indexes to the World Wide Web should also be searched, using the keywords CD-ROM, multimedia databases, library systems, and educational technology.

CD-ROM TITLE RESOURCES

CD-ROM TITLE DISTRIBUTORS

The US Department of Labor's Standard Industry Classification system ("SIC code system") does not include a classification for CD-ROM title distributors. When seeking organizations that supply CD-ROMs to libraries and schools, look under headings related to software sales and service, general business services, and publishing, as well as CD-ROM publishing, distribution, and sales.

Bureau of Electronic Publishing
141 New Road
Parsipanny, NY 07054
800-828-4766
201-808-2700

Educational Resources
1550 Executive Drive
Elgin, IL 60123
708-888-8300

Educorp
7434 Trade Street
San Diego, CA 92121
619-536-9999
800-843-9497
service@educorp.com (e-mail)
http://www.educorp.com

Jostens Learning Corp.
9920 Pacific Heights
San Diego, CA 92121
619-587-0087
http://www.jlc.com

Library Video Co.
P.O. Box 1110

Bola Cynwyd, PA 19004
610-667-0200

Mac Zone and PC Zone (mail order)
800-248-2088
http://www.zones.com/Mac_Zone
http://www.zones.com/PC_Zone

CD-ROM TITLE DEMOS, PREVIEWS, AND REVIEWS

CD Rom Today Magazine
Imagine Publishing, Inc.
1350 Old Bayshore Highway
Suite 210
Burlingame, CA 94010

**Department of Education
   Internet gopher**
1-800-222-4922 (modem)
gopher.ed.gov

Educational Software Selector
Educational Products Information
   Exchange Institute
103 W. Montauk Hwy. 3
Hampton Bays, NY 11946-4006
516-728-9100

CD-ROM TITLE PRODUCERS

Books in Print Plus (and others)
R.R. Bowker
Division of Reed Elsevier Inc.
121 Chauton Rd.
New Providence, NJ 07974
800-521-8110

Broderbund
500 Redwood Blvd.
Novato, CA 94947
415-382-4400
http://www.broderbund.com

Claris
5201 Patrick Henry Drive
Santa Clara, CA 95952
800-325-2747
http://www.claris.com

Compton's NewMedia, Inc.
1 Athenaeum St.
Cambridge, MA 02142
617-494-2000
http://www.cnm.com

Davidson & Associates, Inc.
Learningways Division
10 Fawcett St.
Cambridge, MA 02138
617-238-5800
http://www.education.com

Delrina Software, Inc.
see Other Software: Symantec
http://www.delrina.com

Facts On File
11 Penn Plaza
New York, NY 10001
800-322-8755
http://www.factsonfile.com

The Learning Company
6493 Kaiser Drive
Fremont, CA 94553
800-852-2255
http://www.learningco.com

CD-ROM Workstation Resources

CD-ROM Drive Manufacturers
(contact for device drivers)

NEC Technologies *see* Computer Equipment Manufacturers

Pioneer New Media Technologies, Inc.
800-444-6784
800-LASER-ON
310-952-2309 (fax)
http://www.pioneerusa.com
Device driver information:
http://www.pioneerusa.com/drivers.html

Sony Electronics, Inc.
3300 Zanker Rd.
San Jose, CA 95134
800-352-7669
http://www1.ita.sel.sony.com/products/storage/cddrives/

Toshiba America Information Systems, Inc. *see* Computer Equipment Manufacturers

Computer Equipment Manufacturers

Apple Computer, Inc.
1 Infinite Loop
Cupertino, CA 95014
800-767-2775
http://www.apple.com

AST Research Inc.
16215 Alton Parkway
Irvine, CA 92718
800-876-4278
http://www.ast.com

Compaq Computer Corp.
P.O. Box 692000
Houston, TX 77269-2000
800-345-1518
http://www.compaq.com

Dell Computer Corp.
2214 W. Braker Lane
Austin, TX 78758
800-613-3355
http://www.dell.com

Gateway 2000, Inc.
610 Gateway Dr.
P.O. Box 2000
North Sioux City, SD 57049
800-846-2000
http://www.gateway2000.net

Hewlett-Packard Co.
Personal Information Products Group

3000 Hanover St.
Palo Alto, CA 94304
800-752-0999
http://www.hp.com

IBM Personal Computer Co.
Old Orchard Rd.
Armonk, NY 10504
800-426-3333
http://www.ibm.com

NEC Technologies Inc.
1414 Massachusetts Ave.
Boxborough, MA 01719
800-632-4636
http://www.nec.com

Packard Bell NEC, Inc.
31717 La Tienda Dr.
Westlake Village, CA
800-733-5858
http://www.packardbell.com

Toshiba America Information Systems, Inc.
9740 Irvine Blvd.
Irvine, CA 92713-9724
714-583-3000
800-334-3445
http://www.toshiba.com

OPERATING SYSTEMS

Apple Computer, Inc. *see* Computer Equipment Manufacturers

Microsoft Corp.
One Microsoft Way
Redmond, WA 98052
800-426-9400
http://www.microsoft.com

Novell Inc.
1555 N. Technology Way
Orem, UT 84057
800-453-1267
http://www.novell.com

OTHER SOFTWARE AND UTILITIES

America Online
8619 Westwood Center Dr.
Vienna, VA 22182
1-800-4-ONLINE
http://www.aol.com

Claris Corp.
5201 Patrick Henry Dr.
Santa Clara, CA 95052
800-325-2747
http://www.claris.com

Eastman Kodak Co.
Kodak Information Center
Rochester, NY
1-800-242-2424
1-716-724-9977
http://www.kodak.com

Library Computer Accessories on the Internet
http://www.auburn.edu/~fostecd/docs/accessories.html

QuarterDeck
150 Pico Blvd.,
Santa Monica, CA 90405
800-354-2834
http://www.qdeck.com

Symantec Corporation
10201 Torre Avenue
Cupertino, CA 95014-2132
800-441-7234
http://www.symantec.com

Telematics for Libraries
http://www2.echo.lu/libraries/en/systems.html

PROFESSIONAL ORGANIZATIONS AND ASSOCIATIONS

American Library Association
50 E. Huron St.
Chicago, IL 60611
800-545-2433
http://www.ala.org

Library and Information Technology Association
50 E. Huron St.
Chicago, IL 60611
312-280-4270

National Education Association
101 16th St. NW
Washington, D.C. 20036
http://www.nea.org

Software Publishers Association
1730 M St. NW
Ste. 700
Washington, D.C. 20036-4510
202-452-1600
http://www.spa.org

WORKSTATION SOFTWARE RESOURCES

CD-ROM MASTERING SERVICE BUREAUS

Nimbus CD International Inc.
P.O. Box 7427
Charlottesville, VA 22906
804-983-1100
http://www.nimbuscd.com

Optical Disc Corp.
12150 Mora Drive
Santa Fe Springs, CA 90670
310-946-3050
http://www.optical-disc.com

LIBRARY AND SCHOOL SYSTEMS

Ameritech Library Systems (Dynix, NOTIS, and Horizon)
400 West Dynix Dr.
Provo, UT 84604
801-223-5200
http://www.als.ameritech.com

COMPanion Corporation
Salt Lake City, UT
Technical Support Hotline: 801-943-7752
801-943-7752 (fax)
http://www.companioncorp.com/

CARL Corporation
3801 E. Florida, Suite 300
Denver, CO 80210
303-758-3030
http://www.carl.org

OCLC Online Computer Library Center, Inc.
6565 Frantz Road
Dublin, OH 43017-3395
614-764-6000
http://www.oclc.org

Appendix D: Recommended Reading

Many of the most popular books on CD-ROMs in libraries and schools were published before 1995 and so have not been included here. On the other hand, while technical books listed on older operating systems may be out of print or hard to find, they have been included in order to identify authoritative sources of information. Hard-to-find and some out-of-print books can be purchased from Amazon.com (http://www.amazon.com).

CD-ROM TITLE SELECTION AND COLLECTIONS

Most of the publications listed here include reviews of specific CD-ROM titles and, consequently, are frequently reissued with updated information: more-recent editions may be available.

Berger, Pam and Susan Kinnell. *CD-ROM for Schools: A Directory and Practical Handbook for Media Specialists*. Wilton, CT: Eight Bit Books, 1994.

Dewey, Patrick R. *303 CD-ROMs to Use in Your Library: Descriptions, Evaluations, and Practical Advice*. Chicago: American Library Association, 1995.

Holmberg, Erin E., ed. *CD-ROMs in Print*. Annual. Westport, CT: Meckler Corporation.

Nolan, Kathleen Lopez, Ed. *Gale Directory of Databases*. Annual. Detroit: Gale Research.

Sorrow, Barbara Head and Betty S. Lumpkin. *CD-ROM for Librarians and Educators: A Guide to Instructional Resources*. 2nd ed. Jefferson, NC: McFarland & Co., 1996.

CD-ROMS IN LIBRARIES AND SCHOOLS

CD-ROM LICENSES AND COPYRIGHTS

The articles in the following book may include some outdated information, since both legislation and case law tend to force frequent changes in license and copyright law.

Nissley, Meta and Nancy Melin Nelson, eds. *CD-ROM Licensing and Copyright Issues for Libraries*. Westport, CT: Meckler, 1990.

GENERAL

The following book is considered to be a seminal text. While information in it may now be out of date, Mr. Desmarais continues to publish very useful information for librarians and educators interested in technology.

Desmarais, Norman. *The Librarian's CD-ROM Handbook*. Westport, CT: Meckler, 1989.

WORKSTATION DESIGN, FURNITURE, AND ERGONOMICS

Espinosa, Leonard J. *Microcomputer Facilities in Schools*. Englewood, CO: Libraries Unlimited, Inc., 1990.

Kaplan, Michael, ed. *Planning and Implementing Technical Services Workstations*. Chicago: American Library Association, 1997.

INTERNET AND WORLD WIDE WEB PUBLICATIONS

Web publications are dynamic and transitory. For current Web addresses, refer to one of the popular indexes at http://www.yahoo.com or http://www.lycos.com.

AskERIC: http://www.ericir.syr.edu

CD Bibliography: http://www.cd-info.com

CD Bibliography: http://www.cd-info.com/CDIC/Bibliography.html#idg

LOCAL AREA NETWORKS

McNamara, John E. and John Romkey. *Local Area Networks: An Introduction to the Technology*. Newton, MA: Butterworth-Heinemann, 1997.

Thomas, Robert M. *Introduction to Local Area Networks*. Alameda, CA: Sybex, 1996.

CD-ROM NETWORKS IN LIBRARIES

Elshami, Ahmed M. *Networking CD-ROMs: The Decision Maker's Guide to Local Area Network Solutions*. Chicago: American Library Association, 1996.

OPERATING SYSTEM MANUALS AND GUIDES

To obtain manuals for older or used computers, write to the computer equipment manufacturer. Both Microsoft Corporation and Apple Computer, Inc. are publishers of operating system manuals and other technical books, which are often available through book sellers.

Apple Computer, Inc. *Macintosh User's Guide.* Cupertino, CA: Apple Computer, Inc., 1984+.

Jamsa, Kris. *DOS: The Complete Reference (Covers all versions including DOS 6).* New York: Osborne McGraw Hill, 1993.

Judson, Jeremy, Ed. *The Macintosh Bible.* Berkeley, CA: Peachpit Press, 199+.

Microsoft Corporation. *Introducing Microsoft Windows 95.* Redmond, WA: Microsoft Corporation, 1995.

Microsoft Corporation. *Microsoft Windows 95 Resource Kit.* Redmond, WA: Microsoft Press, 1995.

Microsoft Corporation. *Microsoft Windows User's Guide.* Redmond, WA: Microsoft Corporation, 1990+.

Microsoft Corporation. *MS-DOS User's Guide.* Redmond, WA: Microsoft Corporation, 1988+.

Naiman, Arthur, ed. *The Macintosh Bible.* Berkeley, CA: Goldstein & Blair, 1992.

Sheldon, Tom. *Windows 3: The Complete Reference.* New York: Osborne McGraw-Hill, 1992.

OPTICAL DISC TECHNOLOGY

Berger, Paul. *Desktop Multimedia Bible.* Reading, MA: Addison-Wesley Publishing Company, 1993.

Gosney, Michael, ed. *The Official Photo CD Handbook.* Berkeley, CA: Peachpit Press, 1995.

Lambert, Steve and Suzanne Ropiequet. *CD-ROM, the New Papyrus.* Redmond, WA: Microsoft Press, 1986.

Parker, Dana. *New Rider's Guide to CD-ROM.* 2nd ed. Indianapolis, IN: New Rider's Publishing, 1994.

Purcell, Lee, and David Martin. *The Complete Recordable-CD Guide.* Alameda, CA: Sybex, 1997.

PERIODICALS

CD-ROM Librarian, Meckler Publishing Corp., 11 Ferry Lane West, Westport, CT 06880. (203-226-6967)

CD-ROM Professional (see below, now *E-Media*), http://www.online.com/cdrompro/

Computers in Libraries, Learned Information, Inc., 143 Old Marlton Pike, Medford, NJ 08055-8750. (609-654-6265), http://www.infotoday.com

DATABASE, Online Inc., 462 Danbury Road, Wilton, CT 06897-2126. (800-248-8466) http://www.online.com/database

E-Media, Online Inc., 462 Danbury Road, Wilton, CT 06897-2126. (800-248-8466) http://www.online.com/database

Educational Technology, Educational Technology Publications, 700 Palisade Ave., Englewood Cliffs, NJ 07632-0564. (800-952-BOOK)

Electronic Library. Learned Information, Inc., 143 Old Marlton Pike, Medford, NJ 08055-8750. (609-654-6265)

Information Technology and Libraries. American Library Association, 50 E. Huron, Chicago, IL 60611. (312-944-6780)

Instructional Delivery Systems, Communicative Technology Corp., 50 Culpepper St., Warrenton, VA 22186. (703-347-0055)

Library Software Review, Meckler Publishing Corp., 11 Ferry Lane West, Westport, CT 06880. (203-226-6967)

NewMedia Magazine, Hypermedia Communications, Inc., 901 Mariner's Island Blvd., Ste. 365, San Mateo, CA 94404. (415-573-5131)

OCLC Micro, Online Computer Library Center, Inc. 6565 Frantz Rd., Dublin, OH 43017-0702. (614-764-6277)

ONLINE, Online, Inc., 462 Danbury Rd., Wilton, CT 06897-2126. (800-248-8466) http://www.online.com/onlinemag or olmag@online.com

Teaching and Computers, Scholastic, Inc., 730 Broadway, New York, NY 10003.

T.H.E. Journal, Information Synergy, Inc., 150 El Camino Real, Ste. 112, Tustin, CA 92680-3670. (714-730-4011)

Index

Accelerator software 103–104
Access rate 142
Access to the CD-ROM system 16, 20, 25, 96
Add/Remove Programs *see* Windows 9X, applets and components
Address conflicts 209, 225–226, 256–257; *see also* DMA; Interface; IRQ
America Online 53, 54, 85, 128, 132; *see also* Online services
Analysis, workstation 134–141
Appletalk *see* Networks, types of
Application Fast "Alt-Tab" Switching *see* Multi-tasking
Archiving titles 44–45
ASCII 131–132
Associations, obtaining titles from 55–56
Attributes, file *see* Hidden files
Audio 25, 89–90, 104–105; CD-A format 142; headphones 25, 105, 150; volume controls 150; *see also* CD-A; Multimedia; Sound
AUTOEXEC.BAT: bypassing on system startup 203–204; required lines vs. optional lines 163; use of 151–153, 160, 162–171, 174, 177–178, 191, 200, 203–211, 214, 222–223, 225, 226; Windows 3.X 217–218, 221–222, 225, 228, 231; Windows 9X 191, 238, 240
AutoRun 185; *see also* Windows 9X, features
AUTORUN.INF 185
AutoSetup 185; *see also* Windows 9X, features
AVI files 233

Back-ups: importance of 110, 113–114, 174; when to perform 79–80, 86, 98, 103, 151, 162, 167, 212, 227; *see also* Drives, hard disk
Binary 131
BIOS self-test 203
Boot disk 205; DOS 205–206, 211, 214, 244; Windows 9X 192, 222–223, 241–242; *see also* Startup disk, Macintosh
Boot log 223
BOOTLOG.TXT 224
Budgets 30–32
BUFFERS= 214
Bugs 69, 213, 234, 257; corrected editions of titles 74
Bulletin board systems (BBSs) 128; downloading from, overview of 132–133; downloading from, steps 132
Bus errors *see* Address conflicts

Cables 116–119, 144, 147, 149–150, 254, 259, 260–261; checking connections 209, 224, 254; replacing 149; shorts in 149, 214
Cache *see* Disk cache; RAM, drives; Virtual memory
Card-catalog systems 20; Telnet to 130
CAV 263–264
CD-audio (CD-A) 58, 210, 255, 257
CD formats 144
CD-I 38, 266
CD Match 86, 135
CD Plus 58
CD-R 3, 16, 29, 71, 265
CD-ROM *see* Discs, CD-ROM; Drives, CD-ROM
CD-ROM-XA 58, 66, 264
CD-WR 29, 71, 265
Cdev *see* Macintosh operating system
CDFS.EXE 104, 184
CDSPEED command DOS 138

289

CHKDSK command, DOS: conventional memory analysis 135; hard-disk space analysis 135–136; Windows 3.X, use of 213; /F switch 211
Circulation of disc library 15
Claris 84
Cleanup Coach 238
CLV 264
COM file-name ending *see* Executable file
COM ports 89–90, 139, 147, 226
COMMAND.COM: general use of 204, 206; on a bootable disk 206; Windows 9X, use of 241–242
Compatibility: hardware, drives with disc formats 144–146, 210, 213, 230; hardware, upgrades 11; Macintosh, System 6 with new titles 193; Macintosh and PCs 34, 145; titles with workstations 35, 58–61, 86–87; titles and workstations, how to determine 61, 160; multimedia, how to determine in Windows 3.X 177–178
Compressed disks *see* Drives, hard disk
Compressed files 85, 131, 133
CompuServe 47; *see also* Online services
CONFIG.SYS: bypassing on system startup 203–204; required vs. optional lines 163; use of 151–153, 160, 162–171, 174, 177–178, 191, 199, 203–211, 214, 222, 225, 226, 230, 240–241; Windows 3.X 217–218, 221–222; Windows 9X 191, 238, 240
Configuration: CD-ROM workstation (diagnosing with MSCDEX.EXE) 137–138; CD-ROM workstation (modifying) 162–168; CD-ROM workstation (recommendations) 67–68; DOS (configuration menus): 170–171; DOS (modifying) 206; examining 203; files 90, 98, 111; files (backing up) 111, 113; *see also* AUTOEXEC.BAT; CONFIG.SYS
CONTROL.INI 222
Copyrights 14, 16–17, 70–71
Costs *see* Budgets
CPU 72
CrossTalk 132

Data transfer rate 142
DBLSPACE command, DOS *see* Doublespace
DBLSPACE.BIN *see* Doublespace
Debugging 205; *see also* Troubleshooting
Decompressing: file 85, 131, 133; obtaining decompression programs 133
DEFRAG command: use of in DOS 212; use of in Windows 3.X 213
Defragmenting: PC hard disk 212, 229, 230; Windows 3.X 213, 229; Windows 9X 213; *see also* Macintosh operating system, desktop, rebuilding
De-installing: DOS titles 162, 176, 182, 186; Macintosh titles 196; Windows 3.X titles 176, 217; Windows 9X titles 238
Demos 53–55
Desk Accessories *see* Macintosh operating system
DEVICE and DEVICEHIGH command, DOS 164–166, 177, 208, 223, 225, 230
Device drivers: Apple Computer 84; audio and sound 178, 213, 231; conflicts with sound card 213; corrupted 234; cost 83–84; device-independent and universal 83, 155, 184; DOS 151–152, 208, 177; downloading 85–86, 128–134; DVD 157; general 58, 66, 81–86, 150–157, 209; hardware device names 153; identifying 138; installing, DOS steps 151, 208; Macintosh 156, 194–195, 260; Macintosh, required files 195–96; MSCDEX.EXE 152–153; multimedia 67, 139, 154, 231, 251; networks 82; obtaining 83–85, 129, 244; problems, most common cause of 81; role of 81; updating 82, 84, 223, 234, 241, 243–244, 247; Windows Setup 217
Device Drivers, Windows 3.X: general use in 139, 153–155, 230; printer drivers 139; removing 154–155;
Device Drivers, Windows 9X 155–156, 185, 187, 243–244, 245
Dialer programs 132

Dictionary titles 45
DIR command, DOS 159, 166–167, 211–213
Disabilities 28
Disc caddie 95–96
Disc changer 19; *see also* Stackers, jukeboxes, and towers
Discs, CD-ROM: capacity 2, 37; care and maintenance 94–96; damaging 95–96; durability 94; ejecting from Macintosh 253, 255; inserting properly 95; interleaved 264; master 265; physical description of 95; surface 212; tracks 172; verifying readability 159
Discounts 56, 73
Disk buffer *see* Disk cache
Disk cache 141, 142–143, 201, 218; DOS RAM disk 210; Macintosh 251; Windows 3.X 221, 228; Windows 9X 245–246; Windows 9X, disabling in 190, 246; Windows 9X, verifying 186
Disk compaction *see* Defragmenting
Disk compression *see* Drives, hard disk
Disk FirstAid 238
Disk Optimizer 212
Disk Tools disks *see* Macintosh operating system
Distributors, title 55, 119
DLL file-name ending (dynamic link library) 175
DMA setting 161
Documentation: title updates 69, 196; troubleshooting procedures and policies 109; Windows 9X workstations 189; workstation, guidelines for writing 105–108; workstation, users of 105–108
Dolby AC-3 105, 267; *see also* Audio; Sound
Donations 32, 55–56
DOS: compatibility with Intel processors 68; device drivers, installing 151–152; drive letter designations 152, 208–209; versions, general issues 207, 239; MSCDEX.EXE 152–153; number (identifying) 135; 16-bit vs. 32-bit applications 139–140; *see also* Boot disk; DOS windows; Individual command words; MSCDEX.EXE
DOS, diagnostic tools: version 5.0 and earlier 135–136; version 5.0 and later 137; version 6.1 and later 137–138
DOS, Windows 3.X: relationship to 62–63; returning to from DOS 207
DOS, Windows 9X running DOS titles under 188–189, 236, 239
DOS EDIT 163, 169, 206, 222
DOS windows 63; running titles in Windows 3.X 199, 219; running titles in Windows 9X 238–239; title installation in 177
Double-buffering 218; *see also* Drives, hard disk
Doublespace: program 214, 230; "uncompressed host drive" 214; /LIST switch 214
Downloading 85–86, 127–134; incomplete file or data-transfer during 127, 128, 129; information needed during 128–129; overwriting FAT 128; steps 128; Web browser 130
DRIVERS= 233
Drives, CD-ROM: access rate and seek time 142; cables 149–150; capacity 144–145; characteristics 141; controller and interface types 142–143, 147–148; data transfer rate 142; disk cache and buffer size 142–143; heads 95; identifiers 87, 209–210; DOS letters 153, 208; installation of 102, 116–117, 146; internal vs. external 144; mode 66, 138, 144–146; multiple 19, 153; network 153; operation of 146, 147, 221; removal of discs from 97; SCSI 193–194; verifying proper operation of 152, 159, 172; *see also* CD-ROM-XA; Drives, hard disk; DVD; Format of discs; Kodak Photo CD
Drives, CD-ROM, speed 66, 88–89, 138, 141–142, 245; Macintosh 195, 259; significance of 66; testing 138
Drives, hard disk: backups 29; capacity 64; compression 214, 230; defragmenting 29, 212; double-buffering 218; drive-in-use light 220, 239; fragmented 212, 227, 229; insufficient 136, 210, 226–227, 259;

maintenance 94; software 102–103; storage 64, 102, 161; upgrades to 102

Drives, free space on 64, 127, 135–136, 249; contiguous 226–227, 228, 230; deleting files 227; verifying amount 166–167

DRV file-name ending 154, 175

DRVSPACE command DOS: /LIST switch 214; use of 214

DVD 3, 19, 29, 58, 102, 105, 264, 266–268

E-IDE controllers 143, 147

Editing, of configuration files 217, 240, 245

Educational titles 50–52

Edutainment 51–52

Emergency boot disk see Boot disk

EMM386.EXE: NOEMS value 218; use of 217–218, 223, 231

EMM386.SYS: NOEMS value 183, 218; use of 183, 201, 217

EMS see Expanded memory

Enabler software, Macintosh System 7, 59–60

Encyclopedia titles 46–47

Environment: controls 25; dust 26, 93; electric lines 26; heat 25; humidity 25, 26, 93, 214, 259; static electricity 26; temperature 25

Ergonomics 27–28

Error correction see Troubleshooting

Error messages: accessing drives 152; DOS 112–113, 240; drive controller 143; file, folder, and path names 244–245; how to interpret 110; "insufficient memory," DOS 167, 210–211; missing files 166, 175, 244–245; programs that generate 112, 113, 118; see also Error message, text; Error messages, Macintosh; Error messages, Windows 3.X; Error messages, Windows 9X

Error messages, Macintosh: "bomb" icon 251; "insufficient memory" 197–198, 257–258; numerical codes 256–257; types 114–115, 197, 252–253, 256; "unhappy Mac" icon 259; X-ed out Mac disk icon 194, 254–255

Error messages, text: "application program has performed an invalid oper-ation" 114; "bootable device that has a SCSI id other than 0 or 1 or 2" 260; "CDR-101" 210; "CDR-102" 210; "CD-ROM drive not recog-nized" 244–245; "conflicting SCSI ID" 260–261; "corrupt swap file" 228–230; "desktop file couldn't be created on the disk" 256; "device not found" 225; "device not loaded" 166, 208; "disc is in the CD-ROM drive" 213, 230; "extensions file must be placed into the Extensions folder" 157; "file not found" 166, 179, 204; "free disk space on drive C is frag-mented. If you have a disk-com-paction utility, you should use it to compact this drive" 229–230; "incor-rect DOS version" 207–208, 225, 242; "incorrectly terminated SCSI device" 260; "installing a driver not supplied with Windows" 154; "insufficient disk space" 211–213; "insufficient memory," SMART-DRV.EXE as source of 226–228; "insufficient memory to run applica-tion" 226–228; "invalid device" 208; "invalid drive specification" 208–209; "music" errors 232–233; "no SCSI device found" 260; "not enough drive letters" 208–209; "not enough Finder memory to work with the disk" 258; "not a network drive" 211; "out of memory" 174, 247; "out of resources" 247; "SHARE viola-tion" 211; "this is not a Macintosh disk, initialize?" 258; "unable to cre-ate directory" 244–245; "wrong disc in CD-ROM drive" 230; "wrong file format" 255–256; "wrong SCSI ID" 260–261; "wrong startup disk" 255

Error messages, Windows 3.X: "Exit" vs. "Ignore" 219; types 113–114, 218–219; "insufficient memory" 179, 181;

Error messages, Windows 9X: "con-tact the vendor" 239; types 114, 239, 240

Errors, nonspecific: address conflicts 161, 209, 225–226, 256–257; bus errors 256–257; CD-ROM drive fail-ure 173, 245–246, 254–255, 259; device drivers 243–244, 256, 257;

General Protection Fault (GPF) 234–235; installation failure 205–206, 206, 210, 222–223, 241–242, 253–254; IRQ interrupts 161, 209, 225–226; MCICDA.DRV 231; MIDI 231–232; mouse cursor 230–231; multimedia problems, Windows 3.X 231–234; multimedia problems, Windows 9X 242–243; PIF errors 221; poor sound quality 214–215, 232–233, 246–247, 259; SCSI 259–260, 261; shortcuts 247; system freezes or hangs 213–214, 231, 259; Video for Windows 233–234, 246; Windows 3.X SetUp errors 221–222; Windows 9X (files retained from Windows 3.X) 247

Evaluation criteria, title 35–41; amount of information 37–38; checklist 52; content 38–39, 44, 45; producer reputation 36; technical quality 36–37

Exclude statement 223, 231

EXE file-name ending see Executable file

Executable file: COM file 128, 231; EXE file 128, 231

Expanding, file 85; see also Decompressing, file

Expanded memory 137, 169, 180, 183, 201, 218; emulating 201; general NOEMS 183; see also EMM386.EXE; Extended memory

Extended memory 137, 169, 177, 180, 201

Extensions, Macintosh 156–157, 195–197, 249, 255–256, 257

"Fair use" 70

FAQ (Frequently Asked Questions) 131

FASTOPEN.EXE 200–201, 217

FAT (File Allocation Table) 128, 249

FDCD.SYS 214

File: binary type 131–132; compression format 128–129; definition 128; text types 131–132; Windows 3.X 244–245

FILE0000.CHK 212

Font/DA Mover see Macintosh operating system

Foreign File Access see Macintosh operating system

Format, of discs 58, 144–145; list of 144–145

FORMAT command, DOS: reformatting 212; /S switch 205–206; use of 205–206

Freeware see Copyrights

FTP 128–131

Full screen mode see Windows 9X, modes

Function keys see PC function keys

General Protection Fault (GPF) 113–114, 222, 234–235

GOTO statement, DOS 170–171

Graphics adapter 181

Graphics resolution 210; memory usage 210–211, 231; Windows 9X 246

HFS 255

Hidden files 229, 240–242

High memory, PC 177, 208, 214

High Sierra format 144, 255

HIMEM.SYS 201, 218, 223

"Hot reboot" see Restarting an operating system

Hour, CD-ROM 39

Hybrid disc 61–62, 145

Hypertext 106

IBM-compatible 62

IDE controllers 143, 147

Image-creation software see CD-R

INI file-name ending 113, 154, 176, 181–183; associating with text editor in Windows 3.X 182; modifying accidentally 222; modifying to install titles 221–222; semicolon in 183; Windows 9X 245, 247

INIT see Macintosh operating system, applets and components

Input devices 65

INSTALL.EXE see Installation of titles

Installation of CD-ROM drives 146

Installation of files: downloaded files 134; DOS device driver files 151–152

Installation of titles: costs of 31; DOS, manually 79, 162, 168; re-installation of titles 176, 206, 211, 217, 249; preparations for 86–87; problems in 88–90; purpose of 80; rules for 79–

80; upgrades and new editions 80; utility programs 171

Installation of titles, steps: overview of 87; preparations for 86–87; problems in 88–90; purpose of 80; rules for 79–80

Installation of titles, Windows 3.X: DOS titles under 179–181; titles 217, 222; types of 173

Installation of titles, Windows 9X: titles 238; types of 186; *see also* Specific operating systems

Installer programs: automatic 79, 159–160, 172–173, 174–175, 186–187, 196; failure of 160, 162, 168; how to run 171, 175; INSTALL.EXE 160, 171, 174–175, 186; license required for 72; Macintosh 156–157, 193, 195

Interactivity 39–40, 50, 263

Interface: CD-ROM software, evaluation of 40, 44; conflicts between cards 149; connecting a CD-ROM card and sound card 149–150; drive controller cards 143–144; Internet cards 24; multimedia cards 64, 100; user 40

Interlibrary loan 16–17

Internet 3, 17; CD-ROM titles and 23, 41–43; connections to 24; costs 24; downloading from 129–131

Internet, source of: demos 54; device drivers 84–86; reviews 53; technical support 118; title updates 44, 48, 69–70, 74

Interrupts *see* IRQ

I/O port address 225–226

IRQ 89–90, 138, 161, 209, 225–226; list of settings 226

ISO 9660 format 144, 255

ISP 130

IVI 50, 263–264

Job aids *see* Documentation

Jukebox *see* Stackers, jukeboxes, and towers

Kermit *see* Modem, protocols

Keyboard 66

Keystrokes, Mac; Option/Apple (to rebuild the desktop), 254; Option/ Shift/Delete (to start up system from a diskette) 253; Shift (to disable INITs) 258; Space Bar (to enable or disable Extensions) 253

Kodak Photo CD 29, 38, 58, 66, 255–256, 257, 264–265

LAN *see* Networks

Laserdisc 263–264, 266

Licensing 10, 13–14, 16, 18, 31, 35, 71–74, 120

LINUX 25, 63

LOADHIGH and LH 164–167, 177, 208, 223, 231

Log book, workstation 91–92, 110, 199

Long file names *see* Windows 9X, long file names

LPT 147

Macintosh operating system (Mac OS): compatibility with Motorola processors 68; desktop, rebuilding 254; Disk Tools disks 253–254; Interrupt button 252–253; Extensions, folder 249; Extensions Manager 253, 256; MacTerminal 132; Memory applet 251; memory, contiguous 197, 257; memory, effect of fonts 258; Reset button 252–253; SCSI, disk mode 259–260; SCSI Manager 252, 259; System 6 60, 63, 195; System 7 58, 60, 63, 195–196; System 8 63; System File 249, 257; System File, damaged 257; upgrading 101; version, minimum requirements for 251–252; number (identifying) 140; warranties 252; *see also* Keystrokes, Mac; SCSI

Macintosh operating system, analysis tools: 140–141; available memory 197, 257; hard drive space 140–141; monitor resolution 140; RAM 140, 251

Macintosh operating system, applets and components: About the Finder 140; About This Macintosh 140, 257; Apple Menu 258; Cdevs 156, 257; CD-ROM Speed Switch 259; Control Panel (access to and purpose of) 140; Desk Accessories 141, 156, 258; Font/DA Mover 156–157, 258; INITs 156, 249, 257; MultiFinder 257;

Sound Manager 252; Startup Device 253, 260

Macintosh operating system, device drivers: Foreign File Access 258; System 6 (installation) 156; System 7 (installation) 156–157

Magnetic fields 93

Maintenance 10, 23, 28–29, 31

MCICDA.DRV 231, 232

MEM command, DOS 137, 167

MemMaker.EXE 168–170, 177; Custom Setup 170, 174; Express Setup 168–170

Memory 64, 88, 174; DOS 210–211; errors 93, 161, 202, 210, 249, 257; Macintosh 197–198, 249–252; management 102, 174, 179; Windows 3.X 180

Memory, conventional: DOS 210–211; loading device drivers 214; minimizing use 204; optimizing 162–166, 170, 201, 208, 218, 226; testing with CHKDSK 135–136; testing with MEM 137, 167; unloading files from 164; verifying 166; Windows 3.X 180; Windows 9X 189

Menuing systems see Shell systems

Microsoft Developers Network CD-ROM 138

Microsoft Network (MSN) 47, 84

MIDI 155, 215, 231–232

Minimum requirements, title 61, 67–70, 141

Miniport 185

Modem 16, 127; ports 139; protocols 132

Modularity, designing for 12, 20

Monitors 105

Motorola 68000 processors 62, 68

Mouse 65–66; DOS 164–165; Mac 252; Windows 3.X 178, 230–231

MOUSE.COM 230

MOUSE.DRV 230

MOUSE.SYS 230

MPC and MPC 2, 61, 104, 138, 213, 230, 232, 264

MPEG and MPEG 2 65, 105, 267

MPLAYER.INI 233

MSCDEX.EXE: DOS 207–208, 225; loading in high memory 208; use of 152–153, 165, 208, 214, 218, 224–

225; versions, number 207–208; versions 2.2 and earlier 207, 225; versions 2.21 and later 207, 225; Windows 3.X 173, 218; Windows 9X 184, 242

MSD command, DOS 137–138

MS-DOS Mode 190–192

MSDOS.SYS, [Options], BootMulti=1 240

Multimedia 104–105; adapters and interface cards 64–65, 100; computer standards 60–61; Windows 3.X 217; Windows 9X 237

Multi-session discs 264

Multi-tasking: 386 enhanced mode 177, 222; Alt-Tab keys 182–183, 222, 239; Windows 9X 189, 239

Networks 13, 66–67; choosing 18, 22; device drivers 82; DOS SHARE command 127, 211; installing titles on 79–80, 134; licensing 73–74; multimedia 21, 65, 67, 104; multiple disc formats 146; operating systems 62–63, 66; performance improvement 99; policies 94, 109, 111; security 16; whiteboard systems 105

Networks, components of: clients 20; drives 144; servers 16, 20, 21, 66; see also Stackers, jukeboxes, and towers

Networks, types of 19–22; AppleTalk 20–21; Banyan Vines 21; LANs 10, 17, 20; Microsoft 20; Novell 20–21; peer-to-peer 20; Powertalk 251; WAN 10; Windows for Workgroups 216; Windows NT 216

Newsgroups 53, 128–31

Newsreader software 131

Norton Utilities 135, 212

Notepad see Windows 3.X, applets and components

NTSC video see Video, DVD standards

OEM 154

Online services 53, 85, 127–134

Operating systems 19, 25, 62–64; compatibility with processors 100; device drivers 66; general in specifications process 10, 58;

safeguarding, passwords 15; safe-guarding, shell systems and menu systems 15; upgrading and optimizing 28–29, 99–101, 212, 251
OS/2 63

Packaging and labeling, title 61–62, 87, 88
Page-turner 40
PAL video *see* Video, DVD standards
Parallel port adapters 147
Passwords: FTP 130; use of 72, 113–114; Windows 9X User Profile 114
Patch 213
PC (Personal Computer) 62
PC function keys: Esc (restarting Windows 9X to view start-up messages) 240; F4 (restarting a Windows 9X system in an old version of DOS) 240–241; F5 (overriding start-up files) 203–204; F8 (viewing the execution of start-up files) 204–205, 213–214, 241
PCMCIA cards 100, 102
Photo CD *see* Kodak Photo CD
PIF (Program Information File) 173, 178–181; advanced settings 221; basic settings 179–181; copying 179; creating 179–181; errors 221; overriding 221; PIF Editor 177; recommendations 176
PKZip 133
Plagiarism 70
Player programs 61, 173
Plug-and-Play 63, 101, 155, 185, 244
Policies: copyrights 71; technical support 199, 216, 236, 249–250; workstation use 93
Ports 117
Power on Self-Test (POST) 117, 203, 252
Power supply: line filters 93, 117; strips 26, 117; surges 26, 93, 213, 259; switches 15, 115, 202, 252–253, 260
Power supply, source: backup 93, 117; fan 117; problems 26, 93, 115, 117; problems, checking for source of 209
PowerMac 62
PowerPC 60, 62
PowerTalk 251

Price, CD-ROM 44
Printing: color 49; configuration files 122; and copyrights 16, 71; grayscale 49; how to 107–108; network 23; PC diagnostics 138; from workstations 16
Problem-resolution *see* Troubleshooting
Processors 61–63, 68
Program files *see* Executable file
Program group *see* Windows 3.X, program groups and items
Program Information File *see* PIF
Project phases: budgeting 10, 30–32; design 10, 13, 16; evaluation checklist 52; implementation 11; maintenance and support planning 11, 28; needs assessment 10, 13, 19; pilot program 11; schedules 10; specifications 10; testing phase 11; title selection 52
Project staffing 10
PROMPT command, DOS 159, 217
Public domain *see* Copyrights

QuickDraw 193, 195, 251, 256
QuickDraw GX 251
QuickTime 193, 195, 251, 256, 257
QuickTime Test kit 135

RAM 64, 226; DOS 210–211; drives 209, 251; Macintosh 250; optimization software 102, 210; testing 137; Windows 3.X 180; Windows 9X 189
RAMDRIVE.SYS 201, 210
Rebooting 202–203, 207
Reference titles 41–43, 47
Reformat, hard disk 212
Registration, of titles 120
Registry 114
Re-installation, title *see* Installation of titles
REM command, DOS 162, 164, 168, 206; use of colon 228
Remov-It II 162, 238
Reports: diagnostic 117; MSD.EXE 137–138; system configuration 86, 92; Windows 9X System Resource Report 188–189
Reserve systems 16
Reset button 202, 220, 252–253
Resolution *see* Graphics resolution

Restarting an operating system: Macintosh 251, 252–253, 255, 260; PC 202–205, 220, 239–242
Restoring: configurations 201; recommended procedures 97; to reinstall titles 97; software 174
Retail stores 51, 54, 84, 119
ROM BIOS 203
Runtime program *see* Player programs

SCANDISK command, DOS 212, 213
SCSI 143, 147–148, 259–261; chains 19, 147–148, 194, 259; connecting 193–194; controllers 143, 147–148; Macintosh, powering on 194; terminators 148, 194, 259; Windows 9X 185
SCSI, cables 254, 261; HDI-30-type 193; peripheral-type 193–194; system-type 193
SCSI, IDs: changing 148; Macintosh (determining) 194; overview 147–148, 194
Searches 49, 105–107; Boolean 105, 107; field 106; free-form 106; keyword 105; punctuation 107; search engines 105
Security: computer viruses 14, 16, 23; Internet 23; of data 15; of drives and discs 13, 15; operating system 15; planning for 14; software 10; workstation hardening 14, 15
Seek time 142, 138
Self-running or self-executing files 133
Self-test *see* Power on Self Test
Serialized titles 47, 68; installation of 68–70
Server *see* Networks, components of
Service bureaus 30, 265–266
SET TEMP= 223
SETUP.EXE 171, 174–175, 186–187
SETVER.EXE 207–208, 225
SHARE command 211
Shareware *see* Copyrights
Shell systems 15, 108, 113, 114, 162, 173, 199, 202
Shortcut *see* Windows 9X, shortcuts
"Skuzzy" *see* SCSI
SMARTDRV.EXE 185, 201, 218, 221, 228, 247

SMARTDRV.SYS 218
Shareware *see* Copyrights
Small Computer System Interface *see* SCSI
Smoothing *see* Sound
Soft boot *see* Restarting an operating system
Software utilities 135
Sound 38, 89–90, 259–260; 8-bit vs. 16-bit 65, 89, 104; buffering 214; cards (jacks, cables, and connectors) 65, 149–150; cards, device drivers 165, 178; problems 161, 210, 233; quality 214–215, 246–247; smoothing 214; SoundBlaster 89; *see also* Audio
SoundBlaster *see* Sound
SPART.PAR 229
SPEAKER.SYS 210
Speakers 105
Speed *see* Drives, CD-ROM
Stackers, jukeboxes, and towers 13, 15, 20, 21, 144, 147, 153
STACKS command, DOS 223
StartUp Disk, Macintosh 195, 197–198, 254; how to create 253–254; *see also* Boot disk; DOS
STF file-name ending 133
StuffIt 133
Sun Microsystems 60
Swap file 103, 210, 227
SYS file-name ending 151, 231
System 6, Macintosh *see* Macintosh operating system
System 7, Macintosh *see* Macintosh operating system
System 8, Macintosh *see* Macintosh operating system
SYSTEM.INI: [boot section] 233; [386 enh] section 181, 221; use of 137, 154, 182, 222

Task-switching *see* Multi-tasking
Tattletale 141
Technical support 10, 22, 74, 199, 216, 236, 249–250; fax-back systems 121–122; fees for 119–120; Internet (source of) 23, 118, 128; Macintosh 250; phone numbers 120; questions 122–124; retailers/distributors (source of) 118; users groups (source

of) 118; vendors (source of) 111, 115, 118, 121–124, 242; voice mail 121

Telnet 130

Text editors *see* DOS EDIT; INI file-name ending; Write

386 Enhanced applet *see* Windows 3.X, applets and components

386SPART.PAR 229

Titles, CD-ROM: atlases and maps 49; *BiblioFile* (first commercial) 2, 41, 43; database 18; evaluation process 34; genealogy 48; multi-volume discs 18, 19, 68; newspaper indexes and archives 43; obtaining reviews 127; serial 42, 47, 68; types of 18; useful life 41; versions and editions 35, 37, 42–43, 44, 129; *see also* Dictionary titles; Educational titles; Encyclopedia titles

Titles, CD-ROM, updates 68–70, 98; CD-ROM disc 43; diskette 43–44, 69; online 43, 48

Towers *see* Stackers, jukeboxes, and towers

Tracks *see* Discs, CD-ROM

Troubleshooting: checklist 115–118; procedures 109–111, 115–118, 201–202, 205–204, 222, 223, 238–243, 250, 252–254; Windows 9X, utility programs 243

Troubleshooting, problems: audio 161; causes 111, 113, 115–118, 181, 209, 212, 223, 249; chain of errors 112; DOS as cause of Windows problems 218, 221; interface settings 161; Macintosh 249; memory errors 202, 259; shorts in cables 149; system freezes or hangs up 213–214, 220, 222, 231, 239, 259

TSRs 211

UDF (Universal Disk Format) 267; *see also* DVD

UMB *see* Upper memory

Uninstall It! 162

Uninstaller 176

Universal device drivers *see* Windows 9X, device drivers

UNIX 25, 60, 63; FTP commands 130–131; *see also* Operating systems

Upper memory 170, 174, 223, 231

URLs 129

Users: estimating number of 17; with disabilities and special needs 28

UUENCODING 131

Utility software: hard-drive management 213, 240; installer/deinstaller 175; PC analysis 127–134; third-party DOS 138; Windows 9X 192, 238

VCACHE.EXE 185

VER command, DOS 135, 208

Version number: "incorrect DOS version" error 207–208; identifying, title 120–121; identifying, Windows 3.X 138; MSCDEX.EXE 207; title 63, 74, 97

Version table, DOS 208

Video: adapter cards 65, 105, 214; conflicts with sound cards 214; DVD standards 267; hours per disc 38; *see also* Graphics resolution

Video for Windows 185, 233–234

Virtual disk drive *see* RAM, drives

Virtual memory: Macintosh 251; Windows 3.X 139, 226–230

Virus, computer *see* Security, computer viruses

Volume controls 214, 259

WAN *see* Networks, types of

Warm boot *see* Restarting an operating system

Warranty: cards 120; Macintosh hardware 252

WAV file-name ending 233

Wavetable sound 215

Web browsers: downloading with 129–130; *Internet Explorer* 130; *Netscape Navigator* 130; searching 106

Wheelchair access 28

Whiteboard systems 105

WIN command: /B switch 224; /D:X switch 223; /S switch 223; /3 switch 178, 225; use of 168–169, 177, 223–224, 225

WIN386.SWP 227

Windows 3.0 problems 224

Windows 3.X: analysis tools 138–139; compatibility with Intel processors 68; DOS, exiting to 205, 207, 219–220; DOS, relationship with 62–63,

178; icons, creating for titles 175–176, 188; icons, for CD-ROM drives 172, 224; multimedia use 217, 222; program groups and items, creating for titles 173, 178–179; running titles under Windows 9X 187–188, 236; shutting down 220; 16-bit applications 139–140; temporary files in \TEMP directory 227; version number, identifying 138; *see also* DOS windows; INI files; MSCDEX.EXE; PIF (Program Information File); WIN command

Windows 3.X, applets and components: 386 Enhanced (access to and purpose of) 139; 386 Enhanced (use of) 177, 222; Control Panel (access to and purpose of) 155; Control Panel (use of) 138–139, 217, 222, 226, 233; Drivers 177, 231–233; File Manager 224, 227; Media Player 172, 233–234; Media Player (General MIDI Setup option) 232; MIDI Mapper 231–232; Notepad 182–183, 191, 222, 225; Setup 138–139, 217, 221–222, 230

Windows 3.X, device drivers: installing 153–155; installing (multimedia) 154, 217, 226, 233; MCI CD Audio Player 232; MCI Redbook Audio 232; Microsoft Windows Driver Library 84

Windows 9X: analysis tools 140; CD-ROM, pros and cons of 101; compatibility with Intel processors 68; device drivers, installing 155–156; device drivers, universal 184, 243; emergency startup disk 114, 241; features, CD-ROM-specific 184–185; long file names 244; multi-tasking in 189; performance improvement 237; Properties sheets 156, 237, 242; retaining earlier versions of DOS and Windows 3.X 213, 213, 238, 240, 245; role of AUTOEXEC.BAT and CONFIG.SYS in 238; shortcuts 187–188, 245, 247; shutting down 239; small footprint 185; System Resource Report 188–189; system resources 247; upgrading 237, 238, 241, 243; upgrading disks 237; version number, identifying 138; with Windows

3.X, installing titles under 187–188; with Windows 3.X, running titles under 236; *see also* DOS windows; MS-DOS mode; MS-DOS.SYS

Windows 9X, applets and components: Add/Remove Programs 185–188, 238; Control Panel (access to and purpose of) 140, 237; Drive Speed Switch 245; Explorer 240; Multimedia Properties 185, 242–243

Windows 9X and DOS: running titles under 188–189, 236, 238–239; running titles under old versions of 192; Windows 95 version of 239

Windows 9X, modes: F4 and F8 selection of 192, 240–242; full screen 188, 189–190; full screen (optimizing) 189–190; MS-DOS 188, 190–192; rebooting to change 191; standard 223; 386 Enhanced 223; title installation 186

Windows 95 Upgrade Assistant 238

Windows for Workgroups 216

Windows NT 216

Winfo 139

WIN.INI 137, 182, 222

Wordpad 240–241

Working directory, Windows 3.X 180

Workstation: cleaning 26, 93–94; DOS (modifying configuration) 162–168; examining configuration 203; locating, for multimedia 104; Macintosh requirements 251; maintenance supplies 96–97; optimizing 98–108, 200–201; preparing 69; repairing 28–29, 31–32, 97

Workstation, capabilities: analysis 135; costs 30–31; determining 134–141; portable 15; stand-alone vs. networks 43; World Wide Web (WWW) 128–131

WORM 265

Write program, Windows 3.X 183

Xmodem *see* Modem, protocols

XMS *see* Extended memory

Z file-name ending 131

Zip drives 102

ZIP file-name ending 133

Zmodem *see* Modem, protocols